W9-BMY-430

Race, Liberalism, and Economics

EDITED BY

David Colander, Robert E. Prasch, and

Falguni A. Sheth

THE UNIVERSITY OF MICHIGAN PRESS

Ann Arbor

First paperback edition 2007
Copyright © by the University of Michigan 2004
All rights reserved
Published in the United States of America by
The University of Michigan Press
Manufactured in the United States of America
♾ Printed on acid-free paper

2010   2009   2008   2007   5   4   3   2

No part of this publication may be reproduced,
stored in a retrieval system, or transmitted in any form
or by any means, electronic, mechanical, or otherwise,
without the written permission of the publisher.

A CIP catalog record for this book is available from the British Library.

Library of Congress Cataloging-in-Publication Data

Race, liberalism, and economics / edited by David Colander, Robert E.
    Prasch, and Falguni A. Sheth.
        p.   cm.
    Includes bibliographical references (p.   ) and index.
    ISBN 0-472-11356-9 (cloth : alk. paper)
        1. Race relations—Economic aspects.   2. Racism—Economic
    aspects—United States.   3. United States—Race relations—Economic
    aspects.   4. United States—Economic policy.   5. Liberalism—United
    States.   I. Colander, David C.   II. Prasch, Robert E., 1958–
    III. Sheth, Falguni A., 1968–

    HT1531.R328   2004
    305.8'00973—dc22   2003021576

    ISBN-10: 0-472-03224-0 (pbk. : alk. paper)
    ISBN-13: 978-0-472-03224-2 (pbk. : alk. paper)

To Julie Kidd

*whose generosity
made possible the conference on which
this volume is based*

Contents

PART 3
Policy Issues

Preface

Economics is about policy, and policy by nature is transdisciplinary. This book attempts to look, in a broader manner than is usually done, at economic ideas as they relate to race and to policies that deal with racial inequalities. It was inspired (or maybe the better word is *provoked*) by David Levy's work on the history of economics and its relationship to racism. David's work was, as it usually is, provocative and interesting, but it seemed to us that there was more at stake than was initially evident from his articles and from those he published with coauthor Sandy Peart. Specifically, it seemed that David had a broader agenda of revitalizing the Chicago approach to race. A conference was designed to explore that broader goal and to consider the issue of race in a broader perspective than is usually done. This book is the end product of that conference.

The conference was made possible by the generosity of the Christian A. Johnson Endeavor Foundation, which has funded David Colander's chair at Middlebury College. It was one of an ongoing set of conferences that have been run at Middlebury College on economic issues. These conferences have always tried to bring out, rather than hide, controversy, and this one was no different; we chose a set of very bright participants from a variety of different fields, including philosophy, English, and anthropology as well as economics, and we let them at each other. The diversity of approaches of the conferees was not only from outside economics; there was also a significant diversity of views among the economists who attended.

While this volume is derived from the papers presented at the conference, it diverges from the conference in a number of ways. We used the conference as raw material and then, after the conference, organized the themes that came up in discussion into what we think will be an interesting and provocative volume. This places enormous burdens on the participants, whom we asked to expand on issues that were raised at the conference and that we believe are important for understanding the subject matter. Through this process of direction and editing, we created a set of essays that fit together more like a symphony than like the collection of individual sounds that often make up conference volumes. Even the papers that were presented at the conference were substantially revised to better connect with the evolving theme of the volume.

Because of its transdisciplinary nature, this book should be of interest not only to economists but also to a larger audience interested in the implications of economics for policies dealing with race, including political scientists, feminists, public policy specialists, philosophers, historians, and sociologists, as well as interested laypeople. Some papers in it may make them mad, but all are, we believe, intellectually challenging and interesting.

We placed enormous demands on the participants, and they responded superbly. We would like to thank each of them enormously; the quality of the papers is top-notch, and we appreciate all the work they did. Besides the participants, many people helped with the conference and helped make this book possible. Marie Winner and Amy Holbrook worked hard with the organization of the conference and did a great job. The students in Dave Colander's class on the history of economic thought read the conference papers, discussed them, and played an important role in the initial editing process.

Once we turned to editing the book, our editor at the University of Michigan Press, Ellen McCarthy, was extremely helpful in providing timely reviews and in encouraging us to proceed. Marie Winner, Laurel Houghton, and Helen Reiff also helped with the editing process; Helen also did the index. We thank them all, but most of all we thank the Christian A. Johnson Endeavor Foundation, which made the conference and this book possible.

Introduction

Economic reasoning is often presented as a technical exercise—optimizing, solving for second-order conditions, or relating costs to benefits. It certainly involves such issues, but in reality the techniques of economics are simply elements of a broader reasoning process that leads from basic philosophical principles to policy precepts. As John Maynard Keynes put it, "economics is not a set of conclusions; it is a method of analysis, a way of thinking, that, when used correctly, leads its practitioner to correct conclusions." As the teaching of economics has come to focus more on the technical aspects of constrained maximization, the broader philosophical principles upon which applied policy economics is based have been downplayed—and even lost for many economists. Some highly regarded economists, such as Amartya Sen and Kenneth Arrow, have emphasized that relationship, but in many lay discussions of economic policy (and unfortunately in some discussions by economists), it remains invisible.

An important premise underlying this volume is that the philosophical issues cannot be ignored; to understand economic policy, one must understand how broader philosophical concepts serve as the foundation for reasoning on economic policy. This volume explores this theme while considering a particular subset of issues regarding how economics currently deals with the problem of race and how it has dealt with that problem in the past. The issue of race provides an opening by which to consider the philosophical foundations of economics, since the interconnections between race and philosophical issues significantly affect the policy implications of economic analysis. Specifically, the chapters in this volume explore how economic reasoning relates to the broader concepts of liberalism and racism, each of which reaches deeply into the ethical and conceptual foundations of policy.

The primary issue that emerges from this interconnection is the historical fact that economists have generally been proponents of free markets. In particular, the following question arises: Is it consistent with good economic reasoning (and if so, when) to have government modify market results or even sometimes prevent free markets from operating? Many laypeople think that the answer to that question lies in economic theory. It does not; despite periodic claims to the contrary, economists' support of markets is not based on a technical proof of the superiority of markets; there is no proposition in economic theory that markets are a preferable way of organizing society. Markets have advantages and disadvantages. Instead, economists' support of markets has traditionally been based upon a broader philosophical foundation of liberalism and history—on what markets have and have not achieved in the past and how that past relates to the future.

Modern economics is widely thought to have begun with Adam Smith's *An Inquiry into the Nature and Causes of the Wealth of Nations,* so we shall begin our considerations there. Smith ([1776] 1937) argues that of all systems of production, slavery is one of the most inefficient (80–81). He supports this proposition with the argument that while free individuals have incentives to work hard to improve their lives, that is not so for slaves. He writes, "A slave, on the contrary, who can acquire nothing but his maintenance, consults his own ease by making the land produce as little as possible over and above that maintenance" (366). Since slaves have nothing to gain, they have no reason, other than that they are forced to do so, to work over and above the minimal amount.

Smith also believed that there were few inherent differences among individuals: "The difference of natural talents in different men is, in reality, much less than we are aware of; and the very different genius which appears to distinguish men of different professions, when grown up to maturity, is not upon many occasions so much the cause, as the effect of the division of labor. The difference between the most dissimilar characters, between a philosopher and a common street porter, for example, seems to arise not so much from nature, as from habit, custom and education." Acknowledging the importance of what today's economists would term *human capital* and *path dependence,* Smith goes on to state, "The difference of talents comes then to be taken notice of, and widens by degrees, till at last the vanity of the philosopher is willing to acknowledge scarce any resemblance" (15–16). The preceding quotations suggest that Smith thought that slaves had a potential and capacity similar to that of their masters and that any differences that remained were a result of a lack of training, opportunity, and adaptive responses to the situations in which they found themselves.

Yet Smith also argued that profitable activities and institutions had a tendency to win out over unprofitable ones, and he was thus left with the question, Why did slavery continue if it is economically inefficient? In answer to this question, he offered the view that human nature is more complex than the simple desire for wealth that is so often associated with his work. According to Smith, "The pride of man makes him love to domineer, and nothing mortifies him so much as to be obliged to condescend to persuade his inferiors. Wherever the law allows it, and the nature of the work can afford it, therefore, he will generally prefer the service of slaves to that of freemen" (365). In this way, Smith concluded that slavery could be both inefficient and sustainable over an extended period in some industries, in several parts of the world. In short, the forces of the invisible hand may not be sufficient to eliminate slavery.

While Smith's analysis of the economics of slavery was in accord with what most economists today would perceive to be a sound analysis of the incentive structure and the market process, it was his ability to modify some of his initial assumptions by allowing for a more complex structure to human nature that enabled him to arrive at a richer consideration of the economics of slavery. In sum, Smith demonstrated that people and the social systems they create are multifaceted and respond to a myriad of motives. One possible outcome is that both the institutions that perpetuate inequality and the corresponding social relations that some may find repugnant can become built into the fabric of society. For Smith and for contemporary economists, policies that should be used to change such actions or institutions do not follow directly from economic reasoning. Such policies, to work, would have to be based on an extensive knowledge of the existing system, a set of moral principles, and an understanding of market processes.

The following chapters analyze one of the longest-lasting and most difficult of contemporary issues: race in America, focusing on white racism toward blacks. They do so within this broad Smithian policy approach, rather than within the narrower policy-oriented approach sometimes associated with modern economic considerations of social and economic issues—including race. The volume is meant to serve as a backdrop to discussions of the implications of economic ideas for the policies that our society is struggling with today: affirmative action, quotas, education vouchers, drug prohibition, and other policies that asymmetrically affect the position of minorities within the population. This volume comes to no conclusion on these issues, but it does demonstrate that the implications of economic reasoning are less clear than they are often portrayed as being. In doing so, the volume challenges the beliefs of both those who see economics as necessarily leading to a laissez-faire policy and those who see economics as necessarily leading to a need for government intervention. Economic reasoning alone generates neither of these conclusions. Thus, it is not surprising that the views of a majority of economists, practicing at a given point in time, have changed over the years and will likely continue to change in the future, as their interpretations of human nature, the broader philosophical principles underlying policy, and the policy context change.

History of Liberalism and Racism

In this introduction, we provide a brief overview of the ideas that support the preceding propositions and describe the arguments presented in the chapters that follow. In the first section, we discuss the concepts of liberalism and racism, specifying how they are used in this book. In that discussion, we briefly explore the history and use of these concepts with regard to how they have related to economic thinking and policy in the past. In the second section of the introduction, we provide an overview of the chapters, their relation to the broad themes presented so far, and their relation to the other chapters in this volume.

Liberalism

Liberalism is typically defined as a political philosophy that proposes that the polity should be organized so as to allow for the full and free development of the individual. It has its roots in the Judeo-Christian tradition, which emphasizes the importance of individuality and the idea that the moral worth of individuals can be established independently of the customs, laws, and authorities in existence at a given moment in time. Not surprisingly, over the centuries, this posture has proven to be a challenge to these same customs, laws, and traditions. The individual and the liberty of his or her ideas, actions, and possessions rose steadily in importance, and authority based solely on power and tradition became less legitimate in the eyes of those ruled by it.

Historically, liberalism saw its greatest development at about the same time as the emergence of classical political economy, and indeed, it is no coincidence that these ideas were so closely associated in time—although this is not the place to develop these links. Nevertheless, it is difficult for historians of economic thought to view the evolution of political theory in the nineteenth century without being tempted to say that political economy is largely an application of the theory of political liberalism. In its initial form, the policy recommendations of classical political economy and classical liberalism were each highly supportive of laissez-faire, yet the interpretation of laissez-faire must be seen within the context of the time, and these thinkers accepted the need for government intervention in a number of instances. Adam Smith is probably the most important example of a classical economist who supported the policy of what he termed "Natural Liberty" as a principle but who was still open to exceptions in instances wherein it could be plausibly argued that laissez-faire undermined the public interest.

John Locke's writings play an important role in the emergence of liberalism as a philosophical framework. For Locke, the rights of man emerge from the obligation to protect and enhance God's greatest gift to us, namely, our own lives. Locke argues that from this obligation, which we know through both "Reason" (as a trait accorded us by God) and "Revelation" (Divine Scripture), emerges the set of individual rights and duties that characterize each of our individual lives. Locke further deduces a right to private property and locates the origin of civil society in our collective need to defend and maintain our right to property (Locke [1690] 1952, chap. 5). Property rights, derived from our ownership over our own labor, are themselves thought to be an extension of our own *freedom* to do with our lives as we each believe to be proper. For this reason, the government is obliged to articulate, defend, and arbitrate the rights of property among the citizens of the state. This liberal justification for government displaced the origin and moral ground of civil society away from the will of the king and toward the consent of the governed.

As we know, civil society accommodates a multitude and variety of people, not all of whom possess property or are even recognized as possessing property rights. Initially, liberalism (and its corresponding rights) pertained to an almost exclusively male landed aristocracy. There were few protections and privileges for women, the poor, and the uneducated. In early liberal theory, such issues as whether rights could be in conflict or whether policy might be used to accommodate those who were left out by a dysfunctional distribution of property were not addressed.

Among the (mostly) English theorists of what came to be called the "new liberalism," individuals began to question whether protecting individual property rights in a society, in which some people were starving and others were living in luxury, was consistent with a truly liberal point of view. For this group, the freedom to starve was seen not as liberty but simply as another type of slavery. These considerations motivated a revision of the liberal project, a revision designed to complete liberalism's initial agenda by addressing the problems of individuals whose freedom was effectively nullified by economic misfortune or want. Thomas Hill Green (1917), Leonard Hobhouse (1911), and John Hobson (1974) are some of the thinkers associated with the reassessment and revision of liberalism as a political doctrine.

Perceptions of the necessary conditions for human flourishing changed and were extended over time. Liberalism, and what are considered liberal politics and policies, also evolved, as they dealt with the problems that emerged from the unequal and sometimes arbitrary distribution and assignment of property and property rights. Correspondingly, the legitimacy of various claims to liberal rights has evolved over time. Certain basic rights were initially limited to a group of male property holders and were gradually extended to other men; over the next two or three hundred years, the idea of political liberalism was extended to religious and racial minorities and women. As this occurred, many problems and issues that earlier writers had not perceived or had chosen to ignore had to be addressed.

As we stated already, early in its history, liberalism was closely associated with natural rights and with a belief in the essential fairness of a political regime based on property rights, at least as compared to the other problems faced by society. The increase in wealth that modern economies would soon create for all of society demonstrated to the classical political economists the basic validity of this approach; consequently, they often based their arguments on these observations. By the end of the nineteenth century, however, the existing system of property rights, with its judicially supported policies of liberty of contract and a limited role for government, came to be seen as a basis for inequality in bargaining power and in the consequent distribution of income and wealth. In short, an exclusive concern with formal property rights could be a source of oppression. At this time, termed the Progressive Era in the United States, economists, including many that we would perceive to be neoclassical economists, began to join with those who called for more significant intervention in the economy (Prasch 1998, 2000).

In sum, as Western society changed and as some of the qualities of market economies became better understood, liberalism moved from an ideology largely supporting laissez-faire to an ideology supporting government intervention (Merquior 1991; Schultz 1972). That is why liberalism is not seen today as a political perspective that supports laissez-faire; instead, it is seen as promoting significant government intervention, relative to what Americans today think of as conservatism. The situation is more complicated because liberalism maintains its roots and supports particular types of government market intervention—interventions that some contemporary liberals believe are consistent with the specifically guaranteed rights of individuals. There is much controversy over how to interpret those specifically guaranteed rights. Since the context within which the liberal attitude is brought to bear on policy issues is continually changing, the term must be seen as a continually evolving concept rather than a static one.

Contemporary liberals are not opposed to markets, but they do think that the government must take a role in modifying and controlling the market so as to promote the free and full development of individuals. Contemporary liberals try to take advantage of the market's merits while proscribing some of its more dangerous features. Thus, policies that liberals support must, in principle, be consistent with the achievement of a maximum of economic freedom while maintaining a plausible equality of opportunity. One famous liberal economist, John Maurice Clark (1960, 124), put it this way: "Market mechanisms are not automatic panaceas; they are things that can be made to work, but only by a people that has learned to work together."

While liberalism is a broad political doctrine, it is not consistent with all policies or policy views. For example, most variants of Marxism are inconsistent with the liberal vision of individually-directed economic freedom. Liberalism is, however, consistent with John Maynard Keynes's position on government intervention, because his ideas presented a resolution to some of the outstanding problems of political economy while maintaining intact a commitment to the political philosophy of liberalism (Keynes [1936] 1964, chap. 24). At least this was a perspective that was widely held from the 1930s through the 1970s.

From the preceding considerations, we get a sense that liberalism is consistent with a wide variety of policies—including policies that would have been anathema to the liberals of the nineteenth century. For example, recent debates in political economy have been cast as a contest between markets and socialism, and liberalism has been defined in reference to that debate. Early liberals, who made up the school of Philosophic Radicals, were posing questions in a very different framework. As we suggested earlier, the issue of their day was a contest between the competing principles of aristocracy and liberalism. To read the works of Adam Smith, the parliamentary speeches of David Ricardo, the tirades of James Mill, or the more nuanced writings of John Stuart Mill is to read an extended record of the contention of political liberalism that everyone has a right to free and full self-development as individuals. These writings are in clear contrast to an older notion that was more widely accepted in that era, namely, that there was a traditional—even natural—political order on earth that obliged each of us to accept the rule of our "betters," that is, the landed classes of the old aristocracy. Such a conflict of ideas is evident in the debate between Carlyle and Mill discussed in the first several chapters in this volume. Others, such as their great contemporary Edmund Burke, presented an antiliberal defense of tradition as the only plausible bulwark against political anarchy, such as was evident in the Reign of Terror that came in the wake of the French Revolution (Burke [1792] 2001).

As we have discussed already, today's liberalism is much more expansive a project than the demand for freedom from the arbitrary control and rule by a state that was almost exclusively responsive to aristocratic and landed interests. Depending on the historian one reads, any of several economic and political changes and events in the United States and Great Britain led to this change in vision. Populism, the stresses of early industrialization, a desire to win the emerging working-class vote, and so on, have been advanced as causes.[1] We do know that modern liberalism emerges from within the American Progressive movement as represented by such figures as Herbert Croly and Walter Lippmann. This movement also included some of the most well-regarded American economists of the early twentieth century. John Bates Clark, John Maurice Clark, Henry Rogers Seager, John Commons, Richard Ely, and Wesley Clair Mitchell each argued that under some conditions, the free market could itself become a constraint on liberty, and for that reason, the liberal project would have to consider what reforms would be required to extend liberty to the private sphere of market relations. It was at this time that the liberal agenda came to include health and safety at the workplace, maximum-hours laws, minimum-wage legislation, and so on.

Initially, few American economists maintained a principled objection to this extension of the liberal project—although many continued to debate the wisdom of specific policies and practices. But in the 1920s and

1930s, a dissent from this consensus became increasingly evident. By the 1940s and more so in the 1950s, economists such as Joseph Schumpeter ([1942] 1975), Henry Simons (1948), Friedrich v. Hayek ([1944] 1972, 1973), and Milton Friedman (1962) were beginning to establish their reputations as "classical liberals" in opposition to the new liberals who had championed the modern welfare state in most Western democracies. These liberals stressed the need to protect the sphere of private life, including private property and market relations, from the grasping hand of the state. In conclusion, the positions of both new and classical liberals alike are, in our view, consistent with the ideals and values of liberalism, because they each take individual freedom and human flourishing to be the only legitimate end of a well-ordered society. Hence, it serves little purpose for us to enter into a debate about which vision is entitled to be considered "true liberalism."

Race and Racism

The specific concepts with which this volume is concerned are race and racism. As Brendan O'Flaherty and Jill Shapiro show in their joint contribution to this volume, the evolution of racist ideas has been a subtle process woven into movements in the development of scientific thought in a nonlinear manner. Concepts of racism are related to concepts of nationalism and to inherent tendencies in individuals to be wary of strangers and things that are different from what they have known. While the definition of racism is ambiguous, what we will use as a working definition of racism in this volume is any position that holds that there is a correlation between the inherent superiority of some groups of individuals over others and the set of traits that are ascribed as biologically or physically innate for each group. Generally, this view is based on the acceptance of a causal link between inherited physical traits of individuals with different physical appearances and certain traits of personality, intellect, or culture. Thus, to believe that there are inherited distinctions among groups of people is not necessarily racist, but to suggest that trivial differences have asymmetric ethical, moral, or legal implications is, as is the proposition that one race is inherently superior to another.

O'Flaherty and Shapiro provide an illuminating history of racism in this volume, so we will only comment here on an important catalyst to our modern concern about racism that can be found in the writings of Gobineau, a French diplomat and social thinker of the mid-1800s (Gobineau

1963). Gobineau's racist views were picked up by some in the nineteenth century and combined with nationalism. The result was a set of arguments that asserted the superiority of "Aryans," that is, the Germanic peoples, over other races. Some Germans, interpreting Gobineau as implying that the success of civilizations would be determined by their racial composition, concluded that racial purity was needed to protect Aryan societies. When the Nazis translated some of these ideas into policies, the end result was a widespread revulsion among a majority of persons in modern societies. This outcome, leavened by the ideological rivalry between the West and the Communist bloc, induced some important changes in the discussion of race among American intellectuals and social scientists. In the post–World War II period, a "firewall" developed in which discussions that were premised on racial differences, as well as policy proposals based on these racial differences, were outside the realm of acceptable discourse.

The firewall served its purpose in the immediate postwar era, as the Western world came to address its own racist customs and practices. But there were costs also, one being that it discouraged systemic explorations of the complicated effects of policies designed to address racial inequalities. Objective discussions of issues related to race became difficult to conduct. Moreover, in the postwar period, the academy gradually became a more integrated place. Certainly, this welcome development also added complexity to the implicit "rules" of polite discourse and interaction. Earlier, before the firewall, it was easier to write about theories of race, racism, and racial differences; theories of racial differences—many of which theories were problematic—abounded and were part of mainstream anthropological thought. After the firewall, the quantity of this discussion, good and bad, was reduced or marginalized.

Although racist theories within the social sciences became unacceptable after World War II, they continued to be entertained by several segments of the larger population and remained embedded in many of our cultural and social institutions. This, then, is the situation with which modern perspectives and policies toward race must contend.

Offensive and Communicative Uses of Terminology

We raise these issues at the beginning of this book because the terms *liberalism* and *racism* are often highly charged, making it difficult to have productive discussions of the policies and issues the terms are meant to describe or advance. Language often embodies multiple meanings and referents and can be employed as a weapon as well as a means of communication. Consider the election of 1988, which turned the term *liberal* into a profanity and associated it with the image of Willy Horton, a black inmate who violated the terms of his furlough to travel out of state to commit another capital crime. Horton became a centerpiece of the Republican presidential campaign. Republicans used Horton's image to associate the Democratic candidate, Michael Dukakis, with liberalism (a rather ironic fate since Dukakis had led the centrist group, the Democratic Leadership Council, in its attempts to move the Democratic Party away from its association with Roosevelt- and Johnson-style liberalism). After their success in 1988, Republicans leveled the term *liberal* as a pejorative toward all Democrats, and Democrats scrambled to avoid policies that might represent some of the negative implications of such a classification. Democrats, in turn, although generally more subtly, suggested that many of the Republican proposals were racist, discriminatory, and unjust. In recent times, many of those who have opposed affirmative action, favored "tougher" law enforcement, or accepted some form of racial profiling have been seen as racist.

The use of terminology as a weapon, whatever its strength in politics, makes its use as a means of communication almost impossible. In this volume, we use terms descriptively, and all contributors to the volume are both liberal and antiracist by our definitions. But the contributors differ rather substantially in their views of race and economics. One goal of this volume is to move the discussion away from whether a particular policy may be termed "liberal" or "nonracist" and toward a discussion of whether the policy can be expected to achieve some reasonable or defensible goal or goals better than can some other policy or policies.

The Chapters in This Book

This volume is divided into three parts. Part 1, "Classical Economic and Early Approaches to Race," examines the early history of work on race by economists and social scientists more generally. Part 2, "Neoclassical and Modern Approaches to Racism," presents a survey of American economists on race and features some chapters that embody more modern economic approaches to race. Part 3, "Policy Issues," explores some policy issues that follow from the discussion.

Classical Economic and Early Approaches to Race

The first chapter is by a biological anthropologist, Jill Shapiro, and an economist, Brendan O'Flaherty, and is entitled "Apes, Essences, and Races: What Natural Scientists Believed about Human Variation, 1700–1900." It provides a broad context for the discussion in the following sections. In it, the authors explore the history of the scientific study of human variation or "race" and how the views of natural scientists evolved over time. Their study reveals a winding and paradoxical path. Science in the Enlightenment stressed the homogeneity and adaptability of humans, but in time, they argue, the dominant scientific view would be recast to an "increasing focus on the heterogeneity of humankind and the innate and fixed nature of their condition." They show how seminal themes drawn from classical antiquity resonate as they shape and reshape the nature of "racial ideas." Most notably, O'Flaherty and Shapiro contend that essentialist thinking is still so deeply rooted in our mind-sets that it is difficult for us to see beyond it. In addition, their chapter provides the reader with a healthy skepticism as to the use and abuse of natural science in the formation of ideas in social-scientific discussions. By 1900, natural science had failed to validate discrete racial differences, but this failure made little difference to broader social constructs and concomitant policy. This skepticism is an admonition equally valid today as we listen to the "voice of science" while attending to the formation of policy initiatives.

Shapiro and O'Flaherty show that racist views along the lines of those cited earlier were ubiquitous during the time in which early social science developed, although the substance of these views changed tremendously over that period. Liberalism developed in a society in which racist views predominated. They conclude with the thought that "if clear, simple, convincing answers for these questions do not exist outside the world of biological and cultural racial essentialism, why should we be surprised that for many ordinary people trying to understand the world around them, racial essentialism is still the answer?"

The next three chapters in part 1 examine the interaction between liberalism and racism—the treatment of race as a category in nineteenth-century social science. There we find a serious instantiation of the idea that black people were of an intellectual and morally inferior character that had to be controlled or managed "for their own good."

The exploration begins with the discussion by economists David Levy and Sandra Peart of an important episode in the history of racism, an exploration that is part of a larger research program of Levy and Peart's that investigates the issues of race and economics in the history of economic thought. In "The Negro Science of Exchange: Classical Economics and Its Chicago Revival," they argue that the economists' approach in the mid-1800s to problems of race emphasized individuality and the rights of individuals and is far more consistent with modern views of racism than are the views of others of that time. Essentially, they argue that "Chicago" economists of the latter twentieth century who followed the classical liberal approach were the "good guys" and that several prominent noneconomists who were critical of the emergence of a market society were the "bad guys." This chapter adds to their previous work in that it spells out a larger agenda for the research program. That larger agenda is to reconsider the relationship between blacks and markets, to provide an understanding of why markets and a "classical" economic approach to problems should be seen by blacks as supporting blacks, and to place the modern Chicago approach to problems of race in a more appropriate light.

Levy and Peart point out that for many prominent political philosophers and political economists, such as John E. Cairnes and John Stuart Mill, the incorporation of blacks into the conversation of liberalism broadly defined was not problematic. Blacks were to be accorded the basic rights of property owners and citizenship and allowed to compete in the marketplace. But it was problematic for a contemporary anticlassical liberal tradition—that of Ruskin and Carlyle. Since a number of chapters in this volume consider Levy and Peart's views on this issue, they briefly respond to their critics in the appendix at the end of their chapter.

The next two chapters are critical examinations of Levy and Peart's argument. The first, "Contextualizing David Levy's *How the Dismal Science Got Its Name; or, Revisiting the Victorian Context of David Levy's History of Race and Economics*," is by Susan Zlotnick, an English professor. She takes a critical look at Levy's broader research agenda and argues that it takes many issues out of context and, in so doing, misinterprets the antislavery debates of late eighteenth- and early nineteenth-century Britain. Specifically, it ignores the relationship between three mutually imbricated discourses: antislavery, paternalism, and factory reform. She contends that Levy and Peart conflate the paternalism of Thomas Carlyle and John Ruskin with a proslavery position and thereby misrepresent their thinking. Zlotnick also argues that while the classical liberals, including such political economists as John Stuart Mill, took a praiseworthy stand against slavery, their involvement in British imperial politics, particularly in India, at

least somewhat undermines Levy and Peart's assertion that the classical
liberal tradition is antiracist.

The final chapter in part 1, "John Stuart Mill on Race, Liberty, and
Markets," by philosopher Falguni A. Sheth, also reexamines an aspect of
Levy and Peart's argument. She argues that they have taken a narrow perspective on Mill by interpreting his views on blacks as following from his
economics. Instead, Sheth argues, Mill's progressive attitudes about blacks
(and English women) follow from his more fundamental set of philosophical conceptions, which have to do with his views on human nature, the
value of tradition, hierarchy, and customs, rather than his support of free
markets per se. For Mill, free markets and the growing wealth of the nation
are a means to certain ends, not ends in themselves, as is often implied by
the Chicago school of economists and the libertarians who draw inspira-
tion from them.

Neoclassical and Modern Approaches to Racism

Part 2 carries the consideration of race by economists from the earlier
period to modern days. It also explores the current situation of African-
Americans in reference to the history and experience of racism. The first
chapter in this section, " 'Not an Average Human Being': How Economics
Succumbed to Racial Accounts of Economic Man," by Sandra Peart and
David Levy, continues the exploration of their broader research agenda
discussed earlier, examining the neoclassical period of economic thought.
In this period, they find that rather than economists standing apart and
defending classical liberty as they had earlier, economists fell in with other
social scientists. Neoclassical economics gave up classical liberalism and
adopted modern liberalism. The implication is that the classical economics of Smith and Mill is quite different from neoclassical economics—
which often adopted the racist views of the late nineteenth century. They
make these arguments not just for historical interest but to provide context for the modern Chicago approach to the problem of race, which is to
allow the market to eradicate it. They argue that the modern Chicago tradition of economics continues the nonracist classical approach to liberalism and provides a good foundation upon which modern policy can be
built.

The second chapter in part 2, "One Hundred Years of American Economists on Race and Discrimination, 1881–1981," by economist Robert E.
Prasch, picks up where Levy and Peart leave off. He surveys the way that

the mainstream of American economists has considered the situation of American blacks and what their abilities and prospects were in the economy. He is particularly interested in how they understood the fact of racial difference and discrimination to affect market outcomes, or whether they thought they would have any effect at all. To ensure that this chapter is a retrospective, and to shed some light on current debates within American economics on the issues of race and discrimination, he ends his chapter in 1981, when the coming of the Reagan administration signaled an important turn in the way that these issues would be handled in the political realm. In general, his survey reveals that most economists were of their own era and reflected, even as they contributed to, the racial views of the broader society. Later economists had more nuanced insights into the economics of discrimination. In this sense, there is a clear sense of improvement not only in the sophistication of economists' theoretical discussions of race but also in their sympathies toward black people. This, again, mirrors larger changes in American society. While by 1981 the conversation was not yet that advanced, open hostility toward black people and their aspirations had largely fallen out of the academic discussion.

The next two chapters take a critical look at the neoclassical approach to race. The first, "Racial Discrimination in the Labor Market," by economists William A. Darity Jr. and Patrick L. Mason, begins by considering the empirical work on race and finds that there remains substantial racial disparity in the American economy and that much of it lies in discriminatory treatment within labor markets. Darity and Mason argue that neoclassical models that build discrimination into economics via imperfect competition do not solve the problem, because "the reason for the immutability of the imperfection is rarely satisfactorily explained." They write, "Struggle as it may, orthodox microeconomics keeps returning to the position that sustained observed differences in economic outcomes between groups must be due to an induced or inherent deficiency in the group that experiences the inferior outcomes." They conclude with the observation that to explain the data on racial wage disparities, one needs a model in which the market does not work in the long run to resolve the problem.

The next chapter, "Liberty *and* Equality *and* Diversity? Thoughts on Liberalism and Racial Inequality after Capitalism's Latest Triumph," by economist Marcellus Andrews, also takes a critical look at the neoclassical model. It considers the racial consequences of the hegemony of free-market ideas, exploring the implications of both classical liberalism and various forms of egalitarian liberalism for the economic well-being of racial outcasts in capitalist societies who have been the victims of ongoing racial hatred. He points out that the practical political economy of "actually existing" conservatism is deeply influenced by Nobel laureate Friedrich v. Hayek's classical liberal critique of social justice, which limits the claims of justice to the application of a common set of rules to all persons without regard to identity or economic position.

Andrews observes that two consequences follow from this stance. First, all attempts to intervene in economic processes with the intent of altering the distribution of income and wealth in order to promote social justice are taken to be an illegitimate use of public power to shift the balance of rights and rewards from one social or economic group to another, thereby violating the principle of neutrality at the core of classical liberalism. Second, persistent racial inequality that has its origins in historic slavery and apartheid and that is sustained by contemporary patterns of social discrimination rooted in inherited inequalities in skills, wealth, and political power across color lines is nevertheless taken to be a just outcome as long as these contemporary disparities are the unplanned result of competitive economic activity. Andrews argues that the logic of classical liberalism indicates that those who accept its reasoning and politics must also accept the notion that the victims of historic racism and deprivation should accept a reduced social position as the price to be paid for a regime of liberal neutrality in matters of racial identity.

Andrews next examines the work of four egalitarian liberals—John Rawls, Nobel laureate Amartya Sen, Gerald Cohen, and Avishai Margalit—to assess the extent to which market and capitalist institutions can be reformed so that the lofty ideals of classical liberalism are not transformed into just another instrument of racial oppression. Andrews summarizes how each of these writers has explored the analytical weaknesses of Hayek's liberalism, while proposing alternative formulations of the connection between free markets and equality that retain capitalism's flexibility while promoting a more substantive freedom for all citizens. Finally, Andrews concludes by discussing the failure of egalitarian liberalism in racially divided societies and assessing the implications of Cohen's critique of Rawlsian liberalism and Margalit's critique of theories of justice in favor of a rigorous concept of "decency."

In the last chapter in part 2, "The Anatomy of Racial Inequality: A Clarification," economist Glenn Loury gives a response to several of the strands of criticism that have been made of the arguments that he presented in his recent book, *The Anatomy of Racial Inequality* (Loury 2002). In this chapter, Loury defends some of his core conceptions, including the importance of "contact," rather than simply "contract," discrimination, and how that has led to a variety of observable difficulties in African-American communities. In particular, he advances the idea that racial stigma is a cognitive, not a normative, category and that this category has a place in social scientific analysis of the plight of African-Americans when we consider the facts of differential outcomes in schooling, prison rates, and economic success or lack thereof.

Policy Issues

Part 3 considers policy issues. The first chapter, "Pragmatism, Liberalism, and Economic Policy," by economist David Colander, looks broadly at policy and race. He makes the arguments that successful policy has always been pragmatic policy and that the liberal agenda is broad enough to be used to support a wide range of policies. For Colander, policy, in large part, consists of drawing arbitrary lines and making them seem nonarbitrary and acceptable. To make lines that you have drawn compelling, the policy must often be accompanied by ideological arguments—often deep ones—that purport to tie that policy into deeper traditions or that connect it to emotional and ideological positions.

Colander argues that recognizing this aspect of policy is important to developing new policies that have a chance of gaining political support. He argues, first, that the policies that are most likely to make a difference are those that meld together past approaches to the problem in new ways and, second, that the role of economists and policy entrepreneurs is to suggest the broad outlines of how that new melding can be done. He argues that designing such policies involves the use of Chicago-type reasoning, but that reasoning should be seen only as an input into the final policy decision, not as the arbiter of the decision. He maintains that policies dealing with race are often what philosopher Martha Nussbaum calls tragic questions and must be recognized as such if the policies flowing from them are to be seriously considered. Based on these general arguments, he surveys issues that are being considered today and outlines what he believes will be the structure of a new melding of ideas. He argues that the new social policy agenda will be a combination of market policies blended together in new ways. He then provides some examples of such policies.

He advocates focusing on policies that clearly specify goals, not methods for achieving goals, and that have a zero net cost when considered from the perspective of the group being helped.

In the second chapter in this section, "Better Recreational Drugs: Unleashing Technology to Win the War on Bad Drugs," economists Vanita Gowda and Brendan O'Flaherty argue that America's drug laws have played a role in perpetuating racism by creating a thriving market for illicit recreational and occupational drugs and by concentrating anonymous, open-air selling of those drugs in African-American neighborhoods. They suggest that a way around this problem is to legalize certain recreational and occupational drugs, but not the ones that are illicit now. Instead, they offer a novel approach in which the government is to specify what attributes of drugs are acceptable and then to let recreational drugs that can meet these requirements be sold openly. They argue that such an improvement in laws will change the choice set of many individuals, improve the quality of life in many African-American neighborhoods, and reduce certain kinds of profiling and stereotyping.

Conclusion

Economics is seen as many things. To progressives, it is often seen as a defense of the status quo. To conservatives, it is often seen as a proof of the need for markets. Neither of these views is right. It is a way of thinking that, when used correctly, is incorporated in a broader philosophical foundation and developed within a historical context. If economics is to be useful in understanding the problem of race and in guiding future policy toward race, it is necessary to see economics in this broader framework. Then it will not be a way of thinking that is to be condemned by one side and exalted by another; instead, it will be an approach that is used by both sides to further our understanding and to work toward better policy. The chapters in this volume are a step in that direction.

NOTES

1. "Classic" books that explore this change include Dangerfield 1935, Wiebe 1967, and Fine 1964. More recent, very compelling books include Sanders 1999 and Skocpol 1992.

PART I

Classical Economic and Early Approaches to Race

Apes, Essences, and Races

What Natural Scientists Believed about Human Variation, 1700–1900

Brendan O'Flaherty and Jill S. Shapiro

Throughout the eighteenth and nineteenth centuries, both social scientists and natural scientists addressed the question of why Europeans and some of their descendants dominated the rest of the world militarily and economically. They also tackled the deeper and more fundamental questions of what human beings are, how they fit into the scheme of the natural world, and how they differ from one another.

In this chapter, we will try to give a brief overview of what those answers were and how they changed. We will not try to demonstrate direct links between natural scientists and economists; such close textual analysis is beyond our capabilities and the scope of this chapter. We think it highly likely, though, that economists were influenced by the natural science of the day, just as today's environmental economists pay close attention to what meteorologists say about global warming. We are examining the ocean in which classical and early neoclassical economists swam, not the molecules that passed through their gills.

Our basic story is this: An initial consensus on the homogeneity of humans and on causal theories tied to environmental contrasts would be recast to an increasing focus on the heterogeneity of humankind and the innate and fixed nature of their condition. While the cultural superiority of the European was rarely in doubt, by the close of the nineteenth century, his rank would be validated not only by behavior but by biology as well. This fundamental shift was concomitant with a flurry of scientific research into the nature of human variation, the culmination of which would be the formal birth of the discipline of physical anthropology in the early twentieth century. A fundamental paradox is that while the overwhelming majority of data indicated that discrete interpopulational contrasts among humans were elusive, broader social constructs would rely on a scientific foundation that concluded, to use anatomist Robert Knox's aphorism (1850, 6), "With me, race or hereditary descent is everything; it stamps the man."

Throughout this chapter, we will maintain the assumption that the consensus among leading natural scientists today about human variation and race is correct. That is presumptuous, but it is the best we can do. It follows that almost everything written about race by virtually all of the natural scientists whom we will consider was wrong. Many of them were wrong in a way that we take today to be hideously immoral. This does not come as a surprise—we would not use Galen's writings to treat a sick child or Newton's to hook up a stereo. Following the example of the classical economists, we will think of these natural scientists as neither mean nor stupid.

The puzzle in the record of natural science in this time period is that the bad ideas not only persisted, they became worse in many senses. Ordinarily, most economists think that bad ideas—incorrect beliefs about people or technology—should die out, either quickly or gradually. Over time, evidence accumulates and forces the rejection of more propositions (e.g., believing that centrally planned economies are likely to grow fast in the long run was an easier position to hold in 1910 than it is in 2002). Moreover, people whose beliefs are correct will in most cases do better than people whose beliefs are wrong, and the former will either put the latter out of business or induce them to imitate. Our implicit belief that these two processes are at work means that almost all of us think that scholars know more now than they did forty years ago, that what we ourselves personally believe today is better than what we believed ten years ago, and that technological progress will continue over the next half century.

In our case, though, as evidence accumulated, conclusions got worse. Later scientists had better data, better resources, better methods—but they missed the big point by a much wider margin. One task of this chapter will be trying to understand why. We will concentrate on the question of why better evidence failed to give scientists a better understanding of race.

Why the economic process—prosperity and survival for the fittest ideas—
also failed is a question for other chapters.

We begin our history of thought with a necessary preliminary: the background, both intellectual and factual, that set the stage for the often dramatic changes in reasoning and practice that took place as natural science
grappled with the question of human variation in the eighteenth and
nineteenth centuries. The importance of these underlying constructs cannot be understated, as they will be revived repeatedly, many rising from
the ashes to serve as pillars for racial ideology.

Background

By 1700, the Renaissance and several centuries of overseas voyages had
brought Europeans, northern Europeans especially, into contact with
plants, animals, and civilizations they had never before dreamed of. The
Americas, the Pacific Ocean, most of Asia, sub-Saharan Africa, Russia,
and even northern Scandinavia presented Europeans with new plants and
animals and introduced them to people who looked, talked, and acted differently from all the people they had known. The primary sources of
knowledge, the "empirical" data, were the accounts of travelers, mission-
aries, merchants, and other explorers who recorded what they had seen.
Buffon cited eighty such sources in his *Histoire naturelle* (1749–1804),
including the writings of Marco Polo (Voegelin [1933] 1998). Bernier
([1684, trans. 1863–64] 2000) stands as a rarity, a classifier who had actually traveled and seen those whom he was classifying. Understanding how
all these new discoveries fit together and how they could be made consistent with what Europeans knew already was the fundamental challenge
that Enlightenment science faced.

For the history of race, the discovery of the true apes at this time was
one of the most important discoveries. For Europeans, Andrew Battell's
1625 report of a creature that is likely to have been a chimpanzee is the
first definitive account of a true ape (although short anecdotes appear in
Marco Polo and similar travelogues). Not until 1699 and the publication
of Edward Tyson's dissection of an infant chimp do we see the formal entry
of apes into the consciousness of Western science.

So, when the early taxonomists write about the apes, they reference
newly encountered and barely studied creatures. Not until well into the

1800s, with the increased importation of zoological specimens and the Congress of Vienna agreements allowing cross-national access to materials, could broad-based and comprehensive anatomical analyses be conducted. Geoffroy Saint Hilaire and Cuvier will not clearly differentiate the chimpanzee from the orang utan until 1795. In fact, the first gorilla specimens for study were not obtained until 1847, and the first live gorillas did not arrive in Europe and the United States until 1855 and 1898, respectively. The mountain gorilla was not even known to the West until 1902.

European literature is replete with references to "apes" before Battell and Tyson. But these references are not about true apes at all; they are actually about monkeys, most probably tailless Barbary macaques. True apes approximate human form and behavior much more closely than Barbary macaques do. This aspect is readily evident in the names used by local inhabitants; for example, *orang utan* means "man of the forest" in Malay. Europeans would first meet apes at the same time they met sub-Saharan Africans—an association that would have a long history.

In trying to understand the apes and the myriad of other discoveries, Europeans turned first to their intellectual inheritance in both the classics and Christianity. As Hannaford (1996) cogently demonstrates, the writings of Plato, Aristotle, Herodotus, Tacitus, Strabo, and others would be "plundered," and often distorted and misconstrued, in an attempt at validating the prevailing views of the day. Herodotus, for example, often regarded as the first anthropologist, would be used to categorize the races of Europe, and Plato's "myth of the metals" would be used by Davenport in the twentieth century for eugenicist ideas on race mixing.

The majority of modern classicists support the view that the Greco-Roman world was devoid of a concept of race in the modern sense, that it classified by political status and not by variability of physical form (Hannaford 1996). Nevertheless, classical antiquity would provide seminal philosophical concepts for burgeoning taxonomy, central among them, essentialist thought, the Great Chain of Being, and an environmental theory of human variation.

Plato's gift, essentialistic or typological thinking, would have the greatest longevity; it was intrinsic to racial classifications until after World War II. Some would even argue that it is still with us. Paleoanthropologists Milford Wolpoff and Rachel Caspari explain: "Typological thinking is part of our cultural heritage, a part of our mind-set; it is the way most of us organize the world. And even if we 'know' not to apply it to biology, it seeps in anyway" (Wolpoff and Caspari 1997, 317). Rooted in the concept of the *eidos*, the world is seen as composed of distinct elements that are reflections of pure, fixed ideals or essences. Variations among those elements are merely deviations, imperfections around the ideal type.

The second concept, the Great Chain of Being, would at times be met with direct challenge, but it, too, would play a critical role at several historical junctures. The idea was derived from Aristotle, for whom the universe was filled with distinct biotic elements ordered according to imperceptible continuous gradations. A biological link between forms was not implied, nor could new forms emerge. Rather, every life-form that could exist did already, and each held a fixed position or rank along the continuum from the simplest to the divine—a linear chain of being.

The final element, dating back to Hippocrates, attempts to provide an environmental explanation for human variation. Differences, both physical and behavioral, were seen as resulting from diverse environmental phenomena, not innate contrasts. While there were different variants of this perspective, among them Aristotle's polar principles and Diodorus's global zones, the Greco-Roman environmental theory was the basis for classical views of other peoples (Hannaford 1996). This is not to say that these views represent a monolithic construct in Greco-Roman thought; there was indeed some ambiguity. The vital point, however, is that the taxonomies of the 1700s and 1800s, including the classification of humans, would be built firmly on a foundation of essentialist thinking and, for some, on a static chain and/or an environmental theory of causation.

Classical attitudes toward the apes they knew (i.e., Barbary macaques) also influenced how Europeans thought about true apes. The general attitude was summed up by poet Quintus Ennius: "Simia quam similis turpissima bestia nobis" [The ape, how similar that most ugly beast is to us] (1903). In a classical world with blurry lines between men and gods and apes, Aristotle and Galen were not troubled by their findings of great morphological similarity.

Blurry lines between man and god and ape were not a feature of Christianity, the other great intellectual tradition inherited by the Enlightenment. Its overriding principles were a single origin of all life and the unity of mankind. The basis for this unity was man's rationality and morality. Augustine's formulation was clear:

[E]very real man, that is, every mortal animal that is rational, however unusual to us may be the shape of his body, or the color of his skin, . . . and whatever the strength, portion or quality of his natural endowments, is descended from the single first-created man. (Augustine 1952, book XVI, chap. 8)

Thus, the church discouraged the idea that humans were more than one species. Bruno ([1591] 1950) and Vanini ([1619] 1842) both put forward this idea, but it was not well received. Bruno was burned at the stake; Vanini's tongue was cut out, after which he was strangled at the stake and burned to ashes.

Christianity also forced a change in how apes were viewed. With the rise of Christianity, the ape would turn into a *figura diabolica*, then into a sinner, and ultimately into a fool. Thomas Aquinas's anatomical analysis found, contrary to Galen, that there were no anatomical similarities between "apes" and humans.

The Enlightenment

How Nature and Humanity Fit Together

The big problems that Enlightenment anthropology and biology confronted were, first how to reconcile the apparent fact that creatures very similar to the dogs, cats, sheep, and humans that we now see had always existed with the readily observed diversity of those creatures today. The Egyptians had cats just like we do, but no two cats are exactly the same. Enlightenment anthropologists also had to explain how humans could be animals in physical appearance and bodily functioning but also (obviously) superior to them.

The interfertility criterion for species membership, sometimes attributed to Ray (1691), started the Enlightenment on the way to sorting out these puzzling new phenomena. The basic idea is that two individuals are members of the same species if they can breed together and produce fertile offspring. The utility of this criterion becomes apparent in the grand natural systems of Linnaeus (1740) and Buffon ([1749, trans. 1812] 1950).

Voegelin ([1933] 1998) explains how Linnaeus used the interfertility criterion to solve the first of the Enlightenment's two great puzzles. Since all living creatures emerge from an egg and since each egg produces a creature that resembles its parents, no new species are produced in the current epoch. Thus, each species must have an original ancestor (either a hermaphrodite or a pair differing in gender). Each species is a unity that can be traced back to God.

The essence, or *germ* (to use Kant's term), of each species was thus present at its creation and passes down from generation to generation. But the germ is an algorithm, not a blueprint; it carries a rule for reacting to the circumstances that a member of the species may confront. The phenotypes of various members of the species are just realizations of the underlying invisible essence. Nothing new is added as the history of a species unfolds; contingencies are just played out according to rules that were embedded in the germ in the beginning.

While nothing could be added to the instructions with which each species was endowed, it was possible (various thinkers differed on this point) for parts of those instructions to be lost through atrophy. Voegelin ([1933] 1998, 36) explains: "The potential of developing in one or another direction was already present, but it was realized only when particular external conditions occurred, which then favored the unfolding of one potential while allowing others to wither." The phenotypes of the original members of the species, while not necessarily perfect representatives of the essence, were better representations than subsequent generations because they were closer to God's hand and because no potential had been allowed to wither. The dogs in the Garden of Eden had within them both the instructions for creating collies and the instructions for creating cocker spaniels, but today's collies have lost the instructions for creating cocker spaniels.

This combination of eternal essences and contingent realizations neatly solves the Enlightenment's biological problem. It reconciles the fixity of species and the diversity of individuals.

A second problem, reconciling humans to the natural world, did not call forth such a neat solution. The interfertility criterion would not permit scientists to look at humans as anything other than a single species, since most claimed to be aware of interbreeding between different types of people).[1] Beyond the fact of interfertility, scientists need a way of telling one species from another, a *differentia specifica* (per Aristotle) or a *differentia essentialis* (per Ray). I know that two creatures cannot produce fertile offspring, but how do I know which is a mosquito and which a pig? The Enlightenment's second problem then boiled down to finding a *differentia essentialis* for humans. A *differentia essentialis* that was purely somatic would lower humans to the level of the other animals, where they did not belong; one that was purely spiritual would deny the bodily nature of humans.

Enlightenment writers tried several different approaches to this problem. Linnaeus, in the first edition of *Systema Naturae* (1735), places humans within the category *Anthropomorpha*, the first division of the

Quadrupedia, under the category for clawed animals (the grouping for animals with four incisors, four fingers, and hairy bodies). His classification was based on morphological similarity; for him, the unique distinguishing characteristic of man was the possession of a rational soul (*nosce te ipsum*) and, as such, was irrelevant to this taxonomy:

> I cannot discover the difference between man and the orangoutang, although all of my attention was brought to bear on this point, except for laying hold of some uncertain characteristics. (Linnaeus 1735, as quoted in Stepan 1982, 7)

Linnaeus's 1758 edition offered refinements. He replaced the term *Anthropomorpha* with the term *Primates*, describing the first order, a category that included four genera: *Homo*, *Simia* (monkeys and apes), *Lemur*, and *Vespertillo* (bats). Even with this change, there was insistence that the distinction between humans and other animals be drawn more sharply. Thomas Penant would write, "I reject [Linnaeus's] first division, which he calls Primates, or foremost in creation, because my vanity will not suffer me to rank mankind with apes, monkeys and bats" (Penant 1771, as quoted in Thomas 1983, 110).

Buffon took an approach that was in many ways the opposite of Linnaeus:

> [T]hat there is an infinite distance between the faculties of man and those of the most perfect animal evidently proves that man is of a different nature. . . . one passes all at once from the thinking being to the material being, from the intellectual power to mechanical force, from order and design to blind movement, from reflection to appetite. (Buffon 1749, as quoted in Voegelin [1933] 1998, 48)

Only at the end of the Enlightenment is there a recognizably modern resolution to this problem, in the work of Blumenbach and Kant. They define humans as part of nature in purely somatic terms. Blumenbach would focus on morphology and its concomitant functional ties (including language and reason) to distinguish humans. For him: "[T]hen the subsequent characters, especially if they are looked at collectively, seem to suffice for a definition of mankind: (A) The erect position; (B) The broad, flat pelvis; (C) the two hands; (D) The regular and close set rows of teeth" (Blumenbach [1795] 1865, 164).[2] Based on these characteristics, Blumenbach called for the ordinal separation of humans, with the former in Bimanus and the rest of the primates in Quadrumana.

Varieties of Humans

Enlightenment scientists looked at the different varieties of humans in this context. The human essence was created once and had been passed down to us since then. There were several important implications: variety came from environment, the number of races was small, many different traits mattered, races were not ordered in a hierarchy, and Africans were currently problematic. We will discuss each of these implications in turn.

Variety Comes from Environment

Although all humans shared the same essence, they differed because they lived in different environments. Some people found themselves in the tropics, where the algorithm produced dark skin, wide lips, and woolly hair. Others found themselves in the arctic, where the algorithm produced epicanthic folds, tawny skin, and so on. In general, people who lived in different places were expected to look and act differently, in response to their environment.

Buffon sets forth this theory of causation most emphatically. He offers three causative factors, chief among them climate, followed by diet and, to a minor extent, customs. With such an environmental theory and dynamic view of nature, human differences are seen as superficial. Moreover, they are seen as flexible; change was possible (within eight to twelve generations), and race would persist as long as the milieu remained. Blumenbach ([1775] 1865, 113) echoes the same environmental explanation: "[C]olour . . . is, at all events, an adventitious and easily changeable thing, and can never constitute a diversity of species." He also attributed most of the diversity in head form to mode of life and to art.

The Number of Races Is Small

Enlightenment typologies generally required that the number of principal varieties or races be a half dozen or less.[3] This desire for a small number of races in part grew out of a desire for taxonomic neatness, but it was validated by an implicit theory of natural history. In modern terms, this theory of natural history is called the "ancient candelabra" (and it has very little modern support). The idea is that certain large groups of people have been separated from each other, isolated, and restricted to breeding with cousins, for very long periods of time. Thus, Kant, in defining the term *race*, emphasizes that it is part of natural history, not nature, a source of information about causes, not a static descriptor.

The "ancient candelabra" theory is perhaps best illustrated in the predominant Christian view of the origins of Africans, which probably influenced the scientists of the time. Sub-Saharan Africans were thought to be descendants of Ham, one of Noah's children. More specifically, all of their ancestors after Ham were also considered Ham's descendants, as no interbreeding with nondescendants was to have occurred in the intervening millennia.

Enlightenment scientists knew that environment worked slowly— Europeans who went to the tropics did not develop wide noses—and so long periods of reproductive isolation were needed to produce the diversity they were finding among humans. But because reproductive isolation was plausible only for big bunches of people—blocks on the order of continents, not countries—the number of races had to be small.

Thus, for instance, Bernier and Camper both counted four races (the latter's followed the division of the continents), and Leibniz distinguished five. Blumenbach has four races in his first edition and five in his second. Kant, coming from philosophy, has four races based on climate, the two-by-two interaction of temperature and humidity.

Many Traits Matter

Man's special place in nature implied that salient differences should not merely be confined to the somatic realm. The human essence, in contrast to the essences of other animals, was spiritual and intellectual as well as physical, so the distinctions among human varieties should be made on these grounds as well. Throughout the Enlightenment typologies, then, we find groups distinguished by philosophy, culture, habits of mind, and general beauty.

Giordano Bruno and Jean Bodin both attempted an elementary geographic arrangement of populations using skin color. The latter's account was purely descriptive and included such neutral terms as "duskish colour, like roasted quince, black, chestnut, fairish and white" (Bodin, as quoted in Slotkin 1965, 43). These were followed by philosopher Gottfried Leibniz, who focused on skin color and hair color and form, and by John Ray, who relied on stature, shape, skin color as well as food habits. Brief descriptions of other "peculiarities" were also offered often—comments that today would sound like, "New Yorkers talk fast and they wear black."

Linnaeus, whose approach to taxonomy would be adopted by future generations, does not offer any subdivisions among humans in his first edition of *Systema Naturae* (1735). In the 1740 version, he adds four geographical subdivisions (Europaeus, Americanus, Asiaticus, and Africanus). These divisions would remain through the twelfth and final edition in 1768. Critically, they are presented as categories below level of species, and they are not ranked any more than divisions of a genus. Only with the tenth edition (1758), the edition in which he created the Primates as the first order, does he abandon his heretofore exclusive reliance on anatomical features. The tenth edition is important not only because it marks for many the beginning of taxonomy proper (due to the consistency in methodology) but also because it signifies a dramatic change in the treatment of differences among humans. Here, his approach to humans differs from his classification of other animals, because sociocultural aspects of temperament, character, clothing, and customs become part of the classification. While he is not the first taxonomist to include such data, he was the first to make it scientific. He draws on ancient and medieval theories of the link between the four humors and temperament. For example: Americanus is choleric and ruled by custom, Europaeus is sanguine and ruled by laws, Asiaticus is melancholy and ruled by opinion, and Afer is phlegmatic and ruled by caprice (Slotkin 1944, 461–62). Among Linnaeus's most long-lasting contributions was the legitimization of the idea that humans could be subdivided into groups. As Marks (1995, 52) states, "This assumption is ultimately what students of human diversity owe to Linnaeus."

There Is No Hierarchy

The scientists who enumerated the types of humankind did so without ranking them. They considered the majority of contrasts superficial in nature and the divisions themselves, arbitrary. Europeans were seen by Buffon and Blumenbach as the most likely original form from which changes occurred. This did not imply deterioration, only environmentally produced modification. Linnaeus does not even rank his nonhuman categories. While his attitudes toward the superiority of humans appear evident, his seminal approach was to replace a unidimensional great chain with a two-dimensional pattern, horizontal and vertical, with categories of equal rank. There was a hierarchy, but all classes were considered equally classes and were not ranked.

Blumenbach ([1795] 1865, 264) added another reason for rejecting hierarchy:

> Innumerable varieties of mankind run into one another by insensible degrees. . . . [N]o variety exists, whether of colour, countenance, or stature, . . . as not to be connected with others of the same kind by such an imperceptible transition, that it is very clear they are all related, or only differ from each other in degree.

Blumenbach emphasized that discrete divisions among humans were elusive and that the process was often arbitrary. This lack of discreteness as human form graded from one people to the next would be central to Blumenbach's view of the unity of humankind. As noted earlier, his argument for an ordinal separation of humans was part of an overall goal to emphasize the unity of the species. For Blumenbach, as Flourens explains, all human races were alike; they were united in mind, "The human mind is one. The soul is one" (Flourens [1847] 1865, 57).

Contra Linnaeus, by his third edition, Blumenbach relied solely on physical criteria and explicitly omitted reference to cultural traits and broad inferences about personality. For Blumenbach ([1795] 1865, 270), "there is no single character so peculiar and so universal among the Ethiopians [i.e., Africans], but what it may be observed on the one hand everywhere in other varieties of men."

In his first publication, Blumenbach adopted Linnaeus's four varieties; in his third, he added a fifth, Malay. With this step, as Gould (1994) argues, Blumenbach forever changed the geometry of race from a cartographic model to one that could and would be misinterpreted as indicating a linear hierarchy of worth. As for the Great Chain of Being, Blumenbach's rejection of the concept would serve as the standard for British students of racial science in the early part of the nineteenth century (Stepan 1982).

Africans Are Currently Problematic
Though many different divisions of humankind into races were developed, they had one element in common: almost all Europeans were always in one race, and almost all sub-Saharan Africans were always in another. All the differences in classification are among other groups (and among the Hottentots and Laplanders, the people from the furthest reaches of Africa and Europe).

Enlightenment writers also generally say better things about Europeans than they do about other races, especially Africans. This view that Europeans are better than Africans differs from the similar view that later scientists held in two important dimensions. First, the Enlightenment scientists (except for Sömmering) did not claim to have objective data to support their beliefs; they just took it as a common understanding, a shared social belief. You do not need to write a footnote when you claim, for instance, that India is poorer than the United States or that malaria is bad for people.

Second, little, if any, hierarchy is implied by these distinctions. Europeans are handsome because they live in a better climate; Africans are ugly because they live in a horrible climate. Thus, Buffon ([1749, trans. 1812] 1950, 15) writes:

The most temperate climate lies between the 40th and 50th degrees of latitude, and it produces the most handsome and beautiful men. It is from this climate that the ideas of the genuine color of mankind, and the various degrees of beauty, ought to be derived. The two extremes are equally remote from truth and from beauty.

Consistent with this notion that lousy climate produces lousy people is the low opinion that many writers (Bernier and Buffon especially) held of Laplanders, whom even Blumenbach excluded from the European race. Bernier ([1684, trans. 1863–64] 2000, 3) writes of them: "They are little, stunted creatures with thick legs, large shoulders, short neck, and a face elongated immensely; very ugly and partaking much of the bear. . . . [T]hey are wretched animals."[4]

Not all Enlightenment thinkers were in step with scientists on this environmentally contingent view of European superiority. There was considerable evidence in favor of an alternative position. European military superiority, for one thing, was becoming overwhelming; you could not make money placing bets on non-European countries. Incomes were beginning to diverge notably. Moreover, if you base your belief in the unity of humankind on the Bible and Christian tradition, it is not inconsistent to value possession of that tradition. Thus, Kant writes:

The Negroes of Africa have by nature no feeling that rises above the trifling. Mr. Hume challenges anyone to cite a single example in which a Negro has shown talents, and asserts that among the hundreds of thousands of blacks who are transported elsewhere from their countries, although many of them have even been set free, still not a single one was ever found who presented anything great in art or science or any other praiseworthy quality; even though among the whites some continually rise aloft from the lowest rabble, and through superior gifts earn respect in the world. So fundamental is the difference between those two races of men, and it appears to be as great in regard to mental capacities as in color. The religion of fetishes so widespread among them is perhaps a sort of idolatry that sinks as deeply into the trifling as appears to be possible to human nature. (Kant [1775] 1997, 55)

(By contrast, Blumenbach established a special library in his house devoted exclusively to authors of African descent and especially praised the poetry of Phillis Wheatley.)

An African American Looks at the Enlightenment

Although most Enlightenment writers accepted the current inferiority of non-Europeans, at least implicitly, much of the Enlightenment approach was well received among African American thinkers. As late as 1854, in his address *The Claims of the Negro, Ethnologically Considered*, Frederick Douglass uses familiar reasoning to argue for the unity of the human race: polygenism would throw into question the Genesis account, animals are instinctively subject to the domain of Negroes as well as whites, and mental and physical differences arise from the environment, not from heredity. Douglass argues that, "His flat feet, long arms, high cheek bones and retreating forehead" result from strenuous labor with little intellectual engagement; they are not immutable (520).

Douglass, like John Stuart Mill, is echoing familiar themes from the Enlightenment: humans are essentially united and distinct from the apes, environment causes differences and can eliminate them, and science demands no hierarchy. But he is echoing them in 1854, when science has moved on.

Natural Science after the Enlightenment

As Stanton (1960, 11) states, in the 1700s the "concept of equality was a scientific concept." It rested on the unity of humankind through a single origin, on a similar morphology, and on the importance of environmental factors in explaining human physical and mental diversity. The consensus on equality began to fray at the end of the eighteenth century. As both Europe and North America became embroiled in controversies over slavery and colonialism, new, dramatically different perspectives arose. In Europe, the Great Chain of Being was revived. In the United States, monogenism was contested and lost its primacy. On both sides of the Atlantic, environmental explanations were rejected, and human differences, both physical and behavioral, came to be seen increasingly as fixed, discrete, and indicative of an ordering. As a result, by midcentury, the fate of science and racial thought would be linked. It would be impossible to separate them, and within the broader social sphere, a biologically rooted pessimism about the human condition prevailed.

While economic, political, and social factors all played important roles, this reorientation can also be linked to fundamental changes in science. We may not prefer their conclusions, but the nineteenth century produced better empirical scientists than those of the eighteenth century.

The Great Chain Returns

It is difficult to pinpoint the reasons for the reemergence of the Great Chain. One explanation points to the sheer "naturalness" of it, as increasing complexity in life-forms could be seen at all turns (Stepan 1982). Another alternative is that the association and seeming proximity between humans and apes was too deeply embedded in Western European thought to disappear. A third approach relates directly to methodological and theoretical changes within the practice of science, and while not necessarily precluding the other ideas, it appears to be the most substantial. In brief, the period between 1800 and 1830 saw the development of the fields of comparative anatomy, physiology, histology, and paleontology. The idea of gradation proved central to these comparative studies, and interestingly, it was central to the biological work of both Cuvier and Lamarck, who held polar views on the idea of evolutionary change (Figlio 1976). Friedrich Tiedemann's classic embryological work examined the gradations among life-forms and linked them to the development of human fetuses and children (1816). While he never linked embryology to racial differences,[5] others would make that association, saying that some races are more like children while others are more like adults. By midcentury, the idea that the races formed a graded series had become a foundation in racial science.

Despite the fact that the repudiation of the Great Chain had been a central element of the British monogenist argument, from this time on even ardent monogenists spoke of gradations in form. Situating human diversity on the Great Chain meant that what was once seen as superficial and arbitrary was now rigid and innate, a permanent difference in the essential natures of these groups. This ranking pertained to physical traits as well as to moral, intellectual, and social qualities. It was nature, not man, that prevented civilized behavior. Now that the hierarchy was firmly reentrenched, the only question was how best to measure it. The initial answer through roughly 1850 was an overwhelming (though not mono-lithic) chorus of non-European biological inferiority as voiced by the likes of White (1799), Stanhope Smith (1810), Prichard (1826), Lawrence (1822), Cuvier ([1817, trans. 1831] 1950), Morton (1839), Agassiz (1850), and Broca (1888). The continuing search for answers would be the goal of research for the remainder of the century.

The new position of Africans on the Great Chain would place them in closer proximity to the apes. Now, beliefs that had circulated perhaps since the earliest English encounters (virtually simultaneous) with both the human and ape inhabitants of Africa were given scientific support. As Stepan (1982) notes, while some researchers would avoid or object (Hux-ley 1870; Owen 1852) to any such association, others saw it clearly in one or more features (Hunt 1863–64; Lawrence 1822; Cuvier [1817, trans. 1831] 1950). Charles White, for example, in *An Account of the Regular Gradation in Man* (1799), compared Africans to apes with respect to geni-talia and menstrual cycles. In 1817, Georges Cuvier, continental Europe's preeminent biologist, wrote about the "Negro" race, "The projection of the lower parts of the face, and the thick lips, evidently approximate it to the monkey tribe" (Cuvier [1817, trans. 1831] 1950, 44).

In Britain, too, scientists moved away from fundamental conclusions of Enlightenment science. James Prichard (1826), who held for flexibility and change, looked to biological "sports" as the causative agent for varia-tion. For him, climate could have an influence, though it did not create biological diversity. Further, he saw the original or stemrace as African, with Europeans as the later development. The following comment of William Lawrence (1822, as quoted in Gossett 1997, 57) suggests the looming shadow of the Great Chain: "That the Negro is more like a mon-key than the European . . . cannot be denied as a general observation."

Polygeny Gains Ground

History

Polygeny, the view that different races have different origins and are different species, was the major challenge to Enlightenment science in the first half of the nineteenth century. As noted earlier, the overwhelming consensus of scientists in the eighteenth century was that despite the evident diversity in form and behavior, humankind represented a single type, a single species, bound by a common origin. Toward the end of the 1700s, polygenist theories reappeared. Influential voices, such as those of Voltaire and Kames, would pose their challenge primarily to church dogma rather than to science (as would also later be the case with Nott and Gliddon). Even Hume was a polygenist. In the next century, these ideas would find broad-based support.

The trajectory of this debate takes different courses in Britain, on the Continent, and in the United States. In Europe, the debate was quashed dramatically on March 9, 1830, when Cuvier, a strict creationist, thoroughly routed Geoffroy Saint Hilaire in debate at the Academy of Science in Paris. As a result, the analysis of human variability in Europe was nearly silenced through the first half of the century.

In Britain, where scientists tended to be more religiously orthodox than those in Europe, the leading students of race, Prichard and Lawrence, stood firmly with the views of Linnaeus, Buffon, and Blumenbach on origins (Stepan 1982). They put forth a formidable challenge to the polygenist voices that began to gain strength in the 1840s. By 1860, James Hunt would lead the polygenist voice in British science, but while polygeny would have important implications for the future of anthropology as a discipline in Britain, it clearly remained a minority view.

The United States, in contrast, was the prime battlefield for the debate over origins. Proponents of slavery and of abolition were on both sides of the issue. In fact, among the leading voices championing the monogenist perspective in the United States, most were proslavery (Bachman 1855a, 1855b; Cartwright 1860; Fitzhugh [1854] 1965, [1856] 1960). Further, few would attempt to argue from a scientific perspective. John Bachman, a clergyman, challenged Morton on the fertility of hybrids and "natural repugnance" and Agassiz on the existence of discrete geographic divisions among races (Bachmann 1850, 1855a, 1855b), though increasingly his positions would be rejected as unscientific.

On the other side of the debate, science not only would join other polygenist voices but would take the lead in constructing a formidable argument. Samuel George Morton's classic comparative analysis of cranial capacity, *Crania Americana* (1839), would be coupled with Louis Agassiz's theoretical base (1850). As a result, by 1850, through the allure of numbers and the muscle of data, Morton convinced most of the scientists of this time that the multiple origins theory was the most parsimonious way of explaining human variability. The belief, long held in the wider social sphere, of the relative ranking of Europeans, Native Americans, and Africans was now validated by "objective" scientific evidence. At this point and hereafter, scientific method and theory became integral to any social construct of race.[6]

After Morton's death, Josiah Clark Nott and George Robin Gliddon would cloak themselves in the guise of science to continue as Morton's disciples. Their 730-page tome *Types of Mankind,* published in 1854, was the leading American work on human races at the time. In it, the association between Africans and apes was clearly highlighted through juxtaposed illustrations that typically exaggerated the "simian" features of the former and the "human" features of the later (458–59). The comment on one comparison of an Algerian, a Saharran, and a gorilla states, "The palpable analogies and dissimilitudes between an inferior type of mankind and a superior type of monkey require no comment" (Nott and Gliddon 1854, as quoted in Gould 1996, 67). As with Voltaire, Nott and Gliddon aimed their attack at conservative theology—as Nott would call it, "parson skinning" (Gossett 1997). Still, their lectures on "niggerology," as they described it, brought the issue to a broader audience using the voice of science.

Thought

Why did polygenists replace monogenists in the United States? Why did race become more important than environment? Part of the story is the obvious weaknesses and empirical shortcoming of the Enlightenment theories. Thinking of the essence of a species as an algorithm was a good approach for explaining intraspecies diversity, but it had the unfortunate empirical implications that acquired characteristics could be inherited and that "blacks" should turn "white" within a few generations in a temperate climate (and that the tans that Englishmen picked up in the tropics would be passed on to their children). Even without the efforts of scientists to acquire new information, the Enlightenment view of what species were became increasingly difficult to maintain as the nineteenth century wore on.

Two new kinds of scientific findings also hurt the Enlightenment view. The first was the vast expansion in the variety of plants and animals that scientists were learning about. Each new part of the world opened up to serious study by Europeans resulted in the discovery of new varieties, most of them fairly specific to that place. Simultaneously, knowledge of ancient Egypt was growing rapidly. The pyramids had been dated fairly accurately to about three thousand years ago, and the recovered artifacts indicated that the people, animals, and plants of that era were quite similar to those of present-day Egypt and the Mediterranean.

Together, these new findings made the idea of essence-as-algorithm untenable. Since Noah's ark beached at Ararat about 4,100 years ago—a fact that no one had any reason to question—and since varieties changed very little in the last 3,000 years, there was no reason to think they had changed much in the 1,100 years between Ararat and the pyramids. The algorithms just could not have worked fast enough to produce in only 1,100 years, from only a few species, the vast variety scientists were finding in the natural world. God and Noah must have done far more work 4,100 years ago than the Enlightenment scientists gave them credit for.

Thus, for instance, Louis Agassiz, a great Swiss and American naturalist, developed a theory about "centers of creation": species were created in the locations that were meant for them, and generally did not wander far from those places (Agassiz 1850).

Early nineteenth-century scientists maintained the notions of species-as-essence and of creation (even of the date of creation). The part of Enlightenment science they jettisoned was the idea that the essence was an algorithm. There were more species,[7] and they were less malleable. God hard-wired each being at the time of creation.

In anthropology, the Enlightenment approach also suffered because it seemed old-fashioned. As sciences that made no appeal to spiritual qualities of humans experienced greater success, the paeans that the Enlightenment wrote about humanity seemed increasingly a diversion from the serious study of nature. Similarly, the insistence on a literal interpretation of Genesis—a single creation event—seemed outmoded. Paradoxically, it was the least modern parts of Enlightenment science that created the space that let it sound so modern.

The nineteenth century also saw a growing gap between Europeans (and their descendants) and the rest of the world, not the convergence the Enlightenment foresaw, as Africans abroad adjusted to a better climate and as they and all the other non-European races absorbed European wisdom and religion. European military dominance increased. Miscegenation became prevalent enough that any dark-skinned person who was successful or educated could be assumed to have European blood.

Some peculiarly American forces may have been at work, too. Blumenbach's chief somatic argument for the unity of humankind was the lack of any sharp distinction between races. In the Old World, French shaded into Italians, Italians into Sicilians, Sicilians into Berbers, Berbers into Moors, and Moors into Senegambians. But in the United States, no such intermediate groups existed; with Native Americans either exterminated or transported to the West, there were only Africans and northern Europeans. Under these circumstances, it was much easier to believe that races were discrete.

The extraordinary success that Europeans had enjoyed in displacing Native Americans may also have reinforced the perception of European superiority. So, too, did the prosperity and abundance of the new nation: how could climate count for so much and race for so little when you contrasted what the Native Americans had accomplished in a few millennia in, say, Ohio with what Europeans had done there in a few decades? A friendly and sympathetic review of Morton's *Crania Americana* from the *American Journal of Science* concluded:

> One of the most singular features in the history of this continent, is, that the aboriginal races, with few exceptions, have perished or constantly receded, before the Anglo-Saxon race, and have in no instance . . . mingled with them as equals. . . . These phenomena must have a cause. (Combe and Coates 1840, quoted in Gould 1996, 83)

But while polygeny and the greatly enhanced role for biological inheritance that it implied were good ways of maintaining important elements of Enlightenment thought—essentialism, divine creation, the biblical chronology—in the face of mounting disconfirming evidence, this new way of looking at nature faced a major challenge in partitioning individuals into species. Ray's interfertility criterion and the scholastic *differentia specifica* had done this job for the Enlightenment, but neither tool could be used easily in the world of polygenesis.

The problem that the interfertility criterion presented for polygeny is obvious: one cannot simultaneously maintain that races are different species, that mulattoes are fertile, and that individuals are partitioned into species by the interfertility criterion. The polygenists solved this problem by relaxing both of the other propositions enough that they could still believe the first. They rewrote the interfertility criterion to require only that the offspring of different species have a certain quality; then they argued that mulattos had that quality. The polygenists had some difficulty articulating exactly what that quality was, but our best translation is, "sufficiently infertile that a dynasty will die out after a few generations," which is what they maintained, in the absence of good demographic data to the contrary.[8] As Agassiz claimed, "half-breeds" were "unnatural, as shown by their very constitution, their sickly physique, and their impaired fecundity" (in E. C. Agassiz 1886, 599). He was following popular convention in 1863 when he contrasted the "manly population descended from the cognate nations" with the "effeminate progeny of mixed races" (Agassiz 1886, 603).

Weakening the interfertility criterion helped solve the polygenists' original problem, but not without consequences. Weak or relative infertility of hybrids ensured that at any time, the vast majority of individuals would have inherited the essence of their species undiluted, and so in this regard, it worked almost as well as the Enlightenment's strong infertility. As an operational matter, however, weak infertility is a much more cumbersome criterion than is strong infertility. With the latter, to find out whether individual A and individual B are members of the same species, all one needs to do is breed them and see if the progeny are fertile—a matter of a generation. With weak infertility, one must wait several generations to answer this most basic question. When studying fruit flies, this waiting is not a serious cost, but when studying humans, it is.

Because the weak infertility criterion was a much less useful tool than the strong one for studying long-lived populations, polygenists had to put more emphasis on physical differences instead of fertility behavior in drawing lines between species. For races of humanity, finding a *differentia specifica* (or *differentia essentialis*) became a much more pressing, and in 1850, a still unsolved-problem.

Everything the polygenists did added to the burden that the untestable and unobservable essence of each race had to bear. For the Enlightenment, racial essences did not even exist, since only species could have essences (because only within species was descent restricted). Polygeny created the idea of a racial essence and then forced on it most of the weight of assigning individuals to races in the short run, since the only kind of fertility information that could be used was long-run data and since a *differentia specifica* had not yet been found.

By the publication of Darwin's *Origin of Species* (1859), typological thinking supported the discrete separation of humankind into hierarchically ranked races, each fixed in position along the Great Chain of Being. Environmental theories for diversity had been replaced by the new majority view of separate origins. This helped to fix the contrasts as innate and permanent—part of each person's essential nature. Body form was inextricably linked to behavior (in part a contribution from phrenology) and then abstracted to race.

The Darwinian Revolution

In 1859, Darwin's *Origin of Species* appeared in print and sold out on the first day. Within ten to fifteen years, most biologists accepted evolution as a general theory of the living world.

What Darwin Said

Humankind was once again united as one species, now the product of evolutionary processes. Darwin's theory of a biological continuum of humans and animals, physically, mentally, and morally, should have marked the demise of the Great Chain, but puzzlingly, the key concepts of fixity, ranking, and essentialism remained intact. Researchers would call themselves evolutionists while keeping alive a racial science of fixed essential types, the direct antithesis of Darwin's focus on populational variability, the food for natural selection's continuous change.

Darwin provided an account of natural history that was simpler and more complete than the Genesis narrative. Since one of the strongest arguments for polygeny depended on the biblical timetable, this reduced the appeal of polygeny. Because a major part of the Enlightenment argument also rested on Genesis—Adam and Eve as the source of humankind's unity—traditional monogeny as well suffered.

With respect to fixity, the early Darwinian theorists generally held that natural selection was no longer operating on humans.[9] Thus, the diversity that presently existed, be it a result of adaptation or sexual selection, came about long ago and had since remained fixed. In *The Descent of Man* (1871), Darwin offers a hypothesis of early race formation and stasis (Stepan 1982).[10] Further, as Stepan (1982) says, by viewing races as now fixed units, Darwin unintentionally bolstered the idea of fixed types, rein-forcing, instead of undermining, essentialistic thinking.

Explanations for the persistence of ranking are also complex but may be rooted in the analyses of anatomical gradations that had become central to science in the early part of the century and that had helped to revive the Great Chain. In structuring the argument for a relationship among forms and for the descent of man, Darwin needed small steps of continuity, and the "lower races" would serve this role. In his early notebooks, Darwin had written about the gradation in moral conscience in human races and, later, about the scale of civilization. While Darwin was trying to argue for the continuity of a single human species, it was all too easy to misinterpret his meaning to see races as forming an evolutionary scale. The new evolu-tionary language as applied to race would argue that the "lower races" had evolved the least far, that they had lost the struggle for survival, that they were unfit.[11]

The partial ordering that evolution contained allowed scientists to rank races in terms of "development." Europeans were the most highly devel-oped race because while in the past they had lived like other races, they no longer did so, and because they had also conquered other races. Africans still lived like Europeans had lived a long time ago; therefore, they were not as developed. James Bryce, a British Liberal, for example, gave a well-received series of lectures in 1902 entitled *The Relations of the Advanced and Backward Races of Mankind* (Bryce 1903).

What Race Science Heard

Darwin did not provide any new facts about humans or refute any old ones. The predominant response in biology was to maintain as much of the old way of looking at human variation as possible and to pluck a little of the low-hanging fruit that Darwin had exposed. Thus, Darwin did not upset the stylized fact of relative mulatto infertility that the polygenists had established. Therefore, you could still think of Africans as descendants of Ham and of Europeans as descendants of Shem, even though you no longer believed in "Ham" and "Shem"; the picture of separate strains remained.

As far as causality is concerned, the polygenists' view of the role of envi-ronment was easy to rephrase and replaced the long-held Enlightenment view. Instead of relying on the Creator's wisdom to match type with environment, scientists could now rely on evolution (either natural selection, mutation, or inheritance of acquired characteristics—all three mecha-nisms had their adherents in the late nineteenth century). Unlike the Enlightenment thinkers who believed Europeans were beautiful because their climate was salubrious, post-Darwinian anthropologists thought Europeans were smart and diligent because their climate was harsh:

> [The Negro's] environment has not been such as would tend to produce in him the restless energy which has led to the progress of the white race; and the easy conditions of tropical life and the fertility of the soil have reduced the struggle for existence to a minimum.. . . . [S]kill in reck-oning is necessary for the White race, and it has cultivated this faculty; but it is not necessary to the Negro. (Willcox 1910–11)

Darwinism was thus compatible with the idea that each race has its own essence, so the idea of racial essence survived the Darwinian revolution intact. For each environment, there is some best way of coping, a combi-nation of mental and physical capacities that best allowed humans to thrive. The body and mind that represented these was the ideal type, the essence of the race that inhabited that environment.

With racial essences (and separate lineages) intact, whether or not races were considered separate species became a semantic question to which great attention did not have to be devoted. Perhaps we all had some common ancestors who were recognizably human a long time ago; perhaps we did not. Because races had essences and species did not, race was a more important division than species.

In regard to apes, Darwin's ideas served to provide a natural, not merely a conventional and nominal, tie between them and humans. Darwin oblit-erated Buffon's infinite gap between humans and animals. God did not create humans ex nihilo; they evolved with chimps from an ape ancestor, just as mosquitoes and radishes evolved from other animals and plants.

The other piece of evidence for African inferiority was the alleged sim-ilarity between Africans and apes—in appearance (e.g., prognathism) and habitat. After Darwin, the inference was obvious: because they resembled apes more than Europeans did, Africans had traveled less far on the road of human development, the road that started with apes. Merit was unidi-mensional, and Africans, like apes, lacked it.

In sum, fixity persisted, ranking persisted, and essentialistic thinking persisted. Now, within the framework of evolutionary theory, the association between apes and some humans, specifically Africans, was given "scientific validation."

Racial Science after Darwin

After Darwin and the Civil War, racial science faced two great challenges. The first was scientific: finding a *differentia specifica* to tell the races apart. The second was policy oriented: figuring out how to predict and manage the interface between advanced and less developed races. Neither of these challenges could even be articulated in the language of Enlightenment science or in the language we use today. Still, after the Great Chain's return, polygenism, and Darwin, these concerns were both obvious and pressing.

Telling Races Apart

Why It Mattered
For race scientists after Darwin, finding some physical characteristic that partitioned humans by the geographical location of their ancestors circa A.D. 1500 was crucial for maintaining the reality of races. If races had essences, the essence of each race had to show up in some way (at least in 1500) other than geographical location. Mere correlation would not do (unless, perhaps, it was dazzlingly high). Essences are like noses and mothers; everybody (except half-breeds) must have precisely one essence—no more, no less. To make racial essences part of hard science, you had to find their physical expressions. That is what race scientists set out to do.

How They Tried
In the second half of the 1800s, the basic definition of physical anthropology was the study of human variation defined as group comparison. As the study of race became more professional, new and more precise techniques were developed. Even if racial types were conceived of as fixed in the past and to some extent intermingled now, it was still thought by some that one could discern elements of the original types. Measurement would be used not only to quantify contrasts but to help chart the evolutionary trajectory of human diversity.

In the eighteenth century, Camper had begun modern craniometry with his introduction of the facial angle (another debt to Aristotle).[12] Now, all aspects of the skull would be examined, including cranial dimensions, patterns of growth, suture closure, and the all-important contents of the cranium—the brain. By the century's close, Ripley (1899) would report that over ten million children and half a million adults in the United States and Europe had been measured for their "racial identity." The cephalic index, the ratio of head length to head breadth, was the next standard of measurement scientists used. Developed by Anders Retzius in 1842, it would become the most important measure of head shape used in the second half of the nineteenth century (Stepan 1982). Its most common use was in distinguishing among different European "peoples" or "races." While there was no general attempt at this point to assign relative worth according to the cephalic index, these data would be used in the interpretations of past and present history.

While populations were being sorted by cranial form, other scientists focused on different features, often using them directly to point to the evolutionary inferiority of some races, most particularly of the African (Gossett 1997). Gratiolet (1839, 1854) had earlier argued that coronal suture closure happened earlier in Africans, thus limiting the potential growth of their brains. Now, in the wake of Darwin, this argument could take on evolutionary significance.

Another primary area of research included the brain. In addition to the work conducted by Paul Broca (1888), founder of the Anthropological Society of Paris and father of French anthropology, researchers such as Bean (1906), Broca, Mall (1909), and Deniker (1900), to name just a few, compared weights, convolutional patterns, and various aspects of cerebellar form. Some would find racial differences, but in the end, Bean would virtually stand alone against the wealth of data (Deniker, Mall, Broca) and the conclusion first offered by Tiedemann (1836) that clear distinctions across racial lines could not be drawn.

When skulls and their contents failed to provide a criterion to distinguish among races, many cast a wider net in the search for useful criteria. These included body lice (Darwin, Murray) as well as hair (Bory de Saint-Vincent, Broca, Browne, Haeckel, Huxley, Keane, Muller) (Gossett 1997).[13]

Ultimately, by the end of the nineteenth century, the leading scientists who had studied skulls, brains, hair, skin, and so on had arrived at the same conclusion: the search for distinct human types was an exercise in futility. Keane (1896, 1908), Ranke ([1894], 1938), Deniker (1900), and Virchow ([1896], 1950) would all find insufficient grounds for distinguishing races of humans.

By the end of the century, despite the development of new techniques, scientific rigor, and exhaustive research, physical anthropology, the science of human variation, had failed to validate the reality of racial types. John Wesley Powell, director of the Bureau of Ethnology of the Smithsonian Institution would say in the 1880s, "there is no science of ethnology" (meaning the determination of racial differences) (Gossett 1997, 83). Topinard, Broca's disciple, would also arrive at the conclusion that races were abstractions. His comments sound eerily modern:

> [R]ace is only a subjective notion. The only objective reality is what we have before our eyes: peoples and tribes. Under such conditions one questions whether it would not be preferable to be less free with the word race. (Topinard [1892] 1950, 176)

Yet typological thinking did not disappear. There was still faith in the reality of racial distinctions that were innate, biologically based, and, through their relative worth, indicative of evolutionary success.[14]

Managing the Inferiors: Institutionalizing Anthropology

The institutionalization of anthropology in the United States and abroad would serve to solidify an image of ranked races. Practitioners in this field on both sides of the Atlantic were called on for their expertise in "managing the inferiors." In Britain, the newly formed Anthropological Institute worked to restore respectability to the field of race science and saw its contribution as an imperative for administering a multiracial empire (Lorimer 1997). The same held for the expanding colonial empires of France, the Netherlands, and Germany, as they called on both physical and cultural anthropology for the information needed to deal with populations in Africa, the Indies, and South America.

In the United States, the field was shaped by the unique situation of internal colonialism. The Smithsonian Institution was founded in 1846 and was followed by the Bureau of American Ethnology in 1872. The goal of the latter echoes that of the Anthropological Institute in Britain, as the bureau would study Native Americans in order to know how best to deal with them, "for their own good."

Critically, the dominant intellectual perspective of the day, evolution, now undergirded cultural anthropology (ethnology) as well as the biological sphere. The scientific study of society/culture was based on the "bio-logical laws" of struggle, survival, and adaptation and on progress along an evolutionary scale. The cultural evolution of E. B. Tyler, Herbert Spencer, and Lewis Henry Morgan served as a complement to biological inquiry. Baker (1998) cogently demonstrates the important role of institutional-ized anthropology, most notably that of the Smithsonian, in presenting to the public a "scientific" representation of the hierarchy of races through living ethnology displays at turn-of-the-century expositions and world's fairs.

Lorimer (1997, 23) argues that in Victorian England, the role that sci-ence played with respect to race served to reconcile, at least to some degree, "the contradictions between democracy at home and imperialism abroad." The same argument can be put forth for the treatment of so-called lower races within the confines of the United States. A skewed take on Darwinian theory, "social Darwinism," would be used in the United States to account for social, political, economic, and even physical inequality.

Apes and Medicine

The link between Africans and apes evident at earlier historical junctures was now revitalized, not by the field of physical anthropology, but by med-icine. Physicians made numerous comparisons between apes and the vari-eties of humans, typically finding African Americans approximating apes in one dimension or another. Comments on various aspects of facial form, such as the breadth of the nasal aperture or receding chin (apes lack a true chin and only anatomically modern humans—not even Neandertals—possess one), supplemented the now familiar remarks about the degree of African facial prognathism.

Moreover, the medical profession moved beyond the craniometric focus that had been at the heart of physical anthropology. Through their analy-ses of postcranial anatomy, medical doctors would call into question the African American condition with respect to one of the principle defining human characteristics—erect posture. From Aristotle (man as a feather-less biped), through Blumenbach, and even today, erect posture and con-comitant bipedalism distinguish humankind. While presented in seem-ingly innocuous tones, comments about the "simian nature" of the African pelvis, vertebral column, or limb form clearly resonated the African-ape tie. Haller (1971, 49) notes:

Dr. Van Evrie felt that because of the Negro's physiological place in nature, he was "incapable of an erect or direct perpendicular posture." The structure of his limbs, the form of his pelvis and spine, and the way the head was set on the shoulders gave the Negro a "slightly stooping posture."

In 1899, the *Journal of Anatomy and Physiology* would publish an article by J. Arthur Thomson entitled "The Influence of Posture on the Form of the Articular Surfaces of the Tibia and Astragalus in the Different Races of Man and the Higher Apes" (Haller 1971).

Anticipating Extinction

What happened when advanced and backward races came into contact with each other? Opinions were divided, but the consensus was that the backward race was doomed. In the end, in the evolutionary struggle of the most fit, the fate of the African was sealed. Drawing on the dictum that ontogeny recapitulates phylogeny, the fetal African (and infantile Asian) would be no match for the European. Based on the "hard" data from anthropometry, medicine, and the census, physical and mental decline was inevitable. In 1862, Joseph Camp, statistician and superintendent of the 1860 census, stated that the "gradual extinction of the Negro was an 'unerring certainty' " (Haller 1971, 40). The next census would strengthen this view, as it incorrectly reported that the growth rate for the African American population was only 9.86 percent, a sharp contrast to the average of 29.98 percent for this population from 1790 to 1850 and 24.5 percent less than the population growth of European Americans for the decade (Haller 1970a, 317–18). This supposed decrease in population growth was almost entirely due to severe underenumeration in the Southern states, which were still undergoing Reconstruction. (The Census Bureau now publishes alternative estimates for 1870.)

The strains of Spencer and social Darwinism can be seen in a response to optimistic claims by sociologists that the African American population was increasing. Dr. Eugene R. Corson wrote in the *New York Medical Times* in 1887:

> Thrown into "the struggle for existence" with a civilization "of which he is not the product," the Negro "must suffer physically, a result which forbids any undue increase of the race, as well as the preservation of the race characteristics." (Cited in Haller 1971, 47–48)

A sampling of titles from the medical journals of the time further serves to illustrate this preoccupation: "The Negro Problem from a Medical Standpoint" (1886), "The Future of the Colored Race in the United States from an Ethnic and Medical Standpoint" (1887), "The Effects of Emancipation upon the Mental and Physical Qualifications of the Negro in the South" (1896), "The Effect of Freedom upon the Physical and Psychological Development of the Negro" (1900), "The Future of the Negro from the Standpoint of the Southern Physician" (1902), and "Deterioration of the American Negro" (1903) (Haller 1970b).

The demise of the African in America was one of the most widespread beliefs in medicine and anthropology in the late 1800s (Haller 1971).[15] Policy would match biology with segregation and disenfranchisement among the "first steps toward preparing the Negro race for its extinction" (Haller 1970b, 167). The impact of this belief can be seen on a practical level in that, for example, some of the largest insurers of African Americans reduced the benefits of those who had been issued policies based on European American mortality rates.

While the prognosis of extinction would be amended in the early 1900s, the evolutionary fate of African Americans was far from optimistic. In losing the struggle for survival, they would be left as a remnant and peripheral population.

Partially Dissenting Voices

Not all thinkers agreed that backward races in contact with advanced races were doomed. A sizable neo-Lamarckian minority thought that backward races could be slowly uplifted through the right kind of contact with advanced races. Dyer (1980) explains that the neo-Lamarckian perspective held by a significant portion of U.S. social scientists from 1890 to 1915 was central to their perspectives on race, society, and evolution. Lamarck's theory of the inheritance of acquired traits allowed for morphological and behavioral change due to a variety of factors, including environment as well as wishes and desires. This theory was drawn to argue that society as a whole and its constituent elements, the different races, could be changed by altering the social environment. From this perspective, adherence to an evolutionary perspective did not necessitate the extinction of African Americans.

The best-known proponents of this view at the turn of the century were Theodore Roosevelt and Booker T. Washington. Neither was a professional scientist himself, but both were in contact with leading scientists. As it became clearer, however, that Mendelian genetics, rather than the inheritance of acquired characteristics, was the mechanism through which evolution proceeded, neo-Lamarckianism became untenable and faded away.[16]

Another partially dissenting stream was also represented within the African American community, through such religious writers as Harvey Johnson and in the more secular work of W. E. B. DuBois. Johnson, a Baltimore Baptist minister, argues for the superiority of the African race over the Caucasian because of the more honorable origins of the African race in the biblical story of Ham and the great empire of Egypt, compared with the bizarre and heathen origins of the Caucasian race with Romulus and Remus (Johnson 1891). DuBois rejects the Great Chain of Being and argues, like an economist, that different races have different comparative advantages, that a one-dimensional scale of merit is not appropriate:

> We are that people whose subtle sense of song has given America its only American music, its only American fairly tales, its only touch of pathos and humor amid its mad money-getting plutocracy. (DuBois [1897] 2000, 114)

What is most telling, though, for the purposes of our argument, is that by the end of the nineteenth century, all of the leading voices in the African American community accept racial essentialism, even though they differ among themselves and with the European American mainstream on the future and ranking of the races. Indeed, it is hard to find a more eloquent expression of essentialism than DuBois's ([1897] 2000, 110):

> [T]he history of the world is the history, not of individuals, but of groups, not of nations, but of races, and he who ignores or seeks to override the race idea in human history ignores and overrides the central thought of all history. . . . We see the Pharaohs, Caesars, Toussaints and Napoleons of history and forget the vast races of which they were but epitomized expressions.

The distance from Frederick Douglass less than a half century before is immense—at least as great as the distance from Mill to Marshall.[17]

By the dawn of the new century, the general perspective on human diversity on both sides of the Atlantic was tightly swathed in the language of biology, though not supported by the results of a century of scientific investigation. Differences were innate, fixed, and ranked. The future was clearly marked.

Conclusion

It should not be surprising that economists changed how they viewed race between 1700 and 1900; everybody else did too—most especially natural scientists. At the beginning of the period we have looked at, scientists had a very poor understanding of how nature operated—so poor that they could not explain how Europeans became stronger, richer, and better than other people around the world. Over the course of two hundred years and through the combined efforts of scientists from a variety of newly forming disciplines, vast quantities of information were gathered and digested. Biology and anthropology not only struggled to understand the relationship between humans and other animals and humankind's place in the natural world but also sought insights into the relationships among humans—how they differed from one another and why. By 1900, Europeans and European Americans could finally explain coherently why they were superior. "Science" had provided an answer, nearly.

It is not a happy tale that we tell, but it is an instructive one. Not many people today are smarter than Linnaeus, Darwin, or DuBois or more moral than Kant or Blumenbach. The questions we ask are not that different either: why people in some parts of the world are so much richer than people in other parts, why police are corrupt in Mexico City, why African Americans are about six times as likely to be incarcerated or murdered as are European Americans (Reuters 2002; U.S. Department of Justice 2002a, 2002b), why only five of the 316 people who graduated with one of the authors from a Newark public high school thirty years ago still maintain addresses in Newark, and how humans got to be the way they are.

Of course, today, these questions have solid answers that do not appeal to racial essentialism or to the Great Chain of Being. Each question, in fact, has several such solid answers—and none of them is so convincing and simple that the questions have really been answered. If natural and social scientists today really knew the answers to these questions, they would not have to spend so much time looking for and arguing about those answers.

As we look among ourselves (or to our closest relatives, the other apes),

Plato's gift is still with us. If clear, simple, convincing answers for these questions do not exist outside the world of biological or cultural racial essentialism, why should we be surprised that for many ordinary people try-ing to understand the world around them, racial essentialism is still the answer?

NOTES

1. The term *mulatto* is first cited by the *Oxford English Dictionary* in 1595, and *quadroon* is first cited in 1707.

2. Notice that we are comparing "man" and "the ape" as two essences, not "humans" and "apes" as two populations.

3. Prior to the 1700s, terms like *race* and *species* were used by learned persons in a loose generic sense that was roughly synonymous with *kind*, *type*, and *variety*. Further, none of the terms referred specifically or exclusively to physical traits, though such features were normally a part of the general description. Blumenbach takes *principal variety* as a synonym for *race*, and only in Kant is the term *race* used and formally defined.

4. This concern with good climate and with beauty also led to the naming of the "Caucasian" race. The story begins with Bernier, who encountered Circassian slave women in Turkey and Persia and concluded, on the basis of this evidence, that people from the Caucasus were the handsomest on earth. Buffon echoed this sentiment. Blumenbach, using their accounts and also having in his possession a single skull from the region, came to the same conclusion. He thought it likely, therefore, that humankind in general and Europeans in particular had originated from this region, so he named the European race after Mount Caucasus: "I have taken the name of this variety from Mount Caucasus . . . because its neighborhood . . . produces the most beautiful race of men . . . ; and because all physiological rea-sons converge to this, that in that region if anywhere, it seems we ought with greatest probability place the autochthones of mankind. For in the first place, that stock displays, as we have seen . . . , the most beautiful form of the skull. . . . Besides it is white in color, which we may fairly assume to have been the primitive color of mankind, since, as we have shown above . . . , it is very easy for that to degen-erate into brown, but very much more difficult for dark to become white, when the secretion and precipitation of this carbonaceous pigment . . . has once deeply struck root" (Blumenbach [1795] 1865, 269).

5. In fact, in another famous work (Tiedemann 1836), he would argue, counter to most of his contemporaries, that there were no differences between the brains of Africans and Europeans.

6. For a full analysis of Morton's results, see Gould 1996. For a critique and reanalysis more favorable to Morton, see Michael 1988.

7. Morton, for instance, "regarded several breeds of dogs as separate species because their skeletons resided in the Egyptian catacombs, as recognizable and dis-tinct from other breeds as they are now" (Gould 1996, 52).

8. In a world where most slave traders were polygenists and you were not, you could make money by outbidding them for mulatto women, since fertility expectations for the women were irrational. But you could not make much money, since Fogel et al. (1992, 325) estimate that a fecund woman was worth only about 8 percent more than a sterile woman and that any differential fertility was either small or very far in the future. Most slave traders, moreover, were monogenists.

9. For Wallace (1871), man had escaped it because of his inventiveness.

10. As for explanations for the origin of the diversity, neither Darwin nor Wallace focused on the correlates between physical traits and environmental adaptations. Darwin in fact came to the conclusion that racial traits were not adaptive and explained them in terms of sexual selection (Stepan 1982).

11. In fairness, the lack of consensus among early evolutionists (Darwin, Wallace, Huxley) on aspects of the theory, coupled with an incomplete understanding of the genetics of inheritance (a gap in understanding that would remain until the middle of the following century), contributed to the failure to develop a new concept of race at this time.

12. The facial angle is a measurement based on a line drawn through the lower part of the nose and the orifice of the ear. For Camper, this provided a standard for comparing forms, and it is accordingly regarded by many scholars as the beginning of modern craniology. The smaller the angle, the more apelike the face. Human facial angles range from 70 to 100, from the African to the Greek of antiquity. As orang utans have a facial angle of 58 degrees, Camper placed the African as closer to the ape than to the European.

13. It is interesting and puzzling that the African-ape morphological link, found in common imagery as well as in science at this time, is not similarly applied to the analyses of hair. The hair of Africans was likened to that of another non-human, the sheep: "the hair of the white man will not felt, but the wool of the Negro will felt" (Browne 1850, 8). The fact that ape hair closely resembles that of non-African peoples is not deemed of consequence.

14. Looking at a conjunction of characteristics, rather than at a single trait, makes it easier to identify uniquely the geographic origin of many individuals, but the cost is that many individuals cannot be identified at all. This is the approach of modern forensic anthropology. For example, among the standard "European" features are a narrow face, a sharp nasal sill, a narrow distance between eye orbits, little facial prognathism, and a prominent chin. An "African" cranium has a narrow face (in contrast to a wider, "Asian" face), no nasal sill, a wide distance between the eye orbits, alveolar prognathism, and a chin that only projects slightly (Bass 1987). These combinations of features sort with a high degree of accuracy the skulls that fall in one category or another. But many skulls fall in neither category (or fall in both).

15. Darity (1994) documents the impact of this belief on the American Economics Association.

16. Mendel's work was not resurrected until 1902, and despite August Weismann's theory of "germ plasm" back in 1869, Lamarck's ideas were still powerful in some circles into the 1900s.

17. There is some reason to believe that in the twentieth century, DuBois

became less of an essentialist under the influence of anthropologists such as Franz Boas. See, for instance, DuBois's essay "The First Universal Races Congress" ([1911] 1995). However, as late as 1939, Melville Herskovitz was reporting racial essentialism in DuBois's *Black Folk: Then and Now* (1939). For a discussion of this controversy, see Lewis 2000, 455–56. Whatever DuBois believed later in his life, it is fairly clear that as the nineteenth century drew to a close, he was a strong race essentialist.

The Negro Science of Exchange

Classical Economics and Its Chicago Revival

David M. Levy and Sandra J. Peart

For analytical purposes, are economic agents—humans—the same or not? In this chapter, we argue that, historically, the debate between those who trusted in markets and those who did not followed logically from different answers to this question. Starting with Adam Smith, classical economists held that humans are the same in their capacity for language and trade. They concluded that since markets are useful for some agents, they are beneficial for all of us. But the supposition of homogeneous competence was widely questioned in the nineteenth century by those who held that significant differences exist among humans, only some of whom are capable of language or trade. This presumption of (hierarchical) difference led the critics of economics to argue against markets. In their stead, they offered two alternatives: slavery and, when slavery was no longer a possibility, paternalism.

Thus, our contention in what follows is that, as a historical fact, the controversy over whether markets work or not occurs over the presumption of equal competence, or homogeneity. On the side of homogeneity, we locate all the great classical economists and, much later, the Chicago school of economics associated with George Stigler and Gary Becker. On the side of heterogeneity, we find many "progressives" (Thomas Carlyle, John Ruskin, Charles Dickens, and Charles Kingsley). We hold that the reputation for "progressiveness" of those on the side of heterogeneity is unwarranted. This chapter explains why.

The linchpin of the economists' opposition to both slavery and paternalism is their presumption of human homogeneity that disallows masters, whether they own, rule, or look after their inferiors in a kindly fashion. Supposing that the social world is composed of equally competent optimizers, there is no group that needs looking after and no group that can do the looking after. In economics, there are no victims with whom to empathize: trades are voluntary and, it is presumed, mutually beneficial. This world without victims is surely what gives economics its reputation for hard-heartedness. By contrast, the great charm of paternalistic accounts is doubtless the compassion they allow for the victims of voluntary transactions.

But there is a potential dark side to paternalism. For any victim, it is tempting to find a class of victimizers. In the period we study, we find that paternalistic accounts of market transactions focus attention on both sides of the transaction and suggest that the victimizers are evil and parasitic, feeding and thriving on the blood, sweat, and tears of their victims. Those who are supposedly so adept at using markets as to be in the position of systematically taking advantage of ill-equipped traders are called "harpies," "parasites," "vampires," and "Jews." We conjecture that this aspect of paternalism explains the hatred of market relationships that is still all too obvious.

Economists, such as John Stuart Mill, who have asked how agents become competent demonstrate that it is possible to address the substantive issue of human development—how, in fact, we learn to optimize; how children learn to function as adults—without appeal to a class of victimizers (Peart and Levy 2001). Indeed, one might fairly point to paternalistic aspects of Mill's writing and remember that he nowhere supposes the existence of a class of parasites. Yet appeal to human parasites is the great temptation for those working within the paternalistic tradition. Those we have studied succumbed to it.

We begin the following account with some important history. It is still too rarely appreciated[1] that economics became the "dismal science" in this period because of an avowedly bleak and unrealistic view of human nature that abstracted away from the possibility of racial difference. Early economists were committed to a fixed, race-neutral account of human nature, the hardest possible doctrine of analytical homogeneity, in which all observed outcomes are explained by incentives, luck, and history. As a consequence, they opposed racial slavery and paternalism, and they favored markets instead. Foes of homogeneity might well have called economics "dismal," bleak, or even black—the "Negro science" of trade.

As we will show in this chapter, our view of history runs counter to the commonly held perception that economists earned the phrase *dismal science* because of an avowedly bleak and unrealistic view of human nature that abstracted out the possibility of improving the human condition. Here, "dismal science" ought to be read "sorrowful science," because economists were committed to a fixed world of misery. They opposed schemes for human improvement and favored markets instead. Just as *progressive* is an unwarranted adjective for opponents to classical economics, this telling of our history is unwarranted.

How the Dismal Science Got Its Name

Everyone knows that economics is the dismal science. Almost everyone believes that Thomas Carlyle was inspired to coin the phrase by T. R. Malthus's gloomy prediction that population would always grow faster than food, dooming humankind to unending poverty and hardship.

While this story is well known, it is also wrong. Although he created the phrase, Carlyle's target was not Malthus but economists, such as John Stuart Mill, who argued that it was institutions, not race, that explained why some nations were rich and others poor. Carlyle attacked Mill, not for supporting Malthus's predictions about the dire consequences of population growth, but for supporting the emancipation of slaves. The fact that economics assumed that people were basically all the same, and thus that all were entitled to liberty, led Carlyle to label economics the "dismal science."

Here is the paragraph in which Carlyle first uses the phrase "dismal science" as part of his attack on the antislavery stance of political economy.

> Truly, my philanthropic friends, Exeter Hall Philanthropy is wonderful; and the Social Science—not a "gay science," but a rueful—which finds the secret of this universe in "supply-and-demand," and reduces the duty of human governors to that of letting men alone, is also wonderful. Not a "gay science," I should say, like some we have heard of; no, a dreary, desolate, and indeed quite abject and distressing one; what we might call, by way of eminence, the *dismal science*. These two, Exeter Hall Philanthropy and the Dismal Science, led by any sacred cause of Black Emancipation, or the like, to fall in love and make a wedding of it,—will give birth to progenies and prodigies; dark extensive moon-calves,

unnameable abortions, wide-coiled monstrosities, such as the world has not seen hitherto! (Carlyle 1849, 672–73)

Exeter Hall was the political center of British evangelicalism, the moral center of the antislavery movement. The antislavery movement in Britain was comprised of two groups in coalition: political economists of both a Utilitarian persuasion (James Mill, Harriet Martineau, J. S. Mill) and a Christian persuasion (Archbishop Richard Whately and John Bright) and Christian Evangelicals (William Wilberforce, T. B. Macaulay) for whom Adam and Eve were real people. Carlyle was the greatest enemy of this coalition. His "The Negro Question" revived the pro-slavery movement in midcentury Britain.[2] In a nutshell, Carlyle argued that work was godly and that if people (or horses) would not work under market conditions, slavery was not only justified but also godly. The next step, of course, was to presume that some races were predisposed to want (hence, to work) less than others.

As evidence that blacks had an ungodly attitude toward work, Carlyle pointed to the massive unemployment among emancipated slaves in the West Indies. For him, this unemployment was not the result of economic conditions, such as the decline of island agriculture with the repeal of the protective tariffs that were part of the bargain for emancipation. Rather, it was the result of the nature of blacks, a nature that rendered them insensitive to market incentives. As a result, he thought that the only cure for this (ungodly) unemployment was slavery, under which the "beneficent whip" would be able to improve the "two-legged cattle."

If Quashee will not honestly aid in bringing out those sugars, cinnamons, and nobler products of the West Indian Islands, for the benefit of all mankind, then I say neither will the Powers permit Quashee to continue growing pumpkins there for his own lazy benefit; but will sheer him out, by and by, like a lazy gourd overshadowing rich ground; him and all that partake with him,—perhaps in a very terrible manner. For, under the favour of Exeter Hall, the "terrible manner" is not yet quite extinct with the Destinies in this Universe; nor will it quite cease, I apprehend, for soft sawder or philanthropic stump-oratory now or henceforth. No; the gods wish besides pumpkins, that spices and valuable products be grown in their West Indies; thus much they have declared in so making the West Indies:—infinitely more they wish, that manful industrious men occupy their West Indies, not indolent two-legged cattle, however "happy" over their abundant pumpkins! Both these things, we may be assured, the immortal gods have decided upon, passed their eternal act of parliament for: and both of them, though all terrestrial Parliaments and entities oppose it to the death, shall be done. Quashee, if he will not help in bringing out the spices, will get himself made a slave again (which state will be a little less ugly than his present one), and with beneficent whip, since other methods avail not, will be compelled to work. (Carlyle 1849, 675)

Mill's response—a letter to the editor of *Fraser's Magazine*—came into print a month after Carlyle's "The Negro Question." In it, Mill offered an amazingly dense, multidimensional argument. He condemned Carlyle for what he called "the vulgar error of imputing every difference which he finds among human beings to an original difference of nature" (Mill 1850, 29).[3] After noting the inconsistencies in Carlyle's application of the "gospel of work" (27), Mill attacked the gospel itself. Is it really true, he asked, that work per se is valuable?

> This pet theory of your contributor about work, we all know well enough, though some persons might not be prepared for so bold an application of it. Let me say a few words on this "gospel of work" . . . .
> Work, I imagine, is not a good in itself. There is nothing laudable in work for work's sake. To work voluntarily for a worthy object is laudable; but what constitutes a worthy object? On this matter, the oracle of which your contributor is the prophet has never yet been prevailed on to declare itself. He revolves in an eternal circle round the idea of work, as if turning up the earth, or driving a shuttle or a quill, were ends in themselves, and the ends of human existence. Yet, even in case of the most sublime service to humanity, it is not because it is work that it is worthy; the worth lies in the service itself. (27–28)

Finally, Mill turned to Carlyle's claim that Caribbean blacks were wasting the land by growing food for themselves rather than spices for Europeans. What, Mill asked, was the right or best crop to grow in the West Indies?

> In the present case, it seems, a noble object means "spices." "The gods wish, besides pumpkins, that spices and valuable products be grown in their West Indies"—the "noble elements of cinnamon, sugar, coffee, pepper black and grey," "things far nobler than pumpkins." Why so? Is what supports life, inferior in dignity to what merely gratifies the sense

of taste? Is it the verdict of the "immortal gods" that pepper is noble, freedom (even freedom from the lash) contemptible? (28)

Mill's response in 1850 supposes, as a matter of course, the competence of black people to make their own decisions.

Economics and Common Humanity

Mill's argument builds on Smith's doctrine, enunciated in *Wealth of Nations*, that to be human is to trade. Smith argues that humans are set apart from other animals by their ability to cooperate, an ability that requires them to trade and to talk. Dogs, who vary more physically than humans, could also gain from cooperation. Yet because dogs lack language, they cannot negotiate and thus cannot reap the gains from trade (Smith [1776] 1976, 1:30). As the economist (and soon-to-be archbishop) Richard Whately put it in 1831,

> Man might be defined, "An animal that makes *Exchanges:*" no other, even of those animals which in other points make the nearest approach to rationality, having, in all appearance, the least notion of bartering, or in any way exchanging one thing for another. (6)[4]

So, at the center of classical economics, we have the test for the human: the ability to trade. In fact, Whately proposed that "political economy" be renamed "katallactics"—the science of exchange, from the Greek meaning "reciprocal exchange"—to make it clear that economics is the science of the human and that exchange is a uniquely human act.

The Smith-Whately doctrine—since all language users trade, trade is evidence of our common humanity—was a standing challenge to those who would argue for fundamental differences among humans. This challenge was taken up by Edward G. Wakefield. In his edition of Smith's *Wealth of Nations*, Wakefield disputed Smith's doctrine of common humanity along racial lines. Wakefield argued that the sharp distinction that Smith and Whately supposed to exist between some humans and animals is actually fuzzy. Instead, there are races that will not trade and that are therefore closer to animals than they are to the fully human.

> The savages of New Holland never help each other, even in the most simple operations; and their condition is hardly superior, in some

respects it is inferior, to that of the wild animals which they now and
then catch. (Wakefield 1835, 1:27)

Why do dogs not trade? Contrary to Smith, Wakefield (1:59) argues that
dogs have no reason to trade.

> The wants of every inferior animal are extremely limited. No inferior
> animal wants more than food and shelter; the quantity and kind of food,
> and the kind of shelter, being always the same with respect to each race
> of animals. . . . The wants of man, on the contrary, are unlimited.

So, to what do we attribute a failure to trade? For Smith it is talk not, trade
not. For Wakefield, it is want not, trade not.

When Carlyle responded to the economists in 1850 in the first of the
Latter-Day Pamphlets, he adopted Wakefield's claim that some races do not
trade.[5] There, he argued that the wants of inferior races, like those of
Wakefield's animals, are so limited that there is no reason for them to
trade. He contended that among horses, blacks, and Irish, none would voluntarily trade leisure for wages.

> West-Indian Blacks are emancipated, and it appears refuse to work: Irish
> Whites have long been entirely emancipated; and nobody asks them to
> work. . . . Among speculative persons, a question has sometimes risen: In
> the progress of Emancipation, are we to look for a time when all the
> Horses also are to be emancipated, and brought to the supply-and-
> demand principle? Horses too have "motives;" are acted on by hunger,
> fear, hope, love of oats, terror of platted leather; nay they have vanity,
> ambition, emulation, thankfulness, vindictiveness; some rude outline of
> all our human spiritualities,—a rude resemblance to us in mind and
> intelligence, even as they have in bodily frame. . . . I am sure if I could
> make him "happy," I should be willing to grant a small vote (in addition
> to the late twenty million) for that object!
>
> Him too you occasionally tyrannise over; and with bad result to your-
> selves among others; using the leather in a tyrannous unnecessary man-
> ner; withholding, or scantily furnishing, the oats and ventilated stabling
> that are due. Rugged horse-subduers, one fears they are a little tyrannous
> at times. "Am I not a horse, and *half*-brother?" (Carlyle 1850, 30–31)[6]

Attempting to contract with the subhuman has predictable consequences
that correspond exactly with attempts to contract with two-legged subhu-
mans.

Corn-crops are *ended* in this world!—For the sake, if not of Hodge, then of Hodge's horses, one prays this benevolent practice might now cease, and a new and better one try to begin. Small kindness to Hodge's horses to emancipate them! The fate of all emancipated horses is, sooner or later, inevitable. To have in this habitable Earth no grass to eat,—in Black Jamaica gradually none, as in White Connemara already none;— to roam aimless, wasting the seedfields of the world; and be hunted home to Chaos, by the due watchdogs and due hell-dogs. . . . (Carlyle 1850, 32)

Carlyle's official doctrine, the "gospel of work" to which Mill referred, is that slavery can make one free.[7] If slavery fails, there is extermination.

Work, was I saying? My indigent unguided friends, I should think some work might be discoverable for you. Enlist, stand drill; become, from a nomadic Banditti of Idleness, Soldiers of Industry! I will lead you to the Irish Bogs, to the vacant desolations of Connaught now falling into Cannibalism. . . .

To each of you I will then say: Here is work for you; strike into it with manlike, soldierlike obedience and heartiness, according to the methods here prescribed,—wages follow for you without difficulty; all manner of just remuneration, and at length emancipation itself follows. Refuse to strike into it; shirk the heavy labour, disobey the rules,—I will admonish and endeavour to incite you; if in vain, I will flog you; if still in vain, I will at last shoot you,—and make God's Earth, and the forlorn-hope in God's Battle, free of you. (Carlyle 1850, 54–55).

Economics Versus Poetry: The Eyre Massacre

When Carlyle described political economy as the "dismal science," he juxtaposed it to the "gay science" of poetry.[8] That juxtaposition of economists and poets proved exceedingly apt. With the Governor Eyre controversy in 1865, a terrifying clarity came upon the British debates over social organization and race. Every economist who spoke on the matter—John Stuart Mill, John Bright, Henry Fawcett, J. E. Cairnes, Thorold Rogers, Herbert Spencer—took the position that the principle of impartial justice protected Jamaicans of color every bit as much as it did whites in Britain. Every literary figure of stature who spoke on the matter—John Ruskin, Charles Kingsley, Thomas Carlyle, Charles Dickens, Alfred Tennyson— defended Eyre's methods of state terror.

The controversy was triggered by a seemingly trivial event in the British colony of Jamaica. A contemporary witness wrote:

> On Saturday the 7th October, 1865, a court of petty sessions was held at Morant Bay. A man made a noise in the court, and was ordered to be brought before justices. He was captured by the police outside, but immediately rescued by one Paul Bogle and several other persons, who had large bludgeons in their hands, and taken into the market-square, where some one hundred and fifty more persons joined them also with sticks: the police were severely beaten. . . . On Monday, the 9th, warrants were issued against Paul Bogle and twenty-seven others for riot and assault on the Saturday.[9]

On Wednesday, the police came to enforce the warrants. Stones were thrown. Then the shooting began. The island's governor, Edward James Eyre, took command. Eyre imposed martial law and called in the army to restore order. By the time the army was done, over four hundred Jamaicans were dead, and thousands were homeless. Britons were horrified by the methods of state terror, including flogging with wire whips and the use of military courts to deny civilians their rights.

Among the dead was George Gordon, a Baptist minister and member of Jamaica's legislature. Although Gordon, a civilian, was nowhere near the original disturbances, he was arrested, tried in military court, convicted, and hanged. In a letter written to his wife just before he was hanged, Gordon proclaimed his innocence.

> The judges seemed against me; and from the rigid manner of the Court, I could not get in all the explanation I intended. The man Anderson made an unfounded statement, and so did Gordon; but his testimony was different from the deposition. The judges took the former and erased the latter. It seemed *that I was to be sacrificed*. I know nothing of the man Bogle. I never advised him to the act or acts which have brought me to this end. Please write Mr. Chamerovzow.[10]

Louis Alexis Chamerovzow was the secretary of the Anti-Slavery Society and one of the leaders of the British antislavery movement.[11] When he learned of Gordon's death, he and his colleagues in England formed the Jamaica Committee to protest the governor's actions and demand an investigation. The Jamaica Committee included a host of worthies not usually associated with evangelical Christianity, including Charles Darwin and T. H. Huxley. As head, the members unanimously chose John Stuart Mill. On the other side, it is no surprise that the Eyre Defense Fund was led by Thomas Carlyle, aided and abetted by John Ruskin (Semmel 1962).

That this was how the sides would play out came as no surprise to contemporaries. To onlookers, it was obvious that this was the Carlyle-Mill debate all over again. This time, however, the "beneficent whip" was made of piano wire instead of words.

Eyre's defenders argued that his actions showed the beneficial influence of the work of Carlyle and others in exposing the foolishness of treating a black as "man and a brother." Here are the thoughts of James Hunt (1866a, 16), the moving spirit of British racial anthropology of the day: "We were at first not a little astonished at the decisive measures taken by Governor Eyre: measures which could alone have resulted from a most thorough insight into the negro character."[12] Hunt acknowledged Carlyle's theoretical guidance.[13] Carlyle himself (1867, 14) was quite a bit blunter: "Truly one knows not whether less to venerate the Majesty's Ministers, who, instead of rewarding their Governor Eyre, throw him out of window to a small loud group, small as now appears, and nothing but a group or knot[14] of rabbid Nigger-Philanthropists, barking furiously in the gutter."

On the other side, it was equally clear that Eyre was speaking in the proslavery code that we have encountered in Carlyle. Here is the reaction of G. W. Alexander, treasurer of the Anti-Slavery Society.

> I think it would be somewhat presumptuous in me to refer particularly to the report made by the Governor of Jamaica, but I confess there are two or three passages that have struck me as indicating very great want of judgment on his part. . . . I am sorry to perceive the terms which the Governor of Jamaica has thought fit to use with regard to certain religious bodies in this country, and those whom he calls pseudo-philanthropists. I think it is exceedingly unbecoming in the Governor of a Colony thus to stigmatize persons who had been, it was true, instrumental in procuring the abolition of slavery in the British West-India colonies; and, I hope, in leading to the abolition of slavery throughout the world.[15]

In fact, even before the disturbances that became a massacre, Eyre was proclaiming Carlyle's gospel of labor to all who would listen.[16]

Expelling the "Harpy Jews"

We have looked at two episodes of a debate over racial difference and the
consequent need for the "beneficent whip"—in the first, the whip was theoretical; in the second, it was cut from piano wire. The Carlyle-Mill
exchange and the Governor Eyre controversy were followed in turn by a
hardening of both scientific and popular ideas of racial heterogeneity.[17]
The images in *Punch* and their accompanying squibs reflect this hardening.
After 1865, images depicting the Irish[18] and Jamaicans with apelike characteristics and suggesting that violent measures be used to deal with them
were common. In *Punch* of February 24, 1866 (81), we find a chilling piece
of doggerel under the heading "Responsibility and Rinderpest."

> To "stamp out" the Cattle Plague how could we dare?
> Rebellion was "stamped out" by GOVERNOR EYRE!

In the following issue, the Irish other is now the pest. Below the image of
the "Fenian-Pest" is the imagined dialogue that makes things perfectly
clear.

> Hibernia: "O my dear sister, what *are* we to do with these troublesome
>   people?"
> Britannia: "Try isolation first, my dear, and then—"

The Irish were viewed as parasites, as a class, like cannibals, that takes but
does not give. We shall meet such a class again.

Carlyle's influence extends to the characterization of the victimizer as
parasite. Although his *Past and Present* enjoys unquestioned "progressive"
credentials, it, too, reflects the temptation of paternalism. Carlyle's hero in
the medieval fantasy, Abbot Samson, expels the "harpy Jews."

> In less than four years, says Jocelin, the Convent Debts were all liqui-
> dated: the harpy Jews not only settled with, but banished, bag and bag-
> gage, out of the *Bannaleuca* (Liberties, *Banlieue*) of St. Edmundsbury,—
> so has the King's Majesty been persuaded to permit. Farewell to *you*, at
> any rate; let us, in no extremity, apply again to you! Armed men march
> them over the borders, dismiss them under stern penalties,—sentence of
> excommunication on all that shall again harbour them here: there were
> many dry eyes at their departure. (Carlyle [1844] 1965, 96)

To modify the name *Jew*, Carlyle found a word originating in Greek that the progress of the English language had made into reference to a parasite. The *Oxford English Dictionary* (2d ed.) defines a harpy as "a rapacious, plundering, or grasping person; one that preys upon others"—a parasite.

The thesis that Jews threaten the moral economic order is vigorously pursued in Charles Kingsley's *Alton Locke*. Here, when the old employer dies, his son begins to emulate the Jews, who are portrayed as pursuing wealth at the expense of all moral obligation. Jewish economic practice embodies economic doctrine, but it is morally reprehensible.[19]

> His father had made money very slowly of late; while dozens, who had begun business after him, had now retired to luxurious ease and suburban villas. Why should he remain in the minority? Why should he not get rich as fast as he could? Why should he stick to the old, slow-going, honorable trade? . . . Why should he pay his men two shillings where the government paid them one? Were there not cheap houses even at the West-end, which had saved several thousands a year merely by reducing their workmen's wages? And if the workmen chose to take lower wages, he was not bound actually to make them a present of more than they asked for! They would go to the cheapest market for any thing they wanted, and so must he. . . .
>
> Such, I suppose, were some of the arguments which led to an official announcement, one Saturday night, that our young employer intended to enlarge his establishment, for the purpose of commencing business in the "show trade;" and that, emulous of Messrs. Aaron, Levi, and the rest of that class . . . (Kingsley 1850, 96–97)

In the chapter "The Sweater's Den," we find that Jews threatened Christian workers both in this world and in the next (ibid., 191).

In his review of *Alton Locke* for *Blackwood's Edinburgh Magazine*, W. E. Aytoun (1850, 598) distinguished between "honor" and "competition."

> This is intended, or at all events given, as an accurate picture of a respectable London tailoring establishment, where the men receive decent wages. Such a house is called an "honourable" one, in contradistinction to others, now infinitely the more numerous, which are springing up in every direction under the fostering care of competition.

Jews who run competitive establishments are said to employ "sweaters" so they need not deal with workers on a face-to-face basis.

These sweaters are commonly Jews, to which persuasion also the majority of the dishonourable proprietors belong. Few people who emerge from the Euston Square Station are left in ignorance as to the fact, it being the insolent custom of a gang of hook-nosed and blubber-lipped Israelites to shower their fetid tracts, indicating the localities of the principal dealers of their tribe, into every cab as it issues from the gate. These are, in plain terms, advertisement of a more odious cannibalism than exists in the Sandwich Islands. (Ibid., 598–99)

The moral course of action concerning "human leeches" naturally suggests itself.

In these days of projected Jewish emancipation, the sentiment may be deemed an atrocious one, but we cannot retract it. Shylock was and is the true type of his class; only that the modern London Jew is six times more personally offensive, mean, sordid, and rapacious than the merchant of the Rialto. And why should we stifle our indignation? Dare any one deny the truth of what we have said? It is notorious to the whole world that these human leeches acquire their wealth, not by honest labour and industry, but by bill-broking, sweating, discounting, and other nefarious arts. (Ibid., 599)

Jews are inextricably bound up with classical economic (free-market) policy.

Talk of Jewish legislation indeed! We have had too much of it already in our time, from the days of Ricardo, the instigator of Sir Robert Peel's earliest practices upon the currency, down to those of Nathan Rothschild, the first Baron of Jewry, for whose personal character and upright dealings the reader is referred to Mr Francis' Chronicles of the Stock Exchange. (Ibid., 599)

In the old Greek stories, harpies were agents of divine retribution unleashed on those who victimized others by violence. "Harpy Jews" have now become "vampires" who victimize by exchange.

Read the following account by a working tailor of their doings, and then settle the matter with your conscience, whether it is consistent with the character of a Christian gentleman to have dealings with such inhuman vampires. (Ibid., 599)

Paternalism and Parasites

After 1865, we find that antimarket voices increasingly take on a pater-nalistic, as opposed to a proslavery, rhetoric. Even proslavery accounts were now cast in paternalistic terms. The "paternalistic" explanation for Carlyle's "The Negro Question" is put forward by James Froude when he explains Carlyle's social policy. Carlyle's argument, Froude maintained, was not that any sort of slavery was good but, rather, that reformed slav-ery—a sort of paternalistic looking-after of blacks (in body as well as soul) by whites—would improve the lot of blacks. Economists erred in neglect-ing the well-being of slaves.

> He did not mean that the "Niggers" should have been kept as cattle, and sold as cattle at their owners' pleasure. He did mean that they ought to have been treated as human beings, for whose souls and bodies the whites were responsible; that they should have been placed in a position suited to their capacity, like that of the English serfs under the Planta-genets. (Froude 1885, 2:14–15)[20]

By the late 1870s, paternalism is also explicitly opposed to market-based economics, and the antieconomics rhetoric becomes increasingly violent.[21] The term *cant* was frequently used by those in the paternalistic tradition to attack economists, and "canters" are said to engage in legal reallocations that are not mutually beneficial trades but more like fraud (Levy and Peart 2001–2). Like the Jews, they are therefore human para-sites. Images issued by *Cope's Tobacco Plant* as part of its public-relations campaign (Wallace 1878a, 1878b) juxtapose canting political econo-mists—now explicitly trampled or shown as parasites—to the great pater-nalists of the time: Ruskin, Carlyle, and Froude.

The question that arises is why? What can possibly explain the violence in this and other images and texts of the time? As we noted earlier, we hold that the disagreement between economists and paternalists late in the century follows directly from their two very different starting points concerning human abilities. Paternalism presupposes heterogeneity, dif-ferences that imply that some of us need looking after by the rest. It requires a hierarchy: a notion of who is inferior and who is superior (along with, perhaps, an explanation for the existence of differences).[22] From the supposition of heterogeneity results the claim that, left to their own (market) devices, systematically poor optimizers may be victimized by systematically good optimizers. Paternalists conclude, markets may create human victims and human victimizers, parasites. This difference in ability to pursue one own's interest creates the need to protect inferior decision makers.

Thus, paternalism requires a victim and allows for the existence of a class of parasites. Parasitism extends beyond the range of market transactions to the political realm. In the late nineteenth century, parasites are identified with the Irish home-rule movement. Founded by Isaac Butt, a Whately Lecturer in Political Economy, the home-rule movement is a political center of the katallactic tradition, for it asserts the claim that all language users are capable of self-government. Not only does the paternalistic tradition assert that trade creates parasites, but it also provides a strong indication of who some of those parasites are: political economists of the classical tradition. Why might economists be victimizers? To the extent the economists succeeded in bringing about self-government, they removed the "incapable" from the "protection" of the paternalist. By ending "paternalistic protection," economic policy therefore creates victims and victimizers.

We can use some neoclassical economics to make precise the analytical difference between paternalists and the classical katallactic tradition. Suppose that agents have preferences that can be represented by textbook indifference curves. Place two agents in an Edgeworth box at initial social state α. A "reallocation" occurs so that the agents find themselves in social state β. What warrant do we have to believe that such a reallocation is a Pareto-preferable trade? We observe motion, which we define to be a reallocation, and we ask whether we might correctly judge the reallocation to be Pareto preferable. In the case that it is Pareto preferable, we consider it to be a mutually beneficial trade. As Whately explained when he proposed the katallactics of government, the question is not whether trade is voluntary but whether it is mutually beneficial. In the katallactic tradition, all legal reallocations are mutually beneficial trades, and parasitism cannot exist.

As we noted earlier, Adam Smith pointed out that while all species with desires engage in reallocations, only those with language can trade. In opposition to Smith and the katallactic tradition that followed him, suppose with the paternalists that there are among humans *legal* reallocations that are not mutually beneficial trades. As we have been using the term, paternalism means that some voluntary reallocations are presumed to reduce a consumer's utility. To the extent that reallocations are widespread, one group will systematically be victimized by another. Consequently, such paternalists as John Ruskin denounced katallactics, arguing that in many reallocations, one party benefits *at the expense of* the other.[23]

The most plausible case for paternalism is, not surprisingly, minor children. In many instances that spring all-too-readily to mind to any parent, a child's voluntary reallocation will not be beneficial to the child. As a consequence, such voluntary acts are not regarded as legal trades. There are uncontroversial laws by which reallocations are impeded. But suppose, with the paternalist, that the principle also applies to adults. A "human parasite" might be defined as one who *systematically* benefits from legal reallocations that are not trades. Parasitism is therefore an occupation.[24]

Learning to Optimize

Who shall decide whether a trade is mutually beneficial, the participants or the theoretical onlooker? The Chicago school approach, which, as George Stigler would explain on any and all occasions, is Adam Smith's, is that the agents are their own best judge.[25] The Chicago approach to trade is a worldview without self-victimization. Paternalists who are appalled by such heartlessness might reflect on the historical fact that an intellectual world with victims of trade is also a world with human parasites. We find both the defense of racial slavery and the denunciation of human parasites in the paternalistic tradition. This is not an accident.

But surely there is a reason for the appeal of paternalism. People are not endowed with an ability to optimize; this is something that must be learned. Thus, when the clarion sounded reviving the doctrine of fixed human nature, George Stigler and Gary Becker (1977) sketched a "consumption capital" approach that would explain how (all) people could become competent optimizers. This, too, was a revival of classical katallactic concerns. When Lord Denman (1853, 12–20) attacked Charles Dickens's views on slavery, he contrasted the position of those who would use slavery for the "education" of a slave with real antislavery.

The economists' case for markets—against the paternalists, who wished to see slavery reformed—was that it takes time for people to learn how to be free. One of the most effective speakers for the Act of Emancipation of 1833, Thomas Babington Macaulay, drawing material from Adam Smith, compared the intoxication of freedom with the intoxication of strong drink. Here is evangelical economics policy in one lesson: release the slaves and they grope in freedom to become the same as their masters.[26] This is so even though the masters are white and the slaves are black.

In contrast, paternalists dealt with the proposal to abolish slavery by arguing that reformed slavery could be an instrument of improvement. Here we quote from the review by Henry Morley and Charles Dickens in an 1852 issue of *Household Words*. Several things are made clear in this review. First, Morley and Dickens intend to reform slavery and to delay emancipation until the black slaves are "suited" for freedom (Morley and Dickens 1852, 5). Second, Morley and Dickens appeal to the importance of kind masters, those who would guide by words and not the lash. The reformed slavery would be one without cruelty.

> The stripes! Though slavery be not abolished promptly, there can be no reason why stripes should not cease. Though there *may* be little of lashing and wailing in the slave system, as it is commonly administered in North America, yet men are degraded by being set to work by a coarse action of their fears, when the same men are far more capable of being stimulated by an excitement of their love of honour and reward. (Ibid., 5)

Then, Morley and Dickens reflect on innate racial differences and on how the newly reformed slavery could make blacks nearly white. The educational prospects of reformed slavery are compared in detail with those of the existing model of slavery. In the existing system, the slaves are too stupid to figure out that they ought to resent their situation. This is why Christianity cannot be preached in full.

> The negro has what the phrenologists would call love of approbation very strongly marked. Set him to work for the hope of distinction, instead of the fear of blows. No doubt it has been true that negroes, set to work by any motive which called out their higher feelings as men, would become ambitious and acquire a thirst for freedom in the end. So it is, so let it be. Educate the negroes on plantations, *make them intelligent men and women*, let them imbibe in their full freedom the doctrines of Christianity. It has been true that it was not safe to give knowledge to men who were placed in a position which the faintest flash of reason would resent. (Ibid., 5; emphasis added)

Under the reformed slavery, this defect will be mended, and with the reformation, the slaves will be remade (ibid., 5). Isn't it wonderful how one reforms slavery? One finds kind masters who are willing to teach their slaves how to be humans!

We have been reminded on more than one occasion that while Carlyle's attitudes on race and hierarchy were horrible, those of, say, Dickens were rather more progressive and less hateful. Because they offered a kindly sort of paternalism as an alternative to both markets and slavery, some of the Victorian sages might be salvaged as caring, progressive social commentators who genuinely wished to see the lot of the working poor improved.[27] There may have been some paternalists whose distrust of markets can be contrasted with our characterization of Ruskin and Carlyle (Levy and Peart 2001–2). Those paternalists, we have been told, were not necessarily racists.

But the preceding evidence indicates that, as a matter of fact, they were racists. Posing the problem as a choice among markets, slavery, and (somewhere in between) paternalism suggests why contemporary scholars might be prepared to defend the Victorian sages even today. What they may have failed to confront—and what we have found to be important—is the institutional means by which paternalists sought to "look after" the child-like among us. The paternalists favored slavery—albeit a reformed slavery—because they believed that African-Americans could not look after themselves. Our evidence has also revealed the much neglected darker side of the paternalists' concern for the poor and downtrodden. They demonized groups of people who were said to be particularly adept at preying on the weak and the downtrodden: Jews and the economists who developed the science of katallactics.

APPENDIX: THE PLACE OF ECONOMISTS

In their introduction to this volume, the editors write, "to understand economic policy, one must understand how broader philosophical concepts serve as the foundation for reasoning on economic policy." We agree. An important concern in our contributions has been to ensure that these philosophical underpinnings are called to light and properly understood. We propose that Walras's Law may be applied to the realm of controversy. Just as only one market cannot be out of equilibrium, so, too, when one controversy and the associated ideas are misunderstood, other misunderstandings follow. In this appendix, we provide a short reply to Zlotnick, Sheth, and Colander, each of whom has questioned aspects of our argument. In doing so, we attempt to ensure that the details of the Carlyle-Mill exchange—and the broader philosophical positions in which they are embedded—are correctly represented.

Susan Zlotnick's chapter in the present volume serves to put the reader on notice that there is something important at stake in the question we have raised. At issue is the relation between specialists (here, scholars of English literature) and the ordinary reader (us). We who resist the one way provided by enlightened specialists are characterized by Zlotnick as igno-rant simpletons incapable of grasping Carlyle's *real point*, that capitalism was "inimical to traditional English ways of life."[28]

Here, we can see what the lack of attention to sympathy and ethics, dis-cussed in more detail shortly, has done to economists. For philosophers like Adam Smith, sympathy and ethics are the bridge between private and public considerations. But unlike Smith, modern economists have pre-sumed that economic theorists and specialists in other disciplines all pur-sue the public good of truth, in which case ethical concerns fall away. From truth seeking, we take the easy step to the presumption of trans-parency, because we have assumed that scholars have motives different from those self-interested persons we study.

Economists who suppose specialists pursue truth have long been kept in their place by such specialists. Suppose one were to look up the origin of the "dismal science" in the *Oxford English Dictionary*. Let us compare what the *OED* (2d ed.) does not quote from Carlyle for the first occurrence of the phrase *dismal science* with what it does quote (underlined).

> Truly, my philanthropic friends, Exeter Hall Philanthropy is wonderful; and <u>the Social Science—not a "gay science," but a rueful—which finds the secret of this universe in "supply-and-demand,"</u> and reduces the duty of human governors to that of letting men alone, is also wonderful. Not a "gay science," I should say, like some we have heard of; no, a dreary, desolate, and indeed quite abject and distressing one; <u>what we might call, by way of eminence, the *dismal science*.</u> These two, Exeter Hall Philanthropy and the Dismal Science, led by any sacred cause of Black Emancipation, or the like, to fall in love and make a wedding of it,—will give birth to progenies and prodigies; dark extensive moon-calves, unnameable abortions, wide-coiled monstrosities, such as the world has not seen hitherto! (Carlyle 1849, 672–73)

From the *OED*, we learn that the "dismal science" is in opposition to the "gay science" and that it holds with explanations based on supply and demand. What the OED does not report is Carlyle's loathing of the political economists' coalition with Exeter Hall for the purpose of black emancipation. This distortion of the text suggests why we should not trust the guidance of others without verification.

Let us now turn to some misconceptions in Zlotnick's essay. First, her reading fails to notice a key distinction made by Levy and retained by Levy and Peart: despite her claim to the contrary, we do not ascribe a proslavery stance to all the literary critics of capitalism. Nor do we confuse paternalism with slavery. Indeed, we are very much aware of (at least) three positions among the literary community at midcentury; notwithstanding her claim to the contrary, some writers (such as Carlyle) favored slavery plain and simple, some were paternalistic, and some opposed the abolitionist movement.

The distinction between proslavery and anti-antislavery is not new to us: since it was made by Dickens's contemporaries, a "contextual" reading might easily have detected it. Lord Denman took issue with Dickens's antiabolitionist position.

> We have a still heavier charge against Mr. Dickens. In one particular instance, but the most important of all at this crisis, he exerts his powers to obstruct the great cause of human improvement—that cause which in general he cordially advocates. He does his best to replunge the world into the most barbarous abuse that ever afflicted it. We do not say that he actually defends slavery or the slave-trade; but he takes pains to discourage, by ridicule, the effort now making to put them down. We believe, indeed, that in general terms he expresses just hatred for both; but so do all those who profit or wish to profit by them, and who, by that general profession, prevent the detail of particulars too atrocious to be endured. The disgusting picture of a woman who pretends zeal for the happiness of Africa, and is constantly employed in securing a life of misery to her own children, is a laboured work of art in his present exhibition. (Denman 1853, 9, quoted in Levy 2001, 175)

Even more instructive is Zlotnick's attempt to justify Carlyle's defense of racial slavery by "reconnect[ing] with its historical context." She suggests that rather than calling for a return to slavery, his "The Negro Question" advocated paternalism at home and abroad. Since Zlotnick does not seem critical of Carlyle's "paternalism," let us see what it entails. Here is his doctrine of Romantic freedom, shown to best advantage as the godmaster imparts his knowledge of the one and only way.

No; the gods wish besides pumpkins, that spices and valuable products be grown in their West Indies; thus much they have declared in making the West Indies:—infinitely more they wish, that manful industrious men occupy their West Indies, not indolent two-legged cattle, however "happy" over their abundant pumpkins! Both these things, we may be assured, the immortal gods have decided upon, passed their eternal act of parliament for: and both of them, though all terrestrial Parliaments and entities oppose it to the death, shall be done. Quashee, if he will not help in bringing out the spices, will get himself made a slave again (which state will be a little less ugly than his present one), and with beneficent whip, since other methods avail not, will be compelled to work. (Carlyle 1849, 675)

For Zlotnick, evidently, the god-master *really cares* for his creatures in a way that the hard-hearted economists cannot understand.

Many of the differences between Zlotnick and us relate to "context." By "context," Zlotnick seems to mean listening to the wisdom of specialists like her, whereas we mean considering how the words were taken by Carlyle's contemporaries. The American proslavery discussion (see Levy 2001, 101–2) is easily dismissed by Zlotnick because, after all, it involved slave owners. But Carlyle's "The Negro Question" was reprinted in the *Anti-Slavery Reporter (ASR)* of January 1, 1850, with Mill's response following on February 1, 1850. The attention is explained.

Had this production proceeded from any other pen than Carlyle's, we should have allowed it to pass in silence; but, because it is attributed to him, it must, forsooth, be noticed. Now, what is the staple of his discourse? Stripped of its inflated verbosity, and put into plain English, it affirms that the emancipated slaves of the British colonies are an idle and inferior race of men, whom God has created to be the servants or slaves of white men; who, in the enjoyment of their freedom, are content to live on "pig's food;" that Providence designed them to grow sugar and coffee and spices for the rest of the world, instead of shaping out their own course; and that, if there be no other means of securing that end, the "beneficent whip" must be employed, to compel these "indolent two-legged cattle" to produce the "noble elements of cinnamon, sugar, coffee, pepper black and grey," for their "born lords." In the meantime, and until the "beneficent whip" and the wholesome state of slavery can be restored . . . (*ASR*, January 1, 1850, 9)

The *ASR* reprinted an attack from the *Inquirer* that compared Carlyle's racial attitude to that of a famous economist.

He describes the whole negro race in a tone of scornful vituperation which we cannot call less than brutal. One large branch of the human family, coloured and organised in the manner that has seemed good to the just and merciful Father of us all, and who are thought by competent observers, like Miss Martineau, to possess in peculiar strength some of the most beautiful elements of our nature, Mr. Carlyle stigmatises as being, in morals and intellect, no better than beasts. (ASR, January 1, 1850, 11)

Finally, in our view, the controversy over the New Poor Law is in fact *not* central to the Carlyle-Mill debate over the "Negro question" or the events in Jamaica in 1865, because Carlyle (1904, 29:131–32) *defends* the policies, if not the theory, of the New Poor Law (Levy 2001, 90).

In conclusion, Zlotnick suggests that we might have been led less far astray had we stopped "occasionally to ask a native for directions." She may have a point. But then again, what reason would we have to trust in the directions we received? After all, we did ask this specialist about Governor Eyre, his wire whips, and the judicial lynch and received silence for our edification. Zlotnick's essay contains as much on the "paternalistic" defenders of Governor Eyre's murder and mutilation of Jamaicans as there is in the OED entry on slavery.

Let us now turn to Sheth's comments. In her chapter in this volume, she argues that J. S. Mill's views regarding blacks and emancipation come from his presuppositions concerning human nature, tradition, hierarchy, and customs, rather than from his economics. We have mistakenly, she complains, attributed his position on race (or women) to his economics. Somehow she is able to identify what comes from his economics and what comes from other considerations, without the bother of reading other classical economists.

In fact, one of our main arguments has been that Mill's views on race and on economics all stem from his conception of human nature; that is, they all presuppose equal competence, the analytical commonplace in classical economics. We agree with Sheth that for Mill, the market is a means to development rather than an end in and of itself. Elsewhere (Peart and Levy 2003b), we have cited the key text for this argument, in which Mill clearly allows competent agents to flee civilization for happiness.

To civilize a savage, he must be inspired with new wants and desires, even if not of a very elevated kind, provided that their gratification can be a motive to steady and regular bodily and mental exertion. If the negroes of Jamaica and Demerara, after their emancipation, had con-

tented themselves, as it was predicted they would do, with the neces-
saries of life, and abandoned all labour beyond the little which in a tropical climate, with a thin population and abundance of the richest land,
is sufficient to support existence, they would have sunk into a condition
more barbarous, though less unhappy, than their previous state of slavery. (Mill [1848] 1965, 104)

While these material desires might not be approved in Mill's society, they
are critical steps in the development of the capacity for self-reliance.

The motive which was most relied on for inducing them to work was
their love of fine clothes and personal ornaments. No one will stand up
for this taste as worthy of being cultivated, and in most societies its
indulgence tends to impoverish rather than to enrich; but in the state of
mind of the negroes it might have been the only incentive that could
make them voluntarily undergo systematic labour, and so acquire or
maintain habits of voluntary industry which may be converted to more
valuable ends. (Ibid., 104–5)

Sheth remarks that we cast the debate between paternalists and free-
marketeers in terms of different attitudes regarding human abilities, and
she claims that we fail to provide evidence of this. We believe that our
essays contain remarkable statements from both sides—paternalists and
economists—but since these statements are considered nonexistent, we
add to them here.

First, we might point out that Charles Kingsley's notorious racial views
are a scholarly commonplace. The Kingsley–James Hunt connection is
first published in Levy 2001 (102–11). *Water-Babies'* message of racial
degeneration from man to ape and then to extinction in the nation of
"Doasyoulikes" (Kingsley 1863, 239–40) is detailed in Levy and Peart
2001–2 (article 4). Dickens, too, found blacks unfit for emancipation, in
his review of *Uncle Tom's Cabin*.

When we have clipped men's minds and made them slavish, it is a poor
compensation that their bodies should be set at large. (Morley and Dickens 1852, 5)

Lord Denman (1853, 20) attacked the program of those who would use
slavery for "education."

> These views . . . were discussed by Mr. Macaulay . . . [He] ridiculed the
> notion that such preparation was requisite, comparing it to the prudence
> of a father who advised his son not to bathe until he could swim.

To convey the classical economists' contrasting view of human nature, we
have quoted Smith, Mill, and, in our second contribution to this volume
(chap. 5), J. E. Cairnes.

Finally, let us turn to the arguments of Colander, who, in this volume,
asks us to justify our Chicago-influenced approach. The strength of that
approach is that it places the economic theorist and the subjects on the
same analytical plane and acknowledges that individuals satisfy wants in
diverse ways. To explicate how our concerns relate to the lingua franca of
economics, we consider the discussion in Ariel Rubinstein's *Economics and
Language* (2000). Rubinstein reopens a project that has been mostly dor-
mant since the days of Adam Smith: he uses the same rational-choice considerations to explain aspects of language that economists use to explain
the exchange of goods. Also akin to Smith's approach, the rational-choice
considerations that are used to model the decisions of ordinary language
users are the same in structure as the rational-choice considerations of the
modelers themselves. In Rubinstein's account, there is none of the heterogeneity of motivation or competence that disfigures much modern economics, wherein the subjects of economic theory pursue the private good
of happiness while those who theorize about the subjects are presumed to
pursue the public good of truth.

Rubinstein (2000, 56) asks the central question about the role of economists in the real world: "Why does the utility function $(\log(x_1 + 1))x_2$ in a
two-commodity world lie within the scope of classic textbooks whereas lexicographical preferences do not?" Why is it that we have renounced lexicographical orderings? Consider the two orders as guides that the economic
theorist brings with him to talk to individuals about their choices. How
many ways are there for an ordinary person to attain happiness? The text-
book utility function has, and the lexicographical order does not have, indifference. Indifference allows the ordinary person to attain the goal of utility
maximizing in a diversity of ways. When the order is lexicographical, there
is only one way to attain some agreed-on level of utility: the theorist's way.

This is the choice facing economic theorists: which sort of ordering do
we offer ordinary people in exchange for goods? Adam Smith (1759,
VI.II.42) was critical of the theorist who claimed his was the only way.

The man of system . . . seems to imagine that he can arrange the different members of a great society with as much ease as the hand arranges
the different pieces upon a chess-board. He does not consider that the
pieces upon the chess-board have no other principle of motion besides
that which the hand impresses upon them; but that, in the great chess-
board of human society, every single piece has a principle of motion of
its own.

Others, such as Carlyle, find the lexicographical way appealing and
attacked classical political economy for renouncing the hierarchy in
which the theorist directs the theorized.

We can now explain why we part company with Colander on the
nature and scope of economic policy as it relates to race. Colander urges
the American people to recognize that the legacy of Western ideas about
race and slavery is a long one, with consequences so grave that unfettered
markets cannot seem to correct things. He argues that pragmatic interventions to put things right must be relied on in such "tragic questions."
But such an approach leaves the policy analyst/economic theorist to specify both the tragic questions and—more difficult—*the* solution(s). It places
the analyst in a position that is apparently above the subject of analysis,
and it thus allows that the theorist (and only the theorist) knows what is
best.

Consider Colander's example of racial profiling. How can our view of
the world support the *unconditional* condemnation of the policy? *Our* view
suggests that competent actors inside the market and political process will
come to some equilibrium that seems sensible to them. Our view predicts
that, if circumstances change, "racial" profiling might be viewed as a necessary evil. With the terrorist attacks of September 11, 2001, upon us, the
question of profiling became much discussed. The polling data we have
seen suggests that a majority of black respondents to the statement "Law
enforcement officials may look at people with Middle Eastern accents or
features with greater suspicion and scrutiny . . ." replied "Understandable
but wish it didn't happen."[29] It is hardly surprising that white and Hispanic
majorities were larger.

We do not wish to suggest that the problems to which Colander refers
are not tragic: our research is largely driven by a desire to unearth the terrible and long-lasting influence of "theories" about race and inheritance.
But we find unappealing a policy approach that places the theorist on a
higher plane than the subject.

Perhaps most importantly, we should like to add to our argument concerning the University of Chicago revival of race-blind accounts. We have argued elsewhere (Levy and Peart 2001–2, article 6; Peart and Levy 2003a) that the revival of analytical egalitarianism at midcentury—the presumption that economic and political actors are equally competent—failed to revive a key aspect of classical thinking: notions of sympathy and reciprocity as they constrain transactions in economics, narrowly speaking, and in the wider realm of political economy. When Adam Smith wrote that dogs do not trade because they lack a concept of fairness, a distinction between "mine" and "thine," he sketched the reciprocity norm implicit in market exchange.

When we hail the revival of race-blind theories of human interaction, we do not wish to imply that either sympathy or ethics has also been systematically revived. Without a foundation in sympathy or ethics, economists have little basis to participate in discussions of compensation for the violations of reciprocity that occurred in the dramatic taking of life via slavery or the less dramatic takings via state restrictions on free choice.[30] Our sense of how to move forward on policy issues entails not only race-blind accounts of human action but also the rejuvenation of a classical notion of sympathy—that of individuals celebrating the desires and choices of other individuals, whatever those may be. Policy that acknowledges the desires and choices of only one sort (the theorists') and that presumes that choices of a different sort (the subjects') are to be dismissed as incorrect or unfortunate is inconsistent with our notion of celebrating such diversity. Much rhetoric about diversity in fact serves to stifle a large set of actions.

NOTES

1. Counterexamples are gaining ground. See Persky 1990; Levy 2001; Levy and Peart 2001–2.

2. In his attack on Charles Dickens's opposition to the antislavery movement, Lord Denman (1853, 12) makes the point that proslavery views were being revived at midcentury by the most popular of contemporary writers.

3. With Mill, the doctrine of the analytic irrelevance of race attained its sharpest form: "Is it not, then, a bitter satire on the mode in which opinions are formed on the most important problems of human nature and life, to find public instructors of the greatest pretensions, imputing the backwardness of Irish industry, and the want of energy of the Irish people in improving their condition, to a peculiar indolence and insouciance in the Celtic race? Of all vulgar modes of

escaping from the consideration of the effect of social and moral influences on the human mind, the most vulgar is that of attributing the diversities of conduct and character to inherent natural differences" (Mill [1848] 1965, 319).

4. The extension to involuntary exchange—the katallactics of government—is announced in the second edition (Whately 1832) and begun in Whately 1833. Whately's point is that katallactics depends on the mutually beneficial nature of exchange, not on whether an individual act, such as paying taxes, is voluntary.

5. For the argument that the first of Carlyle's *Latter-Day Pamphlets,* the February 1850 "Present Time," ought to be read as Carlyle's response to Mill, see Levy 2001, 20, 83, 100.

6. The "horse and half-brother" sneer is a response to an antislavery question that was asked on behalf of the slaves out of Africa, "Am I not a man and a brother?" Denman (1853, 12) notes that it was only recently that a "man and a brother" had been ridiculed. Levy and Peart 2001 (2001–2 article 2) has links to the image that accompanied the question.

7. "Liberty? The true liberty of a man, you would say, consisted in his finding out, or being forced to find out the right path, and to walk thereon. To learn, or to be taught, what work he actually was able for; and then, by permission, persuasion, and even compulsion, to set about doing of the same! . . . If thou do know better than I what is good and right, I conjure thee in the name of God, force me to do it; were it by never such brass collars, whips and handcuffs, leave me not to walk over precipices!" (Carlyle [1844] 1965, 211–12).

8. The term *gay science* is described as "a rendering of *gai saber,* the Provençal name for the art of poetry" in the *Oxford English Dictionary* (2d ed.).

9. *Colonial Standard,* quoted in the *Anti-Slavery Reporter* 13 (December 1, 1865): 282. Paul Bogle lives in the lyrics to Bob Marley's "So Much Things To Say."

10. *Anti-Slavery Reporter* 13 (December 1, 1865): 298.

11. We can judge his importance by the following "tribute" from *Punch* 51 (January 13, 1866): 16.

CHAMHEROBZOW
(A Negro Melody)

De niggers when dey kick up row,
No hang, no shoot, say, CHAMHEROBZOW.
CHAMHEROBZOW de friend oh nigger,
In all de world dar arn't a bigger.
    Gollywolly, gorraworra, bow-wow-wow!
    De nigger lum him CHAMHEROBZOW.

De buckra try, de buckra swing;
Yoh! CHAMHEROBZOW, dat ar's de ting.
De nigger am your man and brudder:
You tell de debble take de udder.
    Gollywolly, gorraworra, bow-wow-wow!
    De nigger's friend Ole CHAMHEROBZOW

12. Hunt will figure prominently in our second contribution to this volume. The *Popular Magazine of Anthropology*, in which this comment appears, is a spinoff of Hunt's *Anthropological Review* and seems to have been prompted by events in Jamaica. Hunt's various ventures are discussed in Rainger 1978.

13. In discussing Robert Knox's doctrine of racial war, Hunt (1866b, 25–26) brings in Carlyle as economic prophet: "He [Knox] would have that latest of all ethnological puzzles to some—the present 'insurrection in Jamaica;' an insurrection, however, which he, as we have already seen, foretold upon scientific principles, which Carlyle, in his tract on 'The Nigger Question,' hinted at as probable on grounds of social economy."

14. Levy (2001, 25) gives the Irish connotation of "knot" missed by the *Oxford English Dictionary* (2d ed.).

15. *Anti-Slavery Reporter* 13 (December 1, 1865): 305–6. The entire issue was devoted to the "Jamaica Massacres."

16. Evidence that Eyre promoted the Carlylean worldview, which in turn was fundamentally responsible for the events in Jamaica, is found in the *Anti-Slavery Reporter*. The context is Carlyle's "gospel of labor" embodied in the "Queen's Advice." This evidence is presented in article 3 of Levy and Peart 2001–2. The "Queen's Advice" is given in Holt 1992 (277–78, 280–83), where it is linked to the "Negro Question."

17. Walvin (1973, 172) notes: "After the events of 1865 English racial antagonisms crystallized more clearly than at any time since the collapse of the slave lobby. Eyre found enormous support for his legalized savagery, notably from Ruskin, Tennyson, Kingsley, Dickens and Carlyle. Their public utterances and those from sympathetic newspapers revived the very worst English attitudes towards the Negro." The role of the scientific community is studied in our second contribution to this volume. For the *Punch* images, see Levy and Peart 2001–2.

18. Those who are unfamiliar with the period may not realize that the debate over racial heterogeneity in England focused on the "Irish problem" every bit as much as it did the "Jamaican problem." See Curtis 1968; Levy and Peart 2000.

19. " . . . his wages, thanks to your competitive system, were beaten down deliberately and conscientiously (for was it not according to political economy, and the laws thereof?) to the minimum on which he could or would work" (Kingsley 1850, 245).

20. Martineau (1837) had influential things to say about just what use the American slave owners made of the bodies of their young female slaves. Levy 2001 and Peart and Levy 2003b (141–42) give the details of Martineau's economics of the harem.

21. One of the best examples we have found of this violence is in visual form in the paintings and posters issued by *Cope's Tobacco Plant* (Wallace 1878a, 1878b) and discussed in *Plenipotent Key* 1878. These are studied in detail in Levy and Peart 2001–2.

22. While people can be sorted into a hierarchy along racial lines, paternalism does not require racism. Age, religion, or gender might be the sorting mechanism instead.

23. Here is the relevant aspect of the entry for the term *catallactic* from the *Oxford English Dictionary* (2nd ed.): "A proposed name for Political Economy as

the 'science of exchanges'. . . . 1862 Ruskin *Unto this Last* 132 The Science of Exchange, or, as I hear it has been proposed to call it, of 'Catallactics,' considered as one of gain, is . . . simply nugatory. . . . 1862 Ruskin *Unto this Last* 155 You may grow for your neighbour . . . grapes or grapeshot; he will also catallactically grow grapes or grapeshot for you, and you will each reap what you have sown."

24. As we noted earlier, paternalism is necessary, though not sufficient, for the existence of human parasites: the distribution of benefits might be random over reallocations that are not trades.

25. This does not mean that Smith supposes that individuals have anything like perfect perception of their own interests. He emphatically does not (see Levy 2001). Where a paternalist would appeal to guidance by one's betters, Smith appeals to guidance by evolved social rules of conduct.

26. Macaulay (1961, 1:178–79) claims: "It is the character of such revolutions that we always see the worst of them first. Till men have been some time free, they know not how to use their freedom." Behind Macaulay's analysis of the adjustment to intoxication is Smith ([1776] 1976, 492).

27. "Paternalism" is not exactly ignored in Levy 2001; rather, it is treated as the robust school of statistics treats ordinary least squares. Episode 4 of Levy and Peart 2001–2 is a beginning of a less dismissive treatment of paternalism.

28. Zlotnick's characterization of us and/or our position runs from "deafness," to "crude assertions," to "unfamiliarity with the complicated cultural landscape of nineteenth-century Britain" and "trawling" for evidence.

29. See <http://www.publicagenda.org/issues/red_flags_detail.cfm?issue_type =race&list=3&area=3>.

30. In our second contribution to this volume, we argue that the removal of ethics from economic concerns has also cost economists intellectually—as we have had our history written incorrectly for us.

Contextualizing David Levy's *How the Dismal Science Got Its Name;*

or, Revisiting the Victorian Context of David Levy's History of Race and Economics

Susan Zlotnick

In *How the Dismal Science Got Its Name* (2001), David Levy opens with an analysis of an 1893 depiction of John Ruskin, author of *Unto This Last* (1862), one of the most influential nineteenth-century attacks on classical economic theory. Levy turns to this image, the cover illustration of *Ruskin on Himself and Things in General* (1893), for visual proof that proslavery attitudes are embedded in the early Victorian critique of the free market. The image is a striking one. It represents Ruskin as St. George, doing battle with a man dressed in banker's garb—replete with spats, waistcoat, and moneybag. To anyone familiar with the representational practices of Victorian culture, the figure holding the moneybag, a monstrous hybrid of man, ape, and dragon, is instantly recognizable as a caricature of a capitalist. However, Levy (2001, 5) pegs the figure as an ex–West Indian slave formally attired and thereby signifying the "merger of a black person and the discipline of economics." This original interpretation supports Levy's contention that the critics of capitalism were hostile to both blacks and the free market, but it does not hold up under scrutiny.[1]

Unfortunately for Levy, the capitalist's vaguely racialized features cannot be read as evidence of racial identity. In this case, the features indicate the capitalist's otherness—not his race—and thus underscore his alien-

ation from Englishness and the thoroughly English Ruskin, who is appropriately costumed as the nation's patron saint. Deployed in a variety of
ways throughout the nineteenth century, race was a reality to the Victorians, in that they believed in racial differences that denoted moral, physical, and intellectual divides between people of diverse skin colors. Yet they
also used race figuratively, with race functioning as a floating signifier that
could be attached to any group (e.g., the Irish or the urban poor) to signify
its otherness. Mistaking a figurative use of race for a literal one, Levy fails
to grasp the image's main point, one frequently articulated in the late Victorian period: that capitalism itself was inimical to traditional English
ways of life.[2]

This misreading of the Ruskin image highlights the fundamental problem with Levy's thesis: his unfamiliarity with the complicated cultural
landscape of nineteenth-century Britain. As Levy publicly stated at the
conference, the motivating force behind his scholarship is the desire to
show that the free market is the black man's best friend. Since the daily
headlines in the *New York Times* or even the *Wall Street Journal* do not
offer him much evidence, Levy goes trawling in historical waters in search
of the proof he needs. He drifts back to the early decades of Victoria's reign
in order to argue that the Victorian critics of capitalism (Ruskin as well as
Thomas Carlyle and Charles Dickens) embraced slavery as the alternative
to capitalism, while the political economists of the period, such figures as
John Stuart Mill and Thomas Babington Macaulay, championed the freedom of all men through their advocacy of the free market.

In brief, there are three main thrusts to Levy's argument. First, he
recasts the Victorian critics of capitalism as history's villains: he ascribes
an undeserved proslavery pedigree to them and argues for an intimate link
between anticapitalist and proslavery attitudes. Second, he tries to recu-
perate capitalism by (mis)characterizing the economists as antiracist, abolitionist "good guys" (Levy 2001, 58). Third, Levy accuses the contemporary literary establishment of a reprehensible (and perhaps racist) silence
about the racism of Ruskin, Carlyle, and Dickens, a silence that in Levy's
mind arises from the infamous anticapitalist biases that latter-day English
professors share in common with the Victorian men of letters. Even if
these assertions were correct—and, in my view, they are not—it remains
unclear to me how they would ultimately prove that the free market is a
boon to people of color. However, I will leave that problem for others to
ponder. The modest goal of this chapter is to address the historical inac-

curacies that throw into doubt many of Levy's conclusions about the Victorian era.

Levy's difficulties with history seem to arise out of deafness to the complex racial/imperialist discourses in the period, a disability all too evident in his reading of the Ruskin portrait. Levy's neglect of the recent scholarship on nineteenth-century British culture may partially account for these problems, but the fact remains that one cannot successfully rewrite history by flattening it out into a narrative of good and bad guys. To offer a more nuanced rendering of the Victorian past, this chapter resituates the writings of the political economists and their critics within the overlapping discourses that circulated within nineteenth-century Britain, with the aim of providing the complex historical context missing from Levy's analysis. The chapter's first section constructs a more balanced view of the Victorian critics of capitalism by reconnecting them to important debates, such as factory reform, ignored by Levy; the second section challenges Levy's portrait of the political economists as unqualified heroes, in part by calling attention to the role they played in some controversial aspects of Victorian life (e.g., the empire, the Poor Law Amendment Act of 1834) curiously overlooked in Levy's work; and the final section offers a necessary corrective to Levy's tendentious, misleading view of contemporary scholarship.

Paternalism and Discourse in the Nineteenth Century

In a letter contemplating the future of the enslaved American black, Charles Dickens wrote, "Free of course he must be; but the stupendous absurdity of making him a voter glares out of every roll of his eye, stretch of his mouth, and bump of his head" (quoted in Ackroyd 1990, 544). As Dickens's words make clear, repugnant racism could coexist side by side with an antislavery position in the nineteenth century because racism permeated Victorian culture.[3] "There was," Edward Said (1994, 100) observes, "no significant dissent from theories of Black inferiority." Given its ubiquity, the presence of racism does not automatically signal proslavery sympathies, even though Professor Levy frequently cites the former as evidence of the latter. Indeed, Levy's contention that the early Victorian critics of capitalism—Dickens, Ruskin, Carlyle—were slavery supporters founders on just such basic misunderstandings of the social terrain of nineteenth-century Britain. To properly evaluate the relationship between these three men of letters and slavery, one must be better attuned to the language of racism in the nineteenth century as well as to the important discourses with which it intersects (paternalism, abolitionism, factory reform) in their writings.

For example, only by failing to consider paternalist ideology and its relationship to the factory reform movement in early Victorian England could Levy contend that the critics of capitalism presented their readers with the option of either slavery or the market economy. Throughout his extended analysis, Levy consistently misreads paternalistic utterances as proslavery ones, even though the two are not identical. For Ruskin and Carlyle, the choice was not between slavery and the free market but between liberalism (with its attendant faith in unfettered capitalism) and old-fashioned paternalism. James Oakes (1998, xvii) offers a useful definition of both, which he sees as fundamentally antagonistic socioeconomic orders:

> "Paternalism" suggests a social order which is stable, hierarchical, indeed consciously elitist, and therefore fundamentally antithetical to liberalism. A paternalist assumes an inherent inequality of men: some are born to rule, others to obey. A liberal espouses a far different social fiction: "All men are created equal." A paternalist stresses the organic unity born of each individual's acceptance of his or her place in a stable, stratified social order. A liberal stresses individualism, social mobility, and economic fluidity within a society which promotes equal opportunity.

Along with Southey, Coleridge, Disraeli, and most members of the Tory party, Ruskin and Carlyle were paternalists.[4] Wishing to return to what historians often designate as the old moral economy, Victorian paternalists offered a conservative critique of industrialism that rejected the mechanistic market economy in favor of an organic, hierarchical world associated with the preindustrial past. To be sure, the merry old England conjured up in paternalist texts is deeply tinged with nostalgia, and it frequently features happy peasants, model landlords, and Morris dancing on the village green. Paternalism's most famous instantiation is Victorian medievalism, which depicts the medieval world as a lost golden age and an antidote to the fallen present of factories. Carlyle's and Ruskin's best-known critiques of the infant industrial world are medievalist documents: both Carlyle's *Past and Present* ([1843] 1927) and Ruskin's "The Nature of

Gothic" ([1853] 1985) represent an idealized feudal hierarchy as the divinely sanctioned alternative to the laissez-faire economy of modern times.[5]

To be fair to Levy, his conflation of British paternalism with American slavery has a certain logic to it, given that the Southern slave owner used paternalism as a legitimating ideology to defend his peculiar institution from its critics. Such a defense flowed "naturally from the slave owner's self-image as a loving, paternalistic master who provided for his people" (Kolchin 1993, 194). However, in addition to covering over the cruel and inhumane treatment of blacks, the rhetoric of paternalism concealed the fact that Southern slavery was organized along capitalist lines, exporting its major cash crops to international markets.[6] So not only does paternalism's centrality in early Victorian political debates destabilize the opposition Levy establishes as fundamental to his argument—slavery on one side, free markets on the other—but the economic realities of American slavery undermine Levy's assertions as well. By setting up a false opposition between slavery and the free market, Levy's thesis (like the slave owners' self-justifying use of paternalism) covers over the fact that slavery and the slave trade prospered as part of a global capitalist network and had done so since that network first emerged in the early modern period.

Not only does Professor Levy's argument proceed by setting up false oppositions, but it also claims equivalencies where none exist. Central to Levy's project is his identification of a common trope in nineteenth-century texts—the comparison of the wage "slavery" of white British factory workers and the enslavement of blacks in the New World. However, whenever Levy sees this worker/slave analogy in the writings of Carlyle, Ruskin, or Dickens, he wrongly assumes a dangerous moral equivalency is being drawn, one that indicates a proslavery bias. (Indeed, his condemnation of *Hard Times* as a proslavery text rests largely on the assumption of moral equivalency.) Once again Levy is led astray by his failure to contextualize, in this case to acknowledge the interrelated, intercontinental discourses of abolitionism and factory reform out of which the analogy emerges.

The presence of the worker/slave analogy in a Victorian text does not by itself indicate the author's position vis-à-vis slavery. First deployed during the 1770s by slave owners who maintained in self-defense that black slaves were better off than British workers, the worker/slave analogy quickly entered the political lexicon and was used strategically by abolitionists and factory reformers as well as slavery's apologists throughout the nineteenth century. Catherine Gallagher's *The Industrial Reformation of English Fiction* (1985) traces out with great precision the analogy's genesis and its relationship to the abolition and factory reform movements. Gallagher argues for a complex and often contradictory relationship between the antislavery movement and the critics of industrial society:

> Industrial reformers and social critics appropriated the images, the rhetoric, and the tone of the antislavery movement. Simultaneously, however, they used arguments and rhetorical strategies associated with the advocates of slavery. . . . However, in using the worker/slave metaphor, most critics of industrialism . . . were not revealing pro-slavery sentiments. Rather, they were articulating their objections to the liberal political economists' model of freedom and developing their own alternate ideas of liberty. (4)

By unraveling the tangled history of the worker/slave analogy, Gallagher provides the necessary amendments to Levy's crude assertions that the nineteenth century's political economists, allied with the Evangelicals, were on the right side of the abolition debate, while the critics of capitalism staunchly defended human bondage, evidenced by their use of the worker/slave analogy.

According to Gallagher, critics like Carlyle (and I would add Ruskin) participated in a Romantic critique of political economy that fundamentally challenged the liberal model of human freedom, which emphasized "the ability . . . to contract one's labor—or other commodity—to the highest bidder on an open market" (Gallagher 1985, 7). Denying the reality of this doctrine of free labor for destitute, desperate workers, Romantics like the poet Samuel Taylor Coleridge argued that human free will could best be exercised in a paternalistic community in which the governors assured the workers' well-being. For Carlyle and Ruskin as well as Coleridge, paternalism was the only way to protect and ensure the individual's God-given freedom. Indeed, on close reading, both Ruskin's "The Nature of Gothic" ([1853] 1985) and Carlyle's "Occasional Discourse on the Negro Question" (1849) promulgate this Romantic notion of freedom. So, for example, Ruskin's notorious statement in "The Nature of Gothic" ([1853] 1985, 85) that "men may be beaten, chained, tormented, yoked like cattle, slaughtered like summer flies, and yet remain in one sense, and the best sense, free" is not—as Levy characterizes it—an unfeeling defense of American slavery but a plea for England to return to a quasi-medieval hierarchy that would guarantee the worker the "best kind of liberty—liberty from care" (Ruskin [1853] 1985, 86) by resurrecting a social bond between commoners and nobles, not slaves and masters. One certainly should question Ruskin's breezy dismissal of torture and exploitation here, but his disregard for physical suffering does not make him proslavery: it makes him a Tory paternalist with a Romantic view of human freedom.

This same understanding of freedom operates within Carlyle's "The Negro Question," a text Professor Levy discusses at some length. When reconnected with its historical context, one of widespread racism as well as agitations over abolition, factory reform, and the Irish potato famine, Carlyle's essay no longer appears to be the indiscriminate proslavery text Levy alleges. While the essay reserves slavery as the policy of last resort, it calls on the whole for an authoritarian, paternalist state to "guide" the newly emancipated slaves of the West Indies. It is important to recall the exact moment in which Carlyle wrote the essay, which began its life as an occasional piece written in response to current events. The emancipation of the slaves in the British Empire created a labor scarcity on West Indian sugar plantations, and one publicly discussed solution to this shortfall was the importation of labor to the islands. Derived from the laws of supply and demand, this remedy infuriated Carlyle and led him to hurl the famous "dismal science" epithet. With the tragedy of the Irish potato famine in mind, Carlyle (1849, 672) predicted that a flood of new workers would transform the West Indies into a "*Black Ireland . . .* with pumpkins themselves fallen scarce like potatoes."[7] In this instance, Carlyle draws on a variation of the worker/slave analogy in order to argue, as David Goldberg notes, that the proposed immigration scheme would "render the Negro inhabitants as free to starve as their British counterparts" (Goldberg 2000, 205). By analogizing the situation of West Indian blacks and white British workers, Carlyle exposes the "social fiction" espoused by the political economists in their doctrine of free labor.

Although Levy implies that Carlyle's vehement attack on political economy is intimately connected to his proslavery sentiments, Carlyle's tirade against the dismal science in "The Negro Question" echoes similar criticisms made in his seminal industrial writings of the 1830s and 1840s. Carlyle's anger at Victorian liberals arises from his belief that only a muscular, paternalistic leadership (what he calls "hero worship") can restore health to a diseased body politic and remedy the condition of England. Political economy, Carlyle thunders in "The Negro Question" (1849, 672), "reduces the duty of human governors to that of letting men alone," and that explains why it is a dismal science and not a gay one. In other words, classical economics, with its laissez-faire imperatives, denies certain divine truths. In particular, Carlyle holds to be self-evident the truth that the struggling mass of men, whether they be ex-slaves, Irish peasants, or Manchester mill hands, needs to be led by the enlightened few.

In "The Negro Question," Carlyle calls not for a return to slavery but for a paternalistic hierarchy, at home and abroad, where lower-class whites as well as emancipated slaves could fulfill their divine destinies as workers. "To do competent work, to labour honestly" is the everlasting duty of "all men, black or white," according to Carlyle (673); and the invective he spews at blacks stems from his racist belief in the ex-slaves' laziness. The "idle black man" of Carlyle's imperial imagination must be "*compelled* to work as he was fit, and to *do* the Maker's will who had constructed him with such and such prefigurements of capability" (674). To be sure, the words bespeak Carlyle's authoritarian stridency, but they are not an appeal to reinstitute slavery in British possessions. For as he informs the West Indian blacks a few paragraphs later, "You are not 'slaves' now; nor do I wish, if it can be avoided, to see you slaves again; but decidedly you will have to be servants to those that are born *wiser* than you, that are born lords of you,—servants to the whites, if they *are* (as what mortal can doubt they are?) born wiser than you" (676–77). The distinction between servant and slave is an important one because it underscores Carlyle's quasi-feudal orientation. Not surprisingly, at the conclusion of "The Negro Question," Carlyle invokes the medieval model as the ideal social organization and cites approvingly the arrangements in the Dutch-owned islands, where whites treat the blacks in "the manner of the old European serfs" (677). Carlyle's dream of resurrecting serfdom in the Caribbean is mightily unappealing to us, but no more so perhaps than what Carlyle understood as the solution put forward by the political economists of the day: overpopulating the islands to ensure (or might we say compel?) "free" and "willing" workers to enter the cane fields.

Political Engagements of Nineteenth-Century Economists

Just as Levy conveniently forgets the imbricated discourses that shape the meanings one can assign to the words of Carlyle, Ruskin, and Dickens, so, too, does he fail to recall the range of political engagements that occupied the nineteenth-century political economists. Any mention of the contro-

versial stances they took toward the poor law and factory reform movements or of their direct participation in Britain's imperial adventures is
missing from Levy's account. When we fill in the spaces left blank by Levy,
a less idealized picture of the nineteenth-century political economists
emerges. The Victorian critics of capitalism were not as bad—nor were the
political economists as good—as Levy makes out.

The most significant blank in Levy's argument is the gaping hole left by
Levy's dismissal of the industrial revolution. Levy tries to skirt its impact
on Victorian society by citing Thomas Macaulay's observation that longer
life spans in the nineteenth century proved the beneficial nature of rapid
industrialization (Levy 2001, chap. 7). Whether conditions improved or
worsened for working people in the first half of the nineteenth century—
as well as how to measure or define such improvement—is one of the great
historiographic debates of the last one hundred years.[8] But whatever historians may think, many Victorians, both upper-class and working-class,
viewed the 1830s and 1840s as a time of national crisis. Macaulay's remark
cannot do justice to the world-transforming events faced by Britain's early
industrial workers, nor can it adequately represent the social and political
trauma infant industrialism inflicted on the early Victorian world. Such
problems as rapid urbanization, Irish immigration, and the overcapitaliza-
tion of the textile market produced a disgruntled labor force that coalesced
into the Chartist movement, which seemed to pose the threat of an immi-
nent workers' revolution in the years before midcentury.[9] Novelist Elizabeth Gaskell, a Manchester resident sympathetic to the brave new industrial world, proclaimed in *Mary Barton* ([1848] 1987, 96) that the working
class "only wanted a Dante to record their sufferings." To ameliorate the
condition of England's workers, the abolitionists and Evangelicals, who
had been in coalition with the political economists over the struggle to
end slavery, broke ranks and began to divert "a portion of the humanitarian energy that they had set flowing in the slave trade debate into this new
channel of reform" (Gallagher 1985, 11).

Carlyle, Ruskin, and Dickens belong to this tradition of humanitarian
concern. Faced with the innumerable examples of human wretchedness
associated with early industrialism—from child labor, to urban squalor, to
unsafe workplaces—these social critics called for immediate intervention,
while the political economists seemed willing to accept misery in the short
run because they believed that an unregulated market would benefit everyone in the long run. It is important to recall these years of domestic tur-
moil, because they explain why, for so long, figures like Carlyle, Ruskin,

and Dickens have been celebrated as men of conscience and character while the political economists have suffered some ignominy for their position, however principled it may have been.

Even if we leave aside for the moment the political economists' response to the distresses of early industrialism, there are other grounds on which one can challenge the humanitarian mantle Levy wishes to bestow on them. To reiterate, Levy's argument goes something like this: (1) the political economists are history's "good guys" because of their abolitionism, (2) their abolitionism presupposes an antiracist attitude, and (3) the political economists' abolitionism and antiracism prove that the free market is the black man's friend. However, Levy can sustain such an argument only by repressing the direct involvement of the major Victorian political economists in the notoriously racist project of the British Empire.[10] James Mill and John Stuart Mill, to name just two of the men Levy champions, found lifelong employment with the East India Company, both rising to the important position of chief examiner. What sustained both Mills' engagements with Victorian empire building as well as the imperial activities of numerous other utilitarians and political economists were certain deeply held racist convictions.

Varieties of racism flourished in the nineteenth century. John Stuart Mill may not have shared Carlyle's conservative belief in " 'the Negro's' inherent inferiority articulated by the racist science of the day," but he did promote a liberal form of Victorian racism, a belief in "Europe's historically developed superiority," which justified British control of unenlightened places like India, where colonizers would exert "benevolent despotism" in order to refashion the Other in the image of Western progress and civilization (Goldberg 2000, 204–13). Perhaps the most famous articulation of this liberal racism can be found in Thomas Babington Macaulay's "Minute on Indian Education," which became the basis of the English Education Act of 1835. Intervening in the debate between Anglicists and Orientalists on the side of the Anglicists, who favored giving Indians a solid British education and discontinuing support for the study of Arabic and Sanskrit, Macaulay (1972, 249) declares that "we must at present do our best to form a class who may be interpreters between us and the million whom we govern: a class of persons, Indian in blood and colour, but English in taste, in opinions, in morals and in intellect." Surely this image of transforming Indians into dark-skinned versions of Englishmen is morally suspect for its attempt to create an indigenous upper class divorced from (and despising) its own culture. In his most outrageously racist moments, Carlyle—like Conrad's Kurtz—may imagine the need to "exterminate the brutes," but certainly we can recognize in Macaulay and Mill's liberal vision of cultural erasure an attenuated, but nonetheless kindred, sentiment.

Mill and Macaulay could not escape this liberal racism because it is entrenched within the deepest structures of classical economic theory. One has to read no further than the first chapter of the foundational text of modern economics, Adam Smith's *The Wealth of Nations*, for what postcolonial critics would label an Orientalist moment. Although Smith uses Africa—rather than the East—to construct the West as civilized, the same process is at work, wherein a primitive Other is conjured up to serve as the "contrasting image, idea, personality, experience" to Europe (Said 1978, 2). Smith concludes chapter 1, the famous pin chapter, with this declaration: "Yet it may be true, that the accommodation of a European prince does not always exceed that of an industrious and frugal peasant, as the accommodation of the latter exceeds that of many an African king, the absolute master of the lives and liberties of ten thousand naked savages" (Smith [1776] 1937, 24). In this passage, Smith deploys material prosperity to establish an ascending scale of human progress, with "darkest" Africa at the bottom and Enlightenment Europe at the top.[11] Inheriting from Smith and his eighteenth-century predecessors a certain frame of mind, one that generated Western superiority out of the imagined backwardness of Others, Victorian political economy is racist at its core. Moreover, the arbitrary definition of progress found in Smith (i.e., progress equals material prosperity) became one of the unquestioned standards with which later political economists, such as Mill and Macaulay, measured the civilized and uncivilized world.

Not only when they invoke the image of "ten thousand naked savages" living in remote parts of the globe do the Victorian political economists display unself-conscious racist attitudes: their domestic policies are suspect as well. Take, for example, one of the most controversial pieces of social legislation of the first half of the nineteenth century, the Poor Law Amendment Act of 1834 that instituted the infamous eligibility test, wherein life in the workhouse was supposed to be made "less eligible" than life out of it. Inspired by Thomas Malthus's *Essay on Population*, the legislation registered a triumph of the new political economy over the old, paternalistic order.[12] Two political economists (Nassau Senior and Edwin Chadwick) headed the royal commission authorized by Parliament to investigate the workings of the Elizabethan poor laws and to recommend reforms. As historian Lynn Hollen Lees (1998, 118) notes, the royal commissioners focused on pauperism rather than poverty because "in their analytical framework, poverty resulted primarily from unemployment, the maldistribution of labor, and the misuse of wages, whereas pauperism—the real problem—arose from individual immorality and fecklessness encouraged by public policy." In other words, the same essentializing that is indispensable to racist thinking subtended the royal commissioners' conceptions about the pauper classes in Britain: the pauper's essential moral failings (laziness, licentiousness) caused his suffering, which the punitive workhouses were intended to correct through the imposition of prisonlike discipline. Like Carlyle's lazy ex-slave, who required the strong arm of a paternal government to get him working again, the political economists' pauper needed to be forced—although the economists would have preferred the term *reformed*—into becoming a useful member of the modern state.

The Difficulties of Interdisciplinary Work

The problems in Levy's work can serve as a cautionary tale about the difficulties and dangers of straying beyond the borders of one's disciplinary training. Interdisciplinary work is to be encouraged for the new insights it yields, but the intrepid explorer of far-flung fields should stop occasionally to ask a native for directions: an hour's conversation over coffee with the right specialist might have led Levy to temper his more outlandish claims and perhaps even to reconsider before publicly committing himself to a gross misrepresentation of literary criticism at the present time.

Levy's argument implies that there is a vast conspiracy by left-leaning literature professors (tenured radicals all) to conceal the unsavory truths about the Victorian critics of capitalism. If he were writing two or three decades ago, there would be much truth in his contention that academia has overlooked the racial politics of Carlyle, Ruskin, and Dickens in its rush to hero-worship them for denouncing capitalism, industrialism, and Victorian modernity in strikingly memorable phrases. Yet given the explosion of postcolonial studies in the last decade, with its the focus on the ideological work of race in the production of cultural meaning, Levy's charge rings false. This recent development in the discipline goes unacknowledged by Levy, who only cites critics whose work is either outdated (in the case of F. R. Leavis) or dated (in the case of Raymond Williams). For example, Levy treats Leavis as if he were still an unchallenged authority in the halls of academe, whereas few professors these days invoke Leavis's *The Great Tradition* (1948) without supplying the scare quotes for which English professors are notorious. Like Matthew Arnold's "the best that has been thought and known," Leavis's "the great tradition" has become academic shorthand—a quick way to refer to and call into question traditional notions of canonicity. Williams's *Culture and Society* (1958), a text with more currency than *The Great Tradition*, also has not escaped the notice of postcolonial critics. No less a figure than Edward Said takes Williams to task for disregarding the racial politics of nineteenth-century British intellectuals. Said's *Culture and Imperialism* (1994) revisits the same literary terrain mapped out by Williams and reevaluates a range of canonical figures—from Carlyle and Ruskin to Mill and Macaulay—in light of their imperialist predispositions.[13]

In many ways, Levy's unnecessary vilification of English professors parallels his treatment of the Victorian critics of capitalism. In his revision of the Victorian past, Levy seems compelled to reduce history to a Manichaean battle between the good guys and the bad guys. However, the nineteenth century produced few unconditional villains or heroes: each of the intellectual figures from the period who still instruct, delight, and infuriate bears, in George Eliot's useful phrase, "spots of commonness," possessing cheek by jowl much to admire and much to condemn. Neither the conservative critics of capitalism nor the liberal political economists could step outside their historical moment. So, despite their abolitionism, men like Mill and Macaulay were also tainted by the nineteenth century's racism. Their conservative opponents—Carlyle, Ruskin, and Dickens—held deeply objectionable views on race, class, and gender; nevertheless, they generated a valuable critique of unrestrained capitalism that did *not* lead them to lovingly embrace slavery as the alternative. Thus, the example set by these Victorian thinkers could not convince anyone but a true believer like Levy that the free market will make us all free at last.

NOTES

1. The ideas discussed in this chapter are found in the second chapter in this volume and in the broader research project Levy and Peart are working on. At times in the present chapter, I refer to Levy alone, because I am specifically citing the ideas of, or quoting from, Levy's book *How the Dismal Science Got Its Name*

(2001). At other times, I am engaging with arguments put forward jointly by David Levy and Sandra Peart in the second chapter of the present volume.

2. See Martin Wiener's *English Culture and the Decline of the Industrial Spirit* (1985) for a discussion of the relationship between Englishness and anticapitalist discourses in the nineteenth century.

3. Despite Levy's assertions, Dickens was not proslavery. His biographer Edgar Johnson (1977, 222) notes that when confronted with the reality of slavery on his 1842 tour of America, Dickens's "flesh crawled with moral revulsion," and that the novelist proved to be "a resolute abolitionist." Of course, Dickens's abolitionism did not prevent him from having Confederate sympathies during the Civil War, but even such sympathies do not necessarily betoken a proslavery stance. According to Peter Ackroyd (1990, 1010), a more recent Dickens biographer, the reason Dickens did not support the North in the Civil War was "because he believed the Federal cause to be based on dollars and cents with the antislavery cry as no more than mere camouflage for the grosser economic motives" of wishing to dominate the South economically.

4. Dickens's politics are too amorphous to be easily labeled, but his writing evidences paternalist strains.

5. Both paternalism and medievalism have been amply documented by historians and literary critics. See, for example, David Roberts's *Paternalism in Early Victorian England* (1979), Jeffrey Spear's *Dreams of an English Eden* (1984), Alice Chandler's *A Dream of Order* (1970), A. Dwight Culler's *The Victorian Mirror of History* (1985), and Marc Girouard's *The Return to Camelot* (1981).

6. The extent to which slavery was capitalist has been a major debate among American historians. For a good overview of this debate, see Peter Kolchin's *American Slavery, 1619–1877* (1993). Kolchin (173) concludes that the Southern economy was a mixed one, in that "relations of exchange were market-dominated, but relations of production were not."

7. Throughout this chapter, I cite the 1849 version of Carlyle's "Occasional Discourse on the Negro Question," because that is the text to which Professor Levy refers.

8. For an overview of this debate, see David Cannadine's "The Present and Past in the English Industrial Revolution, 1880–1980" (1984).

9. An introduction to the political and social turbulence of the 1830s and 1840s can be found in Christopher Harvie's "Revolution and the Rule of Law" (1988).

10. Much work has been done on the relationship between the Victorian political economists and imperialism. See Eric Stokes's *The English Utilitarians and India* (1959), Javed Majeed's *Ungoverned Imaginings: James Mill's "The History of British India" and Orientalism* (1992), and *J. S. Mill's Encounter with India* (Moir, Peers, and Zastoupil, 1999).

11. Smith's racism, like Mill's and Macaulay's, is of the liberal variety. Smith was not an essentialist, in that he did not believe in the biological inferiority of blacks, but he did believe in the superiority of Western civilization.

12. For more on the involvement of the political economists in the passage of

the Poor Law Amendment Act, see Raymond Cowherd's *Political Economists and the English Poor Laws* (1977) and George Boyer's *An Economic History of the English Poor Laws* (1990).

13. Professor Levy's unfamiliarity with the simple tools of the literary trade, such as bibliographic databases, may explain why the postcolonial critique of Victorian culture eluded him. Levy claims (2001, 161–62) that a search of JSTOR yielded him no articles addressing his particular concerns, but he does not seem to realize that JSTOR, a database containing a handful of journals available online, is woefully limited. The appropriate databases to begin such an investigation are the MLA Bibliography, Historical Abstracts, and WorldCat. A quick subject search of the name *Carlyle* using the first two databases revealed a spate of recent articles on race in Carlyle's writing, while entering the keywords *slavery in literature* into WorldCat, a comprehensive catalog of books, generated dozens of titles, all published in the 1990s, that investigate the colonial/imperialist context of nineteenth-century British literature.

John Stuart Mill on Race, Liberty, and Markets

Falguni A. Sheth

In the second chapter in this volume, David Levy and Sandra Peart consider classical economics and its revival by the Chicago school and suggest that the racism and proslavery positions promulgated by such writers as Thomas Carlyle and John Ruskin are closely linked to their anti-free-market—or as Levy and Peart call it, paternalist—attitudes. In opposition to Carlyle and Ruskin stands classical political economist John Stuart Mill, whose antiracism and antislavery positions, suggest Levy and Peart, lie in his free-market economics. They imply that the distinction between Mill and Carlyle applies to comparisons of their modern-day inheritors. They see Chicago economists as the descendants of Mill, modern-day liberals as the successors of Carlyle and Ruskin.

In this chapter, I suggest that John Stuart Mill's noted attitudes regarding blacks and political emancipation lie in a different, perhaps more fundamental set of philosophical conceptions than those that Peart and Levy ascribe to free-market advocates generally. These conceptions have to do with his views on human nature and on the value of tradition, hierarchy, and customs. To the extent that there is a consistency between Mill's advocacy of free markets, his antiracism (at least on the issue of slavery), and his antisexism (at least with regard to English women), it emerges from certain key a priori philosophical positions that he has articulated in his writings, not from his economic views alone.

Specifically, I suggest that Mill's ability to argue in favor of the emancipation of politically oppressed groups, such as blacks and women, stems from four philosophical positions: first, his anti-innatist views of human nature (which he appears to borrow from his father, James Mill, and from Jeremy Bentham); second, his avowedly steadfast resistance to the authority of nature, law, tradition, or custom in the sphere of politics and in society generally as a way of restraining or directing the actions of human beings; third, the telos of happiness and moral perfectibility—on the levels of both individual and societal development—toward which both his utilitarian philosophy and his writings on freedom strive;[1] and fourth, his cautious advocacy of the role of free markets as vehicles for human liberation and the emancipation of human potential, which is linked closely to the careful management of those markets to maximize the ability of human beings to develop themselves and to advance in society. It is only to the degree that economists accept these four propositions that they can see themselves as descendants of Mill.

The Context of the Carlyle-Mill Debate on the "Negro Question"

Let me set the context for the origins of this specific philosophical conflict between Carlyle and Mill. Thomas Carlyle's "Occasional Discourse on the Negro Question," first printed in *Fraser's Magazine* in December 1849, addresses the stark lack of labor supply in the British colony of Demerara in harvesting spices, sugarcane, and other local island crops. Carlyle suggests that the recently emancipated blacks on the island had been shirking their God-mandated duty by refusing to attend to the necessary task of harvesting. The framework that Carlyle constructs, which I shall address shortly, leads him to the conclusion that if these emancipated blacks would not engage in their duty voluntarily, they should be coerced into working. They must, insists Carlyle, be forced to submit to a master, either as servant or as slave.

The philosophical tenets, if we may call them that, from which Carlyle is led to his conclusion are as follows: Wise men understand that they must submit to a Law of Nature, which has been handed down to them by their Master. This law of nature compels them to work. It is their duty as wise men to engage in the business of accomplishing the tasks of harvesting the crops of the colonies. Only wise men can grasp the complex relationship of supply and demand, according to which plantation owners who need their crops to be harvested will find a supply of labor to accommodate that demand.

Carlyle (1849, 101) insists that only truly rational—wise—human beings are capable of responding properly to the laws of supply and demand, because they have several needs that constrain their actions into conformity with those laws. The laws of supply and demand, if they are at all relevant for black men, take on a slightly different, perverse configuration, according to Carlyle: The only demand that blacks have is food, pumpkins more specifically. These are plentiful on Demerara, "supplied" by the sun and the soil, and thus made available through very little human effort. Black men, then, have very little need to work to maintain their subsistence. Carlyle's belief that blacks need very little for their existence is a charge to which he returns in a more extensive fashion near the end of his piece, in order to polish his argument concerning the nonhuman—and therefore nonrational—character of blacks: "pumpkins . . . are not the sole requisite for human well-being. No; for a pig they are the one thing needful; but for a man they are only the first of several things needful" (101).

To Carlyle, that "species" that refuses to work must, by inference, be "foolish" and, by extension, also incapable of grasping the law of supply and demand properly. Indeed, this is why he believes that the model of free markets is in such a terrible state of disarray on the good island of Demerara—because it can only be grasped by wise, rational men. For Carlyle, there is nothing wrong with the model of markets. Markets and the laws of supply and demand function for rational men. Men who are rational will work for wages, will work in response to a demand for labor. The problem, as Carlyle sees it, is not with markets per se but within the miscategorization of the labor supply to be found on the island. Said labor supply consists of those creatures barely considered to be human, more akin to beasts, who in their lack of reason do not realize their duty on earth. Thereby, lacking reason, blacks must be made to be submissive to masters on earth, if they are not capable of realizing their master in Heaven. Indeed, Carlyle's preconceptions about the mental, rational state of black ("African") men, whom he ranks at the bottom of the human chain and just above horses on the animal chain, amazingly, coincidentally, appear to accord with his philosophical construction of the nature of the world.

This framework of Carlyle accords closely with the philosophical world found in John Locke's *Second Treatise of Government*, written 150 years prior to Carlyle's notorious essay. There, in similar fashion, Locke suggests that the law of nature bestowed by God to men enables them to infer their duty on earth. Reason is both the law of nature itself and the intellectual capacity to figure out the laws of nature. Men who are reasonable, then, will be able to use the ability that God has given them both intellectually and physically (i.e., their bodies, labor) not only to fend for themselves and to flourish but to take up their God-given duty: "God, when he gave the world in common to all mankind, commanded man also to labor, and the penury of his condition required it of him" ([1690] 1952, par. 32). In this framework, the resources of the earth are infinite, and men need only engage in as much work as necessary to maintain their subsistence. To accumulate more than what is just perfectly necessary to maintain one's subsistence is an example of greed or, alternatively, the origin of barter and exchange markets and currency ([1690] 1952, chap. 5). Says Locke,

> "God has given us all things richly," (I Tim. vi. 17), is the voice of reason confirmed by inspiration. But how far has he given it to us? To enjoy. As much as any one can make use of to any advantage of life before it spoils, so much he may by his labor fix a property in; whatever is beyond this is more than his share and belongs to others. Nothing was made by God for man to spoil or destroy. (Par. 31)[2]

If we were to transpose Carlyle's description of the situation on Demerara onto Locke's labor theory of property, we would be left with the inference that these emancipated slaves are indeed rational men who have the intellectual capacity to figure out the law of nature. They work only as much as needed—Carlyle accuses them of subsisting on pumpkins alone. According to Locke, this is a sign of true human beings who have used their reason to divine and satisfy their requirements. But Carlyle insists that men have several needs, only one of which is subsistence. Another is the need to work; the apparent lack of awareness for this second need on the part of the ex-slaves of Demerara suggests a lack of rationality that justifies, for Carlyle, the use of force to compel them to submit to servitude or slavery.

Mill's Response

For Mill, the situation on Demerara appears to be perfectly in accord with the law of supply and demand and with the role of markets. In his 1850 rebuttal to Carlyle, entitled "The Negro Question," Mill argues that the demand for labor is high enough that the wages that blacks receive enable them to live after supplying only a minimal amount of labor.

> After fifty years of toil and sacrifice . . . the negroes, freed from the despotism of their fellow beings, were left to themselves, and to the chances which the arrangements of existing society provide for those who have no resource but their labour. These chances proved favourable to them, and, for the last ten years, they afford the unusual spectacle of a labouring class whose labour bears so high a price that they can exist in comfort on the wages of a comparatively small quantity of work. (88–89)

Indeed, suggests Mill, perhaps the trick to addressing the shortage of labor is to raise wages, that is, to allow blacks to keep the entirety of the crop that they harvest (91). Mill's rebuttal to Carlyle in this essay is waged on three fronts—I will only discuss two—that are the key philosophical premises (or "principles," as Mill refers to them [89]) of Carlyle's argument.[3]

The first front on which Mill challenges Carlyle is on the idea that work is an end in itself. The honor, the significance of work, lies not in its accomplishment but, rather, in the worth of the object to be attained by it. In other words, asks Mill, is the end for which the service is performed enough to justify the effort put into its attainment (90)? The worth of work, as Mill says, is not "to work upon work without end." It is true, admits Mill, that a minimal amount of work must be done by every individual to subsist and to justly ensure the functioning of society (91). But to work without end precludes the natural telos of human development, namely, the ability to fulfill one's potential in any myriad of ways, as is suitable to one's individual nature. Says Mill, "In opposition of the 'gospel of work,' I would assert the gospel of leisure, and maintain that human beings cannot rise to the finer attributes of their nature compatibly with a life filled with labour" (91). Work, then, is merely a means by which to subsist, in order to clear the way by which to pursue other talents, pleasures, and fulfillments that are intrinsic to the status of being human. The status of being human is a key dimension of Mill's other, later writings. In particular, this status is not substantial, in the Lockean or Kantian sense, but, rather, teleological: being human is a formal category that must be filled out in whichever multiplicity of ways each person is wont to do. I will return to this key aspect of Mill's philosophy in the next section.

The second front on which Mill disputes Carlyle regards Carlyle's argument that work is an obligation, a duty undertaken as a symbol of submission to one's master. This submission can only be voluntarily undertaken by wise—rational—men, according to Carlyle. Immediately conspicuous to Mill is the inconsistency by which Carlyle's argument is applied across the races. Such duty is meant to be undertaken by black men, but not by white men, as is exhibited in Mill's reference to white plantation owners "who do not work at all in exchanging the spices for houses in Belgrave Square." Perhaps to be truly consistent, suggests Mill, white proprietors should not be restricted from "the 'divine right' of being compelled to labour." Instead, they should earn exactly that amount equivalent to the work that they put in (92). Moreover, for Mill, the unfilled demand for labor is proof not only that free markets function quite well but that blacks are indeed quite human and quite "wise." Indeed, suggests Mill, labor would not be in as high demand were blacks entitled to the entirety of their produce; this conclusion appears to be the equivalent of the suggestion that were employers to offer higher wages, perhaps their need for labor would be fulfilled.

On a more profound level, Mill highlights the philosophical speciousness of Carlyle's argument by exploring the character of wisdom that lies at the heart of Carlyle's position on the "Negro question." Mill provisionally explores the implications of the position that it might be each man's duty to submit to his master by undertaking the obligation—the duty—to work. In particular, Mill takes Carlyle to task for his position that men must submit to those who are wiser than they; Mill understands Carlyle to mean that some persons are "born more capable of wisdom" than others (92). Mill argues that the basis on which Carlyle's argument rests— namely, that there is a significant difference in the nature of blacks in comparison to whites—is based on a faulty, presumptive knowledge of the substance of human nature. Mill suggests that the differences between men are too easily attributed to human nature, which is overdetermined as such, when they might just as easily be ascribed to external forces that mold and shape human characters in as many ways as there are people.

Mill's specific response to Carlyle on this point is as follows: He chastises Carlyle for attributing any and all differences in the characters of men to an "original" difference in nature. The question of original human nature, insists Mill, is neither fully known nor a given. Rather, using the metaphor of two trees (a metaphor to which he returns in later writings), he suggests that human nature is fundamentally shaped and evolves through external forces.

As well might it be said, that of two trees, sprung from the same stock, one cannot be taller than another but from greater vigour in the original seedling. Is nothing to be attributed to soil, nothing to climate, nothing to difference of exposure—has no storm swept over the one and not the other, no lightning scathed it, no beast browsed on it, no insects preyed on it, no passing stranger stript off its leaves or its bark? If the trees grew near together, may not the one which, by whatever accident, grew up first, have retarded the other's developement [sic] by its shade? Human beings are subject to an infinitely greater variety of accidents and external influences than trees, and have infinitely more operation in impairing the growth of one another. (93)

In the preceding excerpt, Mill suggests that the set of factors that account for the dramatic growth and advance of one seedling or human being over another are unknown. But even more fundamentally, Mill's point is that the "nature" of a human being is precisely unformed, nebulous, and subject to various contingencies. In this point, Mill's affinity with his father's and Bentham's theory of human nature as a tabula rasa becomes evident (see Donner 1991, chap. 1, especially n. 5; Rossi 1970, 11–12). These dual themes of the external forces that shape human nature and the set of contingencies that create the particular contours of human character (namely, the question of what exactly constitutes the "natural" and, more specifically, human nature), along with the theme of the telos of human development already mentioned, will resurface in Mill's writings for the next twenty years.

The Consistency and Philosophical Basis of Mill's Response

Mill's response to Carlyle in his 1850 essay embodies themes that are consistently borne out in both his prior and later writings. By 1848, in the first edition of *Principles of Political Economy*, Mill has already developed his theory of free markets and his advocacy of the laws of supply and demand. As I will show, for Mill, these two concepts (the theory of markets and the laws of supply and demand) are not dependent on a substantial theory of human nature. This point will become clear through the course of the argument in this section. Here, however, I would like to address Mill's theory of human nature more generally. I have already asserted that Mill's view of human nature, while not necessarily formally empty, is nevertheless a "substantively" thin one. For brevity's sake, I shall refer to his position on human nature as anti-innatism. It is borrowed from his father's and Bentham's espousal of David Hartley's theory of associationist psychology, whereby the mind is a blank slate in which experiences are conjoined together to form pleasurable or painful associations. This view also has its origins in the empiricism of John Locke and David Hume (see Mill [1873] 1989, 70–71, especially editor's nn. 8–9).

There are several important features representative of Mill's position. First, Mill adheres to the view that human nature consists of capacities, needs, and desires rather than core attributes or substances. Desire is actually the most important attribute of human nature for Mill, as I shall argue shortly, and in circumscribing human nature in this way, Mill sets himself apart from other liberal philosophers and economists whose primary understanding of human nature is that it is constituted by a substantive notion of reason. Second, Mill believes that human nature is shaped and transformed by external forces and contingencies, which serve to create a series of experiences, associations, and traits, again none of which are necessary, predetermined, or innate. Third, Mill consistently argues for an agnostic moral telos that, though he himself terms it "happiness," should have the flexibility of being substantiated or "fleshed out" in any number of ways.

If my argument about Mill's view of human nature is accurate, it will show that his political ("anti-racist") views on the "Negro question" and the "woman question" (the latter of which is less immediately relevant to the preceding discussion) are grounded on his decided agnosticism about substantive ontological features of human beings and on the internally driven *potential* of which any given human being is capable, which emerges from desire as the trait that Mill attributes to human beings. Further, it will substantiate my position that Peart and Levy are inaccurate in their claim that free markets are inherently antiracist institutions in and of themselves. Most free market theories insist on the existence of a human rationality that is, as Mill recognizes, inherently exclusionary of various members of the human species, depending on the political mores of the day. Thus, reason is used to exclude blacks from living their lives autonomously, and it is directed in a similar fashion toward the autonomy of women. As I hope will become evident, the way in which Mill specifically advocates free markets is quite singular in character; his advocacy of free markets goes hand in hand with his anti-innatism. Markets, for Mill, are vehicles for human liberation—the liberation of human spirit or desire, human development, potential, and capacities. Markets are also a vehicle for the evening out of the diversity of human talents and capacities. But they are not, as Mill's insistent anti-innatism suggests, dependent on a specific substantial view of human rationality or even on a strong view of human nature more generally.

The three tenets of Mill's anti-innatism mentioned earlier appear, sometimes implicitly, throughout his writings, usually in conjunction. We can see this by considering several of Mill's writings: *On Liberty* ([1859] 1978; hereafter cited as *OL*), *Utilitarianism* ([1861] 1979; hereafter cited as *UT*), "The Subjection of Women" (1869 in Mill and Mill 1970; hereafter cited as SJ), and "Nature" (published posthumously in 1874, but written sometime in the 1850s; hereafter cited as N). In these essays, not only does Mill develop a philosophical understanding of human nature that is consistent with his response to Carlyle in the 1850 essay, but he returns to Carlyle's views over again and develops his own contravening position more explicitly.

For example, in "The Subjection of Women," Mill engages in an examination of the justifications for the explicit subordination of women and in the arguments for the removal of restrictions on women's political and economic emancipation. The first justification that Mill scrutinizes is that of the "law of the strongest," a theme raised by Carlyle in his essay in defense of a forced servitude among the black men of Demerara. Mill suggests that the concept of might has often been invoked to support the subordination of various weaker species, always as a "natural" phenomenon, in order to justify domination. This holds not only for the enforced subordination of women to men but, as Mill recalls, for the subordination of the black race to the white; various "innate" traits, or the absence thereof, are invoked to maintain the domination of various subsets of the human population. Says Mill of the American debate on slavery, "Did they not call heaven and earth to witness that the dominion of the white man over the black is natural, that the black race is by nature incapable of freedom, and marked out for slavery? some [sic] even going so far as to say that the freedom of manual laborers is an unnatural order to things anywhere" (SJ, 138).

Moreover, suggests Mill, everything deemed natural is that which appears "conventional," "usual," "customary"—in other words, as it should be (SJ, 138). Obviously, Mill recognizes the aversion on the part of his contemporaries to women's active participation in the labor force; this resistance is, again, based on a more robust—and detrimental—conception of human nature than Mill is willing to allow. To objections such as the assertion that women are intellectually weaker or physically more fragile than men, he responds that we have no conclusive data on the "innate nature" of women (SJ, 148). In fact, suggests Mill, there is plenty of evidence for the contrary conclusion, that women are products of their environments: education, physical exercise, and administrative training can enable women to excel in whichever field they choose to pursue. To the caution that it is not customary for women to hold jobs, he argues that "custom" is the catchphrase of male authoritarians who cement physical differences, such as women's relative size and strength, into a social and political hierarchy through laws and men's rights (SJ, 129–30).

So, how then are we to understand the proper meaning of human nature? For Mill, all distinct character traits are the result of external forces, stimuli, effort, experience, training, and education—"the result of conscious or unconscious cultivation" (SJ, 194). All distinctions between blacks and whites, between men and women, between any given human being and another, are, if not random, certainly susceptible to the unique, singular experiences weathered by each soul. Mill echoes in his other writings this perspective on the cultivation of human nature and the uniqueness of each individual.

In his essay on nature, for example, Mill expounds at length on the absence of substantial qualities or virtues that are innate in human nature. In fact, he says, all that can be found in human nature is purely instinctive and, for that reason, to be overcome, if not already transcended, through extensive "artificial discipline," external environment, or education (N, 393). In fact, Mill is so insistent that such "virtues" as courage, goodness, and cleanliness are the result of extensive education, even in "savages," that he deceptively seems to lend Carlyle ammunition for his position regarding the supposed inherent vices of the ex-slaves of Demerara: "The courage which is occasionally though by no means generally found among tribes of savages, is as much the result of education as that of the Spartans or Romans" (N, 393–94). Elsewhere, he challenges Rousseau's picture of the natural veracity of the "noble savage," by insisting:

> Savages are always liars. They have not the faintest notion of truth as a virtue. They have a notion of not betraying to their hurt, as of not hurting in any other way, persons to whom they are bound by some special tie of obligation; their chief, their guest, perhaps, or their friend: these feelings of obligation being the taught morality of the savage state, growing out of its characteristic circumstances. But of any point of hon-

our respecting truth for truth's sake, they have not the remotest idea.
(N, 395)

While this quote may seem to condemn Mill on precisely the same racist
grounds of which Carlyle is guilty, it is important to scrutinize his words
carefully: Mill is not suggesting that "savages" are *innate* or *natural* liars.
Rather, in his zeal to illustrate that human nature is almost always overcome by custom, obligations, social mores, or education, he consistently
takes his opponents' pictures of "naturally primitive men" to illustrate that
even so-called "natural behaviors" have always been shaped by external
forces.

It is important to remember here that Mill, unlike other economists of
his day (and unlike his contemporary economistic counterparts), gives no
credence to a substantial, innate notion of reason, much less to a greater or
lesser degree of mental capacity systematically accorded to one group of
individuals (men, blacks, English) over another.[4] Indeed, to the extent
that Mill acknowledges the existence of reason, it is only to show how his
theoretical opposition deploys the concept of reason strategically to but-
tress a notion of an innate natural "Instinct" (N, 392). He has even less
interest in explaining the differences between mental capacities among
individuals through ontological, physical, or biological narratives.

> I have before repudiated the notion of its being yet certainly known that
> there is any natural difference at all in the average strength or direction
> of the mental capacities of the two sexes, much less what that difference
> is . . . so long as the most obvious external causes of difference of char-
> acter are habitually disregarded—left unnoticed by the observer, and
> looked down upon with a kind of supercilious contempt by the preva-
> lent schools both of natural history and of mental philosophy: who,
> whether they look for the source of what mainly distinguishes human
> beings from one another, in the world of matter or in that of spirit, agree
> in running down those who prefer to explain these differences by the
> different relations of human beings to society and life. (SJ, 200)

Furthermore, suggests Mill, because the English are so far from the state of
nature and have become accustomed to governing society through the rule
of law, they are incapable of recognizing what is natural (in women's character) from what is artificial, because they have such limited (i.e., only
English) experience on which to depend. The same charge, for different
reasons, extends to other cultures as well. The French believe women are

fickle because they are prejudiced and can see nature only through a "sophisticated and distorted" form, and besides, their errors are "positive" (SJ, 201–2). In comparison, the errors of the English, who believe women are "constant" but cold, are "negative." The Orientals believe that women "are by nature voluptuous" (SJ, 201). Sounding very Rousseauian here, Mill continues his critique of our understanding of nature: "[T]he artificial state superinduced by society disguises the natural tendencies of the thing which is the subject of observation, in two different ways: by extinguishing nature, or by transforming it" (SJ, 202). Thus, the nature of women and, by extension, other groups of persons, including black men, can never be truly manifested, since we are at a loss to dig beyond the artificial characteristics of human nature to what is "true" and original.

Earlier in the same essay, in language that clearly recalls his debate with Carlyle over nineteen years earlier, Mill continues the discussion of those unfair practices that are justified in the name of the natural order of things. Presenting the position of an imaginary American proslavery advocate, he says: "It is necessary that cotton and sugar should be grown. White men cannot produce them. Negroes will not, for any wages which we choose to give. Ergo, they must be compelled" (SJ, 155). Mill likens this rationale to that offered for restricting women's participation in the workplace: "It is necessary to society that women should marry and produce children. They will not do so unless they are compelled. Therefore it is necessary to compel them" (SJ, 155). This compulsion appears ironical to Mill, in the face of the insistence that certain behaviors are natural, or inherent, to various subsets of the population. The mandating of various behaviors on the parts of women and blacks, suggests Mill, is fruitless if in fact such behaviors are not natural.

Again, then, what does it mean to engage in natural behavior? Is it merely not obstructing human beings—men, women, blacks, Hindus—from doing what they wish? Can it be that simple? Actually, yes and no. In his 1859 essay *On Liberty*, Mill continues the discussion begun in his 1850 response to Carlyle. In his argument against the societal restriction of people's liberty to determine their lives for themselves, Mill reveals his fundamental position on what human nature is constituted of. It is not, as Wendy Donner (1991) suggests, based merely on consent, choice, the ability to make decisions. Were it this simple, then not only would Mill's position be difficult to differentiate from myriad other liberals and economists of his day (and later), but he would also contradict his basic philosophical premise that human nature has no fundamentally developed or core substance and, hence, is inherently susceptible to the shaping and malleability imposed on it by external forces. Rather, for Mill, as he passionately expounds in the famous third chapter of *On Liberty*, entitled "On Individuality as One of the Elements of Well-Being," human nature is primordially constituted by desire and impulse: "[D]esires and impulses are as much a part of a perfect human as beliefs and restraints" (*OL*, 57). Desire is not antithetical to being human, as Kant would argue; on the contrary, suggests Mill, "To say that one person's desires and feelings are stronger and more various than those of another is merely to say that *he has more of the raw material of human nature* and is therefore capable, perhaps of more evil, but certainly of more good" (*OL*, 57; my italics).

But does this really prove that desire, rather than reason, is for Mill the basis of human nature? For him, reason is certainly part of the intellectual faculty that all human beings have, which is used for the purposes of making decisions, choosing for themselves certain ends instead of others. Desire is different from reason, in the same way that human nature is distinguished from a machine. Reason is an instrumental faculty that allows human beings to make choices, whereas desire is what drives human beings to develop themselves. Reason and decision making are faculties that distinguish human beings from automatons who "set to do exactly the work prescribed for" them, not because it is a core constituent of human nature, but because it is the faculty that enables the "free development of individuality" (*OL*, 54), allowing human beings to throw off the yokes of custom, power, arbitrary authority, sheer power, and legal regulations in the name of truth, good, or proper behavior (*OL*, 54), à la Carlyle's mandates concerning blacks in his 1849 essay. Customs, insists Mill, "are made for customary circumstances and customary characters; and his circumstances or his character may be uncustomary . . . though the customs be both good as customs and suitable to him, yet to conform to custom merely as custom does not educate or develop in him any of the qualities which are the distinctive endowment of a human being" (*OL*, 55–56). This endowment—but not the constitutive essence of human nature—is reason. In the following statement, Mill identifies the various intellectual faculties that human beings hold, including "perception, judgment, discriminative feeling, *mental activity*, and even moral preference," all of which can be implemented for the purposes of making choices (*OL*, 56). Mental activity includes "observation to see, reasoning and judgment to foresee, activity to gather materials for decision, discrimination to decide, and when he has decided, firmness and self-control to hold to his deliberate decision" (OL, 56).

But this intellectual capacity is substantively different from that which forms the core element of human nature, because it enables human beings to discriminate among ends, to make decisions, to choose between options. The mental capacity is, in this regard, secondary to the crux of what forms human nature, which are "natural feelings" (Mill 1850, 57). Natural feelings are those that can be managed, controlled, directed toward various ends, cultivated through the intellectual faculty, which includes not only reasoning and judgment but also moral preference, as seen in the preceding quote. In fact, insists Mill, desires and impulses are energy, which can be put to nefarious as well as beneficial uses, and when culture and conscience shape those impulses, one can be said to have character. Moreover, concerning the "person whose desires and impulses are his own—are the expression of his own nature," Mill argues, "[i]f in addition to being his own, his impulses are strong and are under the government of a strong will, he has an energetic character" (OL, 57).

Desire, then, is not instrumental but a drive: desire is what confirms that we are human and not machines. Indeed, more than any other trait that Mill tenuously ascribes to human beings, he is insistent that self-development is driven by desires, along with needs, pleasure, and the seemingly inevitable pursuit for happiness. Mill continues: "Whoever thinks that individuality of desires and impulses should not be encouraged to unfold itself must maintain that society has no need of strong natures—is not the better for containing many persons who have much character—and that a high general average of energy is not desirable" (OL, 58).

This is where Mill introduces his vision of free markets, in which the purpose of such markets is to seduce individuals into realizing their true talents, skills, and various dimensions of authentic self-development. Instead of regulating and restricting individual behaviors, one can merely provide incentives, such as raising wages: "When you have made it worth their while to serve you, as to work for other employers, you will have no more difficulty than others have in obtaining their services" (SJ, 155) The same incentive will work on women: rather than shutting off all other avenues to their self-development in order to compel them to obey their "true natures" by entering into marriage, perhaps allowing women to realize their freedom will lead to the best possible outcome for the realizations of their particular selves. Why educate women, why lure them to taste the possibilities of literacy and literary endeavors, if they are to be restricted altogether later in life? Perhaps if that is the agenda, Mill suggests, "[t]hey never should have been allowed to receive a literary education" (SJ, 156). Here and elsewhere in that essay, Mill notes that society institutionalizes certain practices to compel women—like blacks—to perform certain acts or to behave in certain ways. For Mill, the irony is that such institutionalized coercion might lead some to believe that those practices are antithetical to the "natures" of each group. Thus, Mill argues for lifting the restrictions on women's behavior to allow them to act in accordance with their abilities, without having judgments imposed about which behaviors are natural or unnatural: "What women by nature cannot do, it is quite superfluous to forbid them from doing. What they can do, but not so well as the men who are their competitors, competition suffices to exclude them from" (SJ, 153).

In making this argument, Mill is implicitly reintroducing his belief in the natural telos of human development. This is basically the idea, found in *Utilitarianism* and in *On Liberty*, that the end of human development is happiness. Happiness is a morally worthy end and also an ideal good for human beings to pursue; it is a state that reflects the proper ontological status of human beings.

> No reason can be given why the general happiness is desirable, except that each person, so far as he believes it to be attainable, desires his own happiness. This, however, being a fact, we have not only all the proof which the case admits of, but all which it is possible to require, that happiness is a good, that each person's happiness is a good to that person, and the general happiness, therefore, a good to the aggregate of all persons. Happiness has made out its title as *one* of the ends of conduct and, consequently, one of the criteria of morality. (*UT*, 34)

Mill's notion of happiness is an attempt to salvage his father's and Bentham's utilitarian moral theory by transforming the concept of happiness from a quantitative calculation to a qualitative human ideal, namely, one that can accommodate various noble, refined pleasures that are deemed worthy not of swine (as Thomas Carlyle charged of the philosophy of Bentham and James Mill) but of human beings properly speaking (*UT*, chap. 2; cf. Robson 1969). Happiness is distinct from pleasure. Pleasure is a mental state of which all sentient beings are capable; however, humans can experience pleasure in a way more fitting to their status as human, that is, in a more complex manner than do pigs. Happiness, then, is a formal, potential trait that human beings can realize in their pursuit or development of their particular selves. It is the purpose—the moral telos—of human beings to realize their lives in such a way as to pursue happiness.

To return to the point at hand—Mill's argument for easing the limitations on the proper scope of women's behavior—it may be the case that Mill's anti-innatism and his antinaturalism form the foundations of his economic beliefs; however, as I will argue, his progressive attitudes nevertheless reveal an acute myopia with regard to the obstacles of class and poverty that undermine his "libertarian" message. This myopia is revealed in a number of Mill's essays. For example, in chapter 3 of On Liberty, Mill argues that no individuals should be preempted from pursuing their talents, since such talents pave the way toward diversity. However, he does not surmise how one can pursue one's talents if they do not have the means to obtain an education or training. Rather, he focuses his arguments on the different social conditions that apply to women versus men: women have less time to work on literature than men do (SJ, 209)—because of their household and family management responsibilities, because they have more demands made on their time and faculties (SJ, 211), because women are less ambitious than men ("whether this cause be natural or artificial" [SJ, 212]). These factors may account, Mill suggests, for why their work is less original (SJ, 207 ff.). But these factors, while relevant and pragmatic explanations for the shortcomings of women's potential, do not account for shortcomings due to lack of material means.[5]

I bring this point up because it is relevant to discussions of the role of free markets in contemporary society, especially with regard to the various public policy issues confronting minorities in American society today. Free markets have been used by Mill and by many after him as a vehicle for the liberation of the potential of individuals of all races. However, there are two primary differences between the method of Mill's argument on this count and the way in which contemporary "Chicago" economists and David Levy and Sandra Peart make their arguments. The first basis of difference is, as mentioned earlier, that Mill refuses to make a claim about the substance of human nature as being inherently rational—or inherently anything, for that matter. For contemporary economists, the condition for the possibility of the existence of homo oeconomicus is that he must have a substantial rational nature, which allows him to make a variety of predictable choices based on the specific details of his circumstances and pregiven preferences. The second basis of the difference is that for Mill, free

markets can be treated as vehicles for the emancipation of human potential, but they need not be entirely unregulated. Women who wish to
develop their talents as writers can use the free market to hire themselves
out as writers or reporters or can attempt to sell their novels. Their talent
is neither restricted nor inhibited by regulations on their actions in the
market. However, for Mill, labor is not a commodity like any other commodity. Instead, the conditions of human potential must be carefully protected from the vagaries of business interests and profits, which might lead
to scrimping on health and safety regulations or on other workplace protections and thus might affect laborers detrimentally. For Mill, commodities may not be regulated, but the conditions of workplace employment
should be regulated when necessary to ensure that human beings have the
ability to develop their talents, skills, and general potential in a safe manner. The same cannot be said for contemporary free-market advocates,
such as Milton Friedman and Richard Posner.

None of this is to say that Mill is not a staunch proponent of the role of
free markets in the emancipation of blacks and of women. However, Mill
tends to use the concept of free markets rhetorically—to appease the
opponents of abolition and women's emancipation.[6] Rather, free markets
are the mechanism that enables individuals (whites, blacks, men, women)
to develop their particular talents and inclinations—those things for
which one is most fit (SJ, 154). In On Liberty, Mill disapprovingly suggests
that unions and maximum wages will reduce the incentives of factory
workers to improve their talents and skill (OL, 85–86). But it is important
to note that for Mill, free markets are *means* to particular practical ends—
developing one's talents, earning higher wages, finding a supply of labor to
harvest spices in Demerara. Free markets are not social or political ideals
in themselves; nor are they the *cause* by which individuals can be emancipated. Mill suggests:

> As the principle of individual liberty is not involved in the doctrine of
> free trade, so neither is it in most of the questions which arise respecting
> the limits of that doctrine, as, for example . . . how far sanitary precau-
> tions, or arrangements to protect workpeople employed in dangerous
> occupations, should be forced on employers. Such questions involve
> considerations of liberty only in so far as leaving people to themselves is
> always better, *caeteris paribus*, than controlling them; but that they may
> be legitimately controlled for these ends is in principle undeniable. (OL,
> 94)

In and of themselves, free markets do not lead to greater freedom for any individual; they merely provide an efficient mechanism by which to pursue one's particular interests. Thus, Mill clearly and openly acknowledges that laws and regulations can be instituted to ensure social and political freedom—since the latter are the fundamental ideals that must be protected. Political ideals can be pursued through markets, but they cannot be ensured and protected by markets—only laws can do this.

Likewise, in his essay "The Negro Question" (1850, 92), Mill's view is that markets are less about protecting the freedom of blacks than a means by which to mobilize sufficient labor to harvest the spice fields—provided, of course, that sufficiently high wages are paid. Again, it is important to note that Mill's rebuttal of Carlyle's proposal to compel blacks to work, as serfs or slaves, is based on his prior judgment that using laws to create slavery is wrong. Again, Mill relies on the notion of markets not to rebut the concept of slavery but, rather, to point to a different method by which to harvest one's fields. He is, as usual, careful to distinguish his political and social ideals (freedom, emancipation) from the means to practical goals.

Conclusion

In the second chapter in this volume, Levy and Peart have articulated the debate between the proponents and the detractors of the free market in the following terms: the debate between the paternalists and the free-marketeers lies in their attitudes regarding the ontological status of human beings, that is, in whether the nature, competence, and intelligence of human beings are fundamentally the same or different. The paternalists, assert Levy and Peart, believe that "[f]or any victim, it is tempting to find a class of victimizers. . . . victimizers are evil and parasitic, feeding and thriving on the blood, sweat, and tears of their victims." The accused victimizers are the free-marketeering classical political economists, who strongly advocate for "self-government," thereby removing "the 'incapable' from the 'protection' of the paternalist." The free marketeers have been maligned, suggest Levy and Peart. For free marketeers, there are no victims, since all human beings are fundamentally homogenous in their capacities and intelligence, and thereby "trades are voluntary and . . . mutually beneficial."

Levy and Peart may have aptly described a long-standing general political antagonism between those with paternalist orientations and those who are fundamentally opposed to government interventions. However, in the case of the Carlyle-Mill debate on the issue of Demerara spice colonies and the subject of emancipated slaves, I believe they have mischaracterized the debate. Furthermore, throughout their essay, Peart and Levy offer no real evidence that the political opposition between Carlyle and Mill resembles the schema that they have articulated.

The real antagonism between Carlyle and Mill can be described as follows: Carlyle believes that the shortage of labor supply on the island of Demerara is due to the refusal of emancipated slaves to work. Carlyle also believes that all men who have sufficient reason will be able to infer that engaging in their God-given duty to work is its own reward (the "gospel of work"). From this it follows that anyone who is not working has a deficient intellect. By inference, then, for Carlyle, markets are not pernicious or exploitative; rather, markets and the laws of supply and demand function only for those who are capable of reason. The refusal of slaves to work for wages must be due to their insufficient intellect and thereby their inability to grasp the laws of supply and demand. Those who deliberately refuse to work must be commanded or forced to work—either in servitude or in slavery. This is the gist of Carlyle's argument in his 1849 essay "Occasional Discourse on the Negro Question."

For Mill, markets are certainly liberating—as Levy and Peart would concur, I suspect, but not for the reasons they offer. For Mill, the genius of markets lies in their role as a vehicle to the development of human potential. In other words, for Mill, unlike for other proponents of free markets, markets are not conclusive evidence of the rationality of human beings but, rather, an institution that enhances the ability of human beings to develop and pursue their own conceptions of the good life and their talents and skills and to obtain the items necessary to these pursuits. Moreover, unlike other proponents of free markets, Mill avowedly did not ever articulate a position on whether all human beings had homogenous natures. Rather, he was steadfastly agnostic on this question. If anything, he believed that the question itself had often been answered positively to constrain or restrict the behavior of whichever population was out of favor at the time—blacks or women. Mill believed that human beings had an internal drive that, if bars of various sorts were lifted, would propel them to develop themselves to the best of their abilities and the maximum of their capacities, that is, to their telos.

This drive, I have attempted to argue, is that of desire—the desire to realize one's humanity. Desire is fundamentally a human characteristic for Mill, but it is decidedly different from the rationality that free-market economists tend to believe characterizes all human beings, according to Levy and Peart. Thus, Levy and Peart's characterization of the debate between the paternalists and the free-marketeers is, I believe, a fundamentally inaccurate characterization of the debate between Thomas Carlyle and John Stuart Mill.

NOTES

1. In this chapter, I will not address all of Mill's writings, since to do so would prioritize an intellectual history of his ideas rather than a philosophical reconstruction of certain key concepts that I believe inform his ideas. My treatment of Mill will concentrate on the following writings: *Utilitarianism*, *On Liberty*, "The Subjection of Women," and "Nature."

2. Locke differs from Carlyle with regard to the outcome of the God-given duty to labor. Whereas Carlyle believes that blacks will receive the wages they are due when they undertake their duty to labor, for Locke (1690, par. 32), the duty to labor will result in property: "He, that in obedience to this command of God subdued, tilled, and sowed any part of it, thereby annexed to it something that was his property, which another had no title to, nor could without injury take from him."

3. The third is a disputation of the facts of the situation in Demerara, which has no relevance in this chapter.

4. This is where my disagreement with David Levy and Sandra Peart lies, namely, about whether Mill's economistic framework is typical of free-market economic theory in general. I believe that Mill's position is somewhat unique in the liberal and economic theories of human nature, whereas Peart and Levy take the opposite position.

5. There is one key exception to Mill's position on the limitless potential of individuals to govern themselves. In *Considerations on Representative Government*, Mill asserts that representative government should be the norm for all people, except for those who are not yet evolved enough to be deemed fit to govern themselves. Here, he has in mind those peoples, such as in "Asiatic villages," who, though able to govern their local villages or town interests, have not yet "coalesced into a body and learned to feel themselves one people, except through previous subjection to a central authority common to all" (Mill 1862, chap. IV, 88–89). While this statement is one of several blatant paternalistic exceptions to Mill's general libertarian anti-innatist position, it does not appear to constitute a serious challenge to the argument that I have put forward here.

6. So does his close partner in intellectual collaboration Harriet Taylor. For example, in the "Enfranchisement of Women" (Mill and Mill 1970), to the concern that if women are unleashed as uninhibited forces in the labor market, they

will glut up the market and lower wages for men and women, thereby preventing (married) couples from earning more together than if men were to remain the sole economic provider, Harriet Taylor responds that the dignity gained by women earning their own wages will compensate for a decrease in wages and that, in time, "palliatives" (i.e., regulation?) will be found for the problem of decreased wages. Thus, for Harriet Taylor, free markets are the mechanism by which social and economic chaos can be avoided, rather than a solution to political or economic oppression.

PART 2

Neoclassical and Modern Approaches to Racism

"Not an Average Human Being"

How Economics Succumbed to
Racial Accounts of Economic Man

Sandra J. Peart and David M. Levy

Our earlier contribution to this volume showed how racial theorizing was used to attack the antislavery coalition of evangelicals and economists in mid-nineteenth-century Britain. Classical economists favored race-neutral accounts of human nature, and they presumed that agents are equally competent to make economic decisions. Their opponents, such as Carlyle and Ruskin, presupposed racial hierarchy and argued that some people are incapable of making sensible economic or political decisions. They concluded that systematically poor optimizers will be victimized in either market or political transactions.

In this chapter, we shall show how the attacks on the doctrine of human homogeneity succeeded—how, late in the century, economists came to embrace accounts of racial heterogeneity entailing different capacities for optimization.[1] We attribute the demise of the classical tradition largely to the ill-understood influence of anthropologists and eugenicists[2] and to a popular culture that served to disseminate racial theories visually and in print. Specifically, W. R. Greg, James Hunt, and Francis Galton all attacked the analytical postulate of homogeneity that characterized classical economics from Adam Smith[3] through John Stuart Mill. Greg cofounded the eugenics movement with Galton, and he persistently attacked classical political economy for its assumption that the Irishman is an "average human being," rather than an "idiomatic" and an "idiosyncratic" man, prone to "idleness," "ignorance," "jollity," and "drink" (quoted in full later in this chapter).

By 1870, two theories of race coexisted in the scientific community and the popular press. The more devastating view of the owner of the *Anthropological Review*, James Hunt, held that there were races whose physical development arrested prematurely, dead races incapable of elevation. The second theory, which we call *parametric racism*, held that the inferior race differed from the superior (Anglo-Saxons) along some parameter(s). As both sorts of racial theories entered into economics in the decades that followed, the focus moved from physical differences stressed by the anthropologists—the shape or size of the skull—to differences in economic competence. Economists argued, for instance, about whether the Irish or blacks in America were competent enough to make choices concerning labor supply or to save for their old age. We shall demonstrate how pervasively these racial accounts entered into economic thinking well into the twentieth century, in economists' characterization of choice of family size, intertemporal decision making, and consumption of "luxuries" and intoxicants.

The influence of eugenicists on economics extended to policy. As economists came to accept racial accounts of economic behavior, they allowed that some among us are "unfit," parasites who live off of the rest of society. They endorsed an elaborate "remaking" program for inferior decision makers, and for many economists, the remaking was also to be biological. A major theme in this chapter shall be how such policies were designed to reduce the level of what they called "parasitism" in society.

While eugenics is now commonly understood to have been influential, but mistaken, policy, the tension between economists who presume that agents are equally able to optimize and those who wish to improve the economic competence of various groups has never been fully resolved. Racial accounts won the day well into the twentieth century, but near the middle of the century, the classical tradition of homogeneity was revived at Chicago. Not surprisingly, given the racial characterization focused on intertemporal decision making, time preference was central in the Chicago revival. In his 1931 review of Irving Fisher's *Theory of Interest*, Frank Knight voiced his skepticism about the common link supposed in economists' accounts between time preference and race. Knight and, after him, George Stigler and Gary Becker questioned myopic accounts of intertemporal decision making. As the Chicago school revived the classical doctrine of homogeneity, it also (and by no coincidence) revived the presumption of competence even in political activity.

Eugenics Attacks Abstract Economic Man

The eugenics influence on economics has three signatures. First, the race becomes the unit of analysis. Second, ethical concerns of the sort that underscore Adam Smith's development of the sympathetic principle vanished. Materiality is all. The third signature of eugenics is the argument that the inferior race is a race without variation, unimprovable by eugenic methods of breeding from the top of the distribution of characteristics. This is Hunt's doctrine of racial heterogeneity in its most virulent form.

In the second half of the nineteenth century, theories of racial heterogeneity were much discussed in British anthropological circles, and attacks on equal competence emerged from within economics itself.[4] In January 1869, W. R. Greg used the occasion of a discussion of W. Stewart Trench's "The Realities of Irish Life" in the *Quarterly Review* to argue against the race-blind accounts of human behavior defended by J. S. Mill. Here, Greg (1869, 78) objected specifically to the abstract accounts of human beings put forward by the classical economists, on the grounds that they abstract from race.

> "Make them peasant-proprietors," says Mr. Mill. But Mr. Mill forgets that, till you change the character of the Irish cottier, peasant-proprietorship would work no miracle. He would fall behind the instalments of his purchase-money, and would be called upon to surrender his farm. He would often neglect it in idleness, ignorance, jollity and drink, get into debt, and have to sell his property to the nearest owner of a great estate. . . . In two generations Ireland would again be England's difficulty, come back upon her in an aggravated form. Mr. Mill never deigns to consider that an Irishman is an Irishman, and not an average human being—an idiomatic and idiosyncratic, not an abstract, man.

In his *Enigmas of Life* (1875)—now informed by Galton's *Hereditary Genius* ([1892] 1978)—Greg focused his attack on the homogeneity doctrine implicit in T. R. Malthus's account. Greg (1875, 129) argued that Malthus is concerned only that, on average, marriage be postponed. Greg emphasized a new law in opposition to Malthus.

. . . possibly the danger *ultimately* to be apprehended may be the very reverse of that which Malthus dreaded; that, in fact, when we have reached that point of universal plenty and universal cultivation to which human progress ought to bring us, the race will multiply too slowly rather than too fast. One such influence may be specified with considerable confidence,—namely, THE TENDENCY OF CEREBRAL DEVELOPMENT TO LESSEN FECUNDITY. (103)

Darwin's theory of natural selection profoundly influenced early eugenicists; the admiration was mutual.[5] In 1864, A. R. Wallace had argued that the doctrine of natural selection did not apply to humans because of ethical concerns generated by human sympathy.[6] The eugenics response attempted to counteract such ethical imperatives, to create by policy the "survival of the fittest." Greg (1875, 119) responded to Wallace:

> My thesis is this: that the indisputable effect of the state of social progress and culture we have reached, of our high civilization in its present stage and actual form, is to *counteract and suspend* the operation of that righteous and salutary law of "natural selection" in virtue of which the best specimens of the race—the strongest, the finest, the worthiest—are those which survive . . . and propagate an ever improving and perfecting type of humanity.

Greg's challenge to classical economics relied on Carlyle's supposition that competence varies by race. To see this, compare the following passages from Carlyle's *Shooting Niagara* and from Greg's discussion on the survival of native races, both of which assert that the black race's survival depends on the benevolent despotism of the white.[7]

Carlyle

One always rather likes the Nigger; evidently a poor blockhead with good dispositions, with affections, attachments,—with a turn for Nigger Melodies, and the like:—he is the only Savage of all the coloured races that doesn't die out on sight of the White Man; but can actually live beside him, and work and increase and be merry. The Almighty Maker has appointed him to be a Servant. (1867, 5)

Greg

The Indians of the Antilles, the Red man of North America, the South Sea Islanders, the Australians, even the New Zealanders (the finest and most pliable and teachable of savages), are all alike dying out with rapidity—in consequence of the harshness, or in spite of the forbearance and protection, of the stronger and more capable European. The negro alone survives—and, but for the observation of what is now going

Greg (*continued*)
on in our sugar islands and in the
United States we should say, seems
likely to survive. He only has been
able to hold his own in a fashion,
and to live and flourish, side by side
with masterful and mightier races.
(1868, 357)

The modern theory of statistical racism as first explained by Arrow
(1973) and Phelps (1972) supposes that groups will be divided on the basis
of sample means. The race α will differ from race β on the basis of an estimate of location. While we do not deny that this sort of racialization took
hold in economics, we find another form of racism also of consequence.
The racists we consider, Hunt first and foremost, distinguished race α from
race β on the basis of an estimate of scale. "Inferior" is a judgment applied
to a race β that is supposed with zero variance. The sample mean of some
race, its stereotype in Arrow-Phelps terminology, *is* the "inferior" race.
The reader who thinks that the first β that deviated from the stereotype
would falsify this hypothesis has not encountered Hunt's "mixed-race"
immunization strategy. The intelligent "β" is not a real "β."[8]

For anthropologists such as Hunt, the generating mechanism for the
dead-race claim is simple. Both the mean and variance of intelligence and
other moral characteristics are functions of the length of time one's mind
develops. Cranial development of the "lesser" races stops sooner. If this
notion were localized to Hunt, in his claim that blacks use the big toe as a
thumb and fail to develop language,[9] it would be of no further consequence. This is not the case.[10] Even Galton was influenced by Hunt.

Before his encounter with Hunt, Galton recognized the diversity of
African peoples (Stepan 1982, 127) and pointed out the stupidity of
Hunt's zero-variance assertion.

The Negro, though on average extremely base, was by no means a member of a race lying at a dead level. On the contrary, it had the capacity of
frequently producing able men capable to taking an equal position with
Europeans. The fact of a race being distinguished by the diversity of its
members was well known to ethnologists. There were black and red subdivisions of many North African races, and the contrast between the
well-fed and ill-fed classes of the same tribe of Negroes was often such as
amount apparently to a specific difference.[11]

After the encounter, Galton reads as if he were seeing the world through the theory provided by Hunt.

How is this possible? By contemporary judgment, Hunt was a "quack." Galton's integrity is beyond reproach.[12] But Galton had a weakness: there was a result that he really wanted to believe, a positive correlation between the physicality of a man and his intellect (Pearson 1924). All that has been written on Hunt pictures him with enormous vitality and energy.[13] Galton would not be the first intellectual, nor would he be the last, to have been seduced by charisma. Nor would he be the only African explorer to learn to see the world through Hunt's eyes.[14] As the following passages show, by 1865, Galton's writing on savages in general reads just like Hunt's on the Negro.[15]

Hunt

M. Gratiolet has also observed that in the anterior races the sutures of the cranium do not close so early as in the occipital or inferior races. From these researches it appears that in the Negro the growth of the brain is sooner arrested than in the European. The premature union of the bones of the skull may give a clue to much of the mental inferiority which is seen in the Negro race. There can be no doubt that in puberty a great change takes place in relation to physical development; but in the Negro there appears to be an arrested development of the brain, exactly harmonizing with the physical formation. Young Negro children are nearly as intelligent as European children; but the older they grow the less intelligent they become. They exhibit, when young, an animal liveliness for play and tricks, far surpassing the European child. (1864, 8)

With the Negro, as with some other races of man, it has been found

Galton

Another difference, which may either be due to natural selection or to original difference of race, is the fact that savages seem incapable of progress after the first few years of their life. The average children of all races are much on a par. Occasionally, those of the lower races are more precocious than the Anglo-Saxon; as a brute beast of a few weeks old is certainly more apt and forward than a child of the same age. But, as the years go by, the higher races continue to progress, while the lower ones gradually stop. They remain children in mind, with the passions of grown men. Eminent genius commonly asserts itself in tender years, but it continues long to develop. The highest minds in the highest races seem to have been those who had the longest boyhood. (1865, 326)

Hunt (*continued*)
that the children are precocious, but
that no advance in education can be
made after they arrive at the age of
maturity. (1864, 12)

Popular Representations of Race

Two types of racial models parallel to the anthropologists' treatments also characterize popular representations of race, such as those in *Punch*.[16] There was, first, what we call parametric racism—the theory that Irish (or blacks) are inferior to Anglo-Saxons in some respects.[17] The second, more devastating racial theory holds that the Other is a race without variation, a nonhuman (and nontrading) brute. That both types of racial theories were applied to the Irish is evident from the following remarks by Thomas Huxley (1870, 197) in an address to the Anthropological Society.

> If the writer means to be civil, the Celt is taken to be a charming person, full of wit and vivacity and kindliness, but, unfortunately, thoughtless, impetuous, and unstable, and having standards of right and wrong so different from those of the Anglo-Saxon that it would be absurd, not to say cruel, to treat him in the same way; or, if the instructor of the public is angry, he talks of the Celt as if he were a kind of savage, out of whom no good ever has come or ever will come, and whose proper fate is to be kept as a hewer of wood and a drawer of water for his Anglo-Saxon master. This is the picture of the lion by the man.[18]

In the early 1860s, *Punch* published an increasing number of illustrations by John Tenniel.[19] Initially, Tenniel's Irish subjects reflect some variation, and the treatment parallels the parametric treatment of race already outlined (Levy and Peart 2000). But late in 1865, *Punch*'s caricatures of the Irish (now almost always by John Tenniel) take on a strange uniformity. In "Fenians in a Fix" (October 21, 1865), two Irish Fenians sit slumped in stocks. They have Cruikshank-style faces, with misshapen jaws. They sport distinctive feathered caps that reappear in a number of subsequent caricatures of the Irish. This figure—the apelike Irish—appears again in September, in "Erin's Little Difficulty" (September 30, 1865), where a diminutive but otherwise identical Fenian rebel is receiving a whipping from his (female) master. In "Rebellion Had Bad Luck" (December 10, 1865), a week after *Punch* reports on cannibalism—as gross an instance of human parasitism as one might imagine—in the context of the Jamaican controversy (on which see our earlier contribution in this volume and Levy and Peart 2000) and the Fenian support for the hanged Jamaicans, John Bull again appears with an apelike Fenian.

Early in 1866, a particularly violent cartoon appears, "The Real Irish Court; Or, the Head Centre and the Dis-Senters" (January 6, 1866). Here, the uniformity of the Other is most striking: the Fenians are all dressed alike (all with the same cap as in the earlier cartoons, now minus the feather); all have apelike jaws and odd, protruding teeth. From this point, that jaw and those teeth figure prominently in all characterizations of the Irish in *Punch*. In a characterization of November 10, 1866, we have John Bright selling "medicine" to apelike Irishmen. Here, the message is particularly striking—for these Irish folks are neither violent nor evil, but they have been victimized by an unscrupulous politician. We will return to the capacity for self-government shortly.

"Characteristics" of "Lower" Races

By the mid-1860s, racial hierarchy was everywhere—in literature, anthropology, eugenics, and the popular press. In the decades that followed, the racial accounts moved economics away from Mill's hard doctrine of homogeneity to one of racial heterogeneity. To show this, we present in table 1 evidence of how the anthropologists and eugenicists characterized race. Karl Pearson, the technically most proficient of the eugenics thinkers, a founding editor of *Biometrica*, and the founding editor of the *Annals of Eugenics*, is discussed in Peart and Levy 2003a.

Table 1 then demonstrates how these characterizations carried over to economics literature. It documents claims by economists concerning lack of differentiation among "lower" races, as well as parametric variations in work effort, improvidence, and foresight of the lower classes (especially the Irish). Despite some differences, noted shortly, the common language and themes demonstrate that the influence of the racial theorists was broad and persistent.

In Britain, economists tended to focus on the lower classes, and they argued that the working classes are creatures of passion, unable to plan for the future, and unusually susceptible to alcoholism (Peart 2000). Lurking behind the label of "labouring poor," however, is often a racial explanation. When the Irish were involved, class may signify race (as Jevons [1870] reveals; see Peart 2001b). For Marshall, the "industrial" classes are racially inferior: as conquest and the intermixture of races occurred, the inferior (yet still white) races sort themselves into the lower ranks of industrial society (Marshall [1890] 1930, 195).

Breeding Economic Man

Eugenicists urged that selective breeding be used to improve the genetic makeup of the race. The question that remains is whether economists who embraced racial theorizing also followed eugenicists on policy. They did.

Pigou (1907, 364–65) accepted that the lower classes reproduce at relatively high rates, while the "higher classes" delay marriage and have few children.[20] The biological question remained: "is there reason to believe that bad original properties and poverty are closely correlated?" Pigou's affirmative answer focuses on economic competence.

> For, if we consider the matter, it is apparent that among the relatively rich are many persons who have risen from a poor environment, which their fellows, who have remained poor, shared with them in childhood. Among the original properties of these relatively rich presumably there are qualities which account for their rise. A relatively high reproductive rate *among those who have remained poor* implies, in a measure, the breeding out of these qualities. It implies, in fact, a form of selection that discriminates against the original properties that promote economic success. (Pigou 1907, 365)

Marshall ([1890] 1930, 201) also endorsed Greg's argument concerning differential fertility rate, writing about a "cause for anxiety," "some partial arrest of that selective influence of struggle and competition which in the earliest stages of civilization caused those who were strongest and most vigorous to leave the largest progeny behind them; and to which, more than any other single cause, the progress of the human race is due."[21]

Among British economists, the argument was often that the Irish overbreed, while Anglo-Saxons reproduce at relatively low rates. In America, the Irish were frequently offered as an example of an "inferior" race, but the "Negro problem" and the "immigration problem" formed the backdrop to discussions of eugenics policies. Waves of immigration drawn predomi-

TABLE 1. Anthropologists, Eugenicists, and Neoclassical Economists on the "Lower" Races

	Homogeneity of Race?	"Characteristics" of "Lower" Races
Hunt 1864, 1866c	"In the negro race there is a great uniformity of temperament. In every people of Europe all temperaments exist; but in the Negro race we can only discover analogies for the choleric and phlegmatic temperaments" (1864, 11). "We now know it to be a patent fact that there are races existing which have no history, and that the Negro is one of these races. From the most remote antiquity the Negro race seems to have been what they are now. We may be pretty sure that the Negro race have been without a progressive history; and that they have been for thousands of years the uncivilized race they are at this moment" (1864, 13).	Susceptible to impulse; lack willpower; improvident; cannot resist temptation (1866c, 117); "ungovernable appetite" (1866, 125); lack foresight (1866c).
Galton 1865	"The race [American Indians] is divided into many varieties, but it has fundamentally the same character throughout the whole of America" (321) "Here, then, is a well-marked type of character, that formerly prevailed over a large part of the globe, with which other equally marked types of character in other regions are strongly contrasted . . . the typical	"The Red man has great patience, great reticence, great dignity; the Negro has strong impulsive passions, and neither patience, reticence, nor dignity. He is warm-hearted, loving towards his master's children, and idolised by the children in return. He is eminently gregarious, for he is always jabbering, quarrelling, tom-tom-ing, or dancing. He is remarkably domestic, and he is endowed with such constitutional

		vigour, and is so prolific, that his race is irrepressible" (321). Savages lack instinct of continuous steady labor, possess wild untamable restlessness, wild impulsive nature of Negro (325, 327).
	"West African Negro" (321).	Want of self-reliance; sexual passion; imprudent; feckless; feebleminded; high birthrates (Pearson 1924, 73, 80, 222; Pearson and Moul 1925).
Pearson 1924	Servile, gregarious, herdlike; undifferentiated; remain the Red Man and Negro despite environmental differences (1924, 73–74); oppression reduces differentiation (weeds out physically and mentally fit individuals) (Pearson and Moul 1925, 8).	Intemperate; improvident; lacking foresight (1869, 186–87); ignorant; careless; unsubdued; vicious; want of self-reliance (1870, 196, 200).
Jevons* 1869, 1870, [1871] 1911		"Questions of this kind [work effort] depend greatly upon the character of the race. Persons of an energetic disposition feel labour less painfully than their fellow-men, and, if they happen to be endowed with various and acute sensibilities, their desire of further acquisition never ceases. A man of lower race, a negro for instance, enjoys possession less, and loathes labour more; his exertions, therefore soon stop. A poor savage would be content to gather the almost gratuitous fruits of nature, if they

TABLE 1.—Continued

	Homogeneity of Race?	"Characteristics" of "Lower" Races
		were sufficient to give sustenance; it is only physical want which drives him to exertion" ([1871] 1911, 182–83).
Marshall [1890] 1930	"Strange uniformity of general character" among savages (723).	Savage life ruled by "custom and impulse"; "never forecasting the distant future"; "seldom providing for near future"; "servitude to custom"; fitful; "governed by the fancy of the moment"; incapable of steady work (723) (whereas Anglo-Saxon are steadfast [581]); a great mass of humanity lack patience, self-control, self-discipline (581); England peopled by the strongest members of the strongest races of northern Europe (740); capital-labor division characterizes English race/modern civilization (745); race of undertakers develops in England (749).
Pigou§ 1907, 1920		"Feckless"; high birthrates (1907, 364–65); "faulty telescopic faculty"; "propagation untrammeled by economic considerations" (123); "lack initiative and understanding" (1920, 326), overestimate chances of success (1920, 493).
Webb‡ 1910	American blacks less differentiated than whites (236–37).	Maximum birthrates; thriftless; idle; drunken; profligate; feebleminded; unfit;

lacking in self-respect and foresight (233–40).

Commons 1916	Can perform a limited range of tasks. Unmechanical and unintelligent. Slavery reduced differentiation.	Impulsive; strong sexual passion; debauchery; high birthrate; lack self-control, foresight, self-reliance, willpower, ingenuity; ignorant; unstable; indolent; adverse to solitude; improvident; superstitious; contented; fail to develop language (39, 40, 49, 60, 94, 212–13).
Fisher¶ [1909] 1976, [1930] 1986		Lack foresight and self-control; improvident; impatience; weak wills; weak intellect ([1909] 1976, 73, 376; [1930] 1986, 73).
Fetter 1916	Can master a limited range of occupations (367).	Defective mentally and physically; high birthrates (369, 375).

*1869; laboring classes; 1870 (208 ff.): Irish explanation for mortality rates.
§Lower classes; nonrace.
‡The fecundity characteristic applies both to the lower classes and to American blacks, while the other characteristics are specified in terms of class.
¶Characteristics are specified in terms of lower classes with (Irish) racial components.

nantly from genetically inferior races—Eastern European Jews—are said to
have reduced the genetic quality of the nation (Commons 1916, 200 ff.).
Since such immigrants multiply at high rates, the deterioration is said to
be ongoing.[22] Advances in public health were dysgenic.

> Thus there are increasing reasons for fearing, that while the progress of
> medical science and sanitation is saving from death a continually
> increasing number of the children of those who are feeble physically and
> mentally . . . (Marshall [1890] 1930, 201)[23]

In the eugenics context, economists concluded that laissez-faire policy
meant a deteriorating stock and an increase in parasitism. For example,
Sidney Webb (1910, 236–37) argued that laissez-faire in the biological
sense means the "survival of the lowest parasite."

> The question, who is to survive, is determined by the conditions of the
> struggle, the rules of the ring. Where the rules of the ring favour a low
> type, the low type will survive and *vice versa*. The survivors of an unreg-
> ulated epidemic of scarlet fever or typhus may owe their escape to con-
> stitutional peculiarities which are otherwise perfectly valueless, and
> which may even perhaps only be found amongst persons who, from
> every other point of view, we should call unfit. If, for example, it were
> possible for an epidemic of malarial fever to spread unchecked all over
> the United States of America it is highly probable that the whites would
> be eliminated and the blacks would survive. There is, indeed, always a
> general presumption that the unregulated, unpurposeful struggle will
> distinctly favour the less individually developed and more prolific organ-
> isms as against the more highly developed and less fertile. In short, the
> "survival of the fittest" in an environment unfavourable to progress
> may—as everybody knows—mean the survival of the lowest parasite.

Webb (237–38) endorsed the "social machinery" of eugenics and called for
wide-ranging intervention to prevent breeding by the unfit. Irving Fisher
(1909, 675) maintained that the bottom portion of the genetic pool lives
off the rest, in "social degeneration and gross parasitism."

> Similarly, the "Tribe of Ishmael," numbering 1,692 individuals in six
> generations, has produced 121 known prostitutes and has bred hundreds
> of petty thieves, vagrants, and murderers. The history of the tribe is a
> swiftly moving picture of social degeneration and gross parasitism,

extending from its seventeenth-century convict ancestry to the present-day horde of wandering and criminal descendants.

To reduce this sort of parasitism, economists endorsed both sets of eugenics policies to improve the genetic makeup of the economic unit (generally, in this context, the nation): measures to encourage fertility among the "superior" genetic stock and measures to reduce fertility among the "unfit."[24] In America, the discussion also focused on the need to select immigrants to reduce the numbers from "inferior," "defective," and "undesirable" classes of immigrants (Commons 1916, 230).[25] The practical measure seized upon by Commons (235) in this context was the simple device of a literacy test, to "raise the average standard" of immigrants. Fetter (1916, 378) argued for an overall reduction in immigration, as well as a eugenic selection of immigrants to "improve the racial quality of the nation by checking the multiplication of the strains defective in respect to mentality, nervous organization, and physical health, and by encouraging the more capable elements of the population to contribute in due proportion to the maintenance of a healthy, moral, and efficient population."

While many economists favored some form of eugenic remaking early in the twentieth century, they also resoundingly endorsed policies designed to reduce what they perceived as systematically mistaken decision making among the lower orders. The laboring classes were said to discount future consumption because they were overly impatient and lacking in foresight or self-control. They mistakenly neglected to lay by savings for cyclical fluctuations in labor demand, and they also saved too little for their old age; they were unable to decide correctly what investment to make in human capital or when to marry (and how many children to have). There was little presumption that these "inadequacies" would correct themselves, that agents would eventually learn how to participate in the marketplace. In fact, economists argued the opposite: well into the twentieth century, they disassociated themselves from the Smith-Macaulay position on learning by trial and error, outlined in our earlier contribution to this volume. Increasingly after 1870, they consequently called for interventions aimed at "improving" decision making, strengthening willpower, instilling prudent habits of spending, and enhancing what Pigou would call "faulty telescopic faculties" (Peart 2000). More generally, pauperism and lack of self-reliance resulting from overpopulation and undersaving are regarded as inevitable results of relying on a market system for all consumers, including those among us who, without help, are ill equipped to deal with markets.[26]

Return to Fixed Human Nature

In midcentury, perspectives changed again. The modern revival of the classical economists' doctrine of fixed human nature by the Chicago school is now a matter of common knowledge. However, the contrast between the Chicago view and what came earlier in terms of racial—or hierarchical—theorizing has been neglected. The most sharply questioned issue was that of time preference. When Frank Knight reviewed Fisher's theory of interest, he asserted, against the common racial imputation of time preference, a view of the primacy of culture. Whereas there may be no difference between the Teuton and Jew, these cultures differ radically from the Greek.

> As previously stated, we do not know whether people generally, or the class from which savings come, would "discount" the future or the present or neither, "other things being equal." In general, there is perhaps more ground for the inverse allegation as against the modern European peoples and especially the Teutonic stock (and the West European Jews?), namely, that they "look before and after, and sigh for what is not" and neglect the present moment. Compare Faust and Rabbi ben Ezra with Marius the Epicurean, or the Puritan with the Greek view of life. (Knight 1931, 203)

Perhaps more dramatically, Knight saw no difference in the motivation of different sorts of people. Note how he explains the demand for wealth.

> It seems to me indisputable in fact that people desire wealth for many reasons, of which the guaranty of the future delivery of groceries or other consumable services is sometimes the main and sometimes a quite minor consideration. It is desired for the same reasons a head-hunting hero desires a goodly collection of skulls; it is power, a source of prestige, a counter in the game, an article of fashion, and perhaps a mere something to be "collected." It is wanted to use, but also just to have, to get more, in order to get still more. (Knight 1931, 177)

There is nothing here about the "curious lack of variation" of savages or about parametric variations in behavior across races; instead, Knight offers an illustration of economic problems across time, culture, and race.

The 1977 Stigler-Becker attack on the postulate of positive time preference continued the argument that Stigler made in his dissertation: positive time preference has no role in the making of abstract economic man.[27] In this stigmatization of positive time preference, Stigler remained Knight's faithful student.

Because both Chicago economics and the classical economists have been characterized with the laissez-faire label, it is appropriate that we close with statements in which the competence of agents in the political process is urged. The same arguments that apply to competence in a market carry over to competence in the political process. We view Cairnes and Stigler as advancing the doctrine of politics as exchange, or politics as optimization, rather than as adherents to a doctrine that there is a list, long or short as it may be, of appropriate state action. To make that list is to question the competence of the political agents who find it in their interest to lengthen or shorten it.

The first statement with which we close this discussion comes from Mill's most technically proficient disciple, J. E. Cairnes. His defense of Negro suffrage begins with an attack on anthropological argument. What does body type have to do with competence?

> In approaching the question of the negro suffrage, one encounters the assumption, made with so much confidence by reasoners of a different race, of the inherent unfitness of the negro for political life. The shape of his skull, the prominence of his lower jaw, the size and hardness of his pelvis, indicate, say these reasoners, closer relationship with the chimpanzee than is consistent with the effective discharge of the duties of citizenship. *With such anatomical peculiarities, he must be incapable of understanding his own interest, or of voting for the representative best fitted to promote it.* (Cairnes 1865, 335; emphasis added)

Cairnes then emphasizes that political participation is critical to improvement.

> He must therefore be excluded from the sphere of politics, and by consequence from all the opportunities of improvement which the sphere of politics opens. Montaigne thought, as we have been lately reminded, that it was assigning rather too great value to conjectures concerning witchcraft, to burn human beings alive on such grounds. Whether to consign a whole race to perpetual serfdom be as serious a step as the

burning alive of a small proportion of each successive generation, it is unnecessary to determine; but this at least we may say, that the adoption of either course on grounds no stronger than the prosecutors of witches could formerly, or the advocates of negro subjection can now, adduce, argues, to say the least, very remarkable confidence in the value of conjectural speculation. It would argue this even were there no facts to rebut such *à priori* guesses; but, in truth, such facts abound. (335–36)

Cairnes closes with a devastating implication of the consequence of the sexual usage of slaves, throwing the mixed-race assertions back at the anthropologists. What does race have to do with the discussion of suffrage?

But in truth the consideration of race is almost irrelevant to the question we are discussing. The bulk of the freedmen who are now demanding admission to citizenship in the United States have, it must never be forgotten, quite as much Anglo-Saxon as African blood in their veins. . . . The truth is, the great majority of the freedmen of the South are not negroes, but Anglo-Africans. (336–37)

Finally, Stigler (1975, x) put forward a variation on the public choice theme that policies are the result of competent pursuit of interest in the political sphere.

It seems unfruitful, I am now persuaded, to conclude from the studies of the effects of various policies that those policies which did not achieve their announced goals, or had perverse effects (as with a minimum wage law), are simply mistakes of the society. A policy adopted and followed for a long time, or followed by many different states, could not usefully be described as a mistake: eventually its real effects would become known to interested groups. *To say that such policies are mistaken is to say that one cannot explain them.* (Emphasis added)

Given a choice between laissez-faire policy and the doctrine of human competence, human competence holds.

NOTES

Earlier versions of this chapter were presented at the 2000 History of Economics Society meetings in Vancouver and at the Middlebury College Christian A. Johnson Economics Conference "Race, Liberalism, and Economics" in April

2001. Portions of the chapter draw on material in Peart and Levy 2003a and Levy and Peart 2001–2. We have received valuable comments from David Colander, Sandy Darity, Deirdre McCloskey, and A. M. C. Waterman.

1. Darity (1995) also gives evidence of racism in American economics early in the twentieth century. Our account attempts to provide a context and an explanation for that racism.

2. Using the JSTOR database, we found no use of the word *eugenics* in any of the literally hundreds of articles and reviews written by Joseph Schumpeter, George Stigler, or A. W. Coats. (The results of our search, conducted on May 14, 2000, are available in HTML form on request.) Phil Mirowski (1989) discusses energetics at length with a glance at eugenics. The essays in Mirowski 1994 mention eugenics once, in connection with Marshall. As far as we can determine, only J. J. Spengler has paid attention to eugenics. The eugenic involvement of the neoclassical economists is completely apparent in specialist accounts of eugenics (Soloway 1995).

3. Cf. Smith [1776] 1976, 1:28: "The difference of natural talents in different men is, in reality, much less than we are aware of; and the very different genius which appears to distinguish men of different professions, when grown up to maturity, is not upon many occasions so much the cause as the effect of the division of labour. The difference between the most dissimilar characters, between a philosopher and a common street porter, for example, seems to arise not so much from nature as from habit, custom, and education. When they came into the world, and for the first six or eight years of their existence, they were perhaps very much alike, and neither their parents nor playfellows could perceive any remarkable difference. About that age, or soon after, they come to be employed in very different occupations. The difference of talents comes then to be taken notice of, and widens by degrees, till at last the vanity of the philosopher is willing to acknowledge scarce any resemblance."

4. Perhaps the most explicit challenge to the classical economists' presumption of homogeneity is found in Hunt 1866c (122): " . . . principles of Mr. Mill, who will not admit that the Australian, the Andaman islander, and the Hottentot labour under any *inherent* incapacity for attaining the highest culture of ancient Greece or modern Europe!"

5. Darwin was taken with Greg's 1868 *Fraser's Magazine* article "On the Failure of 'Natural Selection' in the Case of Man" (see Darwin 1989, 138–39). He was particularly struck by Greg's characterization of the Irish: "The careless, squalid, unaspiring Irishman, fed on potatoes, living in a pig-stye, doting on a superstition, multiplies like rabbits or ephemera" (Darwin 1989, 143, quoting Greg with omission 1868, 360).

6. "If a herbivorous animal is a little sick and has not fed well for a day or two, and the herd is then pursued by a beast of prey, our poor invalid inevitably falls a victim. So in a carnivorous animal the least deficiency of vigour prevents its capturing food, and it soon dies of starvation. There is, as a general rule, no mutual assistance between adults, which enables them to tide over a period of sickness. Neither is there any division of labour; each must fulfill *all* the conditions of its existence, and, therefore, 'natural selection' keeps all up to a pretty uniform standard.

"But in man, as we now behold him, this is different. He is social and sympathetic. In the rudest tribes the sick are assisted at least with food; less robust health and vigour than the average does not entail death. . . . Some division of labour takes place. . . . The action of natural selection is therefore checked" (Wallace 1864, clxii).

7. A similar link between Carlyle and Galton is demonstrated in Peart and Levy 2003a. In popular culture, the doctrine linking race survival and benevolent despotism is taught in Charles Kingsley's 1863 *Water-Babies,* in the edifying "History of the great and famous nation of the Doasyoulikes, who came away from the country of Hardwork, because they wanted to play on the Jews'-harp all day long" (Kingsley 1863, 239–40).

8. The details are provided in Young 1995 and Levy 2001. As an example of how this works, cf. Hunt 1863, 16: "The exhibitions of cases of intelligent Negroes in the salons of the fashionable world by so-called 'philanthropists,' have frequently been nothing but mere impostures. In nearly every case in which the history of these cases has been investigated, it has been found that these so-called Negroes are the offspring of European and African parents."

9. Hunt 1864, 19. The language slur resurfaced in economics in the early twentieth century, when Commons (1916, 94) asserted that the Yiddish spoken by Russian Jews "is scarcely a language—it is a jargon without syntax, conjugation, or declension." The reader will recall the importance of language noted in our earlier contribution to this volume, in terms of the ability to communicate as a requirement for trade.

10. Reade (1864, 399) claims: "the growth of the brain in the negro, as in the ape, is sooner arrested than in those of our race." Kingsley (1863, 245) notes: "a Hindoo tailor uses his toes to thread his needle."

11. The quote is from "Anthropology at the British Association" (1863, 388). We find no discussion of this essay in any report in any of the secondary literature, even though Pearson's monumental *Life* (1924) devotes an extensive section to Galton's anthropological writings.

12. At age 85, Galton found technical reasons to believe that majoritarian decision making had desirable properties. He called attention to this "unexpected" result with great clarity, choosing to title the first of a pair of articles "Vox Populi," explicitly challenging his Carlylean assertions already quoted. In Levy and Peart 2002, we reprint the articles and call attention to Pearson's judgment that Galton chose to publish his results in *Nature* to maximize their contemporary (policy?) impact. Porter (1986, 130) notes Galton's antiegalitarianism in the years before these articles were published.

13. The obituary from the *New York Weekly Day-Book* of November 6, 1869, reprinted in the *Anthropological Review* under "Anthropological News" (Death of the Best Man in England 1870), gives some flavor of contemporary opinions: "We are pained to hear of the death of Dr. James Hunt . . . beyond doubt the best, or, at all events, the most useful man in England, if not, indeed, in Europe. . . . Dr. Hunt, in his own clear knowledge and brave enthusiasm, was doing more for humanity, for the welfare of mankind, and for the glory of God, than all the philosophers, humanitarians, philanthropists, statesmen . . ." For additional texts, see Peart and Levy 2003a.

14. Cf. Reade 1864, 399: "Thus it has been proved by measurements, by microscopes, by analyses, that the typical negro is something between a child, a dotard, and a beast. I cannot struggle against these sacred facts of science."

15. Galton never—as far as we know—employed Hunt's "mixed-race" immunization strategy. Without this quackery to distinguish between the theorized "Negro" and actual people of color, Galton later assumes that variance is a constant across observed races. Peart and Levy 2003a provides details.

16. In Levy and Peart 2000, we consider *Punch*'s rival, *Fun*, as well as George Cruikshank's drawings of the Irish.

17. This is the characterization Curtis describes in "The Importance of Being Paddy" (Curtis 1968, 49–65); it parallels Greg's description of the Irish alluded to earlier. Table 1 in this chapter reflects many of these characteristics as well. Cf. Kingsley 1863, 244: "when people live on poor vegetables instead of roast beef and plum-pudding, their jaws grow large, and their lips grow coarse, like the poor Paddies who eat potatoes."

18. The context of these remarks is a debate over differences between the Celts and the Anglo-Saxons, which, Huxley asserted, amounted only to linguistic differences. That position was opposed by the president of the Anthropological Society of London, John Beddoe (1870, 212–13).

19. Tenniel joined *Punch* at the invitation of its editor, Mark Lemon, in December 1850. Initially, Tenniel's contributions were limited to the decorative borders and initials of the journal, but he became *Punch*'s principal artist upon the death of Leech in 1864. The *Dictionary of National Biography* article on Tenniel refers to his "delightful humour which never degenerated into coarseness nor was lacking in dignity."

20. Pigou is singled out by Leonard Darwin (1916, 311) as "as far as I know . . . almost the only economist who has paid serious attention to eugenics in connection with economics." Indeed, a JSTOR search of the term *eugenics* in the economics list finds Pigou 1907 as the earliest resource.

21. The argument is specified in the common terminology of low fertility rates among the "upper classes" and high birthrates among the poor. At least in Marshall's case, however, the racial element is quite clear. Historically, the intermixture of races that followed conquests led him to speculate that the lower races selected into the industrial classes (see Marshall [1890] 1930, 195). Elsewhere, he used the more obvious eugenic phrase, referring to the tendency of the "higher strains of the population to marry later and to have fewer children than the lower" (ibid., 203).

22. In England, economists such as Marshall (1884) feared that such deterioration will occur within cities. Here, the argument is that the Irish form a relatively large and (due to high birthrates) growing constituency in cities (see Jevons 1870; Peart 2001b); cf. Ashby's statement in Reid 1906, 38: "The slums and courts of our large cities are chiefly inhabited by the unfit, who are recruited by the failures in the industrial struggle; and among these early marriages and illegitimate intercourse is more common than among the saner and more intelligent class."

23. Cf. Marshall [1890] 1930, 201 n. 1: "Again, on the Pacific Slope, there were at one time just grounds for fearing that all but highly skilled work would be left to the Chinese; and that the white men would live in an artificial way in which

a family became a great expense. In this case Chinese lives would have been sub-stituted for American, and the average quality of the human race would have been lowered." The contention that, without sterilization or segregation, saving the "feeble" entails a reduction in genetic quality is common (see Fisher [1909] 1976; Darwin 1916; Webb 1910).

24. Webb 1910; Pigou 1907, 1920. Fisher ([1909] 1976, 673) also endorsed government "bounties" to encourage births among the "vital" classes. Proposals ranged from sterilization or segregation, to German-style marriage tests, to devel-oping social prejudice against such reproduction. For Frank Fetter (1916, 366–68), the "Negro problem" was "insoluble": the alternatives of intermixture of races, existence in separate geographical regions, and extinction, are "repugnant," "impractical," and unrealistic. Fetter concludes with "futile expressions of regret."

25. See Cherry 1976; Commons 1916, 198 ff. Pearson also favored restrictions of immigration, arguing that immigration should be restricted to those who are at least 25 percent above the mean for natives in intelligence and physical charac-teristics (Pearson and Moul 1925, 127).

26. Many scholars have noted the increased calls for paternalistic legislation (Peart 2001a) without providing an explanation for the upsurge.

27. "The second ground for valuing present goods more highly is that '. . . to goods which are destined to meet the wants of the future, we ascribe a value which is really less than the true intensity of their future marginal utility.' This is a fail-ure of perspective, an irrationality in human behavior—the only irrationality, it may be noted, that Böhm-Bawerk introduces into his 'economic man'" (Stigler 1941, 213).

One Hundred Years of American Economists on Race and Discrimination, 1881–1981

Robert E. Prasch

It is these problems [social condition and caste] that we are today somewhat helplessly—not to say carelessly—facing, forgetful that they are living, growing social questions whose progeny will survive to curse the nation, unless we grapple with them manfully and intelligently.

—W. E. B. DuBois 1898b

Race, Discrimination, and Economic Theory: What Are the Issues?

Sixty years ago, Gunnar Myrdal observed that American racism represented a pressing dilemma because it coexisted so readily, if somewhat uneasily, with the founding ideas of the United States that it is a "self-evident truth" that "all men are created equal." Understanding the cause, meaning, and persistence of racial injustice has also presented a dilemma to American economists. Moreover, what they have said and taught on this issue has had important implications for the ideas and ideals of social scientists more generally. As I will show, American economists were often imbued with the ethos of their era, although there were important exceptions.[1]

This chapter will survey how American economists addressed and reflected on the category of race in their work and how racism may have influenced the structure, implications, and meaning of economic theory.[2] This is an important consideration for several reasons. Of most importance, our understanding of the world shapes our categories of apperception. These categories, in turn, shape and guide the way we measure, evaluate, judge, and ultimately form policies. The chapter by Glenn Loury in this volume illustrates how our categories of analysis frame our expectations of what is plausible or implausible and how this process in turn determines what we take to be, or not to be, a social problem. In light of the importance of ideas to social theory and policy formation, the following narrative may shed some light on how problems were perceived and addressed, if they were perceived and addressed at all.

Beginnings: The Economic Setting

Racism and discrimination in America have not operated within a static institutional structure. American slavery went through several distinct permutations, and the experiences of American blacks after emancipation were anything but static. Reconstruction, the spread of Jim Crow laws, official disenfranchisement, the great northern migration of blacks, World War II, and the civil rights era each presented a unique situation with a different configuration of both obstacles and opportunities.

Economic history demonstrates that the social and labor market institutions that evolved over this period were the result both of the actions and counteractions taken by a powerful majority and of the responses it induced in a weaker, but not necessarily passive, oppressed minority. Most important, the history of American race relations is not one of a linear advance from a dismal past of slavery into an ever more enlightened present. On the contrary, we have a complex story of advance, punctuated by distinct periods of conflict and even retrogression. Nevertheless, the overall record indicates that advancement toward increased equality and opportunity has taken place over these past fifteen decades—although the cost measured in "life, liberty, and happiness" certainly has been high for a group of persons who ostensibly became full citizens under the Thirteenth through the Fifteenth Amendments to the Constitution (Irons 1999, chaps. 16–18, 28–30; Litwack 1998; Klinkner and Smith 1999).

Examining the postbellum South, Roger Ransom and Richard Sutch observed that an important consequence of emancipation was that newly freed slaves substantially reduced their hours of work relative to the hours they were forced to contribute as slaves. While pre-1890s estimates of

Southern statistics are both problematic and contestable, Ransom and Sutch were able to construct an estimate that black labor supply fell by somewhere between 28 and 37 percent after emancipation (Ransom and Sutch 1977, 44–47). Such a normal and predictable adjustment in labor supply was consistent with the reduction in labor supply that occurred when slaves were freed in the West Indies and that so troubled Thomas Carlyle (Levy and Peart, chap. 2 in this volume; Levy 2001, chap. 1). It was also deeply disturbing to Southern whites who had become dependent on a large supply of cheap and reasonably docile labor: "Nothing in the experience of the planter class had prepared them to deal with blacks as free workers, and in many respects they were far less equipped to make the transition to freedom than the former slaves" (Litwack 1998, 119).

To Southern whites, the "solution," of course, was to limit the political, social, and economic opportunities open to newly freed blacks. Such a sweeping policy necessarily had complex elements but nevertheless could be enacted when its target was a readily identifiable group of people with little education or tangible property, no access to the courts or legislative process, and, most important of all, no serious "exit" option. To this end, Southern whites employed multiple means to ensure that their black neighbors remained poor, ignorant, and landless (Litwack 1998, chaps. 3–4; Wells-Barnett [1893] 1991; Blackmon 2001).

None of the preceding background is offered to suggest that the northern states were a utopia of enlightened race relations. While more formalized in the South, segregation by residence, jobs, and schools emerged as the norm across the United States by the end of the nineteenth century. To make matters worse, the Republican Party, under Presidents William McKinley, Theodore Roosevelt, and William Howard Taft, was anxious to build its electoral appeal in the South, a political agenda that required a deference to "Southern traditions" along with a perceived need to downplay any lingering concern for the rights of black Americans who, since they were increasingly likely to be disenfranchised, would not be voting anyway (Gerber 1976, 248).[3]

Economics and the Evolutionary Perspective
of the Late Nineteenth Century

Social Darwinism is a phrase that usually, and correctly, is associated with the once widespread notion that Charles Darwin's dictum of the "survival of the fittest" could be applied to the social realm. Despite some reservations on the part of Darwin himself, prominent social Darwinists, such as Herbert Spencer and William Graham Sumner, reasoned that some persons come to dominate society at any given moment as a direct consequence of their superior insight, ability, creativity, and intelligence. Such qualities enabled a select few to succeed in the multifaceted competition for the patronage of customers, in the development and application of new technologies, and in the search for cheaper sources of supply. Moreover, it was thought, these "victors" in the struggle for existence deserved the wealth and creature comforts that were the spur that brought forth this socially beneficial effort.

To Herbert Spencer, an increase in the material, physical, and genetic progress of human beings—which he considered society's only ethically defensible goal—depended on the full and unrelenting operation of competitive forces in all areas of economic life. American intellectuals of this time were drawn to his vision since it presented the post–Civil War generation with a notion of a telos—the potential perfectibility of the human race. Spencer and his many enthusiasts among American intellectual, economic, and political elites theorized that the individual striving for the happiness and comfort of himself and his heirs (definitely a male pronoun here) would also improve himself, his family, and the larger society. The increasing perfectibility of the human race would be a necessary outcome. This telos was the source of the popularity of Spencer's doctrine and, simultaneously, its greatest problem from the perspective of improved race relations (Spencer [1874] 1961, chap. 4; Parrington [1930] 1958, 197; Fine 1964, 41–42).

It is less well known or appreciated that evolutionary modes of thought were also attractive to many of the socialists and social reformers of the late nineteenth century. Their version of this doctrine rejected the laissez-faire nostrums of Spencer and his followers, as they perceived an opportunity to improve humanity through the deliberate and calculated construction of supportive economic and social institutions. John Wesley Powell, among other public figures, was associated with this perspective (Hofstadter 1955, chap. 6). The most popular proponent of this view, one who was also criticized by some of his peers for maintaining racist ideas, was the novelist and socialist Jack London. In the academy, prominent intellectuals such as Richard Ely in economics and Lester Ward in sociology were simultaneously social reformers and adherents of an evolutionary approach to social theory (cf. Ely 1903; Dealy and Ward 1905).

The historian Carl Degler (1991, 13) explains:

The aim of social Darwinism was frankly conservative; the rising social scientists were not. Sociologists like Albion Small of the University of Chicago, Franklin A. Giddings of Columbia, Charles A. Cooley of the University of Michigan, and Edward Ross of the University of Wisconsin were reformers to a man. For them, the new social science was intended to shape a fresh and just world for Americans. . . . Scholarship and reformer would work like hand in glove toward an improved and worthy goal.[4]

Regrettably, as Degler illustrates and as I shall show later in this chapter, a reformist sympathy for laborers, women, or society as a whole did not necessarily accompany a charitable outlook on the plight or potential of African-Americans. Sadly, the tendency to champion social reform while maintaining an implicit or explicit commitment to white supremacy was an extensively held view in the late nineteenth and early twentieth centuries. This was especially the case for social reformers who lived and worked in the South, where segregation and the political disenfranchisement of blacks were largely taken to be natural, valid, and just. As the historian William Link (1992, 67) observes, "Most [Southern] reformers assumed that innate racial differences existed and that white supremacy was likely, even desirable."

The feminist novelist and social scientist Charlotte Perkins Gilman is a paradigmatic example of a social scientist who sought to harness evolutionary processes to the cause of social reform and social justice. In her most famous book, *Women and Economics*, she argued that the frailty and economic dependence exhibited by women—in particular, women from the upper and middle classes—were the result of evolutionary dynamics that represented an adaptation, over multiple generations, to the specific environmental and social conditions that women faced (Gilman [1898] 1966). As a reformer, Gilman believed that we did not have to accept as "inevitable" the outcome of any contingent social process. Rather, she argued that if women were to achieve full equality, they would have to be subjected, physically and socially, to an enriched and demanding environment and set of challenges. To be effective, these challenges should be designed to improve women's physical and intellectual fitness to take on important roles in their private lives and in the larger affairs of society (Gilman [1898] 1966; Sheth and Prasch 1996). Whatever the merits of her feminist analysis, Gilman's proposal for the "uplift" of Southern blacks, which called for the drafting of "incompetent" blacks into work battalions to teach them labor skills and a better work ethic (Gilman 1908), was as politically dangerous as it was legally dubious.

The Evolutionary or Historical School of Economists and the Rise of Scientific Racism

Unfortunately, as Brendan O'Flaherty and Jill Shapiro have so vividly described in their contribution to this volume, the newfound reliance on induction and scientific (empirical) methods that typified the late nineteenth century also represented, in general, a retrograde step in our collective understanding of race relations and the economic status of black Americans. As already noted, evolutionary arguments, even those articulated by social reformers, rarely worked to the advantage of blacks. One reason was the methodological hypocrisy induced by strong racist priors (Cherry 1976). Even as environment was advanced as the key determinant of the life chances for most peoples, social scientists would claim that the "facts" demonstrated that blacks retained a residual and immutable inability to compete on equal terms with whites (see Jenks, Lauck, and Smith [1911] 1922, 300–301). Consider the following, fairly typical statement by a professor of political economy at Columbia University, who was also vice president of the American Statistical Association.

> The negroes are by birth and race and previous condition of servitude incapable of representing the full American capacity for political and social life. They have neither the traditions of political life nor practical experience in self-government. The presence of this numerous body of people, who will never fully amalgamate with the white population, will always be a problem for us. The tendency will be for them to remain in a position of inferiority, unable fully to meet the demands on their intelligence and virtue which our system of political liberty and equality makes. (Mayo-Smith 1890, 64–65)

In the scholarly literature of this era, the median narrative would typically begin with the claim that all people, including blacks, had the potential for "improvements and usefulness"; it would then proceed to develop an explanation for the lack of black progress that stressed the degenerative impact of thousands of years in tropical climates on the mental, moral, and cognitive capacities of blacks. The clear implication was that blacks would

be, at best, marginally productive dependents on white society for generations to come. A detailed and widely cited presentation of this perspective
was a book-length journal article that appeared in the *Publications of the
American Economic Association*. Joseph Tillinghast (1902) argued that centuries of natural and social selection in Africa were more important to
understanding African-American social problems than were slavery or the
experience of a mere fifty years of emancipation.

In narratives that began from this perspective, slavery, while conventionally condemned as a "great curse," was, nevertheless, considered a useful first step in the progress of persons of African descent. The historian
William Link (1992, 65) found·that this position was almost universally
held among Southern reformers at this time. To white Southerners, it followed that the emerging postbellum system of black tenancy on white
plantations was a positive development, since it required blacks to work
under the close supervision of white landowners who could aid in the
development of useful agricultural and living skills, even as they imparted
other useful "lessons" on morals, savings, and foresight. A Southern plantation owner who was prominently featured in the economics journals of
this period, Alfred Holt Stone, promoted this perspective in the course of
several articles on the economic prospects of Southern blacks (Stone
1902, 1905, 1906, 1908). According to Stone (1902, 258–60), blacks had
many of the characteristics then conventionally ascribed to them, including a predilection to "sexual looseness," "unreliability," and a "migratory
habit." He also claimed that they "squander more [money] than any similar class of people of whom I have any knowledge."

From today's perspective, it is perhaps remarkable to note that Stone
was, when contrasted to his (white) peers, somewhat enlightened on racial
issues. For example, he thought that the habits and economic condition of
blacks could be improved and that this could occur relatively quickly. In
keeping with the then popular inductive approach to economics, Stone
tested the conjecture, apparently then somewhat in doubt, that blacks
could respond to economic incentives. On the basis of an experiment that
he conducted on his own Mississippi plantation, he found that blacks
responded well to economic incentives and willingly learned better agricultural techniques. It says something about this era that this "result" mer-
ited publication in Harvard's *Quarterly Journal of Economics* (Stone 1905).

Stone's larger concern was that competition in the labor market with a
"superior" white labor force would drive many blacks out of those jobs in
which they were just achieving a toehold. Moreover, he conjectured that

the rivalry between the races for desirable jobs would likely be a source of continuing racial conflict. For these reasons, he thought that the future of blacks lay in farming—in particular, farming in a South that should remain largely segregated for the benefit of blacks (Stone 1906, 1908).[5]

It would be an understatement to say that most of the "scientific" studies by the sociologists and economists of this period were terribly misguided. Often they began with flawed premises and arrived at simply incredible conclusions, particularly in light of what we know of the spread and intensification of both Jim Crow and the practice of lynching in the South during this period. Take, as an example of the thinking of this period, the following quotation from the early work of Carl Kelsey (1903, 74), an empirical sociologist at the University of Pennsylvania.

> One of the most disasterous results of the years following the war was the alienation to so large a degree of the former masters and slaves. The negro respects and trusts the white as he does not a fellow negro. It would be a happy day for the negro if the white women of the South should again take a personal interest in his welfare. . . . In his favor also is that friendliness on the part of the white man, which leads him to prefer the negro as a workman under ordinary conditions.

In light of the attitudes of so many economists and sociologists of the late nineteenth and early twentieth centuries, one may reasonably wonder, as have David Levy and Sandra Peart in their contributions to this volume, if these sentiments were meaningfully different from the attitudes evinced by Thomas Carlyle, the early English anthropologists, and the cartoonists of *Punch* magazine. It is depressingly evident that despite all of the progress in empirical methods and data collection that took place in the late nineteenth and early twentieth centuries—along with the rise of the "modern" method of evolutionary economics, with its close attention to history and social structures—that the depiction of the character, abilities, and prospects of African-Americans in the literature of professional economists declined over these years.

Evolutionary Economics and the Property Rights Perspective: J. B. Clark and W. E. B. DuBois

Today's economists, correctly, associate John Bates Clark with being the first to develop the Marginal Product Theory of Distribution (Clark 1899).

Whatever perspective one takes on the coherence, implications, and meaning of that theory, history reveals that it was a lasting achievement. But Clark was more than an economic theorist. He was a deeply religious man, and his sense of moral obligation induced him to pursue a lifelong search for the "true principles" of social justice, along with the policies and social reforms that would best bring such a vision into everyday practice (Clark [1910] 2002; Prasch 2000).

While Clark did not write extensively on the question of race, what he did write on that subject was remarkably progressive when contrasted with his peers. To begin with, Clark dismissed the idea that blacks were biologically inferior, and he did so years before the major writings of the anthropologists Franz Boas and Alfred Kroeber made their appearance. Clark (1891, 95) noted: "A part of the difficulty lies, probably, in the Negro's psychology; but that is not so deeply rooted that it cannot be eradicated. It is not, at any rate, permanently in the blood."

This premise, in conjunction with his perspective on the economics of competition, led Clark to foresee a day (the great northern migration of blacks had yet to occur) when Southern blacks could earn enough to purchase their own farms, compete as equals, and then, on this material basis, aspire to full social and political equality with Southern whites. Perhaps naively, Clark believed that rivalry between the political parties would ultimately protect and even enhance the value of black suffrage.

> I expect in due time to see the Negro brought to the polls in a coach and four rather than see him repelled. I expect to see fullest suffrage given to him before, from mere education, he is ready for it. . . . The vote of the Negro who owns his farm will be a terror to nobody. It will be a source of safety to the republic as a whole. (Clark 1891, 95)

In short, Clark believed that the diffusion of property would be the ultimate foundation for the economic and social advancement of Southern blacks. Moreover, economic theory, as Clark understood it, was adequate to predict this optimistic, if then radical, outcome (Clark 1891).

Of course, Clark neither lived in nor conducted investigative fieldwork in the South. It is thus reasonable to suggest that his optimism, while refreshing, was somewhat ungrounded. He also cannot be blamed for failing to anticipate the hardening of the legal and social obstacles to economic and political advancement that were soon to be embodied in Southern institutions.

Indeed, historian Loren Schweninger has found evidence that would have supported Clark's conjectures. Schweninger records a surge in black home and farm ownership between 1870 and 1890 that then slows down in the 1890–1910 period. This is consistent with both Clark's optimism and the observation that the Jim Crow regime was formally consolidated during the latter period. Tellingly, while the percentage of blacks who owned their own homes continued to rise after 1877, the bulk of this rise was in the upper South and in urban areas. For example, in the upper South (Delaware, Washington, D.C., Kentucky, Maryland, Missouri, North Carolina, Tennessee, and Virginia), 6 percent of blacks not living on farms owned their own homes in 1870. This expands to 19 percent in 1890 and to 24 percent in 1910. The percentage clearly increases, but at a slower pace, after 1890 (Schweninger 1990, 180, table 19). In the lower South (Alabama, Arkansas, Florida, Georgia, Louisiana, Mississippi, South Carolina, and Texas), nonfarm home ownership was 3.1 percent in 1870, 22 percent in 1890, and 26 percent in 1910 (Schweninger 1990, 170, table 17). Here, the rate of growth was most dramatic during the Reconstruction years, and the rate of slowdown was also more pronounced with the consolidation of Jim Crow after 1890. Nevertheless, there was clear progress in home ownership across the South, if at a diminishing rate, despite the legal and social obstacles to black advancement.

The most striking results are to be found in the ownership of farms, which at this time was the most important capital asset in the predominantly agricultural South. Among black farm families in the upper South, 2.2 percent owned their own farms in 1870, 33 percent in 1890, and 44 percent in 1910 (Schweninger 1990, 174, table 18). But in this statistical story, the rate of black farm owners in the lower South stands out. Here, the percentages are 2 percent in 1870, 18 percent in 1890, 20 percent in 1900, and 19 percent in 1910 (Schweninger 1990, 164, table 16).[6]

In sum, the oppression exemplified by the spread of Jim Crow and disenfranchisement laws between 1900 and 1910 was able to slow down and even turn back black gains across much of the lower South. Judging from Schweninger's data, Florida, South Carolina, and Texas accounted for the greater part of this reduction. It is not a coincidence that the number of lynchings—essentially public extralegal executions—also peaked during these same years, and it is notorious that the deep South was particularly active in this regard. Overall, the dawn of the twentieth century was a period of retrogression in black-white relations. Undoubtedly, this retrogression represented a strong "push" factor behind the great migration of blacks, especially young black men, to northern cities. This migration became pronounced in the 1910s and continued through World War II, with some modest abatement during the Great Depression.

Clark was not alone in his view that the spread of economic independence and opportunity would eventually resolve the problem of race relations. Some prominent Southern blacks who were more fully cognizant of the specifics of the actual situation shared Clark's optimistic perspective. According to Booker T. Washington ([1895] 1965, 156), "No race that has anything to contribute to the markets of the world is long in any degree ostracized." But the merits of Clark's arguments aside, he stands out among his peers, including the other (all white and mostly male) distinguished presenters at the prominent First Mohonk Conference on the Negro Question, for his conjecture that blacks would soon enjoy economic and political opportunities equaling those of whites (Clark 1891).

Another progressive economist of this period was W. E. B. DuBois. While his doctorate from Harvard was officially in history, DuBois had previously completed all the requirements for a doctorate in political economy under Gustav Schmoller and Adolph Wagner at the University of Berlin (he did not receive the degree because the financial support for his studies was from a white-controlled foundation that denied his request for the additional funds that would have been necessary for him to meet the university's formal residency requirement). Not surprisingly, in light of this background, DuBois was steeped in the historical, empirical, and comparative method that was so characteristic of the German approach to political economy. His teachers' emphasis on detailed fieldwork and the inductive method are clearly evident in DuBois's first important book, *The Philadelphia Negro: A Social Study* (DuBois [1899b] 1973; Lewis 1993, chaps. 5–8). In an article related to that book, DuBois stresses the importance of a careful application of the inductive method: "the one positive answer which years of research and speculation have been able to return is that the phenomena of society are worth the most careful and systematic study" (DuBois 1898b, 1). Fieldwork, close observation, and a sustained effort to survey and measure the object of study, be it the black population of the Philadelphia ghetto or poor farmers in a Georgia or Virginia village, was, to DuBois, the necessary first step to a theoretical understanding of the plight of black Americans (DuBois 1898a, 1899a, 1901, 1906b, [1899b] 1973).

DuBois's contribution to an important symposium in the *American Economic Association* illustrates his evolutionary and inductive approach to social science (DuBois 1906a). While the conclusions and policies he proposed were, at that time in his life, not that far from Clark's, his method of research was very clearly different. His article summarized several earlier studies he conducted for the Bureau of Labor Statistics in which he traveled to, and passed a prolonged visit in, several black communities to gather information on the specifics of the situation. It follows that DuBois was cognizant of, and addressed, the prospects for landownership among Southern blacks in light of both white racism and other constraints faced by blacks, including poverty, legal hurdles, lack of savings, and difficulty accessing credit on reasonable terms (DuBois 1906a, 230–32).[7] It should also be noted that DuBois took pains to avoid writing as an activist or a partisan. He made a point of being brutally honest in his economic and social studies. For this reason, he stressed the role that illiteracy, ignorance—and especially ignorance of sound agricultural processes—along with other dysfunctional social pathologies, played in retarding black economic development (DuBois 1898b, 1906a, [1899b] 1973). In addition, the several studies DuBois solicited or directed on the behalf of Atlanta University confirm that DuBois ardently believed that a politically motivated revision of the black condition in white-dominated America would be both bad social science and a poor political strategy.

By contrast with much of the conventional wisdom of his day, especially that of Southerners, DuBois did not think that the plantation experience left black agriculturalists with much of an understanding of either modern or efficient farming processes. Conventional economic analysis supports his view, since the slave economy was premised on an artificially low cost of labor and on the ready availability of new, unexhausted farmland in the West. Commenting on its land-use practices, DuBois called the plantation form of Southern agriculture "land-murder." In his words (1906a, 231), "No graduate of that school knows how to make the desert bloom and the process of teaching must be long and tedious."

After remarking on the increased concentration of the most fertile land among fewer and fewer wealthy whites and on the ruthless exploitation of Southern blacks that was hardening under the conditions of tenancy, black ignorance, arbitrarily enforced property rights, prejudice, and exclusion from craft unions controlled by white skilled laborers, DuBois (1906a, 238) concluded, "The only future of these tenants which means salvation is landholding and this is coming slowly."[8]

Finally, and in contrast to Clark, DuBois saw the political disenfranchisement of Southern blacks as a development that would retard the economic possibilities of both blacks and the larger society. To DuBois, black disenfranchisement would impede the building of necessary infrastructure, such as schools and roads, while obstructing the development of a rational and universal property rights regime. In addition, disenfranchisement was conducive to the development of a biased and legally suspect judiciary. In sum, DuBois thought that the absence of voting rights for any large group of people must inevitably slow down the economic and social progress of the entire society—an argument that supporters of women's suffrage would later advance. As DuBois stated in his presentation to the American Economic Association (1906a, 241–42), "You can twist this matter up and down and apologize for it and reason it out—it's wrong, and unjust, and economically unsound, and you know it."

Institutional Economics

The beginning of the twentieth century was a period of great faith in the influence and benevolence of science along with the "scientific" approach. In an age that saw such marvels as moving pictures, electricity, telephones, and the automobile, there seemed to be very little that the organized intelligence of mankind could not overcome. These notions were not restricted to the sphere of engineering or the applied or natural sciences. What came to be known as the Progressive Era also saw a revolution in the application of the social sciences to social reform. The result was the rise of occupational medicine, scientific management, and social work as distinct fields of study and viable professions for trained scientists and experts (Hepler 2000, chaps. 1–3; Ehrenreich 1985, chaps. 1–3; Kanigel 1997).

In conjunction with the development of several new social sciences, this period saw the rise of a new school of economics—the institutionalist school—that tried to absorb and codify the best lessons of the evolutionary economists of the late nineteenth century, while reiterating, systematizing, and extending the empirical and inductive approach to economic research (Mitchell 1919; Hamilton 1919). In an effort to broaden the hypothesized motivations of people beyond the narrow motives of profit or utility maximization, institutionalists tried to incorporate more of the complexity of human behavior into their studies by examining the process of self-seeking in the context of the rise and decline of the various norms and social conventions that they collectively referred to as "institutions." In this sense, the institutionalists took culture to be an important condition for, and shaper of, economic success and failure.

When considering policy, institutionalists sought out rules that they believed would channel the competitive process into socially beneficial channels, such as improved technology or more efficient management, and away from socially detrimental channels (Commons and Andrews 1916; Clark [1926] 1939). It follows that the consistent theme that underlay such policies as minimum wages for women, child-labor restrictions, or maximum-hours laws was the quest for an improved framework for economic rivalry so as to enhance social efficiency and the quality of life (cf. Groat 1924; Seager 1913a, 1913b; Hutchinson 1919).

Contrary to the statements of some of their detractors among today's economists, the institutionalists were neither antitheoretical nor slavishly prolabor in their general orientation. While it is true that they often took a more interventionist stance in their choice of labor market policies relative to most adherents of the neoclassical school, these positions were neither based on ignorance nor unguided by economic theory. Rather, the institutionalists developed a set of concepts, and theories based on these concepts, that led many of them to conclude that a laissez-faire conception of the labor market was incomplete and even represented an inefficient and pernicious policy in practice. In sum, their theory was different, not absent (Rutherford 2000).

Even a cursory overview of the institutionalists' writings reveals that they did not take a sustained interest in the economics of race relations. When they did, it was usually to consider how blacks newly arrived from the South would affect the operation of modern labor markets. For example, John Commons examined the economic condition and prospects of African-Americans as a specific instance in the larger problem of immigration and the maintenance of standards in northern industrial labor markets (cf. Commons 1908, 1904). In a word, the economic problems of African-Americans were an afterthought to the institutionalists, as indeed, they were to most American economists of the early twentieth century. Since the institutionalist school came to its maturity during the period of the great migration of American blacks to northern cities, it is difficult to understand on purely intellectual grounds why the dynamics of racial inequality, conflict, and discrimination would be anything other than a compelling subject of research.[9]

In their joint contribution to this volume, O'Flaherty and Shapiro illustrate the hold that Darwinism had over theories of race in the United States at the dawn of the twentieth century. This perspective held sway over the public mind and that of many prominent educators and statesmen (cf. Klinkner and Smith 1999, 72–76). Given this intellectual milieu, permeated as it was by the "scientific ethos" of social Darwinism, it is not surprising, though it is still disappointing, to see a figure as important to American economics as John Commons present his uncharitable evaluation of the abilities, dispositions, and potential of black Americans. As with so many of his colleagues, much of his evidence derived from the work of Joseph Tillinghast (1902). The flavor of Commons's thinking is evident in the following quotation.

> Two circumstances, the climate and the luxuriant vegetation, render this region [the Central West Coast of Africa] hostile to continuous exertion. The torrid heat and the excessive humidity weaken the will and exterminate those who are too strenuous; but this same heat and humidity, with the fertile soil, produce unparalleled crops of bananas, yams, and grains. Thus nature conspires to produce a race indolent, improvident, and contented. (Commons 1908, 39)

Tillinghast's previously mentioned study remains the primary reference when Commons states that African-Americans "exhibit aversion to silence and solitude, love of rhythm, excitability and lack of reserve." His description of the characteristics of blacks included the now familiar litany of strong sexual appetites, lack of willpower, and impulsiveness (Commons 1908, 40). While Commons did reference several firsthand reports from the Atlanta University studies, as well as several additional sources, to ground some of his conclusions, he demonstrated an almost studied naïveté as to how whites and other powerful groups had resisted, and would continue to resist, black advancement. In addition, Commons got some facts grievously, embarrassingly wrong, such as his observation that blacks took no part in the Civil War (Commons 1908, 41).[10]

What makes Commons an improvement over some of his contemporaries, such as Richmond Mayo-Smith or Jeremiah Jenks, was his belief that slavery, rather than nature, had to bear the primary blame for suppressing the evolution of the qualities necessary for African-Americans to participate in the larger society and democracy: "The very qualities of intelligence and manliness which are essential for citizenship in a democracy were systematically expunged from the negro race through two hundred years of slavery" (Commons 1908, 41). In addition, Commons believed that universal education in the English language would allow all immigrants and minorities to eventually become upstanding citizens.

> To be great a nation need not be of one blood, it must be of one mind. Racial inequality and inferiority are fundamental only to the extent that they prevent mental and moral assimilation. If we think together, we can act together, and the organ of common thought and action is common language. . . . Race and heredity may be beyond our organized control; but the instrument of a common language is at hand for conscious improvement through education and social environment. (ibid., 20–21)

In matters of race, as in virtually every question dealing with economic policy and the law, Commons's approach was to call for gradual change. Sharing the conventional wisdom as it was then expressed by numerous influential early twentieth-century intellectuals, such as Charles Francis Adams, Commons criticized Northern abolitionists for having pressed for immediate and full citizenship for newly freed blacks. Instead, Commons stressed a program of education, self-help, and other improvements designed to inculcate improved morals, habits, and character. While he acknowledged the presence of white racism, the tenor of his writing suggests that he did not take this racism to be a fundamental constraint on either the life choices of African-Americans or their economic and social progress over time. He also questioned their drive to advance themselves, as when he commented on the paucity of blacks holding skilled positions in the Chicago meatpacking industry: "Notwithstanding the alleged favoritism towards the negroes, they have not advanced to the skilled positions, mainly because they dislike the long apprenticeship and steady work at low pay which lead to such positions" (Commons 1904, 30).

Finally, and of some importance to labor economics as it was then being theorized, Commons thought that blacks, like immigrants, were "accustomed" to a low level of subsistence. For this reason, they would work for a wage that represented a standard of subsistence that was lower than the wage that was necessary to support white Americans in their now customary standard of living.[11] Commons took this sociological "fact" to be a competitive advantage for black and immigrant labor that would make each of these groups more attractive to employers and, he thought, less likely to feel aggrieved by low wages or poor working conditions. He also perceived that conflicts and tensions between the races, in addition to those between the several immigrant communities, would continue to present firms with a bargaining advantage, since they reduced workplace solidarity, as he himself had witnessed in the 1904 Chicago stockyard strike (Commons 1904; Norwood 2002, chap. 3; Tuttle 1969).

As noted, for the most part, institutionalists ignored the economics of race, but there were several important exceptions. One example was Scott Nearing, who was soon to abandon his ill-fated academic career to pursue a pastoral life in Vermont and then Maine. In 1929, Nearing published a vigorous defense of the rights of black Americans as full citizens (Nearing 1929). While the statistical analysis featured in Nearing's book was heavily reliant on secondary sources, and in this way fell short of the standard that had established his academic reputation as an empirical researcher, it presented, in strong contrast to the work of many of his former academic colleagues, both a clear hostility toward racism and his support for equality of opportunity. Chapters in his book covered a range of topics, including rural tenancy, northern residential segregation, life on the job, lynching, and political disenfranchisement. Anticipating the analysis that radical economists were to offer later in the century, Nearing located the root cause of these several calamities in the collective self-interest of white elites. In short, Nearing's book presented a joint indictment of racism and the structure of the American market economy.

A more academically oriented, yet still radical, institutionalist analysis of the economics of race was presented in a book that emerged in 1931 from Columbia University—then one of the centers of American, and institutionalist, economic research. This was Sterling D. Spero and Abram L. Harris's *The Black Worker: The Negro and the Labor Movement*, which was originally presented as the authors' joint doctoral thesis. Spero's chapters were presented for a doctorate degree in political science, and Harris's chapters earned him a doctorate in economics (Harris's degree was only the second doctorate in economics to be awarded to an African-American in the United States). Though their analysis of the political economy of American race relations was not that different from Nearing's, their style certainly was. Spero and Harris's book presented several case studies of the interaction between black workers and white-dominated industries. Separate chapters present a detailed history and assessment of the situation faced by black workers as longshoremen, coal miners, steelworkers, stockyard workers, and railroad workers. The point was to discern patterns behind the dynamics of integration, unionization, and exclusion. While Spero and Harris acknowledged the role that blacks periodically played as strikebreakers, they attributed this choice to ignorance and the long-standing antagonism between black and white labor, dating back to the days of slavery (Spero and Harris [1931] 1972, chap. 7). They also advanced a structural reason for the friction between black and white labor. In their view, blacks served as an "industrial reserve" of labor. This idea, read in the light of several of Harris's early essays, is almost certainly a reference to a Marxian perspective on how the labor market functions (Darity 1989a; Harris 1989). Spero and Harris ([1931] 1972) concurred with Nearing that the true long-term interests of the working class, black and white, depended on the development of labor coalitions that could reach across the color line.

Spero and Harris also placed some of the blame for racist tensions—and, consequently, for the difficult labor market problems faced by blacks—on what they saw as the misguided, if influential, advice of black intellectuals and church leaders in urging black workers to participate in strikebreaking. In their discussion of this issue, Spero and Harris ([1931] 1972, chap. 8) mentioned certain persons by name and presented quotations from published speeches and articles to make their case. One prominent proponent of strikebreaking discussed in the book was Kelly Miller, a colleague of Harris's at Howard University. Miller (1906) took the position that capitalists, some out of benevolence and others out of a search for savings on the cost of labor, would better represent the interests of black workers than any quixotic search for an alliance with, much less hope for admission to, white-dominated trade unions. In retrospect, part of what made Spero and Harris's narrative so interesting is that one could almost read the several detailed studies they present as a brief for Miller's contention that integration into white unions was close to hopeless. Yet despite the dismal record up until then, Spero and Harris ([1931] 1972, chap. 2) maintained that the long-term interests of labor, black and white, depended on the formation of cross-racial alliances.

Gunnar Myrdal and the Beginnings of the Postwar Revival of Interest in the Economics of Race and Discrimination

The economic plight of African-Americans was remarkably understudied over the several decades from 1910 to 1940, especially when contrasted with the more frequent, if more consistently racist, writings of the 1890s and 1900s. In such a context, Gunnar Myrdal's treatise *An American*

Dilemma: The Negro Problem and Modern Democracy (1944), although not
written by an American, was that much more visible and exciting. Here
was the case of a notable European monetary theorist making a substantial
contribution to an understudied problem with a massive and, by the standard of the times, strikingly progressive two-volume tome.

While these volumes were highly descriptive, their major theoretical
argument drew on an important concept that had been a hallmark of
Myrdal's earlier work in monetary economics: cumulative causation
(Myrdal [1939] 1962). In *An American Dilemma*, he joined his idea of
cumulative causation to the evolutionary and empirical tradition already
in widespread use among American economists. Almost single-handedly,
Myrdal and his research associates were able to reinvigorate the economic
analysis of race and discrimination. Both as a monetary economist and in
his theory of the economics of race, Myrdal's core idea was that social systems do not necessarily feature unique and inherently stable equilibriums
that can be fully analyzed through the time-honored approach of comparative statics. On the contrary, Myrdal argued that social structures adjust
like monetary systems, in that they create both new realities and revised
expectations even as the adjustment process unfolds, thereby changing the
underlying structure of the system (Myrdal [1944] 1962, vol. 1, chap. 3,
sec. 7; vol. 2, app. 3). In this insight, he was ahead of his own time, as models that incorporate such dynamics are only now becoming increasingly
prominent in the writings of economists on the subject of race and discrimination (cf. Andrews 1999; Loury 2002).

Myrdal argued that a widely held perspective on the nature of things—
even if that perspective were incorrect—could push a system in one way or
another, which, in turn, would set in motion a variety of secondary adjustments between and among the various subgroups and other actors within
the system. The result may be an outcome far removed from and seemingly
unrelated to the initial cause. When the dynamics that emerge represent a
continuing cycle of activity that moves the social system further and further from a socially desirable outcome, this process is termed a *vicious circle*. For example, Myrdal states that white prejudice has stifled black ambitions and left them, on the whole, in a condition of poverty that includes
low levels of health, education, and workplace efficiency. This condition,
in turn, affects the attitudes, expectations, and behavior of African-Americans—rendering them less accomplished and capable as measured by both
objective and subjective criteria. These learned behaviors, in turn,
"confirm" the initial prejudices of whites, thereby validating and even

contributing to the initial prejudices of whites in an ongoing vicious circle (Myrdal [1944] 1962, 1:75).

Myrdal's detailed narrative maintained that African-Americans had been caught in just such a vicious circle for some time. For this reason, he thought that it would take more than a simple change in policy, even if forcefully applied, to change the status, opportunities, and expectations of African-Americans. Myrdal believed that a solution would require, initially, a careful and detailed understanding of the system, its interrelations, and its dynamic tendencies. Myrdal was confident that once the situation was properly understood in its constitutive and theoretical parts, the social system could be reconstituted in a manner more consistent with American ideals. He proposed, perhaps optimistically, that a relatively small change in several key variables could work with and through the cumulative social processes that were already inherent in the system. For this reason, argued Myrdal ([1944] 1962, 2:1070), "A rational strategy in the Negro problem also assumes a theory of dynamic causation." Perhaps more implausibly, Myrdal (1:76–77) also believed that, done properly, these changes could occur at relatively low cost.

Gary Becker and the Canonical Neoclassical Model

It is widely agreed that, with the exception of a short article by Francis Y. Edgeworth on women's wages, Gary Becker is the person most responsible for codifying the neoclassical approach to the economics of discrimination (Becker 1971; Edgeworth 1922). Soon after its original publication in 1957, Becker's book *The Economics of Discrimination* became the conventional starting point for virtually all of the surveys and discussions of the economics of discrimination that would be written over the next several decades (cf. Marshall 1974; Wolff 1997, chap. 12; Kaufman 1994, chap. 9).

Becker's neoclassical perspective on the economics of discrimination is best introduced with a thought experiment, the structure of which will be familiar to teachers (and students) of introductory microeconomics. Suppose we posit a perfectly competitive economy that assumes

1. many small firms, none of which are large enough to influence market prices;
2. a standardized (homogeneous) product;

3. complete freedom of entry and exit into the market;
4. free and costless movement of productive resources, including technologies, capital, and labor across the economy; and
5. perfect information on the part of all participants with regard to
   prices, production processes, and the location of competing opportunities.

Logic dictates that in such a scenario, economic discrimination, in the
sense of a refusal by one or even many businesses to hire an otherwise
qualified individual or set of individuals of a particular race, religion, or
gender at the market wage, must be a momentary phenomenon. The reason behind this strong conclusion is that any discriminating firm will of
necessity be denying itself the use of the talents and abilities of a portion
of the available labor pool. The preceding assumptions collectively affirm
that those discriminated against will be able either (i) to work at other,
nondiscriminating firms or (ii) to turn to perfectly and costlessly operating
capital and technology markets to borrow funds with which to start their
own firms. The worst-case scenario that could result in the preceding
thought experiment would be the emergence of highly segregated workplaces, but each group, both those who are discriminated against and those
who are not, would experience full employment at equal wages.

This, then, is the result that should emerge if we lived in a perfectly
competitive neoclassical world. In light of the preceding analysis, Gary
Becker set out to examine the economics of discrimination while making
minimal adjustments to this core model. Again, the project was to understand discrimination while working within the framework of neoclassical
economics, which was then rapidly ascendant within the American economics establishment. While his methodological commitments were
attractive to Becker's many supporters, it must be made clear that they
ruled out, categorically, the possibility that discrimination could be caused
by a persistent failure in the market itself. In other words, any observed discrimination could only be an artifact of some premarket preference, condition, or constraint.

It is important to reiterate this last point. Becker's argument did not
prove that the market mechanism could not be a contributing factor;
rather, it ruled out this possibility a priori through the premises of the theory. Since neoclassical models usually presume that the economic system
is a fully functioning competitive model, it follows that any lingering discrimination must be the result of some extramarket restriction, condition,

or preference. In a neoclassical model, the market cannot be an independent cause or contributor to any social pathology (Levine 1980).

To illustrate his model, Becker worked through three cases wherein
economic actors exhibit and act on a "taste for discrimination."[12] This
taste can be held and acted on by a majority group—say, whites—in their
several roles as owners of firms, workers, or customers. In each case, the
discriminating group acts to maximize its utility, rather than pursuing the
more narrow goal of maximizing profits, wages, or, in the case of customers,
the lowest prices. In each case, prejudiced and discriminating persons—in
this case, whites—perceive their interaction with the persons discriminated against to be, to some degree, distasteful, such that they require a
higher than average reward to induce them to hire, work with, or buy from
African-Americans.

To illustrate the major themes of Becker's theory, I will review the case
in which firms are hiring workers. Let us begin by supposing that only
members of the majority group—in this case, whites—own businesses. Let
us also suppose that all workers, black and white, are of identical ability.
Moreover, let us further suppose that minority workers—in this case,
blacks—have no assets of their own, so they must obtain employment
from someone to earn their "daily bread." Finally, let us assume that some,
but not all, white employers are biased against blacks and that those dis-
playing this "taste for discrimination" will only hire blacks if they can pay
reduced wages, that is, wages below what the productivity of black workers
would otherwise command in a free and fair market. Finally, the size of the
demanded wage discount will vary with the intensity of the prejudice felt
by each individual employer and is zero in the case of nondiscriminating
employers.

In figure 1, I present these ideas in the form of a standard graph of the
labor market, illustrating the supply-and-demand curves for black labor.
Notice that the wage for black workers (W_b), presented as a ratio of the
wages of equally capable white workers (W_w), would be equal to the latter—such that $W^* = 1$—in the event that there is no discrimination. This
condition holds (i) if there are only a few blacks seeking employment or
(ii) if there are many nondiscriminating employers in the market, a condition illustrated by supply curve 1 (S_1).

When all positions at nondiscriminating employers are filled, black
workers must begin to accept positions at discriminating employers. Black
workers will, rationally, seek out the least discriminating employer, since
they will search for the smallest possible discount on their wages when

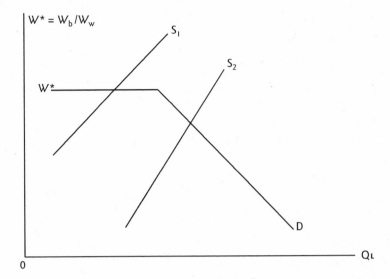

FIG. 1. The market for black laborers

accepting a position. When the least discriminating jobs are filled, black workers will then turn to the next least discriminating employer, and so on, until everyone is employed. Other black workers, discouraged by the low wages now offered, will abandon the labor market (supply curve 2 [S_2]). In this case, W^* is now less than unity, indicating that black labor is paid less than white labor as a result of this discrimination. Since we are assuming a perfectly competitive market in which the wages of all the (presumed homogeneous) black workers must be identical, it follows that in the presence of effective wage discrimination, the wages of all black workers must fall. It also follows that nondiscriminating employers will enjoy a windfall profit associated with their hiring black employees, while the most prejudiced employer who actually hires black employees will be just satisfied with his hiring decision. To the latter, the reduced wage he is able to offer will just offset the perceived "disutility" from hiring black workers.

Again, all black workers, regardless of the kind of firm they are associated with, will be paid less than their white counterparts, because of a core proposition of neoclassical economic theory—the law of one price—that holds that all equivalent commodities or labor services must trade at an equal price in a perfectly competitive market. How far black wages will fall depends on the supply of black workers relative to the number of positions at nondiscriminating employers and on how rapidly the wage discount rises as a consequence of the "tastes" of discriminating employers. A larger supply of black workers relative to the number of nondiscriminating employers means that many black workers will have to work for increasingly prejudiced employers. Again, this fact reduces not only their own wage but the wages of all black workers. Finally, for this theory to work, we must make the counterintuitive assumption that the productivity of black employees will not be reduced through low morale or a reduced willingness to invest in their own job skills, education, and so on in response to the fact that their wage is less than the wage being paid to their white coworkers for the same quality of service.[13]

The dynamics of Becker's model indicate that when white employers indulge a "taste for discrimination," they simultaneously create an inefficient allocation of society's labor resources. Specifically, if we assume that the supply of all workers, black or white, is a positive function of the rate of wages, we must conclude that less labor will be supplied to the market in the event of effective discrimination on the part of some owners. This implies an excess of "leisure" for black workers and less total output for firms and the economy as a whole.

Happily, the behavior of discriminating owners creates a profitable opportunity for the owners of nondiscriminating firms—including start-up firms. To understand this, suppose we introduce a perfect, nondiscriminatory capital market into the preceding model. In such a case, black workers now have the option to "opt out" of a labor market dominated by white owners—a market wherein wages are determined by the most prejudiced of white owners—and start their own firms. Presumably, this will occur until all black workers either are owners or work for other blacks or nondiscriminating whites who have become owners of firms. In this event, Becker's theory would predict the emergence of a highly segregated economy—albeit one in which everyone would have access to the same levels of wages and opportunities for employment. While such segregation may remain a lingering social problem, at least the economic effects of discrimination would no longer be present in the take-home pay of black workers.[14]

A second modification of this model, related to the first, has to do with mobility. If workers could "exit"—as occurred with the onset of the great migration of blacks, especially young black men, from the South to the northern states—wages could rise until blacks achieved equality with whites.[15] Once again, the model predicts that highly segregated workplaces would be the likely outcome but that discrimination in take-home wages would be diminished or even cease.

Finally, nondiscriminating firms earning above-market rates of profit, who do not require these above-market returns to overcome a "psychic" barrier to hiring qualified black workers, would have an opportunity to reinvest their additional profits and thereby to expand the size of their operations. The result would be an expansion of the nondiscriminating sector relative to the discriminating sector of the labor market, because discriminating employers, who require above-market rates of return to overcome their "distaste" for hiring blacks, would not perceive these extra returns to be a "market signal" to expand the size of their operations. Hence, Becker's model predicts a diminished market share for discriminating employers. Over time, only a few discriminating employers would be able to compete while employing an all-white workforce, while other discriminating employers may even be driven from the market by the more efficient, nondiscriminating firms (more efficient because they can recruit from a larger labor pool and are willing to continue operations with a lower level of profit).

Becker's model stood out for its optimism and, specifically, for its suggestion that the market mechanism, if given full reign, would eventually erode the effects of discrimination. Workers of all races could expect equal treatment in the market, even if they end up in segregated workplaces. Interestingly, Becker himself presented some data suggesting that the status of black workers was changing rather slowly (Becker 1971, appendix, table 16). While he did not directly make this argument in his book, the implication that best followed from his model was that the persistence of discrimination affirmed either that there were monopolistic tendencies in the market or that government rules had lessened competitive forces (Becker 1971, chap. 3). Again, the inference that consistently emerged was that more, not less, competition was needed to end the effects of discrimination. Commenting on government rule-making to assist minorities, Becker observed, "In the United States, the evidence provided by the states with such [fair employment] legislation suggests that it somewhat increases both the earnings and unemployment of minorities" (Becker 1968, 210; Friedman 1962, chap. 7; Sowell 1981b, chaps. 3–4).

To recap, Gary Becker's neoclassical model indicated that market forces protected workers subjected to discrimination by providing substantial alternative options even as competition reduced the profit and market share of discriminating firms. Becker argues that the more competitive the market, the stronger these ameliorative forces would be, and the more rapidly would wages and opportunities converge. Becker did allow that monopolies, especially those created, assisted, or protected by government policies, might be able to sustain discriminatory hiring practices over time. By extension, other anticompetitive restrictions, such as union wage-setting policies, fair-employment legislation, or a legislated minimum wage, would also inhibit the ability of discriminated-against persons to enter the labor market. According to those who consider the economics of such policies from Becker's perspective, such well-intentioned laws prevent minorities from undermining the economic position of privileged workers and discriminating firms by using the greatest instrument at the disposal of any poorly treated worker—a willingness to provide as good or better labor services for a reduced cost. Becker and his followers maintain that the willingness of minority persons to do more for less would rapidly undermine discriminating institutions because it appeals to the most corrosive power at work in a market economy—the profit motive. Drawing on this neoclassical perspective, economists of a "Chicago" orientation have consistently objected to market interventions "on the behalf" of those who have been discriminated against. In their view, such policies inevitably present a barrier to entry that, perversely, enables discrimination to persist. Moreover, they have argued, when such policies are targeted at unskilled or youthful minorities, they become an even more pernicious palliative (cf. Kosters and Welch 1972; Moore 1971; Sowell 1977).

Four Approaches to Modifying or Overturning
the Neoclassical Theory of Discrimination

Not all economists were persuaded by Becker's approach. Specifically, some were doubtful of its accuracy in light of the persistence of wage and employment inequality and other discriminatory practices despite America's history of largely free labor markets. But this disagreement could not take any form. As I have already mentioned, in the postwar period, the mainstream of American economists were increasingly attracted to the neoclassical approach to economics, with its highly analytical form and its penchant for tidy and mathematical resolutions to problems (Bernstein 2001; Weintraub 2002). Put another way, American economists of the 1960s and 1970s faced an interesting dilemma: if they were (pre)committed to the neoclassical approach to the analysis of markets, the seeming coexistence of a (relatively) free market economy and persistent discrimination presented something of a conundrum. Essentially, four explanatory strategies presented themselves as ways to resolve this tension.

The first was advanced by the defenders of Becker's theory. They questioned whether the data, especially highly aggregated data, did in fact reveal a pattern of persistent discrimination, or whether convergence was actually occurring—even if at a frustratingly slow pace. If the latter was indeed the case, one could conclude that Becker's theory was essentially correct and that the best policy would be to increase the competitiveness of the economy or, at a minimum, "stay the course."

Few reasonable people in the social sciences argue with the idea that we could benefit from more or better data. In addition, all social scientists would readily agree that overly aggregated data may inadvertently overrepresent or underrepresent the strength or persistence of discrimination. For example, when comparing labor market outcomes across races, it is reasonable to hold constant such variables as age, education levels, experience, family structure, urban-rural residence, and so on. Doing so will undoubtedly lead to a more accurate estimate of the unexplained wage differences, due to discrimination or other causes, that remain in the labor market. Nevertheless, when holding these variables constant, a clear and persistent difference in earnings remains (Darity and Mason, this volume; Mason 1995, 1999a, 1999b, 2000). Moreover, the substantial increases in educational attainment by blacks since the mid-1960s have failed to induce an equally marked change in levels of remuneration or rates of employment relative to whites (*Economic Report of the President* 2002, table B-33). So, researchers must ask, is a variable missing? Is some variable being mismeasured?

A second explanation that directly addresses the fact of persistent differences in economic success is culture. To explore this possibility, economist Thomas Sowell has studied the comparative pace of assimilation across several distinct ethnic groups and concluded that cultural factors were a critical determinant of the relative speed of acculturation and economic success experienced by different ethnic groups in America (Sowell 1981a). For example, Sowell examined the percentage of children across several ethnic groups being raised in two-parent households and found large differences across them, including between groups that shared a common religious heritage, such as Irish and Italian immigrants. He argued that a pattern of broken families and other dysfunctional cultural norms or characteristics has slowed the acculturation, and therefore the economic progress, of certain ethnic groups—including African-Americans (Sowell 1981a).

Sowell advanced another comparison that he took to be particularly indicative of his culture hypothesis. This was his observation that persons of Afro-Caribbean descent were assimilating much more quickly than African-Americans. Yet, Sowell pointed out, both groups shared an ethnic heritage in Africa, the economic and social disadvantage of a background in slavery, and a similar physical appearance in the eyes of potentially prejudiced employers, coworkers, and customers. Sowell argued that the distinct difference in the economic progress between these two groups undermined the proposition that discrimination and a heritage of slavery are the crucial determinants of the economic status of African-Americans (Sowell 1981a, chap. 8).[16]

Simply put, Sowell argued that "culture matters" and that some cultures are more readily adapted to success in a market economy than others. Specifically, Sowell concluded that a strong peasant culture is poorly suited to success in a market-based urban location. The reason is that peasants are generally suspicious of education (especially education provided by "outsiders"), risk-averse with regard to entrepreneurship, and less likely to achieve high savings rates. Collectively, these traits are an obstacle to economic success. Sowell thinks that such attitudes were particularly prevalent among immigrants of Irish (1840s and 1850s), southern Italian, and African-American descent (he dates the African-American "immigration" to the internal migrations of the 1920s through the 1940s). He contrasts these adjustment experiences with that of Jewish and Japanese immigrants, who were more culturally prepared for the educational and social requirements of a modern industrial and market-driven economy. Indeed, in several ways, Sowell's argument is reminiscent of the arguments of the evolutionary economists and institutionalists described earlier in this chapter, albeit without the racist attitudes that marred too many of their writings (Sowell 1981a).

Examined from this perspective, Sowell argued that it takes somewhat longer to adjust the ideas, ideals, outlooks, and values of a peasant culture to those required for success in an urban, capitalist, and competitive environment. He points to the old stereotypes of the Irish, partially grounded in observable behaviors, such as a higher incidence of public intoxication, a reputation for sharp tempers, fearsome gangs, and disintegrating families. He observed that we no longer associate these qualities with the Irish. Sowell suggests that in time we would no longer associate such qualities with African-Americans either if the normal, albeit wrenching, processes of assimilation and the cultural adjustment that accompanies it were allowed to unfold. His concern was that modern social policies, by providing economic support for dysfunctional behaviors, had the undesirable effect of slowing the adjustment of premarket attitudes and cultures toward more functional norms and practices. This position provides the foundation of Sowell's criticism of the modern welfare state (Sowell 1981a).[17]

A third response to Becker was grounded in both the neoclassical tradition and the literature on the economics of information that came into vogue in the early 1970s. It was proposed at virtually the same time by Kenneth Arrow, Edmund Phelps, and Joseph Stiglitz in the early 1970s. In several independently authored essays, they developed innovative, but somewhat complex, analyses of the potentially adverse effects of imperfect information in otherwise perfectly functioning labor markets (Arrow 1973; Phelps 1972; Stiglitz 1973).

Their essays posed the following inquiry: in light of the remarkable cultural and legal changes that took place during the civil rights era, and assuming highly competitive markets, suppose that discrimination is no longer an important factor in hiring decisions. It would then be the case, they argued, that relative productivity and ability would be the crucial determinants of who got hired. If we also posited imperfect information, it would be reasonable to conjecture that a worker's inherent ability might be either expensive or impossible to access in the course of a regular job interview. What remains is a state of imperfect information concerning the relative ability of several applicants for any given jobs. Theorists of imperfect information argued that such a common market imperfection could have a lasting importance and effect on market processes. They observed that such a market imperfection could lead to an economically rational, if socially perverse, practice that has come to be known in the literature as *statistical discrimination*. This literature suggests that in a world of imperfect labor markets some readily observable physical characteristic of a person could act as a "signal" to employers in the event that the gathering of "true" information about the abilities or disposition of individual workers was prohibitively expensive. Schwab (1986, 228) explains, "Statistical discrimination differs from the classic taste-for-discrimination model in assuming no prejudice or invidious motive by employers or employees, but rather that employers use average characteristics of groups to predict individual worker attributes."

Kenneth Arrow argued that profit-making firms might make the inference, whether warranted or not, that a worker's race is the cheapest way to judge a given worker's underlying abilities and qualities and hence the worker's suitability for a particular job. In such a case, the employer, lacking specific information, treats each worker as if his or her individual ability was equal to the employer's current estimate of the average ability of the worker's race. In such a case, employers would be inclined to hire predominantly from the group that they believed had the superior average ability—in this case, workers of European descent (Arrow 1973).

A modification that makes the preceding approach even more interesting is the possibility that the discriminated-against workers, knowing that they are less likely to be selected for the highest paying jobs, may now be inclined, on the basis of an economically rational calculation of their life chances, to underinvest in education and other skill-enhancing activities when the labor market features widespread imperfect information and statistical discrimination. The final result would be a new equilibrium in which the initial expectations of employers, whether correct or incorrect, are actually affirmed by the tendency of the discriminated-against workers to underinvest in skills and education as a rational response to discrimination. Commenting on Arrow's approach, Berkeley economist Michael Reich (1981, 104–5) noted, "If the employer's belief that race is associated with low productivity is false, a feedback mechanism may nonetheless set up a self-fulfilling prophesy that will confirm that belief."

Happily, the situation with regard to most African-Americans is not as dire as the preceding reasoning might suggest. Approaching the question from different starting points, Thomas Sowell and Marcellus Andrews have each pointed out that the direct evidence, both in school attendance and in rising test scores, indicates that the predicted underinvestment in the enhancement of one's education and skills seems not to be happening. In fact, young African-Americans are staying in school longer, and their scholastic performance is converging on that of other ethnic groups, including whites (Andrews 1999, chap. 1; Sowell 1981b).

In addition, Sowell and Reich have each challenged one of the core assumptions of the statistical discrimination story: the suggestion that it is prohibitively expensive to assess the relevant underlying characteristics of a job applicant and that, for that reason, statistical discrimination may be the result of a distasteful, but nevertheless profitable, market strategy on the part of firms. Sowell and Reich have each argued that a clear incentive will exist for maverick firms or managers to challenge the conventional assessment and to hire and train black workers. Drawing on the theory of competitive markets, Sowell observes that "those transactors with more accurate assessments would gain a competitive advantage over those more blinded by prejudice or inertia." Indeed, "the more competitive the market, the more the costs approach a prohibitive level" (Sowell 1981b, 28). Writing from a very different political position, Michael Reich concurs with Sowell: "The statistical-discrimination and signaling arguments require very strong assumptions about the unobservability of individual abilities" (Reich 1981, 105).

Finally, several economists have proposed a fourth response to Becker that I will collectively label the "structural theory" of discrimination. This approach has taken a number of forms, and some authors, for sound reasons, may object to having their views presented together under a single category. Keeping this reservation in mind, I will nevertheless maintain that what I call structural theories share several broad characteristics. One is the proposition that for some reason—it varies across authors—the labor market is segmented by race, gender, class, caste, and so on and that some powerful group (or groups) both is able to profit by this fact and acts so as to make this fact somewhat permanent in an otherwise competitive market economy.

The reasons offered for the segmentation of the labor market are various, with entrenched racist attitudes and openly practiced discrimination often listed. A posited ability of unions or others to control the number and quality of apprentices is another; entrenched hiring and promotion practices by firms may be another; and so on. The neoclassical economists discussed earlier were well aware of all of these problems. What makes the structural theory different is that it also hypothesizes that the observed labor market discrimination is persistent because some group (or groups) achieves, and is able to sustain, direct gains from discrimination. For that reason, these same influential parties have a direct interest and incentive to ensure that racist attitudes and the consequent market segmentation are maintained. Typically, structuralist theories posit a "dual" labor market. Privileged workers (in this case, whites) dominate the primary market, which is thought to provide better wages, benefits, and working conditions. A posited secondary market is less desirable and, because of barriers to entry into the primary labor market, is thought to be overcrowded with unlucky or unskilled whites and virtually all minority workers regardless of skill.

Drawing broadly from the characteristics of the dual labor market hypothesis, Anne Krueger (1963), Michael Reich (1981), and Barbara Bergmann (1971, 1974) each proposed models in which privileged white workers accrue, at least over the short term, a tangible gain from collaborating or colluding in the exclusion of black (and women) workers from the primary labor market. In essence, they form a cartel to pursue and maintain the collective economic reward to be had from the continuing exclusion of otherwise qualified black workers. In each of these models, black workers are largely excluded from jobs in the primary labor market. It follows that the supply of labor in the secondary labor market is artificially high, while the supply of labor in the primary labor market is now artificially low. In such a case, the wages earned in the primary labor market will remain higher than the wages in the secondary labor market, although everyone continues to earn at a rate where their wage is equal to their marginal product. Because of restrictions on labor mobility, wages nevertheless remain higher for workers in the primary labor market than for those who are consigned to the secondary labor market. Again, this is true independently of a worker's education, inherent productivity, work ethic, or any other personal characteristic. Another implication is that society's labor resources are misallocated and that efficiency and output are reduced for the economy as a whole. How severe this misallocation is depends on several measured "elasticities" that, in turn, are a function of the slopes of the labor supply and demand schedules in each of these submarkets. A third implication is that workers relegated to the secondary job market face a reduced incentive to cultivate additional skills, advance their own educations, or maintain an outstanding work ethic, given that they cannot reap the full reward of such investments. Once again, we would have a case of a self-fulfilling prophesy at work in a labor market where discrimination is the norm.

However, this misallocation does not imply that all individuals will perceive their situation as being worse off. There are two clear groups of "winners." First, workers in the primary sector have a direct monetary interest in continued discrimination (Bergmann 1971; Glenn 1963). Second, employers in the secondary sector also have an interest in the status quo, since they enjoy access to a larger workforce and can produce more output at less wages per unit of labor.[18] The difficult cases, and the ones whose persistence has to be explained, is that of firms in the primary market and undervalued workers in the secondary market.

If the structural explanation of persistent discrimination sketched in the preceding paragraphs is to make sense, it is necessary to appeal to some facts or conditions external to the model itself to explain these two difficult cases. In defense of such models, the necessary conditions they posit are not inherently implausible in light of the broad outline of American history. As a thought experiment, suppose that the losses incurred by employers in the primary market were not too large, perhaps because they are capital-intensive producers anyway or have become capital-intensive as a rational response to their artificially high wage bill. It might also be the case that primary-sector firms value the lower turnover costs that they experience with higher wages. Lower turnover may allow such firms an opportunity to invest more heavily in its staff and to promote from within (Wolff 1997, 451; Dickens and Lang 1993). Moreover, suppose the costs associated with changing the institutional arrangements of the labor market—for example, by challenging a strong primary-sector craft union—were rather high (descriptively, this is similar to the situation that Sterling Spero and Abram Harris described in 1931). To complete our scenario, we could readily imagine a situation wherein the losses experienced by those workers crowded into secondary labor markets are not capable of being registered, because of the disenfranchisement of these workers, because of the degeneration of their skills, abilities, or morale as a rational response to their situation, or because of a learned passivity or acceptance of "their place." In such a situation, the pressures to change this system would be modest relative to the strength of those interested in maintaining the status quo, and we would have a sustainable "equilibrium" of sorts, in which a clearly discriminating situation can persist.

Michael Reich (1981, 97) was correct to observe, "The argument that blacks are restricted from some occupations does not explain how this restriction takes place, who enforces it, and why." But in the case of race and discrimination, it is exactly these extramarket and extratheoretical factors that have played such important roles historically. It follows that structural models can be of use when we examine cases in which certain labor markets have been restricted by law or widespread social practices, as actually occurred across the nineteenth and early twentieth centuries in the United States. In the northern states, union agreements, social norms, and periodically legal restraints were sufficient. In the South, social norms were reinforced by Jim Crow legislation and by periodic episodes of lawlessness on the part of whites (Litwack 1998; Earle 2000, 98–99).

Conclusion

In this historical chapter, it is not my task to address the current state of the now enormous economics literature on race and discrimination. Indeed, one might plausibly suggest that the existence of this literature is itself evidence of an erosion in the harshness and degree of discrimination in America. It is also evident that American economics has itself undergone several significant changes since the end the period surveyed in this chapter. The most important is a significant increase in the number of African-Americans employed in academia, specifically as economists. While complacency is not in order, it is worthwhile to note the contrast between the situation today and that of 1936 when, even if we account for all disciplines, there was a total of three African-American Ph.D.s employed in all of the white-dominated universities in America (Sowell 1981b, 47). The style and content of research within the academy, especially research on the history, meaning, and effects of race and discrimination, cannot help but change after the substantial demographic shift of the last few decades.

One hundred years of writing by economists on race has revealed a wide diversity of theories on the cause, context, importance, and meaning of race and discrimination to the functioning of American labor markets and the distribution of income and opportunity. While the methods and the content of the economics of race and discrimination have certainly changed over these one hundred years, these changes have largely taken place at the level of ideas. At no point was a "crucial experiment" or "compelling proof" put forward that could provide a complete refutation or confirmation of a particular theory or approach to this issue. What has changed is society itself. Social scientists, being a part of this larger society, have clearly changed along with the society in which they live and work and on which they depend for their inspirations, ideas, and livelihoods. It has been said that each generation must write its own histories. Perhaps it is also the case that each generation must rethink and write its own theories of the political economy of race and discrimination.

NOTES

1. As I will show, the insights of African-American economists have periodically informed the larger economics profession and shaped some of its conclusions. However, I would like to reemphasize that this chapter is concerned with

the mainstream of economic thought in that English-speaking country that has, historically, been most immediately confronted with the dilemma of race and its implications—the United States. Because African-Americans have been substantially underrepresented in American elite circles, including the ranks of prominent professions, such as economics and its related disciplines, their contributions have been underrepresented in mainstream deliberations and consequently are underrepresented in the body of material surveyed in this chapter.

2. The role of race and liberal political ideology in the early formation of economic theory is the subject of the first part of this volume.

3. One of history's ironies is that with the end of Reconstruction, Southern whites had even more influence in the halls of Congress than before the Civil War. Each black person now counted as a full person—as opposed to three-fifths of a person under slave status—with regard to the apportionment of congressional seats, yet black people still could not vote. It follows that Southern whites were even more overrepresented in the Congress and the electoral college at the end of the nineteenth century than at the beginning. It is not surprising, even if it is still disappointing, to see that most politicians with national ambitions catered to these realities.

4. While Degler classifies these persons as sociologists, the distinction between economists and sociologists at this time could be a fine one. For example, Ross was trained as an economist, and Frank Giddings, while a sociologist, published a book with John Bates Clark on the economics of income distribution (Clark and Giddings 1888).

5. Not surprisingly, DuBois (1908) was critical of Stone's recommendation of continued segregation.

6. Of course, the highly aggregated data presented by Schweninger do not account for the quality of land. One direct observer, W. E. B. DuBois (1906a, 232), concluded on the basis of his several extended field studies in the South: "There are still other regions in the south, and large regions, where black men can buy land at reasonable terms but it is usually land poorly situated as regards market, or unhealthful in climate, or so placed as to afford the owner poor schools and lawless and overbearing white neighbors." Regrettably, it is difficult to see how we can account for DuBois's observations in any quantitative study of black landownership that we might conduct today, but we cannot dismiss such evidence either.

7. Roger Ransom and Richard Sutch were able to confirm that the nineteenth-century South featured extraordinarily high rates of interest. Indeed, they blame much of the South's economic stagnation in the postbellum period on the interaction of racism and racist institutions with poorly functioning financial markets (Ransom and Sutch 1977).

8. DuBois did note the steady increase in landownership among blacks in the South. On this point, his analysis was in accord with Schweninger's data, summarized earlier in this chapter.

9. The numbers are dramatic and, for that reason, need to be mentioned. In the single decade from 1910 to 1920, Mississippi, Alabama, Georgia, South Carolina, North Carolina, and Virginia each lost over one hundred thousand black residents. Between 1910 and 1920, New York's black population rose by 66 per-

cent, Detroit's by 611 percent, Cleveland's by 308 percent, and Chicago's by 148 percent. From 1920 to 1930, the numbers were 115 percent, 194 percent, 109 percent, and 114 percent, respectively (Harris and Spero 1933, 343, table II). In absolute numbers, white outmigration from the South at this time was also substantial, although as a percentage of total residents, it was much smaller than that experienced by blacks (Earle 2000, 102–3). According to a table prepared from U.S. census data by Gary Becker (1971, chap. 9, table 14), the ratio of blacks to whites in the South fell from 43 percent in 1910 to 28 percent in 1950. In the North over those same years, it rose from approximately 2 percent to 5 percent.

10. Good sources on the extent of black participation, on both sides of this conflict, existed at this time. These included an exhaustively documented book by Joseph T. Wilson (1888), who was himself an African-American and Civil War veteran.

11. The notion that some people are "accustomed" to a lower standard of living can be interpreted in a way that makes it other than a snobbish or meaningless idea. For example, the philosopher Martha Nussbaum (2000b, chap. 2) has recently argued for the notion that preferences are "adaptive" in the sense that people adapt their sense of what they can hope for and legitimately desire to the circumstances they face. This is, of course, an exact reversal of what is taught in introductory economic classes. In this reversal, we might say that people learn to want what they get, rather than get what they want. This may be the reason behind our conventional understanding that upward and downward mobility are not symmetric with regard to their effect on people's psyches and sense of well-being.

12. *Taste* is the conventional economic term used in this class of models, which has induced more than a few critics to think that Becker was belittling a complex sociological phenomenon. In a sense, given the implicit rules of economic modeling, this was true. The term *taste* was consistent with the positivistic approach that was beginning to capture the imagination of mainstream economics at the time Becker wrote and revised his book. In principle, such neutral terminology was supposed to set aside questions as to the sources and moral status of such attitudes as racism—or, at a minimum, to marginalize such considerations—while prioritizing the objective study of market phenomena and the formation of "testable" hypotheses.

13. As I discussed earlier in this chapter, such a possibility was considered by Gunnar Myrdal. It was also suggested, but not developed, by Kenneth Arrow, as will be discussed later in this chapter. The incorporation of this idea in the context of a model featuring asymmetric information is presented in Schwab 1986. Glenn Loury has put the issue of "self-fulfilling negative stereotypes" at the center of several of his works on the economic effects of race and discrimination (Coate and Loury 1993; Loury 1998, 2002, and this volume).

14. Arguably, such a scenario emerged in major league baseball in the 1950s through the mid-1960s. David Halberstam (1994, 153–54) recounts that during these years, "National League scouts were pushing the more integrated quality of their league to young black prospects, while the American League scouts were quietly emphasizing to white prospects from the South that if they signed with an American League team, they would play with fewer blacks."

15. To be exact, if we assume that the only motivation to move north was an

enhanced wage, then wages would adjust until the discounted present value of the wage differential offered to blacks in the North, relative to what they earned in the South, was exactly equal to the cost of relocating to the North. Of course, such a rendering of the motivation to migrate assumes that the "psychic costs" of living in the South, with its consequent loss of dignity, erratic and arbitrary enforcement of the laws, and so on, were the same as that experienced in the North. While the North was far from a perfectly equal society during the period surveyed in this chapter, it was a clear improvement over the South in several tangible ways—such as more secure property rights, better housing and schools, and fewer lynchings.

16. Of course, Sowell's considerations on the relative progress of Afro-Caribbeans have not gone unchallenged. Specifically, Stephen A. Woodbury (1993, 244–48), using a more elaborate test to decompose the various causal factors, finds that the difference in economic success achieved by African-American and Afro-Caribbeans, respectively, can be largely attributed to observable factors, such as years of schooling and labor market experience. Sowell's hypothesis is also subjected to a critical review in an article by Patrick Mason (1996) that is both interesting and very accessible.

17. Another approach related to, although distinct from, the culture approach is to simply posit that the minority group is less able intellectually. This would replace the story about culture with another narrative that points to human genetics and innate capacity (or lack thereof). This is an approach that was strongly—and, I would add, persuasively—undermined by Thomas Sowell (1981a, 281–82), among others, as long ago as the 1970s. However, as we have seen in several chapters in this volume, it is an approach with a long heritage that apparently reappears every few decades. (Actually, I believe that such explanations tend to revive during periods when the distribution of income gets markedly worse and that they retreat as the middle class is [hopefully] reconstituted, but such speculations take us away from our topic.) Regrettably, with the resurgence of sociobiology and IQ testing in our era and with the clear success of Richard Herrnstein and Charles Murray's 1994 book, such explanations are returning to our public discourse. Indeed, the fact that standardized tests have made such a comeback in the educational philosophy of this country is in itself a remarkable development, a social pathology that merits its own essay. That these fatally flawed tools that were in the throes of their death rattle by the late 1970s were able to make a comeback and are now being relentlessly advanced by "experts" is, to say the least, a wonderful testament to the power that ideas take on when they are backed by large sums of money.

18. To be perfectly accurate, under the standard assumptions of free entry into the market, "economic profits" for firms in the secondary sector will still be zero although such firms will probably operate on a larger scale than firms in the primary sector. Nevertheless, these firms will still retain a stake in the status quo, because any lifting of the barriers preventing the movement of labor into the primary sector will force them to pay higher wages and because, during the transition, they will experience negative rates of economic profit until enough firms exit the market and the equilibrium level of zero economic profit is restored. In short, firms in the secondary market have a collective interest in avoiding the costs associated with the transition to a free and fair market.

— doesn't include
labor market segmentation

we need
basic descriptive
stat. on
what the
labor market
looks
like

Racial Discrimination
in the Labor Market

William A. Darity Jr. and Patrick L. Mason

There is substantial racial disparity in the American economy, and a major cause of this is discriminatory treatment within labor markets. The evidence is ubiquitous and includes careful research studies that estimate wage and employment regressions, help-wanted advertisements, audit and correspondence studies, and discrimination suits that are often reported by the news media. Yet there is broad agreement that there have been periods of substantial progress. For example, Donohue and Heckman (1991) provide widely accepted evidence that racial discrimination declined during the decade 1965–75. Nevertheless, there are some unanswered questions. Why did the movement toward racial equality stagnate and eventually decline after the mid-1970s? What is the role of the competitive process in the elimination or reproduction of discrimination within the labor market? In this chapter, we review recent literature on these topics.

The Civil Rights Act of 1964 is the signal event that brought abrupt changes in the black-white earnings differential (Bound and Freeman 1989; Card and Krueger 1992; Donohue and Heckman 1991; Freeman 1973). Prior to passage of the federal civil rights legislation of the 1960s, racial exclusion was blatant. The adverse effects of discriminatory practices on the life chances of African Americans in particular during that period have been well documented (Wilson 1980; Myers and Spriggs 1997, 32–42; Lieberson 1980). Cordero-Guzman (1990, 1) observes that "up until the early 1960s, and particularly in the south, most blacks were systematically denied equal access to opportunities and in many instances, individuals with adequate credentials or skills were not, legally, allowed to apply to certain positions in firms." Competitive market forces did not eliminate these discriminatory practices in the decades leading up to the 1960s. They remained until the federal adoption of antidiscrimination laws.

Newspaper help-wanted advertisements provide a vivid illustration of how open and visible such practices were. We did an informal survey of the employment section of major daily newspapers from three northern cities (the *Chicago Tribune*, the *Los Angeles Times*, and the *New York Times*) and from the nation's capital (the *Washington Post*) at five-year intervals from 1945 to 1965. (Examples from newspapers from southern cities are even more vivid.) Many advertisements in the 1960s explicitly indicated the employers' preference for applicants of a particular race, far more often for white applicants. Representative advertisements appear in table 1.

Among the newspaper editions we examined, the *Washington Post* of January 3, 1960, had the most examples of help-wanted ads showing racial preference, again largely for whites. Nancy Lee's employment service even ran an advertisement for a switchboard operator—presumably never actually seen by callers—requesting that all *women* applying be white. Adver-

TABLE I. Representative Advertisments

Chicago Tribune	Los Angeles Times	New York Times	Washington Post
January 3, 1960	January 2, 1960	January 3, 1960	January 3, 1960
LABORATORY TECHNICIAN Experienced, Modern southside medical center. White. Salary open. Call Vincennes 6-3401	COMPANION. White. Lite hswk. for single lady. Must drive. Local refers. CR 1-7704	COOK, housekeeper, Negro preferred, experience essential, prominent family, permanent position, high salary, MA 7-5369	NURSE (practical) white, for small nursing home, Silver Spring area. Car nec. Good salary. EV 4-6161
WAITRESS—White. Good tips. 7611-15 Stoney Island RE 4-8837	GIRL, white, 25–40. Lite household duties Rm, board, sal. Apply eves. after 5, 10572 S. Vermont Ave.	COOK-hswkr., fine position, top salary + bonus. Start Jan. Must be capable, white; ref. HU 2-7222	BOYS—WHITE Age 14 to 18. To assist Route manager full or part-time. Must be neat in appearance. Apply 1346 Conn. Ave. NW, room 1006, between 9 to 11 a.m. or 3:30 to 4:30 p.m.

tisements also frequently included details about the age range desired from applicants, such as men aged 21–30 or women aged 18–25. Moreover, employers also showed little compunction about specifying precise physical attributes desired in applicants.[1]

In January 1965, following the passage of the Civil Rights Act of 1964, none of the newspapers we examined carried help-wanted ads that included any explicit preference for "white" or "colored" applicants. However, it became very common in the mid-1960s to see advertisements for "European" housekeepers (a trend that was already visible as early as 1960). While race no longer entered the help-wanted pages explicitly, national origin or ancestry seemed to function as a substitute. Especially revealing is an advertisement run by the Amity Agency in the *New York Times* on January 3, 1965, informing potential employers, "Amity Has Domestics": "Scottish Gals" at $150 a month as "mothers helpers and housekeepers"; "German Gals" at $175 a month on one-year contracts; and "Haitian Gals," who are "French speaking," at $130 a month. Moreover, in January 1965, prospective female employees still were indicating their own race in the "Situations Wanted" section of the newspaper.

The case of the help-wanted pages of the *New York Times* is of special note because New York was one of the states that had in place long prior to the passage of the federal Civil Rights Act of 1964 both a law against discrimination and a state commission against discrimination. However, the toothlessness of New York's state commission is well demonstrated by the fact that employers continued to indicate their racial preferences for new hires in help-wanted ads, as well as by descriptions of personal experience, such as that of John A. Williams in his semiautobiographical novel *The Angry Ones* ([1960] 1996, 30–31).

Help-wanted ads were only the tip of the iceberg of the process of racial exclusion in employment. After all, there is no reason to believe that the employers who did not indicate a racial preference in ads were entirely open-minded about their applicant pool. How successful has the passage of federal antidiscrimination legislation in the 1960s been in producing an equal-opportunity environment where job applicants are now evaluated on their qualifications? To give away the answer at the outset, our response is that discrimination by race has diminished somewhat but is not close to ending.

The Civil Rights Act of 1964 and subsequent related legislation has purged American society of the most overt forms of discrimination. However, discriminatory practices have continued in a more covert and subtle form. Furthermore, racial discrimination is masked and rationalized by widely held presumptions of African American inferiority.

Statistical Research on Employment Discrimination

Economic research on the presence of racial discrimination in employment has largely focused on black-white earnings and occupational disparities. The position typically taken by economists is that some part of the racial gap in earnings or occupations is due to average group differences in productivity-linked characteristics (a human capital gap) while some part is due to average group differences in treatment (a discrimination gap). The more the gap can be explained by human capital differences, the easier it becomes to assert that labor markets function in a nondiscriminatory manner and that any remaining racial inequality in employment outcomes must be due to differences that occur between African Americans and whites or between men and women outside of the labor market. The typical approach here is to estimate regression equations where earnings levels or occupations are the dependent variable, to be explained by some combination of factors like years and quality of education, experience, job tenure, region of country, and dummy variables for race. If the coefficients on the race variables are significant, after controlling for other factors, that is taken to be evidence of discrimination within the labor market.

Regression Evidence on Racial Discrimination

When we consider economic disparities by race, a difference emerges by gender. When women are compared by their various racial and ethnic subgroups based on U.S. census data for 1980 and 1990, little evidence can be found of systematic wage discrimination (Darity, Guilkey, and Winfrey 1996).[2] However, when males are examined using the same census data, a standard result emerges. A significant portion of the wage gap between African American and white males in the United States cannot be explained by the variables included to control for productivity differences across members of the two racial groups, and this finding is robust to different methodological approaches.

African American women are likely to have the same school quality and omitted family background characteristics as African American men (the same is true for white women and men); hence, it strains credibility to argue that the black-white earnings gap for men is due to an omitted labor-quality variable, unless one also argues that African American women are paid more than white women conditional on the unobservables. The results of Darity, Guilkey, and Winfrey (1996) and Rodgers and Spriggs (1996) can be interpreted as indicating that in 1980 and 1990, African American men in the United States were suffering a 12 to 15 percent loss in earnings due to labor market discrimination.

There is a developing body of evidence that uses color or "skin shade" as a natural experiment to detect discrimination. The approach of these studies has been to look at different skin shades within a particular ethnic group at a particular place and time, which should help to control for factors of culture and ethnicity other than pure skin color. Johnson, Bienenstock, and Stoloff (1995) looked at dark-skinned and light-skinned African American males from the same neighborhoods in Los Angeles and found that the combination of an African American racial identity and a dark skin tone reduces an individual's odds of working by 52 percent, after controlling for education, age, and criminal record. Since both dark-skinned and light-skinned African American males in the sample were from the same neighborhoods, the study *de facto* controlled for school quality. Further evidence that lighter-complexioned African Americans tend to have superior incomes and life chances than darker-skinned African Americans in the United States comes from studies by Ransford (1970), Keith and Herring (1991), and Johnson and Farrell (1995).

Similar results are found by looking at skin color among Hispanics. A research initiative conducted by Arce, Murguia, and Frisbie (1987) utilizing the University of Michigan's 1979 Chicano survey involved partitioning the sample along two phenotypic dimensions—skin color ranging from very light to very dark on a five-point scale and physical features ranging from very European to very Indian on a five-point scale. Those Chicanos with lighter skin color and more European features had higher socioeconomic status. Using the same data set, Telles and Murguia (1990) found that most of the income differences between the dark phenotypic group and other Mexican Americans could not be explained by traditional human capital differences and other variables affecting income. Further supporting evidence on this finding comes from Darity, Guilkey, and Winfrey (1996) and Cotton (1993). Evidently, skin shade plays a critical role in structuring social position and life chances in American society, even between comparable individuals within minority groups.

Cross-national evidence from Brazil also is relevant here. Despite conventional beliefs in Brazil that race is irrelevant and that class is the primary index for social stratification, Silva (1985), using the 1976 national household survey, found that blacks and mulattos (or "browns") shared a relatively depressed economic condition by comparison to whites and that mulattos earned slightly more than blacks. Silva also found slightly greater unexplained income differences for mulattos than for blacks vis-à-vis whites, unexplained differences he viewed as evidence of discrimination. A more recent study by Telles and Lim (1998), based on a random national survey of five thousand persons conducted by the Data Folha Instituto des Pesquisas, compares economic outcomes based on whether race is self-identified or interviewer-identified. Telles and Lim viewed interviewer identification as more useful for establishing social classification and treatment. They found that self-identification underestimates white income and overestimates brown and black incomes relative to interviewer classification.

Despite the interesting results on skin shade, some continue to argue that the extent of discrimination is overestimated by regression techniques because of missing variables. After all, it seems likely that the general pattern of unobserved variables—for example, educational quality or labor force attachment—would tend to follow the observed variables in indicating reasons for the lower productivity of African American males (Ruhm 1989, 157). As a result, adjusting for these factors would reduce the remaining black-white earnings differential.[3]

As one might imagine, given the framework in which economists tackle the issue of discrimination, there has been considerable searching through different data sets to find measures of human capital that could be used to test hypotheses about labor market discrimination. These searches have uncovered one variable in one data set for human capital which, if inserted into an earnings regression, produces the outcome that all or nearly all of the black male–white male wage gap is explained by human capital while none is explained by labor market discrimination. No one, however, has suggested a reasonable missing variable for skin shade. The particular variable that eliminates evidence of discrimination in earnings against African American men is the Armed Forces Qualifying Test (AFQT) as it appears in the National Longitudinal Survey of Youth (NLSY).

A number of researchers have confirmed, with somewhat different sample sizes and methodologies, that including AFQT scores in an earnings equation will nearly or completely eliminate racial differences in wages. For example, June O'Neill (1990) examined the 1987 sample of men aged 22–29 who had taken the AFQT when they were interviewed for the armed forces seven years earlier. The average AFQT score was 48 for African American men and 73 for white men.[4] The unadjusted hourly wage ratio for these men was 83 percent. The ratio adjusted for region, schooling, and potential experience was 88 percent. The ratio adjusted for region, schooling, potential experience, and AFQT score was 95–96 percent, close to parity. Similarly, Maxwell (1994) looked at a cohort of men six years after leaving school and found that the inclusion of AFQT scores in a wage regression explained two-thirds of the gap. Ferguson (1995) used the 1988–92 samples of males aged 25–35 years. Ferguson found that unadjusted gaps in earnings ranged between 13 to 20 percent and that the AFQT score could explain one-half to two-thirds of that difference. Neal and Johnson (1996) found that AFQT scores could explain three-quarters of the black-white gap for men and the entire black-white gap for women. Neal and Johnson also found that AFQT's inclusion in logarithmic wage equations can completely explain wage differentials for Hispanic males and females.[5]

The conclusion of this body of work is that labor market discrimination against African Americans is small or nonexistent. Using Neal and Johnson's (1996) language, the key to explaining differences in African American and white labor market outcomes must instead rest with "premarket factors."[6] But matters are not so straightforward. The essential problem is what AFQT scores are actually measuring and therefore what is being controlled for. There is no consensus on this point. AFQT scores have been interpreted variously as providing information about school quality or academic achievement (O'Neill 1990), about previously unmeasured skills (Ferguson 1995; Maxwell 1994; Neal and Johnson 1996), and even about intelligence (Herrnstein and Murray 1994), although the military did not design the AFQT as an intelligence test (Rodgers and Spriggs 1996).[7] The results obtained by O'Neill (1990), Maxwell (1994), Ferguson (1995), and Neal and Johnson (1996) after using the AFQT as an explanatory variable are, on closer examination, not robust to alternative specifications and quite difficult to interpret.

The lack of robustness of using the AFQT can be illustrated by looking at how it interacts with other variables in the earnings equation. Neal and Johnson (1996), for example, adjust for age and AFQT score in an earnings equation, but not for years of schooling, presumably on the assumption that same-age individuals would have the same years of schooling, regardless of race. However, this assumption does not appear to be true. Rodgers, Spriggs, and Waaler (1997) find that white youths had accumulated more schooling at a given age than had African American or Hispanic youths. When AFQT scores are both age and education adjusted, a black-white wage gap reemerges; as the authors report (3):[8]

> [E]stimates from models that use our proposed age and education adjusted AFQT score [show] that sharp differences in racial and ethnic wage gaps exist. Instead of explaining three-quarters of the male black-white wage gap, the age and education adjusted score explains 40 percent of the gap. Instead of explaining the entire male Hispanic-white gap, the new score explains 50 percent of the gap. . . . [B]lack women no longer earn more than white women do, and . . . Hispanic women's wage premium relative to white women is reduced by one-half.

Another specification problem arises when estimating wage equations that include both AFQT scores and psychological measures of motivation and effort from the NLSY data. Joint inclusion of the measures of "psychological capital" restores evidence that being black has a negative effect on wages (see Goldsmith, Veum, and Darity 1997, 2000). This pure adverse race effect suggests the persistence of differential treatment against blacks or of antiblack labor market discrimination. Furthermore, with the inclusion of measures that capture motivation and effort as variables on the right-hand side of a wage equation, researchers also become more likely to find statistical evidence of discrimination against black women as well as men (Goldsmith, Veum, and Darity 1997, 2000).[9]

Yet another specification problem becomes relevant if one interprets AFQT scores as providing information about school quality. There is a school survey module of the NLSY that can be used to provide direct evidence on school quality, using variables like the books-to-pupil ratio, the percent of students classified as disadvantaged, and teacher salaries. Surely, it would be more helpful to use this direct data on school quality rather than AFQT scores. In another method of controlling for school quality, Harrison (1972) compared employment and earnings outcomes for African Americans and whites living in the same African American ghetto communities, on grounds that school quality would not be very different between them; Harrison found sharp differences in earnings, favoring whites.[10]

One severe difficulty in interpreting what differences in the AFQT actually mean is demonstrated by Rodgers and Spriggs (1996), who show that AFQT scores appear to be biased in a specific sense. These authors show that if AFQT scores are treated as an endogenous variable—rather than being used as an exogenous explanatory variable—and if equations for AFQT are estimated separately for African Americans and whites, controlling for family background, school quality and psychological motivation, the coefficients for generating AFQT scores differ substantially between African Americans and whites. White coefficients generate significantly higher scores for given characteristics than African American coefficients.

Rodgers and Spriggs then create a hypothetical set of "unbiased" African American scores by running African American characteristics through the equation with the white coefficients. When those scores replace the actual AFQT scores in a wage equation, the adjusted AFQT scores no longer explain black-white wage differences. A similar result can be obtained if actual white scores are replaced by hypothetical scores produced by running white characteristics through the equation with African American coefficients.[11] Apparently, the AFQT scores are a consequence of bias in the underlying processes that generate AFQT scores for African Americans and whites.[12]

To muddy the waters further, focusing on the math and verbal subcomponents of the AFQT leads to inconsistent implications for discriminatory differentials. For example, while a higher performance on the verbal portion of the AFQT contributes to higher wages for African American women versus African American men, it apparently has little or no effect on the wages of white women versus white men, according to work by Currie and Thomas (1995). However, white women gain in wages from higher scores on the math portion of the AFQT, but African American women do not. Perhaps this says that white women are screened (directly or indirectly) for employment and pay on the basis of their math performance while African American women are screened based on their verbal skills. Perhaps this is because white employers have a greater "comfort zone" with African American women who have a greater verbal similarity to whites. Or perhaps something not fully understood and potentially quirky is going on with the link between these test results and wages.

Finally, since skill differentials have received such widespread discussion in recent years as an underlying cause of growing wage inequality in the U.S. economy, it should be pointed out that growth in the rewards to skill does not mean that the effects of race have diminished. If the importance of race and skill increase simultaneously, a rising skill premium will explain more of the increase in intraracial wage inequality than changes in interracial wage inequality. For example, when Murnane, Willet, and Levy (1995) ask whether test scores in math, reading, and vocabulary skills for respondents in the National Longitudinal Study of the High School Class of 1972 and the High School and Beyond data sets have more explanatory power in wage equations for 1980 graduates than for 1972 graduates, their answer is yes—the rate of return to cognitive skill (test scores) increased during 1978–86. However, in these same regressions, the absolute value of the negative race coefficient is larger for the 1980 graduates than it is for the 1972 graduates. So Murnane, Willet, and Levy confirm that there are increasing returns to skills measured by standardized tests, but their work does not indicate that the rise in returns to skills can very well explain changes in the black-white earnings gap.

The upshot is the following: There is no doubt that African Americans suffer reduced earnings in part due to inferior productivity-linked characteristics relative to nonblack groups. It is important to account for racial skills differentials or school-quality differentials. However, evidence based on the AFQT should be treated with extreme caution. Given that this one variable in one particular data set is the only one that suggests that racial discrimination is no longer operative in U.S. employment practices, it is far from convincing evidence. It appears likely that African Americans, especially African American men, continue to suffer significantly reduced earnings due to discrimination and that the extent of discrimination may have begun to increase during the mid-1970s.

Direct Evidence on Discrimination: Court Cases and Audit Studies

One direct body of evidence of the persistence of employment discrimination, despite the presence of antidiscrimination laws, comes from the scope and dispensation of job discrimination lawsuits. Throughout the 1990s, there have been large numbers of lawsuits against major corporations involving discriminatory practices. For example, in 1993, Shoney's International paid out $105 million to thousands of black employees, and in 1996, Pitney Bowes paid out $11.1 million for racially biased harassment from colleagues. Suits such as these reveal racial discrimination in employment, training, promotion, tenure, layoff policies, and work environment, as well as occupational segregation.

Perhaps the most notorious recent case is the $176 million settlement reached between Texaco and African American employees, after disclosure of taped comments of white corporate officials making demeaning remarks about African Americans, remarks that revealed an outlook that translated into corresponding antiblack employment practices. Clearly, neither federal antidiscrimination laws nor the pressures of competitive markets have prevented the occurrence of discriminatory practices that have resulted in significant awards or settlements for the plaintiffs.

Another important source of direct evidence are audit studies of the type conducted in the early 1990s by the Urban Institute (Mincy 1993). The Urban Institute audit studies sought to examine employment outcomes for young African American, Hispanic, and white males aged 19–25 looking for entry-level jobs. Pairs of African American and white males and pairs of Hispanic and white males were matched as testers and sent out to apply for jobs at businesses advertising openings. Prior to application for the positions, the testers were trained for interviews to minimize dissimilarity in the quality of their self-presentation, and they were given manufactured résumés designed to put their credentials on a par. The tests involving black and white testers were conducted in Chicago and in Washington, D.C., while those involving Hispanic and white testers were conducted in Chicago and in San Diego.

A finding of discrimination was confirmed if one member of the pair was offered the position and the other was not. No discrimination was confirmed if both received an offer (sequentially, since both were instructed to turn the position down) or if neither received an offer. This is a fairly stringent test for discrimination, since, in the case where no offer was made to either party, there is no way to determine whether employers were open to the prospect of hiring an African American or a Hispanic male, what the overall applicant pool looked like, or who was actually hired. However, the Urban Institute audits found that African American males were three times as likely to be turned down for a job as white males and that Hispanic males also were three times as likely as non-Hispanic white males to experience discrimination in employment (Fix, Galster, and Struyk 1993, 21–22).[13]

The most severe methodological criticisms of the audit technique have come from Heckman and Siegelman (1993). At base, their central worry is that testers cannot be paired in such a way that they will not signal a difference that legitimately can be interpreted by the prospective employer as a difference in potential to perform the job, despite interview training and doctored résumés.[14] They are concerned, for example, with such intangibles as a person's ability to make a first impression and with the fact that certain resumes may be unintentionally superior to others.

One way to overcome some of the difficulties of the audit approach is the "correspondence test," which originally was used overseas in Britain and Australia. This test involves investigators sending letters of inquiry from prospective "applicants" to employers, where the letters signal the "applicants'" ethnicity by using a surname that provides a strong clue about ethnic affiliation. Of course, the letters of inquiry are designed to demonstrate comparable written skills across the hypothetical members of each group, and, again, manufactured résumés are submitted with the letters to present comparable credentials to employers. Riach and Rich (1991–92) report that in the British studies, letters that appeared to be from Afro-Caribbean, Indian, or Pakistani applicants often received replies that indicated that the positions had been filled, while, simultaneously, letters that appeared to be from Anglo-Saxon applicants received responses from the same employers inviting them to interviews. A similar pattern occurred in the Australian audits: inquiries from applicants with Vietnamese- or Greek-sounding names met with information that the position had been filled, while "applicants" whose names sounded Anglo-Saxon were asked to come for interviews. This is impressive direct evidence of discrimination from a powerful test procedure. However, the correspondence test is limited to identifying discrimination at the initial stage of the hiring process; it cannot identify discriminatory practices during the interview stage, at the point of job offer, or in the terms of a job offer.

A compelling U.S. based audit study is a correspondence test recently conducted by Bertrand and Mullainathan (2002). Responding to help-wanted advertisements in Chicago and Boston, the two researchers submitted quality-matched resumes to prospective employers under randomly assigned black-sounding names (e.g., *Keisha Washington* or *Rashad Jackson*) and white-sounding names (e.g., *Brad Kelly* or *Meredith Sullivan*). They then evaluated how the resumes "performed," given the racial associations with the names, based on whether the "applicant" received a callback for a face-to-face interview.

The researchers found that race-linked name assignments yielded major variations in callback rates. Specifically, they discovered that "a 'white' applicant would need to send out eight resumes to get one call back, [while] a black applicant would need to send out fourteen resumes," nearly twice as many. Moreover, they also found that increasing the positive information in the résumé did raise the odds of a callback for a "white" applicant but had no effect on the callback odds for a "black" applicant. Hence, Bertrand and Mullainathan conclude that "small increases in observable skills of applicants cause a rise in discrimination."

Two major implications follow from this study. First, this evidence of race-linked, name-based differential treatment weakens the empirical basis for the statistical theory of discrimination. In a context where the researchers exercise complete control over the information flow to the prospective employer about the "applicant," additional information signaling greater skills on the part of the "black" applicant fails to equalize labor market outcomes between the two racial groups. Second, Bertrand and Mullainathan's finding that antiblack discrimination relatively increases with résumé improvement for the "black" job candidate suggests that the degree of discrimination is sensitive to the applicant's competitive characteristics. Thus, the study hints at the possibility that as blacks become better qualified, labor market discrimination against them may intensify.

The direct evidence from the court cases and audit studies confirms the persistence of discriminatory practices in employment. The evidence is consistent with the characterization of employer beliefs and actions found in the joint Russell Sage–Ford Foundation Multi-City Study of Urban Inequality (MCSUI), newly reported by Holzer (1997). Employers seem to possess strong racial preferences in hiring. These preferences are the consequence of enduring stereotypical beliefs about expected performance on the job, which leads them to set up a racial/ethnic gender ranking of potential hires: white men are generally preferred over white women (unless the job is female-typed); Hispanics of either gender are preferred over African Americans; African American women are preferred over African American men.[15] The MCSUI findings suggest the primacy of race/color as a marker for disadvantageous treatment by employers.

Theoretical Work

Standard neoclassical competitive models can be forced by their own assumptions to reach the conclusion that discrimination can only be temporary. Perhaps the best-known statement of this position is Becker's

Becker

famous "taste for discrimination" proposition (Becker 1971; 1st ed., 1957). If the two groups share similar productivities, under competitive conditions where at least some employers prefer profits to prejudice, then eventually all workers must be paid according to their marginal productivity. The eventual result may involve segregated workforces—for example, with some businesses hiring only white men and others hiring only African American women—but as long as both groups have the same marginal productivity, they will receive the same pay. Thus, discrimination can produce only temporary racial gaps in earnings. Moreover, alternative forms of discrimination are separable processes; that is, wage discrimination and employment segregation are unrelated in Becker's model.

Despite the theoretical implications of standard neoclassical competitive models, we have considerable evidence that the Civil Rights Act of 1964 did have an impact on the extent of racial discrimination. It did not, by any means, eliminate either form of discrimination. This may have been a temporary effect, since there is some evidence that the momentum toward racial equality came to an abrupt halt in the mid-1970s (even though interracial differences in human capital were continuing to close). Moreover, we believe that the forms of discrimination have altered in response to the act. These outcomes suggest that it is not useful to argue that racial discrimination is inconsistent with the operation of competitive markets, especially when antidiscrimination laws have reduced the impact of discrimination within the market. Instead, it is much more beneficial to examine market mechanisms that permit or encourage discriminatory practices.

Since Becker's work, orthodox microeconomics has been massaged in various ways to produce stories of how discrimination might sustain itself against pressures of the competitive market. The tacit assumption of these approaches has been to find a way in which discrimination can increase business profits or in which deciding not to discriminate might reduce profits.

In the customer discrimination story, for example, businesses discriminate not because they themselves are bigoted but because their customers are. This story works especially well where the product in question must be delivered via face-to-face contact, but it obviously does not work well when the hands that made the product are not visible to the customer with the "taste for discrimination."

Perhaps the best of these attempts to explain in a neoclassical framework how discrimination might persist is the statistical discrimination story, which, at its base, is a story about imperfect information. The notion is that potential employers cannot observe everything they wish to know about job candidates and that in this world of imperfect information, they will have an incentive to seize onto group membership as a signal that allows them to improve the employers' ability to predict a prospective candidate's ability to perform.

However, this model of prejudicial beliefs does not ultimately wash well as a theory of why discrimination should be long lasting. If average group differences are perceived but not real, potential employers/selectors should learn that they are mistaken. If average group differences are real, the test for employers in a world with antidiscrimination laws is to find methods of predicting the future performance of potential employees with sufficient accuracy that there is no need to use the additional "signal" of race. It seems implausible that with all the resources that corporations put into hiring decisions, the remaining differentials are due to an inability to come up with a suitable set of questions or qualifications for potential employees.

Models of imperfect competition as explanations of discrimination do not solve the problem completely either. The reason for the immutability of the imperfection is rarely satisfactorily explained—and often not addressed at all—in models of this type (Darity and Williams 1985).

Struggle as it may, orthodox microeconomics keeps returning to the position that sustained observed differences in economic outcomes between groups must be due to an induced or inherent deficiency in the group that experiences the inferior outcomes. In the jargon, this is referred to as a deficiency in human capital. This deficiency is associated sometimes with poor schooling opportunities, other times with culture (Sowell 1981a). But the thrust of the argument is to absolve market processes, at least in the long run, of a role in producing the differential outcome; the induced or inherent deficiency occurs in premarket or extramarket processes.

We certainly believe that human capital, quality of education, years of work experience, and even culture can have a role to play in explaining racial differences in earnings. However, we do not believe that these explanations taken alone come close to explaining the wage differentials and employment patterns that are observed in the economy. Instead, it seems to us that discrimination has managed to sustain itself, both in the United States and elsewhere, for generations at a time. Such discrimination does not always even need direct legal support, and it is not ended by market pressure. Instead, changes in social and legal institutions are needed to reduce it. James Heckman (1997, p. 406) draws a similar conclusion in his examination of a specific sector of employment, the textile industry:

> [S]ubstantial growth in Southern manufacturing had little effect on the labor-market position of blacks in Southern textiles prior to 1965. Through tight and slack labor markets, the proportion of blacks was small and stable. After 1964, and in synchronization with the 1964 Civil Rights Act, black economic progress was rapid. Only South Carolina had a Jim Crow law prohibiting employment of blacks as textile workers, and the law was never used after the 1920s. Yet the pattern of exclusion of blacks was prevalent throughout Southern textiles, and the breakthrough in black employment in the industry came in all states at the same time. Informally enforced codes and private practices, and not formally enforced apartheid, kept segregation in place, and market forces did not break them down.

Nontraditional alternatives to orthodox microeconomics can lead to a logically consistent basis for a persistent gap in wage outcomes. These alternatives can involve breaking down the line so often drawn by orthodox economists between in-market and premarket discrimination. The first alternative involves a mechanism of self-fulfilling prophecy. Suppose employers believe that members of group A are more productive on average than members of group B. Suppose, further, that they act on their beliefs, thereby exhibiting a stronger demand for A workers, hiring them more frequently and paying them more. Suppose that members of group B become less motivated and less emotionally healthy as a consequence of the employment rebuff. Notice that the original decision not to hire may have been completely unjustified on productivity grounds; nonetheless, the decision made *in* the labor market—a decision not to hire or to hire at low pay—alters the human capital characteristics of the members of group B so that they become inferior candidates for jobs. The employers' initially held mistaken beliefs become realized over time as a consequence of the employers' initial discriminatory decisions. In their development of this argument, Elmslie and Sedo (1996, p. 474) observe, "One initial bout of unemployment that is not productivity based can lay the foundation for continued future unemployment and persistently lower job status even if no future discrimination occurs."

More broadly, depressed expectations of employment opportunities also can adversely affect the inclination of members of group B to acquire addi-

tional human capital—for example, through additional schooling or training. It is also possible that the effects of the past are passed along by the disadvantaged group from generation to generation. For example, Borjas
(1994) writes of the ethnic intergenerational transmission of economic
advantage or disadvantage, although he does not use the word *discrimination* to discuss such patterns. Other evidence along these lines includes
Tyree's (1991) findings on the relationship between an ethnic group's status and performance in the past and the present and Darity's (1989b)
development of "the lateral mobility" hypothesis based on case histories of
ethnic groups.

More narrowly, the group-typed beliefs held by employers/selectors also
can have a strong effect on the performance of the candidate at the interview stage. In an experiment performed in the early 1970s, psychologists
Word, Zanna, and Cooper (1974, 109–20) found that when interviewed
by "naive" whites, trained African American applicants "received (a) less
immediacy, (b) higher rates of speech error, and (c) shorter amounts of
interview time" than white applicants. The psychologists then trained
white interviewers to replicate the behavior received by the African
American applicants in the first phase of their experiment and found that
white candidates performed poorly during interviews when they were
"treated like blacks." Such self-fulfilling prophecies are familiar in the psychology literature (Sibicky and Dividio 1986).

A second nontraditional theory that can lead to a permanent gap in
intergroup outcomes is the hypothesis of noncompeting groups that is
advanced by the late W. Arthur Lewis (1979). Related arguments emerge
from Krueger's (1963) extension of the trade-based version of the Becker
model and from Swinton's (1978) model blaming "labor force competition" for racial differences, but Lewis's presentation is the most straightforward. Lewis starts with intergroup rivalry for the preferred positions in a
hierarchical occupational structure. Say that group A is able to control
access to the preferred positions by influencing the required credentials,
manipulating opportunities to obtain the credentials, and serving a gate-
keeping function over entry and promotion along job ladders. Group B is
then rendered "noncompeting."

One theoretical difficulty with this argument—a difficulty that its proponents rarely address—is that it requires group A to maintain group solidarity even when it may have subgroups with differing interests. In
Krueger's (1963) model, for example, white capitalists must value the sol-

idarity of their racial group sufficiently to accept a lower return on their capital as the price they pay for a generally higher level of income for all whites (and for higher wages for white workers).

This hypothesis of noncompeting groups blurs the orthodox distinction between in-market and premarket discrimination, by inserting the matters of power and social control directly into the analysis. This approach then links discrimination to racism, rather than to simple bigotry or prejudice. It leads to the proposition that discrimination—in the sense of differential treatment of those members of each group with similar productivity-linked characteristics—is an endogenous phenomenon. "In-market" discrimination need only occur when all the earlier attempts to control access to jobs, credentials, and qualifications are quavering. One interesting implication here is that growth in skills for what we have been calling group B, the disadvantaged group, may be accompanied by a surge of in-market discrimination, because that form of discrimination has become more necessary to preserve the position of group A. There are three instances of cross-national evidence to support this notion. First, Darity, Dietrich, and Guilkey (1997) find that while black males in the United States were making dramatic strides in acquiring literacy between 1880 and 1910, they were simultaneously suffering increasing proportionate losses in occupational status due to disadvantageous treatment of their measured characteristics.

Second, geographer Peggy Lovell (1993) finds very little evidence of discrimination in earnings against blacks in northern Brazil, where blacks are more numerous, but substantial evidence of discrimination against them in southern Brazil. Northern Brazil is considerably poorer than southern Brazil, and the educational levels of black Brazilians are more depressed in the north than in the south.[16] It is easy to argue that the exercise of discrimination is not "needed" in the north, since blacks there are not generally going to compete with whites for the same sets of jobs. Indeed, there is relatively more evidence of discrimination there against mulattos than against blacks, the former being more likely to compete directly with whites for employment.

Third, in a study using data for males based on a survey taken in Delhi in 1970, Dhesi and Singh (1989) find that the most dramatic instance of discriminatory differentials in earnings was evident for Sikh men vis-à-vis Hindu high-caste men. Most of the earnings gap for Hindu middle-caste, lower-caste, and scheduled-caste men was due to inferior observed charac-

teristics. Since these latter groups could be excluded from preferred positions because of an inadequate educational background, it would not be
necessary for the upper castes to exercise discrimination against them.
Sikh males, however, possessed the types of credentials that would make
them viable contestants for the positions desired by the Hindu higher
castes.

The orthodox approach also ignores long-term effects of past discrimination. Borjas (1994) makes no mention of discrimination in his work, but
a potential interpretation of his findings on ethnic intergenerational transmission of economic advantage or disadvantage is that past discriminatory
effects are passed on to subsequent generations. Tyree's (1991) findings on
the relationship between an ethnic group's status and performance in the
past and group status and performance in the present also suggests the
same potential effects.

A final alternative approach at construction of a consistent economic
theory of persistent discrimination evolves from a reconsideration of the
neoclassical theory of competition. Darity and Williams (1985) argued
that replacement of neoclassical competition with either classical or
Marxist approaches to competition—where competition is defined by a
tendency toward equalization of rates of profit and where monopoly positions are the consequence, rather than the antithesis, of competition—
eliminates the anomalies associated with the orthodox approach
(Botwinick 1993; Mason 1995, 1999a).

A labor market implication of this approach is that wage diversity—different pay across firms and industries for workers within the same occupation—is the norm for competitive labor markets. In these models, remuneration is a function of the characteristics of the individual and the job.
The racial composition of the job affects worker bargaining power and
thereby wage differentials. In turn, race exclusions are used to make some
workers less competitive for the higher-paying positions. Although this
approach does not preclude different pay for similar work, it emphasizes
that the major elements for the persistence of discrimination are racial differences in the access to better-paying jobs within and between occupations.

Whatever alternative approach is preferred, the strong evidence of the
persistence of discrimination in labor markets calls into question any theoretical apparatus that implies that the discrimination must inevitably
diminish or disappear.

NOTES

This chapter is based on an article that was first published in *Journal of Economic Perspectives* 12 (1998): 63–90. We are grateful to Cecilia Rouse, Alan Krueger, Samuel Myers Jr., the late Rhonda Williams, William Rodgers III, William Spriggs, and Timothy Taylor for exceptionally helpful suggestions and criticisms. Maiju Johanna Perala provided valuable research assistance.

1. The C. W. Agency, advertising in the *Los Angeles Times* on January 1, 1950, wanted a "Girl Model 38 bust, 25 waist, 36 hips"; "Several Other Types," with physical characteristics unspecified in the advertisement, apparently also were acceptable.

2. The 1980 and 1990 censuses provide only self-reported information on interviewees' race and ancestry, which makes it possible to partition the American population into fifty different detailed ethnic and racial groups—for example, women of Asian Indian ancestry, Mexican ancestry, Polish ancestry, French Canadian ancestry, and so on. The explanatory variables were years of school, years of college, number of children, married spouse present, years of work experience, years of work experience squared, very good or fluent English, disabled, born in the United States, assimilated (that is either married to a person with a different ethnicity or having claimed two different ethnic groups in the census), location, region, and occupation. Annual earnings was the dependent variable.

There was no control for the difference between potential and actual experience; hence, to the extent that the gap between potential and actual experience and the rate of return to actual experience varies by race, the results for the female regressions may be less reliable than the results for the male regressions.

3. For a view that unobservable factors might favor African American male productivity and, thus, that the regression coefficients are underestimating the degree of discrimination, see Mason 1997a.

4. For Maxwell's (1994) sample, the average AFQT scores were 48.5 for African American men and 72.1 for white men. Neal and Johnson (1996) also found sizable gaps in AFQT scores. African American men and women had standardized age-adjusted scores of -0.62 and -0.52, respectively. For white men and women, the scores were 0.42 and 0.47, respectively. Ferguson (1995) did not report average AFQT scores.

Although interracial differences in AFQT scores appear to be more substantial than the interracial differences in the Scholastic Aptitude Test (SAT) and the National Assessment of Educational Progress (NAEP), the general pattern is the same: whites have higher scores than African Americans. For example, for 1993–94, SAT verbal and math scores for African Americans are 352 and 388, respectively, while the white verbal and math scores are 443 and 495. So the interracial verbal ratio is 79.50 percent, while the math ratio is 78.40 percent. These ratios stood at 73.60 percent and 71.80 percent during 1975–76. For the most part, white scores were stagnant during 1975–94, while the scores of African Americans increased from 1975 through 1987–89 and begin to stagnate thereafter.

NAEP scores are reported for five levels of proficiency in reading, writing, mathematics, and science. These scores are also reported for three age-groups: students aged 9, 13, and 17. Campbell, Voelkl, and Donahue (1997, 17) report:

> Although in 1996 White students attained higher average scores than their Black peers in each age group across the four subject areas, there was some indication that the gaps between White and Black students' average scores in science, mathematics, and reading have narrowed across the assessment years. Despite some fluctuations, however, the trend in writing scale score gaps demonstrates no consistent pattern of increases or decreases at any grade level.
>
> In science, the trend toward smaller gaps among 17-year-olds is due predominately to a one-time decrease in the gap between 1982 and 1986. However, the gap in 1996 was not significantly different from that in 1969. The narrowing of the gap between average scores of White and Black students aged 9 and 13 occurred in the late 1970s or 1980s. Although there has been little change in the 1990s, the gaps for both 9- and 13-year-olds in 1996 were smaller than those in 1970.
>
> In mathematics and reading, scale score gaps between White and Black students aged 13 and 17 narrowed during the 1970s and 1980s. Although there was some evidence of widening gaps during the late 1980s and 1990s, the scale score gaps in 1996 were smaller than those in the first assessment year for 13- and 17-year-olds in mathematics and for 17-year-olds in reading. Among 9-year-olds, scale score gaps in mathematics and reading have generally decreased across the assessment years, resulting in smaller gaps in 1996 compared to those in the first assessment year.

5. Similar results emerge from preliminary research performed with the General Social Survey (GSS), which includes a ten-item test of cognitive skills, called Wordsum (White 1997). The mean African American score on Wordsum in the GSS sample, out of the maximum possible score of 10, was 4.72, and the mean white score was 6.21, a difference similar in magnitude to the racial differences in AFQT scores. In an income equation controlling for age, sex, father's education, mother's education, occupational prestige, and religious affiliation, but not for Wordsum scores, the coefficient on the race variable is negative and statistically significant. But when Wordsum scores are included, the race variable becomes positive in sign and statistically significant. From this standpoint, once cognitive skill is controlled via the Wordsum scores, African Americans receive a positive racial premium relative to their productivity-linked characteristics. Once again, the interpretation could be advanced that there is no statistical evidence of wage discrimination based on these findings.

But matters are not so straightforward. First, if occupational prestige, rather than income, is used as the labor market outcome to be explained, results change rather sharply. Even with Wordsum scores as an included variable in the prestige equation, the race coefficient remains strongly negative.

6. Neal and Johnson limited their sample to persons aged 15–18 in 1980.

This sample restriction reduces the possibility that test outcomes could be influenced by interviewees' exposure to labor market discrimination after secondary school. Neal and Johnson also compute age-adjusted AFQT scores, since the interviewees were not all the same age at the time they took the test in 1980.

7. Indeed, if one uses a measure that, unlike the AFQT, was explicitly designed as a measure of intelligence, it does not explain the black-white gap in wages. Mason (1997b, 1999a) demonstrates this by using in a wage equation an explanatory variable that comes from a sentence completion test given to 1972 respondents to the Panel Study of Income Dynamics (PSID)—a test designed to assess "g," so-called general intelligence. Mason (1997b, 1999a) finds that the significant, negative sign on the coefficient for the race variable is unaffected by including the score on the PSID sentence completion test as an explanatory variable. Indeed, Mason (1997b) finds that although discrimination declined during 1968–73, discrimination grew by 2 percent annually during 1973–91. In comparison, the rate of return to cognitive skill (IQ) was relatively constant during 1968–79 but had an annual growth rate of 1.6 percent during 1979–91.

8. Mason (1997b) finds a similar result when age- and education-adjusted IQ scores are used.

9. Attention to the psychological measures provides evidence that African Americans ceteris paribus put forth more effort than whites, a finding consistent with Mason's (1997a) speculation that there may be unobservables that favor African American productivity. Mason argues that effort or motivation is a productivity-linked variable that favors African Americans, based on his finding that African Americans acquire more schooling than whites for a comparable set of resources.

10. Card and Krueger (1992) also directly control for school quality. They find that there is still a substantial wage gap left after controlling for this variable.

11. Systematic racial differences in the structural equations for the determination of standardized test scores also are evident in the General Social Survey data. Fitting equations for Wordsum scores separately for African Americans and whites also yields statistically distinct structures (White 1997). See n. 4 in the present chapter.

12. Maxwell (1994) reports a coefficient of −0.274 on the race variable in her AFQT regression. This coefficient indicates that after adjusting for differences in family background, race accounts for a difference of less than one percentile in the test scores. However, in a private exchange with William Rodgers, Maxwell has agreed that this reported coefficient is incorrect. The true coefficient is 16.89, which indicates that after adjusting for family background, race accounts for nearly 17 of the 24 percentile points that make up the unadjusted interracial gap in AFQT scores. At most, then, Maxwell can account for 30 percent of the black-white difference in AFQT scores.

Maxwell's correction provides additional weight for the validity of Rodgers and Spriggs's correction. There are two alternatives. First, it may be argued that AFQT is a proxy for skill but does not capture all types of skill; that is, there are other unobserved skills not captured by the AFQT. However, there is no a priori reason to believe that these additional unobserved skills favor a particular group; hence, we do not know whether the coefficient on race is biased upward or downward. Second, it may be argued that there are other predictors of the test that are correlated with race but that are left out of the AFQT explanatory equation.

13. An audit study conducted in Denver, Colorado, independent of the Urban Institute, found no evidence of discrimination against either African American males or Hispanic males (James and DelCastillo 1991). It remains unclear whether this result occurred due to the fact that the Denver labor market is different or because of methodological differences.

14. Some of their criticisms along these lines—for example, concerns about facial hair on the Hispanic male testers used by the Urban Institute—frankly strike us as ridiculous.

15. See especially Holzer 1997, 77–106. Holzer's conclusions are derived from survey data. He surveyed employers in the Atlanta, Boston, Detroit, and Los Angeles metropolitan areas. This data was coordinated with household surveys of the same cities. The surveys were conducted between May 1992 and May 1994. See also Kirschenman and Neckerman 1991, for detailed confirmation of the presence of this racial hierarchy among employers in the Chicago area.

16. The portion of the gap that can be explained by discrimination is much lower in the region of Brazil with the largest black population, the northeast, than in the rest of Brazil. We know of no evidence that suggests that this is or is not true for the U.S. South.

Liberty *and* Equality *and* Diversity?

Thoughts on Liberalism and Racial Inequality after Capitalism's Latest Triumph

Marcellus Andrews

Can civil society be a space where free people of divergent and even antagonistic faiths—including tribes in the grip of the delusion of race—live peacefully on the basis of a social contract where all agree to provide for the basic needs of each in the name of equality? No, say the classical liberals, particularly Nobel laureate Friedrich Hayek, whose midcentury warnings about the dangers of centralized government power in the pursuit of egalitarian dreams—socialism—are now seen as the wisdom of a prophet. Capitalism is ascendant in the wake of socialism's collapse, promising to eliminate mass poverty and provide an endless bounty of goods if only we would accept the necessity of inequality and a margin of required poverty on the part of some portion of the people. The deprivation of the many might—but only might—be overcome if markets are permitted to work their magic, leaving behind a perhaps sizable incompetent remnant whose feeble folkways and broken genes make them losers in the struggle for wealth.

Yet there is a nagging doubt about the necessity of poverty and humiliating inequality under capitalism. A persistent band of egalitarian liberals try to remind us that Hayek's visionary assault on bureaucratic socialism in no way forecloses the possibilities of economic justice. Egalitarians sing only qualified hymns to markets, because they recognize that market failure and economic inequality are social creations that can be met by social action in ways that enhance freedom. Liberty, equality, and diversity are a triplet that flourish or perish together in society, since liberty without a scheme for providing basic resources to all adults and, especially, all children is an invitation to a thick web of private tyrannies and ceaseless strife among classes and tribes. The egalitarians scribble away in the shadows of capitalism's uneasy triumph, like monks preparing for the time when giddiness gives way to shock as images of the broken bodies and empty minds of the neglected, abused, and insulted once again invade the pretty parlors of the powerful and satisfied.

Racial inequality under capitalism, particularly American capitalism, is a standing rebuke to classical liberal sermons about the possibility of promoting freedom without worrying about inequality. Indeed, persistent racial inequality is a slow disaster for capitalism if, as the liberal egalitarians fear, unmonitored free markets lock despised groups into submission and despair, systematically blocking the development possibilities of pariahs. A review of classical liberalism and the egalitarian alternative on the possible cohabitation of freedom, equality, and diversity will expose the weakness of the Hayekian case while providing a brief glimpse of a couple of liberal capitalist roads to racial and economic justice.

The Liberal Perplex

Liberalism, in all of its many varieties, is based on profoundly powerful observations about human diversity and the prospects for social peace. Men and women, as individuals and as members of the bewildering array of social groups that they create, are driven by an almost endless stream of passions, desires, ideals, faiths, and principles that can rarely be reconciled by reasoned argument or debate. This profusion of forms of life is both a fruitful source of innovation that creates knowledge and economic well-being as well as the origin of lethal conflicts that make diversity and peace uneasy partners. A liberal presumes that each man or woman is the best judge concerning his or her own vision of the good and concerning the best means for realizing his or her goals and dreams. The law and the state are social devices—conceived and managed for the benefit of the citizenry—whose primary function is to create harmony between the divergent interests and projects of individuals and the social groups they create and inhabit. While the law and the state may curtail the particular projects of some in the interest of promoting the maximum degree of equal liberty for all, a society that allows government to suppress the choices of a great mass of the people will create conditions of social discord that undermine its authority, thereby setting the stage for individual and collective revolt. Liberal statecraft becomes the delicate art of balancing the conditions for individual creativity and self-assertion against the requirements for social stability under conditions of friction and disagreement about the purpose of life.

Yet liberalism is keenly aware that the individual's capacity to choose and the social demand that persons be responsible for their choices are qualities that are nurtured by families and communities in the context of economic and political institutions. Private property and markets are social devices that liberals support to harness the power of self-interest and material incentives to mobilize resources, talents, and ambition in the service of creating wealth. Democracy is a form of political rule that (theoretically) permits each person to play a part in the formation and evaluation of public policy, thereby tying the use of governmental power to the needs and goals of the people. These institutions are based on the reasoned choice of competent people who are capable of formulating and executing plans in light of the opportunities and restrictions embodied in the law and made manifest via the price mechanism.

The creation of intelligent and responsible persons in a liberal society is the joint task of families, communities, and the state, each of whom provides part of the emotional and material resources that are required for the development of active human beings. Children are born into the world without the capacity to judge, or to act on the basis of reason. The choosing individuals whose actions drive markets, culture, and politics begin their lives as dependent and vulnerable wards of others—parents, teachers, clergy, and many more—until they acquire the habits of mind and action that make them capable of rational choice. Liberal statecraft not only must find a way to balance the divergent projects of free people with the demands for social order but must also somehow attend to the interests of weak, incompletely formed human children while respecting and safeguarding the intimate sphere of family life.[1] Liberal society is obliged to provide a great deal of material support for those children who have the bad fortune to be born to poor, stupid, feckless, or disturbed parents; in disorganized or unstable communities; or to despised social groups.

Finally, liberal society must somehow cope with situations where men and women are miserable and potentially dangerous to themselves and others—including their own children—because they are poor, sick, or incompetent. Many poor adults are without skills or economic resources because they are the children of people who were themselves lacking means or skills. However, other people are poor because they made bad choices in their youth that led to economic incompetence in their adult lives—for example, choosing to bear children while young or to participate in criminal activities that landed them in prison, thereby ruining their chances of acquiring knowledge and skills. What do we do about people who are formally free but who lack the means to act in ways that promote their own well-being or the well-being of weaker persons—especially children—who depend on them?

Race, Rights, and Capabilities

We may sum up the liberal dilemma by adopting Amartya Sen's useful distinction between rights and capabilities in the context of his evaluation of theories of economic justice. Some forms of liberalism, particularly libertarianism and some varieties of classical liberalism (misnamed "conservatism" in America), insist on the primacy of property rights as the object of public policy in liberal society.[2] The purpose of the law and the state is to define and protect each person's freedom to do what he or she wants to do, consistent with an equal range of action for all other citizens. In most libertarian and conservative formulations of rights-based liberalism, property rights are an essential component of liberty because the ownership and control of property confers material independence to all owners, thereby drastically limiting the claims of society on each person. Property allows each person to act in concert with or in isolation from others on the basis of personal preference and mutual advantage.

However, the centrality of property rights to libertarian perspectives explicitly acknowledges the fact that rights can only exist if each person has some access to the material resources with which to implement his or her plans of action. The right to self-ownership, for example, requires each of us to be independent of others, which in turn means that our physical existence must not ultimately depend on the wishes of others. A man or woman can hardly be called free if he or she must violate their own sense of self-respect and value by submitting to the demands of others in order to survive. Rights can only exist substantively if men and women are capable of exercising judgment and taking responsibility, which in turn requires that resources are invested in the formation of their minds and bodies as well as being available for use by adults.

This distinction between rights-based and capabilities-based approaches to liberalism, which echoes Isaiah Berlin's distinction between positive and negative liberty, is used by Sen, Ronald Dworkin, and other writers to explore the promise and problems of liberal egalitarianism.[3] This stream of writing aims at shifting the Left's intellectual center of gravity away from socialism toward market-based forms of economic justice that can stand up to the libertarian and conservative critique of social justice. I will show that Sen's division of the vast field of liberalism into rights-based and capabilities-based theories has the added advantage of exposing the special problem that race poses to libertarian and conservative defenses of free markets.

One might believe that racial diversity, like religious or lifestyle diversity, is simply another species of the wide range of beliefs and faiths that guide the behavior of self-seeking free persons in a liberal society. In a liberal society, the state is supposed to be neutral in matters of faith and, more recently in the United States, in matters of race and color as well. Government is to refrain from sponsoring a particular religious perspective or a racial group's claims about the rank and worth of people based on their color. Yet race differs from religion in that "race," as a social fact, transforms morphological distinctions between people into social cues that guide the allocation of material resources in markets that create and reinforce color lines. For instance, for many whites in American society, black skin is a signal of intellectual inferiority and moral culpability, and this attitude influences the decisions that these whites make in their daily economic lives. These choices, in turn, alter the structure of economic opportunities that blacks face, thereby affecting the extent to which blacks can develop their own capacities to act in the economy and the larger world. White employers who refuse to hire blacks for particular jobs on the basis of their color are not only making self-interested choices in light of their own needs or the needs of their principals; these employers are also reducing the demand for black labor, cutting the income prospects of black workers, and reducing the pool of resources that blacks may use to fund health care, housing, schooling, or other crucial developmental resources for themselves and their children. The fact that racial discrimination redistributes economic resources from despised groups toward favored groups (a point first made long ago by Gary Becker) means that markets in racially divided societies necessarily contribute to the creation of unequal capabilities between social groups in response to the pattern of beliefs and myths about the relative worth of persons based on their color.[4]

The problem here is simple enough: the distribution of wealth, income, and skills bequeathed by the history of racial domination and abuse in the United States permits the white majority to convert its beliefs about the low value of black life into concrete material barriers that deprive blacks of the means for competing in markets. In the parlance of economic theory, the demand-side disdain that whites have for blacks initially leads to low wages, limited employment prospects, and limited access to crucial developmental resources. Over time, the inequality generated by demand-side discrimination is converted into concrete supply-side limits to black achievement, since low incomes, unemployment, and limited access to developmental resources restrict the capacity of blacks to acquire knowledge and skills, accumulate capital and experience, and build up the productive and competitive capacities of their communities. Once black underdevelopment is established, racial inequality between blacks and whites can persist in the face of a gradual reduction in the social legitimacy of race hatred in private and public life.

How can a racially divided liberal society deal with the fact that the rights of whites to act on their racial phobias, given the economic advantages that slavery and apartheid have bequeathed to them, is translated into persistent black economic underdevelopment by virtue of the operation of free markets? Can racial inequality in a free-market society be a just outcome as long as the state refrains from supporting racial hierarchies? If racial inequality is unjust, why? What do terms like *justice* and *injustice* mean in a society where economic rewards are distributed along color lines but where the racial allocation of opportunities and burdens are the unintended outcomes of the legitimate, self-serving choices of millions of individuals in light of their own, petty racial enthusiasms and gripes?

The Irrelevance of Social and Racial Justice
in a Free Society: Hayek

A sophisticated, antiracist American classical liberal would shake his or her head at these kinds of questions, seeing them as examples of the sort of undisciplined thinking that gets in the way of serious analysis and constructive public policy. The root of the problem, from a classical liberal point of view, is that the word *justice* is a very slippery term that lends itself to all kinds of mischief, particularly in the matter of color.

Three ideas combine to make the classical liberal case against the idea of racial justice. The first idea is that demands for equality across class and color lines in economic and social life in the 1960s and 1970s had gone too far, thereby clashing with the need to promote economic incentives by rewarding initiative and deterring antisocial behavior. The slogan "Big government is the problem, not the solution" not only is catchy but also summarizes a complex argument about how the regulation of the fine grain of private dealings is necessarily clumsy and usually counterproductive. The key idea here, developed by Friedrich Hayek in *The Mirage of Social Justice* (1976) and extended to American conditions by Thomas Sowell in *Knowledge and Decisions* (1980), is that government, as an outside enforcer of abstract rules, cannot make informed and effective judgments to promote social and economic justice, because it cannot know why particular persons or organizations make particular choices. At best, a government can review the hiring, admissions, arrest, lending, rental, or business decisions of persons or institutions to judge the resulting distribution of economic rewards and burdens according to some justice or efficiency criteria. However, this after-the-fact approach may well inhibit creativity and efficiency, no matter how well-intentioned the regulations may be, because the state will always lack the relevant and specific information possessed by the participants.[5]

The second big conservative idea is dear to the hearts of most mainstream economists: government attempts to repair the damage that the choices of individuals and organizations may do to the life chances of the poor, to the quality of the environment, and to the prospects for equality and social justice frequently go too far by ignoring the effect of policies on the incentives to work, save, take risks, and develop skills and technologies. The economist's form of this claim simply asks us to remember that there is an inevitable tension between promoting equality and promoting economic efficiency. This tension is due to the fact that the desires of men and women regularly outstrip our limited economic and social resources, thereby requiring us to make painful choices between the things we want. Free markets are a very effective scheme for channeling scarce resources to their most highly valued uses, but the values that markets register— through prices and profits—have no particular correspondence to the needs of the poor or of children, to virtue, to the conditions for environmental or social protection, or to requirements for creating and maintaining a safe, peaceful, and cooperative society out of a bloodstained past of racial hatred and oppression.

The market's main flaw—that its mobilization of resources for those uses that can be expressed in terms of prices and profits occurs without regard for the lives of those whose poverty makes them silent in the economic auction—can be corrected by the judicious use of government power, but only if the wealth-creating prowess of capitalism is respected. According to economists, social policies that run afoul of the central role of self-interest in guiding human behavior will usually fail to reach their goals and will frequently make matters worse. The triumphant conservative critique of the welfare state in America is simply an application of this logic. Conservatives have won the day in economic policy matters by convincing the nation that redistribution taxes the successful for the sake of economic failures, thereby punishing the productive classes of society for pursuing wealth, while encouraging the dumb, feckless, reckless, and lazy to persist in their bad habits and shameful ways.

The third big idea of conservatives, again taken from Hayek, is a direct corollary of the previous two ideas. For such rigorous thinkers as Hayek or Sowell, social justice is a dangerous illusion that poses a threat to liberty as well as to efficiency. With no qualifying adjective, the term *justice* refers to the rules governing relationships between free persons and relationships between individuals and the state. A just society is one that (1) applies the same rules to everyone, without regard to their identity or social station, and (2) establishes clear and transparent rules that facilitate the self-interest of all persons while respecting the need to protect property—including property in one's self (Hayek 1976, 70–73). In other words, justice is concerned with establishing a system of rules that respects each person's freedom without discriminating in favor of any particular person, group, or set of purposes. Therefore, a free-market system is just if the outcome of competition is the result of the unregulated interaction of self-interested people following the rules. Since the results of market competition are the unintended outcome of group activity rather than the goal of a particular individual, the pattern of economic rewards and burdens may be unfortunate but cannot be unjust. Poor people are poor because they do not have resources or skills that can command a high price in the market. So long as their condition cannot be traced to the deliberate activity of particular individuals or to the activity of the government as an agent of a particular class, caste, racial group, region, or purpose, then poverty is sad or disgusting but is not unjust. Injustice is the result of particular patterns of economic rewards that result from the deliberate creation of rules that favor one person, group, or set of purposes over others. According to this view, the term *social justice* is an oxymoron, because it envisions a particular pattern of economic rewards in light of the interests of one section of the community and at the expense of another. Therefore, policies that aim to benefit one person or group by restricting the opportunities of others—such as affirmative action, income redistribution, farm price supports, rent control, or any other restriction on economic opportunities in the name of an outside value—are unjust (Hayek 1976, 80–85).

Two courses of action follow from these insights. First, efficiency and free-market justice can be restored in society if the nation makes work and lawful behavior the only appropriate claims to economic reward. Any other claims to economic resources, including claims of historic injustice by racial and social outcasts or claims based on poverty status or infirmity, only encourage presumed victims to become unproductive consumers who live off the work and wealth of producers. While the winners of the market and merit wars may (but are not required to) make provision for the "truly needy"—those who work hard but who nonetheless fail to achieve an adequate standard of living through no fault of their own—care should be taken to force the lazy, the wicked, and the careless to live with their mistakes. In other words, the only people who have a legitimate claim to a piece of the economic pie are those who have contributed to producing the pie, in proportion to the value of resources they have contributed.[6] Second, the egalitarian preoccupation with the division of the economic pie into more equal slices has undermined ambition and initiative in society, thereby restraining the rate at which the pie can grow. Accordingly, economic rationality requires that we be less concerned with how the economic pie is divided between its various claimants and more concerned with increasing the size of the pie as much as possible.

Serious conservative thinkers have always accepted inequality, perhaps severe economic inequality, as the price of a "free" society that relies on prices and profits to distribute opportunity. These thinkers have not been deluded into the belief that poverty in market society is a reflection of the inferiority of the poor or a proper penalty for "dysfunctional" cultures. For example, Hayek has consistently noted that free markets are devices for promoting the untrammeled exercise of initiative with a minimum of constraint, not schemes for rewarding hard work or virtue (Hayek 1976, 107–23, especially 120). This means that markets are systems for decentralizing power and promoting innovation, but it also means that people can be poor through no fault of their own.[7] Worse, poverty locks the poor out of crucial markets, including markets for housing, health care, education, and other resources, thereby guaranteeing that the poor pass their poverty on to their children. It is convenient for some to pretend that persistent poverty is a reflection of what is wrong with poor people. However, Hayek, at least, knows better than to engage in this sort of nonsense. For him, poverty is simply the condition that some people lack money and wealth. In turn, Hayek is willing to support a free-market system that condemns a portion of the population to permanent penury as the price of a particular form of freedom.

At bottom, the three big conservative ideas I have just reviewed ask us to see society as nothing more than a web of market transactions, where people are tied together by the mutual gains from exchange under a commonly agreed set of "rules of the game" that favor no particular player or group on the basis of their race, caste, region, class, or gender. Indeed, the victorious conservative attack on affirmative action is simply an extension of the Hayekian vision to matters of racial policy in an American context.

Yet the free-market vision of American conservatives has a dangerously utopian aspect. Unregulated capitalism requires the losers of the free-market game to accept the humiliation associated with their lot in life, as well as to teach their children that they, too, deserve their lousy fate. Indeed, the worship of markets and the high tolerance of many conservatives for the pain and misery that follow in the wake of economic and racial inequality is a fundamentalist vision that places competition and efficiency above the concrete needs of human beings for security, good work, and a fair chance to achieve. John Gray makes the point nicely in his essay "The Undoing of Conservatism," in *Enlightenment's Wake: Politics and Culture at the Close of the Modern Age.*

> [Market liberalism or what Americans call "conservatism"] maintains that only a regime of common rules, perhaps embodying a conception of shared rights, is required for the stability of market institutions and a liberal civil society. This species of *liberal legalism* (emphasis in the original) overlooks, or denies, that market institutions will not be politically stable—at any rate when they are combined with democratic institutions—if they do not accord with widespread conceptions of fairness if they violate other important cultural norms. In short they [in America, conservatives] deny the evident facts that the wholly free market is *incompatible* (emphasis added) with social and political stability, while

the stability of market institutions themselves depends far more on their political and cultural acceptability than upon the legal framework which supposedly defines and protects them. (Gray 1995a, 102)

Reconciling Liberty and Diversity: The Classical Liberal Solution

Many varieties of classical liberalism—particularly the Hayekian strain—implicitly begin the argument for free markets and limited government with the claim that the most important social problem confronting society is the creation of institutions that allow liberty and diversity to coexist. Competitive capitalism contributes to social peace by diverting activity and conflict away from collective institutions—especially the state—toward smaller, specialized organizations and activities that cater to the particular needs of people and groups. The displacement of social rivalry from competition for state power to the creation of wealth through market competition and the pursuit of individual or group goals outside the orbit of government shrinks the zone of conflict over ultimate values to a small set of concerns about the principles of social cooperation. Liberals want all potential adversaries in society to agree to create institutions that permit each person to live in ways that he or she has reason to value under conditions of equal freedom for all other persons.

The classical liberal solution to the problem of diversity and social conflict over values tries to eliminate the danger that the state might be captured by some groups to coerce and intimidate others by divorcing government authority from the control of economic resources. However, the classical liberal program does not eliminate the more general problem of the domination of the weak by the strong; it instead relocates the battle over values and social control from the state to the marketplace. Competitive capitalism can be a useful device for fragmenting power—and can thereby contribute to maintaining diversity in society—only if property is widely distributed between rival social groups, to prevent the emergence of social monopolies whereby some groups have the material means to dictate the terms of social intercourse to others. However, the structure of property and contract law and the principles of inheritance from one generation to another play a critical role in either dissolving or reinforcing social monopolies that can use markets to exclude despised social groups from economic opportunities and crucial developmental resources.

Consider the role of markets in shaping the predicament of members of despised sexual and racial minorities. Most gay people in the United States, as elsewhere, are subjected to a long list of nongovernmental discriminatory practices that block their access to jobs, housing, health care, and even physical safety, because of the antigay animus of the majority of their neighbors, coworkers, employers, and landlords, among others. Even if the United States extended the full protections of the Constitution to gay men and women (an unlikely prospect for the foreseeable future), most gay men and women will face insults, abuse, harassment, and unfair treatment on the job, in real estate, and in other markets, because they have limited wealth and depend on their capacity to sell their labor for wages in the labor market. People who depend on the custom of others to make their living are not free to live their lives as they see fit, unless (1) they are independently wealthy or (2) they do not offend the sensibilities of potential trading partners. An openly gay man seeking employment as an engineer or lawyer must be careful to consider his employer's and coworkers opinions about homosexuality, with the consequence that his capacity to live as he chooses is constrained by his need to alter his public persona so as not to offend others. If the community in which he works or lives is marked by substantial hostility toward gay people, a gay man in a market society is "free" to leave the area to find a more civilized place, just as he is "free" to hide his sexual preferences from his neighbors and coworkers. The key problem here is that the existence of free markets and constitutional government (even in the absence of overt violence and intimidation by homophobic thugs) does not eliminate the potential for the nongay majority to coerce and intimidate gay people. Liberal institutions limit the government's ability to persecute sexual outcasts in the name of the majority, while leaving intact the capacity of phobic citizens to use markets to constrict a gay person's freedom.

One can imagine a Hayekian liberal objecting to the foregoing remarks on two grounds. First, discrimination against gay people is far less lethal in a liberal society than in illiberal regimes, precisely because the state may not use its power to persecute gays at the behest of a hostile antigay majority or even to endorse any particular form of sexuality. The unfortunate fact that governments in actually existing liberal democracies regularly practice sexual bigotry by endorsing marital heterosexuality and persecuting sexual outcasts is not a proper condemnation of liberalism but a sad example of how democratic practice may undermine the freedom-enhancing possibilities of liberal institutions. Similarly, racial discrimination in competitive capitalism is not responsible for the long and shameful ordeal that blacks have experienced in American life at the hands of the white majority, even if discriminatory practices in labor, housing, and other markets do limit blacks' access to crucial developmental resources. American racism, in its slavery, apartheid, and now post–civil rights incarnations, has always been a democratic phenomenon that consistently violates liberal principles in order to invest particular visions of whiteness with public authority at the expense of blacks, among others. Had liberal principles of strict neutrality guided American statecraft in matters of race in the postslavery period, for example, blacks may have had to contend with the racist attitudes of whites in the marketplace but would have been spared the government-sponsored abuse that has so wounded them all these years.

Second, wealthy gay men and women or gay people who possess rare and highly remunerative skills can escape most of the economic consequences of antigay animus. Indeed, gay people can defend themselves from the sexual bigotry of the mainstream by acquiring human and financial assets, thereby ending their need to please homophobes to meet their economic needs. Conversely, gay people who lack skills or wealth are more likely to be at the mercy of the antigay mob, because they are poor as well as gay. In a liberal society that endorses basic sexual freedom and enforces the criminal law against those who would physically assault gay men and women, the freedom to live as one chooses depends on one's capacity to literally purchase a zone of isolation, thereby eliminating one's need to depend on the approval of others. Men and women who are treated as racial outcasts can also purchase a zone of freedom—perhaps a very substantial social space where they can pursue their life plans free from the interference and abuse of those who despise them—if they are able to acquire wealth or valuable skills that the larger world is willing to pay for. While it is certainly true that liberal societies warped by race hatred are likely to be balkanized into mutually distrustful enclaves, capitalism and liberalism also hold out the possibility of a "cold peace" that permits each group to develop without the need to share many economic resources. Once again, the classical liberal solution to the problem of peace in a diverse society hinges on the ability of the demos to accept constraints on the will of racial or cultural majorities to impose their hegemony on other groups. In other words, liberalism can preserve diversity and formal equality if men and women are mature enough to refrain from using the state to acquire power over groups and people that they despise.

The racial "cold peace" of classical liberalism conveniently ignores the hard realities of social class and the impact of racial conflict on the allocation of resources in a market society. The classical liberal solution to reconciling liberty and diversity has a seductive charm because it suggests that effort and talent can protect despised people from the noxious views and actions of their bigoted countrymen and countrywomen. But a person's talents are a social product, the end result of a complex process of material, emotional, and intellectual investments by families and communities. Talent is a moment in the intergenerational transmission of wealth, where the income earned by those with skills is the return to the accumulated efforts of previous generations as well as the base for further investments in the skills and capacities of those who are yet to be born. This intergenerational exchange, where one generation hands the baton of ever greater resources and skills to the next, is the backdrop that shapes the rigorous competition for wealth and power within any particular generation. Acts of primitive accumulation rooted in social oppression—for example, American chattel slavery, followed by apartheid, or the near genocide inflicted on the first nations of North America—convey privileges to the dominant racial groups that are transferred from one generation to the next within tightly regulated racial boundaries. The persistent economic and social inequalities that appear across color lines in competitive capitalism are built on the initial crimes that shaped the primordial distribution of economic resources and institutions, only to be compounded by the routine inequalities associated with success and failure in markets that are tied to unequal access to developmental resources. A classical liberal regime constructed in the aftermath of a regime of slavery, genocide, and apartheid cannot logically or ethically ignore that the distribution of economic resources, and therefore the distribution of skills, capacities, and opportunities across a population, ratifies a specific pattern of social domination that permits the ruling racial groups and ethnic tribes to maintain control of a society's central economic and political institutions by virtue of their collective wealth.

An intellectually astute classical liberal could play his or her trump card when confronted with the ways in which a regime of competitive capitalism "à la Hayek" becomes, in practice, a system of persistent, race-based inequality. The trump card consists of two connected observations. First, a liberal capitalist society, even one founded on the basis of staggering moral crimes, is capable of reforming itself precisely because it can safeguard the rights of individuals to self-determination, free from the depredations of racial psychotics or those unscrupulous capitalists who would use racist populism as an instrument of class domination. Capitalism can be a liberating scheme if a constitutional regime uses law to protect all persons, regardless of their color or gender or sexual orientation or faith identity, from the rule of the mob, as long as the state is rigorously neutral in matters of color, gender, and faith. In other words, a liberal capitalist regime can be the answer to historic oppression if it is radically liberal—even libertarian—in its approach to most social questions. Second, a liberal capitalist society is the best economic scheme for redressing the persistent inequalities that flow from historic oppression, precisely because it uses competitive markets, instead of divisive political or moral criteria, to distribute economic resources. The principles of private property and merit are widely viewed as legitimate by all sectors of a diverse society, because each of these principles ties effort to reward in a transparent fashion. Disputes between the poor and the rich about the levels of income received by agents in return for their efforts or for the use of their property, though frequent and occasionally violent, nonetheless concede the legitimacy of the claim that the use of someone's property or the expenditure of mental and physical energy should be rewarded. The relatively tight connection between effort and reward in a market society contrasts with schemes that base access to resources on claims of historical right or redress that require political processes to redistribute income, wealth, and opportunities from one group to another, thereby converting politics into a form of intergroup economic competition at best or even into a form of civil war if things get out of hand.

A wise liberal society that seeks to preserve individual liberty and avoid ruinous conflict over the unequal distribution of economic resources among racial or ethnic groups would do well to promote conditions of equal opportunity and fair competition in the present and future, thereby assuring all individuals that they will receive equal treatment before the law as well as rewards based on their efforts. Merit in the context of a racially divided market society might become the social glue that binds an otherwise disparate population into a cohesive whole that seeks to preserve liberal institutions. This classical liberal response to the problem of racial inequality rules out reparations as compensation for historic oppression—whether such reparations are offered in the form of explicit transfers of monetary wealth or through the use of redistributive taxation and public expenditure policy in order to create opportunity for historically abused social groups. Such reparations are viewed as violations of the principle of

racial and ethnic neutrality in government policy. But relying on a principle of merit to bind a diverse society is a dubious procedure that could well
lock the victims of racial and social oppression in subaltern positions, for
reasons explored in the following section of this chapter.

Merit

Common sense tells us that merit is, in the first instance, the reward that
accrues to all persons who possess talents or property that can fetch a high
price in markets. High returns are the incentive required to induce tal-
ented people to exercise their skills or to encourage property owners to use
their resources in particular ways. Further, high returns are also necessary
to induce men and women to invest time and toil in order to develop and
hone their knowledge and skills through study in school or extra effort on
the job. Yet, as Amartya Sen (2000) has recently noted, the high prices
and resulting high incomes received by those persons who own scarce
resources or skills are not, in and of themselves, measures of merit—in the
sense of just or morally appropriate compensation for the use of personal or
impersonal assets. Instead, high incomes simply reflect the underlying balance of supply and demand in different markets at different points in time.

The price mechanism's much heralded capacity to mobilize talent and
resources in order to fulfill the most profitable purposes does not entitle
property owners to high incomes. Economic efficiency is a morally empty,
though practically important, criterion that can be promoted through
competition among property owners under very stringent conditions, but
it may also require significant intervention by the state, thereby limiting or
even abrogating the free exercise of property rights in some cases.[8] The
owners of highly valued property, including those men and women who
possess valuable skills, merit their high incomes and high social positions
because the larger society values the high levels of output and productivity
that result from competition and the free pursuit of initiative. In turn, high
levels of economic activity and rapid economic growth are socially
beneficial—and therefore are acclaimed to be meritorious—because most
of us believe that wealth and income contribute greatly to human well-
being (Sen 2000, 10–11). We support the claims of property owners to
their high incomes and great social esteem (and condemn unsuccessful
people, particularly unskilled workers and untalented students, to low
earnings and social disrespect) because we think that high returns provide

powerful incentives for people to work, save, study, invent, and endure the
pain and boredom associated with production. By the same token, we condemn economic incentives whenever the consequences of self-interest
undermine well-being by encouraging pollution, crime, or socially destructive outcomes, and we use social policy to alter those incentives that may
be the source of trouble.

Sen is particularly keen to remind us of the instrumental nature of economic rewards and therefore of merit, so that we may not fall into the trap
of conflating merit as a judgment about the outcome of an activity with
judgments about actions themselves or, even worse, with merit as a property of persons quite apart from their actions. This distinction is very
important to keep in mind in modern times, where debates about income
redistribution policy (or the dismantling thereof), affirmative action, and
other social policies tend to confuse merit with judgments about the value
of rewards per se or even the social value of different types of persons. For
example, one often encounters complaints about affirmative action policies that claim that race-conscious employment and college admissions
practices are inconsistent with merit-based criteria for selecting workers
and students. Yet this sentiment is clearly mistaken if we remember that
our criteria of merit are directly tied to our ultimate judgments about the
goals of the activity in question. Hence, college admissions based solely on
standardized tests are consistent with merit if our objective is to select students with a record of high levels of achievement *and* if past test scores are
the most accurate predictor of future achievement *and* if we value the
activities of high achievers. However, there is nothing special or particularly valuable about tests scores or past grades or recommendations as such;
each of these aspects of a student's dossier provides imperfect evidence of
a person's potential to achieve at high levels, if we want to allocate scarce
places in universities to those who may earn the highest marks in the
future. The ultimate economic goal of a test-based regime of college admissions is to select a student cohort that will make the greatest contribution
to the nation's overall economic health, thereby maximizing the rate of
return associated with investments in higher education.

Our notion of merit would change substantially if colleges and universities were charged with the task of distributing educational resources so as
to offset the existing patterns of economic, social, and racial inequality in
society. This equality concern would argue against an exclusive focus on
efficiency criteria and test scores and would favor instead such concerns as
the class origin of students or their capacity to achieve relative to others

facing the same degree of economic and social advantage or disadvantage, thereby changing the nature of "merit" to include different forms of achievement. Such a system would still have to meet the objection to race-based forms of affirmative action from those who see race-based public policies in employment and college admissions as morally indefensible. Further, admission schemes that allocate scarce places in colleges by substituting egalitarian criteria for test-based criteria may well be less efficient than narrower schemes in promoting long-term economic growth. However, a scheme that tilted college admissions in favor of those who have achieved despite serious social and economic obstacles would still be rewarding merit in the interest of promoting economic and social equality.

We can apply Sen's analysis to the distribution of income and wealth in society to see why a Hayekian defense of inequality avoids confusing merit with efficiency, thereby allowing us to see the necessary social role that Hayekian liberalism assigns to brute inequality and the related human suffering. I have already noted that Hayek's approach to matters of justice explicitly disavows any connection between justice and merit. For Hayek, justice is the equal application of rules to all persons as well as the enforcement of property rights in the interest of securing for each person the maximum feasible degree of liberty that is consistent with the same liberty for all. Merit has an instrumental place in this scheme, because the economic rewards or burdens that emerge from vigorous economic competition and the free choice of men and women is an unintended consequence of the price mechanism's alchemy, rather than the design of a conscious agent. People with high incomes "merit" their good fortune only because that is what is required to induce them to use their skills or property for the benefit of others. The distribution of high and low income and wealth is simply the result of competition and exchange in the marketplace, with no moral implications whatsoever.

The central difference between Hayek and Sen on this point is over the legitimacy of using collective action to overturn the results of the market process. Hayek views any attempt to alter the distribution of income, wealth, and opportunity in ways that promote the interests of the poor or social outcasts as a violation of the principles of justice, since these policies require a central state to champion the interests of some people at the expense of the liberty and property of others. By contrast, Sen believes that democratic politics in the context of an open society with a free press and vigorous intelligentsia are the ultimate source of legitimacy in public affairs, up to and including the definition and protection of a regime of private property rights. At bottom, Sen denies that the market is an unplanned social mechanism that is beyond the reach of collective decision making. He thus argues that the citizens of a liberal community regularly and legitimately exercise citizens' control over their social environment through the tightly restrained exercise of state power (Sen 2000, 146–51).

Justice, Humiliation, and Incentives

Profit and merit are far too weak to serve as social glue in a racially divided capitalist society. Conservative political philosopher John Gray has recently broken with the free-market variant of conservatism precisely because it is a public philosophy that has forgotten that markets are devices that serve more profound purposes than wealth accumulation or even the promotion of the maximum degree of individual liberty. Gray reminds the Right, in vain, that the market is valuable because it is an institution that contributes to human well-being by promoting autonomy, "the condition in which persons can be at least part authors of their lives, in that they have before them a range of worthwhile options, in respect of which their choices are not fettered by coercion, and *with regard to which they possess the capacities and resources presupposed by a reasonable measure of success in their self-chosen path among these options* (Gray 1995b, 78; emphasis added)." Autonomy has definite material preconditions that are all too frequently ignored by those free-market enthusiasts who proclaim the efficiency properties of competitive capitalism without also acknowledging the horrendous distributional patterns associated with lightly monitored markets. One of the great advances in modern economic theory, particularly theories of income distribution and economic growth, has been the development of analytically rigorous accounts of the intergenerational transmission of class status and therefore the dynamics of economic and social mobility. A primary insight of this branch of economics is that the capabilities of each generation of men and women in society are the result of deliberate investments of time, attention, and resources on the part of families, communities, and governments. One consequence of this fact is that the capacity for men and women to act autonomously—to decide their own life paths and act competently on their plans, in competition and cooperation with others—is largely the product of the decisions that societies make. Modern conservatism, which is the unfortunate public face of classical liberalism, is an abysmal failure because, as a matter of policy, it has permitted markets to allocate resources in ways that put a brake on the intellectual, social, and personal development of the weak in the interests of the strong.

Yet classical liberalism's failure also provides an opening for egalitarians to press their case for a "decent" society that can reestablish a proper balance between markets and equality. The idea of a "decent" society explored here is derived from Avishai Margalit's *The Decent Society*, a brilliant work of political philosophy that combines an egalitarian's optimism with a coldly realistic assessment of the ethical consequences of the political and social institutions that govern modern life. A "decent society," according the Margalit (1996, 1), is one "whose institutions do not humiliate people." Humiliation, in turn, is "any sort of behavior or condition that constitutes a sound reason for a person to consider his or her self-respect injured" (ibid., 9). This definition pays close attention to someone's reasons for viewing their situation as humiliating rather than to their feelings of humiliation (ibid., 9–29). For example, a black motorist in New Jersey has a reasonable and defensible account of how his or her self-respect is assaulted by a government-sponsored program of racial profiling that targets drivers on the basis of their race. The State of New Jersey's presumption that the skin color of black drivers is sufficient cause to coerce black citizens to submit to higher levels of police scrutiny than are directed at nonblacks increases the anxiety of black drivers, thereby robbing them of the opportunity to live free of the fear that they will be subjected to the arbitrary use of force (possibly violent force) in the name of public safety and the rule of law. Similarly, poor families have reasons for their sense of humiliation when a nation chooses to allow the distribution of educational opportunity as well as opportunities for child health, safety, and overall well-being to be tightly tied to the prevailing and highly unequal distribution of wealth and income. The deliberate social decision to permit parental income and wealth inequality to damage the life chances of poor children is also a judgment of the relative value of poor and nonpoor children in the eyes of the nation's governing institutions. Indeed, the apparent comfort that conservatives display in the face of the pervasive and avoidable unequal opportunity for well-being among children in the United States is a double humiliation because (1) it sanctions unequal opportunities between children even though children cannot possibly be held responsible for their own condition and (2) conservative economic policy contributes to the inequality of life chances among children by prohibiting policies that favor the poor on very narrowly defined ·efficiency grounds.

The primary source of humiliation in each of the cases I have noted is that as a matter of policy, blacks and poor children are being treated as inferior persons by government authorities. Blacks' interest in being free of suspicion and coercion is deliberately set aside to promote the alleged public safety interests of the rest of society, just as the interests of poor children are subordinated to the economic interests of the nonpoor. These deliberate discounts on the well-being of some citizens in the interests of others offends Margalit's definition of decency, which requires social institutions to refrain from humiliating people. However, this concept of decency also implies that economic policy is inherently indecent, to the extent that it requires the humiliation of the poor and racial minorities by promoting policies that prevent the development of capabilities among some members of the nation in order to promote the interests of others.

Margalit's concept of decency is clearly at odds with the Hayekian idea of justice that is the foundation for a great deal of modern free-market conservative thinking. Recall that Hayek's concept of justice is founded on the claim that the distribution of income and wealth that is generated by the activity of free persons in a market economy is legitimate as long as it is the *unplanned* outcome of the pursuit of self-interest. The fact that no person or agency deliberately created the pattern of well-being and deprivation associated with the distribution income, assets, and capabilities means that there can be no claim that the market's verdict is socially unjust, since injustice requires that the interests of one group of persons is advanced by curtailing the liberty of others. In turn, justice requires that public policies refrain from favoring the interests of any particular person, class, region, or racial or ethnic group over the interests of another. In particular, the Hayekian idea of justice demands that the state specifically refrain from any and all redistributive activity, because the use of fiscal measures to transfer resources from one group of people to another necessarily means that public power is being used to favor the interests of one group of persons over another by limiting an individual's control over the use of his or her property. Therefore, any policy that takes resources from the nonpoor with the intent of improving the well-being of the poor is unjust because it violates the principle of governmental neutrality with regard to the liberty interests of all citizens.

Margalit's concept of decency strongly suggests that the Hayekian idea of justice is perfectly consistent with the perpetual humiliation of society's weaker members through the operation of a free-market economy. Hayekian justice and a great deal of conservative economic policy are humiliating because each ignores the role of social deliberation and design in the construction of such core institutions as the market, property rights, and the law. The Hayekian claim that the unplanned outcome of market activity is just regardless of the distribution of well-being forgets that the range and general pattern of market outcomes is the product of deliberate social plans that are formulated, executed, and revised through collective political institutions, particularly in democratic societies. The nature and extent of liberty rights and property rights, the laws governing transactions and the enforcement of property rights and the laws safeguarding liberty rights, and the system of institutions that are developed to regulate macroeconomic conditions, police the nation's borders, and provide other essential public goods are all the product of deliberation on the part of political agents working for their principals, the citizenry. In turn, changes in the content of property or civil rights, in the definition of the public good, or in the institutions designed to address collective needs will necessarily alter the range and pattern of the distribution of well-being. Therefore, a social decision to promote the formal liberty interests of citizens without considering the impact of the resulting distributional patterns of well-being on the poor represents a decision to place a portion of the population in poverty or to subject the poor element of the population to abuse at the hands of private and public power, since a person's capacity to act in his or her own interest is largely determined by that person's access to crucial developmental resources at various stages of life. The decision to arrange social institutions in ways that require a portion of the population to live without adequate schooling, health care, safety, employment, or the capacity to develop and exercise their capabilities is not a neutral stance; it is a deliberate decision to deprive some persons of the ability to exercise their liberty rights. Indeed, a society that requires a portion of the population to live without the opportunity to develop and use their capabilities—by denying them access to crucial developmental resources—is one that chooses to humiliate its poorer and weaker members by treating their life chances as inferior to the life chances and projects of favored others.

A Further Complication

I have already noted that the usual argument in favor of merit, based on incentives, is not as clear-cut as it first appears, once we have taken account of the wholly derivative character of merit. My brief accounts of Sen's critique of merit-based arguments and of Margalit's analysis of humiliation become particularly powerful when coupled with G. A. Cohen's doubts about justice-based arguments for economic inequality.[9] John Rawls's *A Theory of Justice*, arguably the most important work in political and moral philosophy in the second half of the twentieth century, lays out a complete liberal theory of justice that includes a powerful justification for economic inequality, usually referred to (following Rawls's original exposition) as the *difference principle*. The difference principle claims that economic and social inequalities can satisfy the demands of justice in a liberal society if they are (1) of benefit to the least advantaged members of society and (2) linked to the offices, positions, rewards, and prizes that are open to all members of society under conditions of fair and equal opportunity (Rawls 1971, 52–58, 65–73). The difference principle has a great deal of appeal to many on the liberal Left, because it suggests that a competitive capitalist society can arrange its affairs so that the inequalities resulting from the struggle for wealth and position in a market economy are of benefit to the poorest members of the community. Equally important, the difference principle ties inequality directly to the requirement that a community create conditions of equal opportunity, making equality of opportunity an absolute precondition for the acceptability of the unequal distribution of income and wealth in a market order.

According to the difference principle, a market society's reliance on unequal economic rewards to encourage effort, innovation, savings, and growth are not, in and of themselves, suspect, as may be the case under other egalitarian theories of justice. Instead, in a competitive market economy, economic incentives that lead to persistent inequality in income, wealth, and well-being while encouraging growth and development are justified if these inequalities can be shown to maximize the well-being of the poorest members of society. One implication of this principle is that liberal societies that use tax-and-transfer schemes to redistribute income and opportunity from the well-off to the poor must set their policies in ways that balance the inequality-reducing effects of social assistance—for example, in-kind transfers and subsidies to the poor—against the disincentive effects of taxation and redistribution on work, saving, investment, and risk taking in society as a whole. In practical terms, the disincentive effects of redistributive policies act as a brake on the reach of egalitarian policies whenever the latter threaten to reduce economic activity in ways that ultimately cut into the well-being of the poor.

Cohen (2000, 117–33, especially 120–29) has expressed doubts about the ethical legitimacy of the incentive argument that grounds the difference principle, thereby casting doubt on the egalitarian credentials of Rawls's A *Theory of Justice* and wrecking many moral justifications in support of economic inequality. Cohen's argument is straightforward. The claim that inequality can be justified when it is to the benefit of the least well-off already presupposes that the prevailing pattern of inequality in society has come about "naturally" or, in any event, without the deliberate choice or action of a sector of the community in the near or distant past. But existing forms of social and economic inequality are a complex combination of contemporary trends that unfold on the stage of inherited inequalities. The brute facts of the intergenerational transmission of class and social status interacts with the slow evolution of custom and deep-structure social and political institutions to serve as the backdrop for current market events. The inertia of inherited social inequalities, once recognized, casts a cloud over the difference principle because contemporary social policies, even egalitarian policies, are usually enacted on the basis of thoroughly illegitimate inherited conditions.

Consider, for example, a policy of tax cuts enacted on the dubious proposition that the incentive effects of low taxes on the well-off in society are so great that the economic position of the poor will improve. Such a policy takes the existing scheme of economic inequality for granted.[10] Yet it is certainly reasonable for the poor to ask the following three questions of anyone who might make this incentive-based argument for tax cuts.

1. Is our current poverty connected to your current riches through contemporary events and policies or on the basis of inherited social inequalities?

2. What is the justification for the distribution of rewards and burdens associated with inherited inequalities if many of these social inequalities can be directly traced to deliberate social policies or are the result of historical regimes of cruelty, slavery, or abuse?

3. Why should the well-being of poor people depend on further enriching the well-off when the prevailing distribution of advantage and disadvantage in society is the product of unjust actions and policies in the past?[11]

If the inherited set of inequalities cannot be justified by an appeal to the difference principle—that is, if current inequalities did not contribute to the well-being of the poor in the past or present—there is little prospect that inequality-promoting policies enacted in the present can satisfy the conditions of justice. In particular, an incentive-based argument that supports inequality on the claim that such disparities as may arise will improve the circumstances of the poor assumes that both the choices of the well-off and the existing pattern of inequality are immune from criticism. Justice in such a setting is then limited to judgments about the capacity of policy to ameliorate the inevitable and brutal inequalities associated with capitalism, through the use of appropriate tax, expenditure, and regulatory policies. A policy is just or unjust to the extent that it improves the lot of the poor, even though the current condition of the poor can be traced to the self-interested behavior of the well-off in the past or present. If the disincentive effects of the policy on the economic behavior of the well-off are so great that the well-being of the poor is harmed, the policy is unjust. Yet attention to the disincentive effects of egalitarian policies on the poor ignores the fact that the well-off are the ultimate arbiters of the "efficiency" of policy. A policy that worsens the condition of the poor because it dissuades the well-off from pursuing activities that yield side benefits to the poor is certainly troubling. However, the more basic problem in this instance is that the poor are dependent on the well-off. Indeed, the more fundamental problem here is that the poor depend on the satisfaction that the well-off derive from policy, which puts poor people in the wretched position of hoping that the bounty reaped by their richer fellow citizens is so great that some small bit might slop over the edge of the table and fall to them in the lower depths.

The ugly nature of dominance and submission implied in Cohen's analysis of Rawlsian liberalism—and, by extension, classical liberalism and its cruel American conservative offspring—is crystal clear. The rhetoric of formal equality and the difference principle announced by Rawls masks a grotesque type of patron-client relationship between the well-off and the badly off. The Rawlsian form of the ill-favored relationship between the well-off and the poor is far superior to the almost sadistic interdependence between the higher and lower classes displayed during the past two decades of conservative hegemony in the United States. A Rawlsian republic would use its tax, transfer, and regulatory powers to redistribute a fair portion of the national product to the poor, only stopping when the position of the poor was worsened by further egalitarian moves. A conservative, free-market regime would never allow the well-being of the poor to become the measure of policy, not least because poverty is a sign that the poor have chosen their fate freely, are the hard-luck carriers of inferior cultural traits, or are the pitiable product of defective genes. Yet both classical and Rawlsian liberalism ultimately subordinate the interests of the poor to the interests of the well-off, turning the poor into clients whose well-being hinges on the gratification of others. A Rawlsian state limits the prospects of the poor by respecting the rights of the nonpoor to go on strike whenever redistribution becomes too burdensome. By contrast, a conservative regime simply respects the wishes of the nonpoor. This arrangement gives the well-off a permanent, legitimate veto over the structure of economic and social policy on the basis of their own narrow self-interest. The well-off then do not have to justify their actions or preferences on the basis of the difference principle or any other concept of justice.

Cohen's analysis of the problems with the difference principle helps us see why an argument in support of inequality based on merit and incentives is thoroughly humiliating to poor or despised social groups. Poor or despised people without power or resources must capitulate to the brute fact that the well-off control resources and politics, with the consequence that social outcasts can only improve their lot if they propose policies that benefit the well-off. It may be prudent for the poor to recognize and adapt to the realities of power and privilege in society, particularly when the choices of the well-off have substantial effects on the life chances of the poor. However, the fact that the poor must knuckle under to the whims of the well-off to improve their dreary lot is certainly a reason to believe that economic and social arrangements are humiliating.

Another, far more bitter example will drive the point home with great force. Racial inequality in the United States could be justified according to the difference principle, if (1) the prevailing pattern of distribution were a "natural" or accidental outcome unrelated to the structure of existing social institutions and (2) the existing pattern of economic and social inequalities benefits the least advantaged members of society—in this case, the members of the least advantaged racial groups. Of course, the pattern of economic and social inequality between, for example, blacks and whites in the United States surely fails to satisfy the difference principle, since these inequalities can be directly traced to the deliberate design and operation of the nation's political and social institutions as well as to the consequences of widely shared social customs. Further, no person with an interest in matters of justice could argue that modern racial inequality in

the United States benefits blacks, though writers convinced of the intellectual and moral inferiority of blacks might contend that unequal access
to power and opportunity across the color line actually rescues black people from their own incompetence.[12]

We are all too familiar with the obstacles that the hideous legacy of
slavery, apartheid, and present-day race-inspired norms of family and community place before efforts to create a just or even decent society in the
United States. The current debate over affirmative action, which features
an ever more feeble defense of so-called racial preferences in employment
and hiring by liberals, against an ascendant conservative attack on such
preferences in the name of race-blind public policy, provides a perfect
example of the brutal relationship of domination and humiliation between
blacks and whites in America. The argument over affirmative action is a
grand diversion from a serious consideration of the roots of racial inequality in the United States, largely because the debate implicitly assumes that
racial inequality cannot be addressed by a more fundamental reconstruction of economic and social institutions that finally breaks the tight link
between color and class. A brief meditation on this debate will show how
racial humiliation is an essential consequence of existing classical liberalism in the United States.

Humiliation as Political Sport: Affirmative Action

The classical liberal attack on racial preferences in defense of "merit" in
employment and college admissions is, at bottom, a defense of the principles of free and fair competition according to a common set of rules that
are to apply to all members of society. Yet the particular criteria of merit
being used—test scores in college admissions or in hiring and promotion
in employment—are treated as if they are exempt from scrutiny. For example, testing is frequently treated as a neutral and objective device for allo-
cating scarce school resources or job slots to those who will use these
resources most efficiently. It is perfectly plain that a concept of merit based
on efficiency alone, rather than a more subtle merit claim connected to
distributive justice, presumes that increasing wealth is the primary purpose
of procedures of school or job selection. It is also clear that the choice of
efficiency criteria for selecting students or employees without any connected concern for the distribution of the resulting economic rewards

across class and color lines is a decision to accept the legitimacy of the institutions that create and sustain the current distribution of economic well-being across color lines.

Blacks are faced with a terrible dilemma that illustrates Margalit's concept of humiliation in a most painful manner. Black children are forced to attend inferior schools because their parents cannot afford better schools. Black parents are forced to accept less prestigious and less lucrative jobs because they are themselves victims of a regime of racial and class segregation that deprived them of adequate schooling. Whites support a system of college admissions that is officially race-blind but that distributes access to schooling on the basis of class, which is tightly tied to race by virtue of the nation's history and the operation of modern institutions, most particularly labor markets, housing markets, local school finance, and the petty race hatreds of the white majority that guide the choices whites make concerning housing, voting, and hiring. This commitment to color-blind admissions puts further limits on the chances that blacks might acquire high-quality college training. Blacks can resign themselves to the fact that race-blind admissions limit their access to higher education, they can improve their capacity to compete in the merit wars (though how one does this without money or resources is an open question), or they may engage in protest in the vain hope that they might change the hearts and minds of whites.

The issue here is not that blacks are shut out of college schooling by virtue of the death of affirmative action. If whites continue to go against the grain of white American history by allowing colleges to select their students without regard to race, blacks will in time gradually increase their access to colleges and universities if they can somehow bypass the veto power of whites and gain access to developmental resources in other ways. The most important aspect of the end of affirmative action for our purposes is that the conservative stance is indifferent both to the unjust social origins of the current distribution of incomes, wealth, and capacities across color lines and to the antiegalitarian consequences of policies that distribute crucial resources on the basis of wealth and "ability" alone.

Liberty, Equality, and Diversity

Must capitalism in a racially divided society turn markets into an anvil that smashes the life chances of the racial and social outcasts who lack skills and wealth? Can liberal capitalist societies become just social spaces whose economies honor liberty, diversity, and equality? Liberal regimes are, among other things, webs of rules and institutional roles that are designed to facilitate each person's pursuit of the self, free from the domination of the masses as well as from the weight of popular conventional ideas of the good. Economics is the study of the material consequences that flow from the exercise of initiative in the service of the self, where the only limits placed on the self are those imposed by property rights, by the need to maintain essential collective institutions, and by the need to restrain society from smothering individuals by the weight of tradition, authority, or politics.

Liberalism protects freedom and autonomy by disarming the state, by limiting government power in the hope that men and women might be able to choose lives that they have reason to value. Classical liberalism's considerable achievement in crippling the ability of theocrats and zealots to seize state power is tainted by its blindness to the threat that the economic power of racial and moralistic coalitions pose to the liberty of social outcasts, particularly racial pariahs. This dangerous omission in the classical liberal project is repaired by egalitarian liberals, whose work has shown that a liberal society must use economic resources, through some form of redistribution, to protect diversity, by granting all members of society access to fundamental capabilities, thereby granting each citizen the substantive liberty to choose, to compete, and to accept responsibility for his or her actions.

Racial animus coordinates the otherwise separate fears and hatreds of economically dominant racial groups into concentrated private power that can retard the economic and social development of despised groups. Classical liberalism's dual attack on concentrated public power and on the economic power of monopolies and cartels must be extended to properly acknowledge the destructive power of racial, ethnic, and religious hatred in a market setting. Racial embargoes against commerce and social intercourse with outcasts in the shadow of foundational crimes like slavery or apartheid can become holding pens that constrict the life chances of the despised, even though the restricted dealings across the color line are the unintended outcome of the self-interested actions of millions of otherwise unconnected racial phobics. Customary racist practices in private and economic life are the legitimate expression of self-interest and desire that all liberal societies must protect, so long as these practices do not interfere with the formal freedom of others. But the protection of substantive liberty for all requires a racially divided liberal society to construct institutions to prevent cultural and racial animus from wounding the prospects of presumed Others.

Liberal egalitarians have proposed a wide range of strategies for protecting the substantive liberty of all in the context of a market economy. For example, a considerable part of the welfare state—both the system of social insurance and means-tested poor relief and assistance—can be replaced by a basic income scheme of the sort proposed by James Meade (1993) or Philippe Van Parijs (1995). These alternative schemes provide individuals with a (low) guaranteed income that is adjusted for age, infirmity, region, number of children, and a few other elements that affect the standard of living. The economic consequences of a basic income scheme combined with a flat tax has been studied by Anthony Atkinson (1995). Alternatively, the welfare state could be cut back or eliminated in favor of a system of "social endowment" proposed by Roberto Unger (1998) or a "stakeholder scheme" proposed by Bruce Ackerman and Anne Alstott (1999). These latter systems would have the state provide each individual with an initial stock of wealth at the time they reach young adulthood, which could be used by an individual to start a business or finance schooling or toward some other purpose. The primary goal of proposals of social endowment is to provide individuals with the material means to pursue their individual goals (so that they might enjoy the rewards of success or suffer the consequences of failure based on their own efforts and decisions), while reducing the effect of the advantages or disadvantages associated with their class, race, region, religion, or ethnicity.

Each of these proposed alternatives, which seek to combine egalitarian ambitions with economic efficiency in matters of work and savings incentives and with the incentive consequences of taxes used to finance equality, will have to be subjected to rigorous short- and long-term formal analysis to assess the balance of costs and benefits that can be expected to emerge in each case. Yet the egalitarian liberals are steadily clearing ground for the return of equality in liberal societies, thereby allowing us to hope that genuine liberty in the midst of diversity might flourish under capitalism. Otherwise, one sinks into despair at the prospect that the tyranny of the state might be replaced by populist market-driven tyrannies in which the hateful choices of racial phobics and bigots of all sorts cut into the real freedom of abused people.

NOTES

1. An excellent summary of the liberal stance that pits the rights of families against the requirements of liberal societies to protect and promote the develop-

ment of children into autonomous adults is provided by Brighouse in chapter 2 of his recent left-liberal defense of school choice, *School Choice and Social Justice* (2000).

2. See John Gray's brief, but complete, discussion in *Liberalism* (1995b, 61–67) of the link between private property and the protection of liberty in society.

3. See Sen's discussion of contrasting theories of freedom in chapter 3 of *Development as Freedom* (1999, 54–86). Ronald Dworkin's exploration of liberal equality is summed up in *Sovereign Virtue: The Theory and Practice of Equality* (2000).

4. Becker's original analysis of the economics of discrimination in competitive markets included the claim that capitalist institutions, left to their own devices, would gradually eliminate wage and income disparities between racial groups due to discrimination, as long as members of different racial groups displayed similar levels of effort and productive ability. Becker's key finding has been disputed by many writers, who have shown how competitive capitalism can generate persistent racial inequality. One of the most important recent statements of the economic causes of racial inequality is Glenn Loury's *The Anatomy of Racial Inequality* (2002), which brings together the insights of the economic theory of imperfect information and an analysis of the limits of human cognition in social life, to craft a general theory of intergenerational inequality across racial categories that have no "scientific" legitimacy. In an immanent critique of Becker's position, Andrews (1999) shows why competitive markets can reinforce racial inequalities if income inequalities across color lines lead to persistent gaps in rates of human capital accumulation and skill development across color lines.

5. For example, the right-libertarian's chief complaint against antidiscrimination laws and policies is that they interfere with the right of property owners to the full use of their possessions. First, antidiscrimination laws criminalize a certain subset of choices (in this case, a refusal to trade with racial undesirables), thereby reducing, with the threat of punishment, the autonomy and well-being of property owners. Second, proving that particular refusals to let apartments to blacks, to hire blacks, or to admit them into a college or university are due to racial factors is extremely difficult, in large part because governments necessarily lack the relevant information for making these types of decisions. The specific, local information about the quality of applicants for housing, jobs, or schools is in the hands and heads of the buyers and sellers involved, whose knowledge in these sorts of transactions is based on more accurate information than are the judgments of outside observers. An outside observer, such as a government, can see that a corporation has few black employees or that a school has few black students, but it cannot see whether there are black students or black job seekers who are qualified for the positions. Antidiscrimination laws are, accordingly, a source of economic inefficiency, to the extent that they give individuals, enterprises, and other organizations (including other agencies of government) incentives to avoid the costs of punishment that might distort their decisions in favor of candidates who, on their merits, should not gain access to valuable resources or jobs. Firms that fear the costs of antidiscrimination lawsuits or penalties imposed by the state for violations of

antidiscrimination regulations may hire blacks with lower grades and fewer skills than whites or Asians as a rational, profit-maximizing strategy, though the net result of these actions is to disrupt the market's ability to appropriately allocate jobs among the most suitable individuals. See Thomas Sowell's *Knowledge and Decisions* (1980) or Richard Epstein's more recent argument for abolishing antidiscrimination law in *Forbidden Grounds: The Case against Employment Discrimination Laws* (1992), for the most rigorous statements of the right-libertarian position.

6. Hayek's critique of social justice is based on a stringent liberal stance that seeks to protect each person's liberty—in terms of both freedom of action and freedom of thought—from coercive majorities bent on imposing their will. However, Hayek is careful to note that a free society can certainly choose to provide a social safety net, even in the form of a guaranteed minimum income, in ways that are consistent with individual liberty. The provision of a minimum income or minimum living standard only offends Hayek's strict concept of justice if the method for funding and distributing a minimum income treats citizens unequally by imposing unequal economic burdens on some to promote the well-being of others. Therefore, a basic income financed by a lump-sum tax or even by a proportional income or wealth tax is consistent with the conditions of justice laid down by Hayek, because these forms of taxation impose the same absolute or proportionate sacrifice on each citizen (Hayek 1976, 87).

7. Hayek insists that the power of markets to protect individual liberty and to mobilize talent, resources, and information in a complex and highly decentralized society brings with it the inevitable and acceptable risk that many people will fail to realize their goals despite their best efforts. An extended passage from chapter 9 of *The Mirage of Social Justice* (1976, 72) illustrates Hayek's clear view that merit is not the primary purpose of a market society: "The long and short of it all is that men can be allowed to decide what work to do only if the remuneration they can expect to get for it corresponds to the value their services have to those of their fellows who receive them; and that *these values which their services will have to their fellows will often have no relations to their individual merits or needs*. Reward for merit earned and indication of what a person should do, both in his own and in his fellows' interest, are different things. It is not good intentions or needs but doing what in fact most benefits others, irrespective of motive, which will secure the best reward. Among those who try to climb Mount Everest or to reach the Moon, we also honor not those who made the greatest efforts, but those who got there first."

8. Stiglitz's *Whither Socialism* (1994) presents a powerful critique of the Hayekian analysis of markets and the infirmities of socialism, a critique based on modern theories of imperfect information and market failure. Stiglitz's primary point is that socialism failed because it could not cope with a wide array of principal-agent problems that led to destructive patterns of resource misallocation and incentive incompatibility in matters of work. However, Stiglitz makes a point of ripping Hayek's critique of socialism for providing a thoroughly unrealistic assessment of the strengths of market institutions by ignoring the ubiquity of market failure due to imperfect information in capital, labor, and product markets that undermine the coordinative function of the price mechanism.

9. The initial version of this argument can be found in Cohen's Tanner lec-

ture "Incentives, Inequality, and Community" (1995). A sharper and more suc-
cinct statement of this argument is developed in lectures 8 and 9 of Cohen's book
If You're an Egalitarian, How Come You're Rich? (2000).

10. Cohen (1995, 338–53) uses the example of tax cuts to explore the logic
and limits of Rawls's difference principle in the context of a community. In particular, Cohen considers the difficulties of a dialogue between the rich and the
poor in a democratic community where a tax-cut proposal is being considered.
The problem with such a dialogue is that a defense of a tax cut on the grounds that
the incentive effects of lower taxes would encourage the rich to engage in behavior that has a side effect of helping the poor already concedes the point that the
rich refuse to help the poor unless it is to their advantage. This self-interested
behavior on the part of the rich undermines any claims to justice associated with
the tax-cut proposal, with damaging implications for the difference principle, as
explained shortly in text.

11. Of course, the poor do not get to ask these questions of the well-off,
because their poverty prevents them from participating in politics or public policy
in any but the most formal and least effective ways (like voting in a party-based
democratic system dominated by the influence of wealth). In practice, "the poor"
are reduced to the status of an abstraction that is bandied about in political debate
to hide self-interested advocacy behind a screen of social concern. Poor people are
"invisible people" in modern politics and social science, in the same sense that
black people were "invisible" in Ralph Ellison's *Invisible Man:* the social identities
of the poor are molded to fit the rhetorical needs of contending sectors among
social elites in the course of debates over social and economic policy. The marginal status of the poor within the world of policy, politics, and social science
sometimes makes it hard to see that arguments like the difference principle are
ultimately rationalizations on the part of the socially powerful to retain their control over the deployment of resources. The list of three questions that the poor
could ask of the nonpoor put the well-off in the uncomfortable position of
acknowledging that their current power and therefore the well-being of the poor
ultimately depend on the capacity of socially powerful people to exact a price from
the poor if the latter are to improve their lot.

12. One particularly important example of this line of thought is the infamous
chapter 21 of *The Bell Curve* by Charles Murray and the late Richard Herrnstein
(1994), with its dystopian vision of a custodial state that must monitor the behavior of an intellectually incompetent class of citizens, who are also disproportionately dark by virtue of the presumed tight link between race, color, and intelligence.

The Anatomy of Racial Inequality

A Clarification

Glenn C. Loury

In *The Anatomy of Racial Inequality*, I have tried to do three things: outline a theory of "race" applicable to the social and historical circumstances of the United States; sketch an account of why racial inequality in our society is so stubbornly persistent; and offer a conceptual framework for the practice of social criticism on race-related issues—criticism that might encourage reflection among our political and intellectual elite and, in this way, promote social reform. In my book, these objectives are subsumed, respectively, in the successive chapters entitled "Racial Stereotypes," "Racial Stigma," and "Racial Justice" (Loury 2002).

Any theory of "race," it seems to me, must explain the fact that people take note of and assign significance to superficial markings on the bodies of other human beings—their skin color, hair texture, facial bone structure, and so forth. This practice is virtually universal in human societies. Scientists have conjectured that it has a deep neurological foundation. This is the point of departure for my analysis. I refer to a society as being "raced" when its members routinely partition the field of human subjects whom they encounter in that society into groups and when this sorting convention is based on the subjects' possession of some cluster of observable bodily marks. This led to my claim that, at bottom, "race" is all about "embodied social signification."

Let us call this the *social-cognitive* approach to thinking about "race." It may be usefully contrasted with an approach derived from the science/art of *biological taxonomy*. There, one endeavors to classify human beings on the basis of natural variation in genetic endowments across geographically isolated subpopulations. Such isolation was a feature of the human condition until quite recently (on an evolutionary timescale), and it permitted some independence of biological development within subpopulations, which can be thought to have led to the emergence of distinct races. When such philosophers as Jorge Garcia or Anthony Appiah deny the reality of "race," they have in mind this biological-taxonomic notion, and what they deny is that meaningful distinctions among contemporary human subgroups can be derived in this way. Whether they are right or not would appear to be a scientific question.[1] But, whatever the merits of this dispute, it is important to understand that the validity of racial classification as an exercise in biological taxonomy is distinct conceptually from the validity (and relevance) of my concern with racial categorization as an exercise in social cognition.

Moreover—and this, too, is absolutely critical—to establish the scientific invalidity of racial taxonomy demonstrates neither the irrationality nor the immorality of adhering to a social convention of racial classification. Even if Garcia and Appiah are correct and the scientists who think that "race" is a useful biological-taxonomic category are wrong, it would not follow from this that seeing oneself or other people as belonging to "races" is akin to believing that someone with exceptional talents or an odd personality has come from another planet. We can adopt the linguistic convention that when saying, "person A belongs to race X," we mean, "person A possesses physical traits that (in a given society, at a fixed point in history, under the conventions of racial classification extant there and then) will cause him to be classified (by a preponderance of those he encounters in that society and/or by himself) as belonging to race X." Whereas this maneuver would seem deeply unsatisfactory if applied to the question of someone being a planetary alien, I hold that this is a plausible way to proceed when discussing the social reality of "race." This is a pragmatic judgment on my part, not an a priori logical claim; that is, I hold this view because the social convention of thinking about other people and about ourselves as belonging to different "races" is such a long-standing and deeply ingrained one in our political culture that it has taken on a life of its own. Belief that "alien beings are with us" has no comparable salience. If it did, the subjective reality of this belief (and of the practice of classifying people on this basis) would be of interest, regardless of its objective correctness. Thus, for students of the history and political economy of the modern multiracial nation-state, the logical exercise of deconstructing racial categories by trying to show that nothing "real" lies behind them—an exercise that critics of the "race" concept seem to be so fond of—is largely beside the point.

This perspective is supported by the theory of "self-confirming stereotypes" that I advance in my book. My point here is subtle, and judging by reactions to the book, I am not sure that all my readers have grasped it. Suppose people believe that fluctuations of the stock market can be predicted by changes in sunspot activity. This predictability may occur because, as an objective meteorological matter, sunspots correlate with rainfall, which influences crop yields, thus affecting the economy. Or solar radiation might somehow influence the human psyche so as to alter how people behave in securities markets. Each of these possibilities proposes objective causal links between sunspots and stock prices. Making decisions based on these possibilities can be likened to grounding one's cognizance of "race" on the validity of a race-based biological taxonomy. But suppose that no objective links of this kind exist between sunspots and stock prices. Still, if enough people believe in the connection, monitor conditions on the sun's surface, and act based on how they anticipate security prices will be affected, then a *real* link between these evidently disparate phenomena will have been forged out of the subjective perceptions of stock-market participants. As a result of this process, a belief in the financial relevance of sunspot activity will have been rendered entirely rational.

Here is a concrete illustration, drawn from recent discussions of race in American society, that may assist in understanding this point. In my book, I use the example of cab drivers in a big city (Loury 2002, 30–31). Suppose that drivers are reluctant to stop for young black men because they fear being robbed; that is, they think that chance of robbery conditional on race (and, perhaps, conditioned on other information, such as age and sex) exceeds some prudential threshold if the prospective fare is a young black man, but not when that fare is an older white woman. Imagine that their surmise is objectively correct, as a matter of the crime statistics. A very simple process of what economists call *adverse selection* could, at least in theory, explain how such a circumstance might arise, even in the event that each subgroup is no more inclined to rob a taxi driver than any other. The process is the following: If I know the taxi is not going to stop for me or is unlikely to, and if I do not intend to rob the driver, then I will not want to rely on taxis for transportation, because I have very long waits, on the average. Plausibly, this waiting is less costly for someone who intends to rob the driver than for someone who does not. After all, to get in a night's work, the robber may only need one cab to stop at some time during the night. The fact that cab drivers are reluctant to stop for a certain group of persons may discourage all members of that group from using taxis, but those persons intent on robbing will be relatively less discouraged than those who have no such intention. Thus, should the cab drivers begin with an a priori belief that a certain group of people is more likely than another group to harbor robbers, and should the drivers become reluctant to stop for people in that group as a result, then the drivers will end up creating incentives for people to self-select in such a way as to make it relatively more likely that someone hailing a cab who belongs to the targeted group is a robber.

We can see from this example that no *objective* racial taxonomy need be valid (the proportion of robbers in each group might have been the same) for the *subjective* use of racial classifications to become warranted (cab drivers have a rational justification for their use of racial information). It is enough that influential social actors hold schemes of racial classification in their minds and act on those schemes. Their classificatory methods may be mutually inconsistent, one with another, and they may be unable to give a cogent justification for adopting their schemes. But once a person knows that others in society will classify him on the basis of certain markers, and in the event that these acts of classification affect his material or psychological well-being, then it will be a rational cognitive stance—not a belief in magic and certainly not a moral error—for him to think of himself as being "raced." In turn, that he thinks of himself in this way and that his societal peers are inclined to classify him similarly can provide a compelling reason for a newcomer to the society to adopt this ongoing scheme of racial classification. Learning the extant "language" of embodied social signification is a first step toward assimilation of the newcomer, whether foreigner or newborn, into any "raced" society. I conclude that "races," in the social-cognitive sense, may come to exist and to be reproduced over the generations in a society, even though there may exist no "races" in the biological-taxonomic sense. It follows that calling attention to the scientific dispute on the existence of races need have no bearing on the legitimacy of the social practice of racial classification. Despite several critical comments from readers, I continue to insist that, for the purpose of understanding how "race" operates in the American social hierarchy, my viewpoint—thinking of "race" as "embodied social signification"—is both logically coherent and analytically useful.

The foregoing may be unsatisfactory to many ethicists, as they are often keen to move from the cognitive to a normative plane of discussion. They would imagine there to be something "wrong" with seeing others (or, for that matter, oneself) in racial terms—with preferring to associate with people because of their racial identities, with feeling obligated to coracialists, and so on. Just as one might think it wrong to punish people (witches) for the crime of being "the devil's handmaiden" when, in point of fact, no people actually are, so, too, one might think it wrong to condition one's dealings with others on the basis of "race" when, in point of fact, there are no (biological-taxonomic) "races." If there are no races, what possible justification can there be for the embrace of racial identity? My view is that the existence of "races" (in the biological-taxonomic sense) and the ethics of the practice of racial classification are largely distinct problems. I do not think we can get at the latter problem by interrogating the human heart, one person at a time. It is a mistake, in my view, to judge the propriety of social conventions in terms of whether individuals behave virtuously or viciously when they elect to comply with those conventions. To be taken seriously, an ethical critique of race-based thinking must get beneath (or behind) the cognitive acts of individual persons and investigate the structure of social relations within which those individuals operate.

Racial Stigma

This brings me to the topic of racial stigma—which I take to be the central innovative concept in my book (Loury 2002, chap. 3). Critics have charged that I am unclear about my meaning here. Some even see me as reiterating, in a slightly modified form, the tired liberal charge that blacks do not succeed because whites are guilty of moral malfeasance. Both charges are groundless. To reiterate, my basic approach to the problem of racial inequality is cognitive, not normative. I eschew use of the word *racism*, not to avoid sounding like an outdated civil rights leader, but because the word is imprecise. More useful, I think, is my core concept—"biased social cognition." The term *racial stigma* is not a bludgeon with which I hope to beat "whitey" into political submission. It does not refer to "sinister" thoughts in the heads of white people. Nor is it an invitation to passivity for blacks. Rather, what I am doing with this concept is trying to move from the fact that people take note of racial classification in the course of their interactions with one another, to some understanding of how this affects their perceptions of the phenomena they observe in the social world around them and how it shapes their explanations of those phenomena. I am asking: When does the "race" of those subject to some problematic social circumstance affect whether powerful observers perceive there to be a problem, and what follows from such perception?

Given the evident sensitivity of racial discourses, it is perhaps best if I make the point with a nonracial example. Consider gender inequality. We know that there is disparity in the social outcomes for boys and girls in two different venues—the schools and the jails. Thus, suppose that, when compared to girls, boys are overrepresented among those doing well in math and science in the schools and also among those doing poorly in society at large by ending up in jail. There is some evidence to support both suppositions, but only the first is widely perceived to be a problem for public policy. Why? I think this is so because the fact that boys and girls have different levels of achievement in the technical curriculum of our schools offends our basic intuition about the propriety of underlying social processes. Although we may not be able to put our fingers on exactly why this outcome in school achievement occurs, we instinctively know that it is not right. In the face of this disparity, we are inclined to interrogate our institutions—to search the record of our social practice and examine myriad possibilities to see where things might have gone wrong. Our baseline expectation is that equality should prevail here. Our moral sensibility is offended when it does not. An impetus to reform is spurred thereby. We cannot easily envision a wholly legitimate sequence of events that would produce the disparity, so we set ourselves the task of solving a problem.

Gender disparity in rates of imprisonment occasions no such disquiet. This is because tacitly, if not explicitly, we are "gender essentialists"; that is, we think boys and girls are different in some ways relevant to explaining the observed disparity—different either in their biological natures or in their deeply ingrained socializations. (Note that the *essentialism* with which I am concerned need not be based solely or even mainly in biology. It can be grounded in [possibly false] beliefs about profound cultural difference as well.) As "gender essentialists," our intuitions are not offended by the fact of vastly higher rates of imprisonment among males than females. We seldom ask any deeper questions about why this disparity has come about. In this sense, we do not perceive there to be a problem, and so no solution is sought.

We may be either right or wrong to act as we do in these gender disparity matters. My point with the example is to show that the bare facts of gender disparity do not, in themselves, suggest any course of action. To act, we must marry the facts we observe to some model of social causation. This model need not be explicit in our minds. It can and usually will lurk beneath the surface of our conscious reflections. Still, it is the facts *plus* the model that lead us to perceive a given circumstance as indicative (or not) of some as yet undiagnosed failing in our social interactions. This kind of reflection on the deeper structure of our social-cognitive processes, as they bear on the issues of racial disparity, is what I had hoped to stimulate with my discussion of "biased social cognition." The role of "race" in such processes is what I am alluding to when I talk about "racial stigma."

To show how the argument goes, I would like to invoke a thought experiment not unlike the ones I analyze at length in my book. But before I continue, let me make a methodological observation. A few readers have labeled these thought experiments "anecdotes" and have then accused me of playing fast and loose with the facts. This is, to be blunt, a gross misunderstanding. Hypothetical cases and counterfactual speculations are commonplace in both philosophy and social theory. They convey general conceptual distinctions in the context of a larger analytical development. That is how I use them in my book and here.

Returning to my thought experiment, imagine that an observer notes (correctly) that, on the average and all else being equal, commercial loans to blacks have a greater risk of default and black residential neighborhoods are more likely to decline. This may lead that observer to withhold credit from blacks or to move away from any neighborhood when more than a few blacks move into it. But what if "race" conveys this information only because when a great number of observers expect it to do so and act on that expectation, the result (through some possibly complex chain of social causation) is to bring about the confirmation of their beliefs? Perhaps blacks default more often precisely because they have trouble getting further extensions of credit in the face of a crisis. Or perhaps nonblack residents panic at the arrival of a few blacks, selling their homes too quickly and below the market value to lower-income (black) buyers, thereby promoting a neighborhood's decline. If, under such circumstances, observers were to attribute racially disparate behaviors to deeply ingrained (biological or cultural) limitations of African-Americans—thinking, for example, that blacks do not repay their loans or take care of their property because, for whatever reasons, they are just less responsible people on average— then these observers might well be mistaken. Yet since their surmise about blacks is supported by hard evidence, they might well persist in their error.

Such an error, persisted in, would be of great political moment, because if one attributes an endogenous difference (a difference produced within a system of interactions) to an exogenous cause (a cause located outside that system), one is unlikely to see any need for systemic reform.

This distinction between endogenous and exogenous sources of social causation is the key to understanding the difference in our reformist intuitions about gender inequalities in the schools and in the jails. Because we think the disparity of school outcomes stems from endogenous sources, while the disparity of jail outcomes is tacitly attributed in most of our "causal models" to exogenous sources, we are differentially moved to do something about the observed disparities.

Thus, I talk about "racial stigma" and employ the apparently loaded phrase *biased social cognition* because it is a politically consequential cognitive distortion to understand the observably disadvantageous position of a racially defined population subgroup as having emerged from qualities taken to be intrinsic to the group when, as a matter of actual social causation, that disadvantage is the product of a system of social interactions. I argue that a given instance of social disparity is less likely to be thought to constitute a social problem when people see the disparity as having been caused by what they take to be the deficiencies of those who lag behind (e.g., the boys in the jails, but not the girls in the schools). I reiterate that it hardly matters whether the internal qualities mistakenly seen as the source of some group's observed laggardly status are biological or deeply cultural.[2] What matters, I argue, is that something has gone wrong if observers fail to see systemic, endogenous interactions that lead to bad social outcomes for blacks and if they instead attribute those results to exogenous factors taken as internal to the group in question. My contention—despite the misgivings of several critics—is that in American society, when the group in question is blacks, the risk of this kind of causal misattribution is especially great.

I believe the disparate impact of the enforcement of antidrug laws offers a telling illustration of the value in this way of thinking. There can be no drug market without sellers *and* buyers. (Just so, there would be no street prostitution without hookers and johns.) Typically, those on the selling side of such markets are more deeply involved in crime and disproportionately drawn from the bottom rungs of society. When we entertain alternative responses to the social malady reflected in drug use (or in street prostitution), we must weigh the costs likely to be imposed on the people involved. Our tacit models of social causation will play a role in this process of evaluation. To ruin a college student's life because of a drug buy (or a businessman's reputation because of a pickup in the red-light district) may strike us as far more costly than to send a young thug to Riker's Island (or to put a floozy in the hoosegow). One consequence of racial stigma, I suggest, is that because those bearing the brunt of the cost of our punitive response to the broad social malady of drug usage are disproportionately black, our society is less impelled to examine what we are undertaking in this area of policy and to consider reform. I could be wrong about this, but the speculation is certainly not implausible. How "serious" a given crime is seen to be in the minds of those who, through their votes, indirectly determine our policies, and how "deserved" the punishment for a given infraction is considered to be, can depend on the racial identities of the parties involved. This, I am holding, is human nature. There need be nothing "sinister" in any of it. But if we want to *analyze* what is going on around us and not limit ourselves to *moralizing* about it, we will want to take such possibilities seriously.

In my book, I use the theory of biased social cognition that I have just sketched to argue that durable racial inequality can best be understood as the outgrowth of a series of what Myrdal ([1944] 1962) called "vicious circles of cumulative causation." Tacit association of "blackness" with "unworthiness" in the American public's imagination affects cognitive processes and promotes essentialist causal misattributions (Loury 2002, chap. 2). When confronted by the facts of racially disparate achievement, the racially disproportionate transgression of legal strictures, and racially unequal development of productive potential, observers will have difficulty identifying with the plight of a group of people whom they (mistakenly) think are simply "reaping what they have sown." In such a case, there will be little public support for egalitarian policies benefiting a stigmatized racial group. The absence of some policies of this sort in turn encourages the reproduction through time of racial inequality: the low social conditions of many blacks persist, the negative social meanings ascribed to blackness are then reinforced, and so the racially biased social-cognitive processes are reproduced, completing the circle.

I argue that this situation constitutes a gross historical injustice in American society. Again, some have disagreed. Garcia (2002) has counterargued that we act legitimately to reduce racial equality only when we are moved by a desire to promote comity and community, not when we are pursuing "racial justice." Thus, he praises me for my opposition to slavery reparations but simultaneously takes me to task for seeing racial inequalities on a scale so evident in contemporary American life as a justice problem. Yet these two positions of mine are very closely linked. My view is that present racial inequality is a justice problem because it has its root in past unjust acts that were perpetrated on the basis of race. I see past racial injustice as establishing a general presumption against indifference to present racial inequality. To see why this matters, suppose it could be shown that a posture of official public indifference to racial inequality would enhance our comity and community. (So, it would seem, many advocates of a "color-blind" America believe.) Even so, I would still want to urge that some efforts to reduce racial inequality would be warranted. However, I do not think that the degree to which social policy should be oriented toward reducing present racial inequality—the weight to be placed on this objective in the calculus of social decision, if you will—can or should be conceived in terms of "correcting" or "balancing" for historical violation. This is what leads me to reject reparations. My view is that although the *quantitative* attribution of causal weight to distant historical events required by reparations advocacy is not workable, one can still support *qualitative* claims. Much of moral consequence rests on this distinction.

My discussion of racial justice (Loury 2002, chap. 4) stands in the great American tradition of progressive social criticism. I seek to extend and generalize conventional notions of "racism" and "discrimination" so as to deal with the post–civil rights reality of our time. Central to this new reality, in my view, is the fact that there has opened between the races a wide gap in productivity-enhancing behaviors—acquisition of cognitive skills, law-abidingness, stability in family relations, attachment to the workforce, and the like. I place this disparity in human development at the center of my analysis and put forward an account of it rooted in social and cultural factors, not in blacks' inherent capacities. What I am saying in so many words is that even if there were no overt racial discrimination against blacks, powerful social forces would still be at work to perpetuate into future generations the consequences of the universally acknowledged history of racism in America. A corollary of this position is that combating such racism as continues to exist will be insufficient to achieve racial justice.

In stating this, I do not mean to suggest that conventional efforts to combat discrimination should be suspended. Nor do I imply that racism is an empty concept or a historical relic irrelevant to the study of present-day social relations in the United States. The evidence of continuing racial unfairness in day-to-day social intercourse in this country is quite impressive. But the evidence that a gap in acquired skills at least partly explains racial disparities is also impressive. There is a difference of one standard deviation between the mean scores of young blacks and whites on the Armed Forces Qualification Test, only about half of which is accounted for by racial differences in schooling and family backgrounds (Neal and Johnson 1996). The National Assessment of Educational Progress shows the average black at age 17 performing only slightly better in reading and mathematics than the average white at age 13 (National Center for Education Statistics 1996). Two of every three black infants are born to an unmarried mother. Young black men are upwards of five times more likely than whites to be arrested and convicted of criminal offenses. In central cities throughout the country, one can observe nonwhite immigrants of relatively recent arrival overtaking native-born blacks in terms of their economic and social performance.

My central proposition is that to understand this horrible situation, one must take account of the indirect and subtle effects of racial stigma, as distinct from discrimination. I argue in my book that racial stigma leads not only to biased social cognition but also to biased processes of human development deriving from the extreme social isolation of many blacks. There is fairly strong support for this view in the literature. Anderson (1990) provides an ethnographic account of life in inner-city Philadelphia in which peer influences significantly constrain the acquisition of skills by adolescents in those neighborhoods. Waldinger (1996), in a study of immigrant labor in New York City, concludes that poor blacks suffer less from the racism of employers than from the fact that they do not have access to the ethnic networks through which workers are recruited for jobs in construction and service industries. Cutler and Glaeser (1997), comparing U.S. cities with varying degrees of racial population concentration, estimate that a 13 percent reduction in segregation would eliminate about one-third of the black-white gap in rates for schooling, employment, earnings, and unwed pregnancy. Mills and Lubuele (1997) argue that students of urban poverty have yet to explain why "low income black residents actually or potentially eligible for jobs that have moved to suburbs [have] not followed such jobs to the suburbs."

Some observers of the American scene, and not only conservatives, see this situation as reflecting a deep incapacity or immorality of the black lower classes. Accordingly, they deny that this circumstance raises any question of social justice for our nation. I think they are wrong, but I do not think that calling them "racists" is an effective rebuttal of their argu-

ments. I seek grounding for the demand for racial justice that requires neither a showing of contemporaneous discrimination nor an insistence on
some kind of transgenerational historical debt.

Reparations advocates conceive the problem of our morally problematic racial history in compensatory terms. By contrast, I propose to see the
problem in interpretative terms; that is, I seek public recognition of the
severity and (crucially) the contemporary relevance of what has tran-
spired. I stress that this is not merely a question of historical fact; it is also
a matter of how we choose to look at the facts. My goal is to encourage a
common basis of historical memory—a common narrative—through
which the past racial injury and its continuing significance can enter into
current policy discourse. What is required for racial justice, as I conceive
it, is a commitment on the part of the public, including the political elite
and the opinion-shaping media, to take responsibility for the plight of the
urban black poor and to understand this troubling circumstance as having
emerged in a general way out of an ethically indefensible past. Such a commitment should, in my view, be open-ended and not contingent on
demonstrating any specific lines of causality. Should a critic agree with my
proposal but prefer not to use the word *justice* in reference to it, that would
be a matter of little consequence.

The Larger Political Context

I turn now from the argument of my book to a consideration of the larger
political context into which my argument has been injected. More than a
few critics and casual observers (e.g., McWhorter [2002]) have taken *The
Anatomy of Racial Inequality* to be a "coming out" for me as some kind of
leftist after my many years of faithful service as a conservative voice in
debates over racial issues. This is a serious misreading. This book is an
exercise in social theory, not in polemics, and those who have been willing to briefly acquaint themselves with it will quickly find this to be so. My
goal with this exercise has been to understand something of how race,
racial identity, and racial classification work in the social life of this
nation. Such an endeavor self-consciously undertaken as an expression of
political ideology is bound to fail. There are literatures in economics, sociology, and social psychology to which I hope to contribute with this work.
While I hope and believe that I have done so, this is a question that my
scholarly peers will ultimately decide.[3] Some people will inevitably be dis-

appointed to hear this, but I must insist that in the writing of my book, I have had no political agenda.

I should also say a word or two about how some have misinterpreted my concept of racial stigma. That it plays a central role in my theory of racial inequality should not be taken to mean that I believe nothing can be done or that passivity is the only rational response to the situation (as charged by McWhorter [2002]). Nor am I promoting the idea that blacks can make no progress until whites become more magnanimous and giving (as alleged by Early [2002]). These charges seem to confuse two quite distinct realms of analysis. Whether or not the racial stigma that I discuss in my book and the social isolation of many blacks to which it leads are important impediments to blacks' social advancement is an empirical question answerable by social science. Despite the inferences of some critics, this is quite different from the proposition that "history is destiny" for black people. Whether racial stigma or any other obstacle we might encounter along life's path should be seen as fundamentally determining our destinies is a moral and philosophical question—even an existential/spiritual matter— answerable by reference to the values and traditions of black American people. An analysis of the social-structural factors impeding black progress need not be a counsel of passivity. To the contrary, such an analysis is the essential first step in any program of rational action.

Some of my more politically charged critics (e.g., McWhorter [2002]) who have accused me of quietly endorsing leftist positions do so because they imagine that some leftists may agree with what I have written. This is then taken as a valid reason to reject my argument. It has been said that I have forgotten what I used to know about the history of black people and particularly about the origins of the underclass. The substance of these forgotten truths, it is argued, is that the tragic conditions in today's ghettos are "due less to slavery's legacy than to the rise of the New Left in the 1960s" (McWhorter 2002, 29).

I most certainly have not "forgotten" this purported truth about black American history. I never knew any such thing, for the good and sufficient reason that it is not true. I believe that most readers of the present chapter are probably familiar with the general, if misguided, narrative: the ideology of black power led to an oppositional culture in the ghettos; in partial response, guilt-ridden whites gave the black poor free handouts with AFDC (Aid to Families with Dependent Children) programs that paid them to have children and lured them into dependency; racial preferences kept black students from ever learning what serious effort entails; and so on. Indeed, it was my fatigue in having to confront this cartoon version of American social history, with its accompaniment of mindless sloganeering about the serious problems afflicting poor black people, that drove me from the conservative ranks in the first place. My own intellectual integrity simply demanded that I move on. Missing from such an underclass morality tale are a few factors that most social historians think could be significant: deindustrialization in the cities of the "rust belt"; a huge, relatively low-skilled immigration quickening competition at the labor market's bottom rungs; fierce resistance by working-class whites to housing and school integration for decades after segregation had been legally proscribed; technological innovations like the birth-control pill, which helped to alter sexual mores across the class structure, and crack cocaine, which, along with the easy availability of guns, changed life in inner cities across America; the tearing-down of low-rent housing through slum clearance, only to replace these units with massive high-rise public housing projects sited almost exclusively in the black residential districts. One could go on in this vein, but this should suffice to make my point: a person who thinks the underclass is the product of a bunch of 1960s moral relativists knows not what he or she is talking about.

Were such a critic to take a glance at the wealth of historical scholarship on the roots of social decay in American cities (Sugrue 1996, a prizewinning study of Detroit in the quarter century after World War II, is a good place to start), he or she would know just how superficial and tendentious his characterization appears. The greatest of the ideologues of black power was the Nation of Islam's Malcolm X—a Victorian puritan on cultural matters. If the family values, work ethic, and concern with self-improvement on display at the 1996 Million Man March gave any indication of what an "oppositional culture" can produce, such "opposition" can hardly explain poor social performance among black people. Real welfare payments fell continually for a quarter century between 1970 and the advent of welfare reform, even as the size of the ghetto underclass constantly grew. If paying women to have babies led to black welfare dependency, did they elect to increase their "supply of babies" as the pay rate fell? Race preferences at the college level affected a miniscule fraction of black students until well into the 1980s and even now reach only a minority (since three-fifths of American colleges and universities admit all who apply and meet minimal qualifications). How, then, could this set of policies account for the behavior of millions of black students?

A Confession

Having gotten the arguments in the preceding section off my chest, let me now make a confession. I think I know where the animus in the kind of reviews discussed in the preceding section is coming from, and I admit that I am partly to blame. A few political conservatives, including many of my former comrades, are disappointed in and confused about my current position, for good reason: I seem now to be contradicting some of the most powerful arguments that I advanced against racial liberalism in the past. Ten years ago, in the journal *First Things*, I wrote:

> It is time to recognize that further progress toward the attainment of equality for black Americans, broadly and correctly understood, depends most crucially at this juncture on the acknowledgment and rectification of the dysfunctional behaviors which plague black communities, and which so offend and threaten others. Recognize this, and much else will follow. It is more important to address this matter effectively than it is to agitate for additional rights. Indeed, success in such agitation has become contingent upon effective reform efforts mounted from within the black community. . . .
>
> The [key] point . . . is [that] progress such as this must be earned, it cannot be demanded. . . . [W]hen the effect of past oppression is to leave a people in a diminished state, the attainment of true equality with the former oppressor cannot depend on his generosity, but must ultimately derive from an elevation of their selves above the state of diminishment. It is of no moment that historic wrongs may have caused current deprivation, for justice is not the issue here. The issues are dignity, respect, and self-respect—all of which are preconditions for true equality between any peoples. The classic interplay between the aggrieved black and the guilty white, in which the former demands and the latter conveys recognition of historic injustice, is not an exchange among equals. Neither, one suspects, is it a stable exchange. Eventually it may shade into something else, something less noble—into patronage, into a situation where the guilty one comes to have contempt for the claimant, and the claimant comes to feel shame, and its natural accompaniment, rage, at his impotence. (Loury 1992, 20–21)

I imagine several of my critics and a great many others asking, how can the man who wrote those words make racial stigma the central organizing principle of his "anatomy of racial inequality"? While this is not the venue for me to fully address that question, I can offer a partial reply. It is not inconsistent to hold simultaneously that black parents, like all other parents, are responsible for the values embraced by their children and that the nation also bears some responsibility for the suffering of the ghetto poor. Nor is it a contradiction to assert, at one and the same time, that profound behavioral problems afflict many black communities and that these maladies are not an alien imposition on an otherwise pristine Euro-American canvas but, instead, products of economic and political structures indigenous to American society. Both positions can be true, and if both are true, the question becomes one of emphasis. While my emphasis has definitely changed, I do not repudiate the earlier claims.

The deeper issue, though, is the difficulty of coherently and effectively voicing both truths when one endeavors to practice social criticism in the context of what I have elsewhere called a "multiple audience" (Loury 1994). Whenever he or she advances an argument for any kind of reform, a black critic faces two audiences—a communal and a civic one. The 1992 passage quoted earlier was an exercise in social criticism directed, ironically, at black American intellectual and political leaders. (This is ironic because the piece was surely better known among and more widely cited by whites.) My 2002 book is an exercise in social criticism directed at the broad American elite as a whole. A decade ago, I was preoccupied with the questions of dignity and self-respect for black people. These are inherently communal questions. (This is not to say that only blacks can speak of such matters or that blacks must speak only among themselves about them. It is merely to acknowledge that, for the most part, these are matters where blacks must take the lead in defining the goals and managing the processes of moving toward them.) But questions of social justice and fair opportunity are the fit subjects of a broader public discourse, and where the historical echoes of the racial subordination of African-Americans continue to bear on such questions, an honest social critic must say so.

The ultimate difficulty here is that while self-development is an existential necessity for blacks as an ethnic community, its advocacy by black social critics in the larger civic discourse often undercuts the pursuit of racial justice. People feel authorized to perceive a black culture problem, rather than a racial justice problem, when in fact both problems may be present. (Conversely, advocacy for racial justice can undercut communal reform by leading blacks to not see the culture problem.) This difficulty is reflected in the dual meaning of "we" implicit in the signature question I raise in my book, "What manner of people are *we* who accept such degradation in our midst?" (Loury 2002, 159). There are two implied imperatives—getting the "cultural trains to run on time" in black communities and addressing the structural legacy of generations of racial oppression—and they rest on very different grounds. Whereas the first draws on ties of blood, shared history, and common faith, the second endeavors to achieve an integration of the most wretched, despised, and feared of our fellows along with the rest of us into a single political community of mutual concern.

This problem is closely related to the age-old conundrum, going back to Kant, of reconciling individual and social responsibilities. We humans, while undertaking our life projects, find ourselves constrained by social and cultural influences beyond our control. Yet if we are to live effective and dignified lives, we must behave as if we can indeed determine our fates. Similarly, black Americans are constrained by the residual effects of an ugly history of racism. Yet seizing what the iconic black conservative Booker T. Washington once called "freedom in the larger and higher sense" (quoted in Storing 1964) requires that blacks accept responsibility for our own fate even though the effects of this immoral past remain with us. Our doing so cannot, however, be allowed to excuse the nation from acknowledging a basic moral truth—one that transcends politics—which is that the citizens of this republic bear a responsibility to be actively engaged in changing the structures that constrain the black poor, so that the latter can more effectively exercise their inherent and morally required capacity to choose.

Acting on the above considerations, I was on a moral crusade in 1992. I am engaged in a rather different quest now, but I maintain that these are complementary, not contradictory, endeavors. A decade ago, I was sure that the largest obstacle to incorporating the ghetto poor into the commonwealth was that their leaders had the wrong ideas. Today, I think that position was a mistake, and I am laboring to correct the error. (Of course, some of these leaders still have bad ideas, but they are not alone in this.) As I said in the conclusion of my book, the role of a responsible black public intellectual today is to keep in play an awareness of the need for both communal and civic reforms, finding a way to make progress in either sphere complement that in the other (Loury 2002, chap. 5).

Still, playing that role credibly is not easy. Sadly, the larger currents of American public life inhibit nuance in discourse about race and social policy (by commentators of all races). Moreover, there is something inevitably emblematic about the role that a prominent black intellectual like myself plays in such discussions.[4] This role of "tacit testifying" that black dissenters inevitably play when they publicly break ranks from their coracialists accounts for why we tend to be so easily pigeonholed in, and are so willing to remain confined to, one ideological camp or the other. It also helps to explain why when we change our minds, many people—liberals and conservatives alike—act as if they smell a rat. But in my case at least, they are quite wrong.

The great economist and public intellectual John Maynard Keynes is reputed to have said: "When circumstances change I change my opinion. What do you do?" Like all scholars, I hope to continue to think, to learn, and to grow. I wish my critics and sympathetic readers alike the same pleasures.

NOTES

1. A number of distinguished modern scientists disagree with them. Steven Pinker of the Massachusetts Institute of Technology, in his recent book *The Blank Slate* (2002), stresses that races are not discrete, nonoverlapping categories, but he nevertheless argues that what we perceive as race has some biological reality as a statistical concept. A similar position is adopted by geneticist James Crow and zoologist Ernst Mayr, both fellows of the American Academy of Arts and Sciences, writing separately in the winter 2002 issue of *Daedalus*.

2. Thus, Jorge Garcia's (2002) distinction in this regard—between Charles Murray (who, he says, *may* be an essentialist, since Murray thinks blacks are intellectually inferior for genetic reasons) and Dinesh D'Souza (who, he says, could not possibly be an essentialist, since he *only* thinks that blacks are uncivilized)—is largely beside the point.

3. For evidence giving credence to expectations in this regard, see Raphael 2002.

4. Consider how the race of the author has contributed to the credibility of the arguments in such books as McWhorter's *Losing the Race: Self-Sabotage in Black America* (2000) or Randall Kennedy's *Nigger: The Strange Career of a Troublesome Word* (2002). The importance of the author's race in each of these cases is not so much due to the possibility that he has access to inside information. Rather, the key point is that the argument's legitimacy, not its accuracy, can be enhanced by an author's race (e.g., with the statement "Even some blacks can see that . . ."). But legitimacy depends on what a reader can safely assume about an author's motives. As a result, social criticism on race-related topics by black writers inescapably entails an ad hominem element.

PART 3

Policy Issues

Pragmatism, Liberalism, and Economic Policy

David Colander

Debates about esoteric topics in history often are conducted because they have importance in setting a context for modern policy debates. The Carlyle-Mill debate discussed in the first part of this book seems to fit that mold. It is important for the modern policy debate about what set of policies is most appropriate to deal with race-associated problems that our society is experiencing. This chapter concerns that modern debate and the contributions that economic reasoning has for that debate.

Arguments about race, economics, and policy can quickly become complicated. Since the points I want to make with this chapter are simple and do not, I believe, depend on deep philosophical issues, I will reduce the multifaceted debate about race and economics to a simple two-sided debate between classical liberals and modern liberals. On the Right is the Chicago-school, laissez-faire approach to race, which supporters like to classify as a classical liberal approach. The classical liberal side argues that the best policy is one relying on market forces, with the government doing as little as possible, avoiding affirmative action and other programs designed directly with race in mind. On the Left is the modern liberal approach, favoring government intervention. The modern liberal side argues that we need government-designed programs to redress the inequities of the past; it supports affirmative action and race-centered activist programs.[1]

In this debate, an overwhelming majority of blacks support the modern liberal position. In fact, a black classical liberal is likely to find himself or herself a pariah in the black policy community. The historical argument laid out by Levy and Peart in this volume addresses this phenomenon. They argue that, historically, the problack moral high ground belongs to the Chicago liberal position; it was classical liberal economists and laissez-faire advocates who opposed slavery, because they saw blacks and whites as equals.

Levy and Peart also suggest that the true predecessors of the modern-day liberals' interventionist approach are not classical liberals but paternalists. Paternalism supported not only slavery but also treating blacks as less than human. The implicit suggestion of the work of Levy and Peart is that by allowing identity, such as racial identity, into the policy equation, as must be done to design any policy with specific elements favoring one group or another, one is forced to view one group as less than equal and another group as more than equal. Once one does so, one is likely to slide down a slippery slope of racism and blame. The logical continuation of this line of reasoning is that, given the history that Levy and Peart recount, blacks should be much more receptive than they are to laissez-faire positions and to Chicago economics generally. The work of Levy and Peart is an invitation for blacks to come to Chicago.

In this chapter, I present three simple arguments. The first argument is that blacks and modern liberals should be more open to Chicago-type policy approaches than they currently are, but not for the reasons that Levy and Peart give. My second argument is that an important reason why modern liberals and blacks have such a difficult time accepting Chicago policies is the Chicago style of argumentation for their policies. My third argument is that a pragmatic, rather than theoretical, argument for markets, which recognizes the tragic nature of most questions about race, can lead to imaginative and achievable policy initiatives that can garner more black support for market-based solutions than can the arguments Levy and Peart present.

Why Blacks and Modern Liberals Should
Consider Chicago-Style Arguments

Noneconomists often see the purpose of economic theory as providing support for the market and for laissez-faire policy. If that was the initial intent of some economists (from my study of history, it was not), it certainly is not how it turned out. Theoretical analyses of markets have shown how fragile normative arguments for markets are. They have shown that, based on economic theory, there is nothing necessarily fair about market outcomes and that efficiency arguments for markets are based on highly restrictive assumptions that are never met in the real world. Since real-world markets are inundated with externalities and market imperfections that make them far from ideal (even in a very limited, Pareto-optimal sense), economic theory does not provide support for laissez-faire.

A stronger argument for markets rests not on theory but on history. As pointed out in the work of such economic historians as Angus Maddison (1995), markets have been associated with growth that has freed billions of people in the world from the burden of the scarcity of basic needs. Markets have also been associated with technological change that has opened up new ways of doing things, ways that nonmarket economies were not open to. If we want growth and new technology (a debatable goal, I admit, but one that most societies seem to have), markets are a good way to achieve it. Similarly, policies that take incentives seriously tend to work better than policies that do not.

The failure of socialist command-and-control economies was a telling natural experiment that convinced many of the power of markets. The power of market-type solutions can also be seen in the effect of the Earned Income Tax Credit Program and the U.S. welfare reforms of the 1990s, which instituted a work incentive in the U.S. welfare system. Since their introduction, rates of poverty and welfare dependency are down, and the support for welfare policy among the general population has increased. While there is debate about the issue, a majority of lay observers and popular press now agree that the reform has led to an improvement not only for society but also for many low-income individuals.[2]

This historical argument in favor of markets and incentive-based policies must be muted; markets have serious problems, and the markets that existed were regulated, not laissez-faire, markets. Similarly, market economies have generally included significant reliance on government-sponsored redistribution programs, although those programs have been less successful in reducing inequality than many would have liked. History has little to say about the general question of whether regulated markets or nonregulated markets are better; there are many examples on both sides. The answer inevitably depends on specific institutional and contextual issues; there are no general answers.

History does, however, suggest the need for a market economy to have a reasonably strong government committed to establishing rules within which a market can function. If those governments are also committed to democracy and to rejection of policies that lead to repression of the poor, there will inevitably be political pressure for policies to bring about more equality through policy action.

The preceding historical, pragmatic argument for markets can be contrasted with what I see as the Chicago view of markets—the view implying that theoretically, or for some other very deep reason, markets, with as little regulation and redistribution as possible, comprise the ideal institution by which to organize society. Such arguments are often not explicitly stated, but they are generally easily discernable when you look at Chicago economists. (In some ways, they are defining characteristics of Chicago economists.) The Chicago view of markets sees markets that are left to their own accord as leading to reasonably fair outcomes. In the Chicago approach, there exists some law of central tendency that leads to outcomes that reflect people's abilities, as well as a belief that the distribution of abilities is fair. In this Chicago view, if one gets less in a market system, it is because one has less ability; if one gets more, it is because one has more ability. This argument applies to the long run; in the short run, inequities may occur, but if the market is left to its own accord long enough, it will arrive at an acceptable level of inequality for society—a level that allows the income of the society as a whole to be higher than what it otherwise would have been, so that even the poor benefit to the degree that the system lifts everyone higher. That view makes it possible to equate the market with some type of fairness.

In my view, the law of central tendency toward equality in markets is a weak one. As Robert Prasch and Glenn Loury argue in this volume, it is easy to construct economic models showing cumulative processes and systemic monopolies in which one group continually holds down another. Such processes are pervasive in the real world; they tend to expand small initial inequalities caused by historical happenstance and luck into large systemic inequities. In short, differences in wealth create differences in power, and those differences in power perpetuate inequalities that themselves become built into institutions.

Despite my view of the problems with markets, I can support markets and incentive policies on pragmatic grounds because the policy option of government intervention has grave problems as well. Recognizing that there are serious costs of using governmental programs to help any group does not mean that one views the market result as in some sense fair. It simply means that the practice of using government policies to try to fix problems of the market has serious troubles of its own. For example, helping a group to offset past inequities can create a psychology of dependence that can be debilitating. Moreover, the government that has to impose the policies reflects the power structure that exists in the market. This power structure is unlikely to make a significant change in the existing inequities, which are based on that power structure; it is far more likely to transfer wealth from one group in power to another group in power than it is to transfer power to groups without power. Pushing for the politically impossible undermines the possible. Any government that reflects the existing power structure is likely to impose far less than ideal regulations if the goal of the regulation is to help people who do not have power. In many cases, the instituted programs do little for the group they are supposedly helping. Moreover, the programs that are initiated to help a particularly appealing group often create a bureaucracy that pushes for a continuation of the program independent of the program's social worth. Faced with this choice, markets, even highly unregulated markets, do not look so bad.

This combination of positions—pragmatically promarket, but not theoretically promarket—goes against the grain of Chicago economists and modern liberals alike. The modern liberal position tends to share my theoretical view of markets as highly imperfect, but it tends to downplay the pervasive problems with government action. Modern liberals generally dismiss these problems with government programs as being simply a way of supporting the status quo and justifying continued inequality. In my view, modern liberals recognize the problems with government policy but fear that if they admit that government solutions have problems, they are placing themselves in a Chicago-style position. Because Chicago-type solutions are associated with Chicago views of markets, modern liberals generally are not equally open to pragmatic arguments favoring either market solutions or government-led solutions.

Certain policies, such as support of complete public provision of schools and of affirmative action, have become ingrained in modern liberal ideology, and anyone who questions those policies is automatically tagged as "antiliberal." Because these policies are so engrained in its thought, modern liberalism has become closely associated with the means to achieve a goal as well as with the goal of the policy. Acceptable means to achieve a goal for modern liberals often preclude market- and incentive-based solutions. Thus, a modern liberal cannot support such solutions in the way that I tend to support them—that is, not as ideal answers, but as pragmatically the best we might be able to do, given the existing structure of society.[3]

Why Are There So Few Black Chicago-Style Economists?

The difficulty that modern liberals have in supporting markets is compounded for blacks. The Chicago position denies what most people consider a reality: blacks have been and continue to be discriminated against in morally unacceptable ways that the market alone will not fix. There has been a serious injustice committed, which has systematically held down blacks and which continues to discriminate against them. To be black is to admit that, so blacks who do not admit that have to give up their black identity. Chicago economics does not admit that, so to be a black Chicago economist means giving up one's identity as a black.

If the preceding view of markets is required of a Chicago economist, the question is not why you find so few black Chicago economists, the question is why you find any. In my view the reason you find some black Chicago economists is not the reason suggested to me by some modern liberals—that blacks who support a Chicago position are enticed by the money and prestige that it gives them. Rather, it is because, even with the problems, the Chicago policy solutions have much to be said for them, not as theoretically justifiable policies, but as pragmatic policies that, used judiciously, can lead to the ends that blacks and modern liberals want.

The reason it is so hard to be a black Chicago economist goes to the foundation of how one thinks about policy and arrives at a solution. Policies dealing with race are not economic questions; they are moral questions deeply embedded in emotion. In all such moral questions—for example, questions involving race, the role of women, or the Palestinian dilemma—standard economics is not especially good at dealing with policy issues. Economics likes to see itself as this dispassionate, objective analysis that is uninfluenced by emotion. But with moral questions, it is impossible to ignore emotion. Policy is inherently based in a normative structure, and while analysis, especially if judged from a common normative base, may be more or less objective, it can never be perfectly objective.

Standard economics, by which I mean mainstream economics defined broadly to include both the progressive Left and the libertarian Right, is primarily a field of middle-class white males who are eccentric by business standards but who are quite comfortable with the structure of society in which they find themselves. That must be seen as the ideological starting point of the analysis of economic policy. For the most part, even those who were radical in their youth have mostly made their peace with reality; they have found their place in society. Dispassionate, objective analysis is not an instrument of change; it is generally an instrument of support for the status quo.

Recognizing the limits of objective analysis requires one to recognize that moral issues are issues about which economic theory has little to say; it certainly does not have definitive answers. Instead, it is an analysis that can be an input into a wider decision process that integrates the ethics and the passions about previous wrongs—the passions that can lead one to say, "Efficiency be damned; do what is right." I am arguing that for policy, there are two types of questions—questions that Martha Nussbaum (2000a) calls *obvious questions* and *tragic questions*.

Obvious questions that contain no moral issues can be readily handled by the economic approach of reducing all issues to commensurate value. Tragic questions are those questions that involve moral issues and in which there is no morally acceptable choice. Nussbaum argues that not making an admission of the tragic nature of a question—an admission that economic reasoning, applied directly, does not make—demeans the choice that we take. An example is having to decide which of two persons to save when only one can be saved; either choice involves a moral wrong, so the choice is a tragic question. Nussbaum argues that tragic questions need to be handled differently than obvious questions. By not admitting the moral dimension of race questions, Chicago-type analysis makes it impossible for anyone who recognizes the moral dimension of the racial problem to accept the analysis. That, in my view, is why it is so hard to be black and a Chicago economist.

Chicago economics essentially asks us to use a cost-benefit framework for the race question and not to admit that it is a tragic question—that is, not to admit that existing institutions and culture are violating the rights of blacks. In imposing this condition, Chicago economics makes it impossible for the moral difficulty of the decision to be acknowledged and for it to be seen that one's heart is on the right side.

How one should answer tragic questions is unclear. Clearly, cost-benefit analysis is one input into the equation, but it is only an input; it is not the arbitrator. My argument is that the role of economics and economic policy reasoning is different when dealing with such moral dimensional questions than when dealing with obvious questions. Economists can provide historical understanding of what has worked in the past; some input into the decision, with its "objective" analysis; and suggestions about ways of proceeding. But the final decision about policy must be made within a broader philosophical context that is outside the confines of narrow economic reasoning.

Accepting the limitations of applying economic analysis to policy questions is, in my view, a necessary element of making economic analysis relevant within a modern liberal framework; it makes it possible to accept economic conclusions that are otherwise morally unacceptable. Even if, in the end, broader consideration leads one to accept the economic answer, the fact that the solution was reached through broader philosophical consideration might make that solution acceptable, whereas an economic answer arrived at directly would be unacceptable. An example concerns racial profiling. A policy of racial profiling arrived at through cost-benefit analysis would be unacceptable because it involves a moral wrong—singling out an individual on the basis of an irrelevant detail. But if it were arrived at through a broader consideration that recognized the moral issue but was concerned with avoiding another moral wrong—for example, the commission of terrorist attacks—it might be acceptable. Because the Chicago approach does not recognize that the reasoning process through which the solution was arrived at plays a role in determining the acceptability of the solution, it makes it almost impossible for modern liberals to accept market solutions.

The Limits of Liberalism as a Guide to Policy

Where Chicago liberalism errs on one side when dealing with tragic questions, modern liberalism, in my view, errs on the other. In the real world, rights conflict, and the definition of liberalism as a philosophy focused on certain inalienable rights does not allow for the ambiguity that results when those inalienable rights conflict. The reality is that liberalism is a philosophy that is consistent with many different policies, depending on the political and economic context of the times.[4] Thus, I find it more helpful to think of liberalism not as a well-defined set of philosophical principles emphasizing inalienable rights but as a basic attitude of policy analysis that emphasizes the rights of individuals. It leads us to recognition that certain questions are tragic questions and thus cannot be answered by cost-benefit analysis alone, but it does not tell us the answers to those tragic questions. It tells us that we have to struggle with the questions. That struggle will lead to different answers at different times, which is why both classical and modern views fall under, and should fall under, the broad liberal umbrella.

Consider racial profiling again. For most modern liberals, the very consideration of racial profiling as a practical policy is seen as evidence of racism. That is precisely the type of position that prevents fruitful dialogue. The practical reality is that statistical racial profiling will occur and is a natural part of individual psychology. In terms of social policy (when the policy is designed to prevent another moral wrong), where to draw the line about what is acceptable and what is not is a tragic question that cannot be decided on cost-benefit analysis alone. But the fact that it is a tragic question does not mean that an economic consideration of the issue should not be an input into the decision. Economic reasoning suggests a policy of racial profiling in which individuals incorrectly profiled are sincerely apologized to and monetarily compensated for the wrong. Public policy would then have to decide whether the costs of the policy, which would now be born more by society than by the individual, are worth the benefit. In short, racial profiling can be, but is not necessarily, a racist policy, and a careful consideration of the costs and benefits should be an input into, although not necessarily the deciding factor of, a decision about such policy. The tendency of liberal discourse not to allow discussions of those advantages and disadvantages undermines the ability to come to an imaginative compromise.

Toward an Imaginative and Pragmatic Approach to Racial Policy

The argument that the approach one takes to a problem plays a role in determining the acceptability of the solution is a commonplace argument for many humanists but is quite foreign to many economists, just as using the cost-benefit approach as a natural input into a policy decision is quite foreign to many humanists. Policy discussions would be moved along if humanists would get a little economics in their thinking and if economists would get a little humanity. Somehow, the approaches need to be melded together in a different way than they are now. To have a productive policy discussion of racial policy, we need movement away from positions firmly associated with classical liberalism and modern liberalism and toward positions that are more eclectic and pragmatic. Such a pragmatic discussion would allow the development of policies that meld classical and modern liberal approaches in new ways. In my view, these hybrids are the policies that are most likely to provide direction for future policy.

To achieve imaginative hybrid policies, we need a pragmatic approach to racial policy that is based on two propositions. The first is that policy questions dealing with race are tragic questions. This approach recognizes that blacks have been and continue to be discriminated against and that there is no justification of the starting point. Thus, market outcomes cannot be taken as fair or justified. Government policy action is needed. The second proposition upon which this pragmatic approach to race is based is that government policy in a variety of areas is currently failing both blacks and whites. That 1.2 million blacks are incarcerated in U.S. prisons is a tragedy for all U.S. society and is an unacceptable outcome. In education, the fact that blacks have lower scores on standardized tests and have much lower graduation rates, not because of any inherent differences, but because of institutional and cultural realities, is similarly unacceptable. The fact that because of those same institutional and cultural realities, about 23 percent of blacks but only about 7 percent of whites fall below the poverty line is similarly unacceptable. These are problems that cannot be ignored, and as Loury argues in this volume, changes in these outcomes must be central goals of policy. But in designing solutions for these problems, I think it is important to recognize that the pragmatic argument for markets has an important role to play and can help bring about more effective policy as long as the goal of those policies is consistent with expanding the rights and capabilities of blacks.

Individuals more directly involved in racial policy than I am will have to determine specifically what this new approach to racial policy will lead to; tragic questions must be handled by individuals closely associated with them. But I can discuss the framework within which a pragmatic policy would be constructed, with some examples of how I see that framework affecting the ongoing debate.

Clearly Specifying Goals, Not Methods for Achieving Goals

The first characteristic of a pragmatic liberal policy is that it will be focused on achieving goals, not on the method of achieving those goals. Successful pragmatic policy clearly specifies the goals one wants to achieve and then, with as little bias as possible, considers all methods of meeting those goals. Let's consider an example from education policy. Although there is a general consensus among blacks that in many places public education is failing blacks, modern liberals have been slow to consider voucher alternatives. Blacks, who have experienced the problems inherent in the current public educational system, are less committed to public provision of education, and according to polls, 60 percent to almost 70 percent of blacks favor some type of voucher system.[5]

There are many reasons many modern liberals oppose vouchers. Among them are a belief that public education provides a social benefit to society in homogenizing the population and a correlative belief that voucher systems will lead to segregation and cream skimming, leaving public schools with an even harder job than they currently have. These are legitimate concerns but are not necessarily good reasons for a blanket opposition to vouchers. In the pragmatic approach, the policy discussion needs to be in terms of the ability of a range of solutions to achieve the combination of goals one wants. No policy should be seen as inevitably inconsistent with any goal. In a pragmatic approach to policy, one would not automatically brand voucher plans as rearguard plans designed to undermine the goals of public education but, instead, would examine them as pragmatic policies designed to deal with current institutions that have become so bureaucratic and limiting that they prevent the current system from operating effectively in many circumstances that affect blacks.

If there are goals that the public school meets but that currently proposed voucher systems do not, the need is to make those goals explicit and to consider equally any methods of education provision that might meet those goals. Poor blacks do not support vouchers because of any grand theoretical argument for incentives or markets; they support vouchers as a pragmatic way of dealing with a problem that is not being solved by current institutions. Vouchers empower them in the same way that well-off individuals are currently empowered when they send their kids to private schools. Vouchers are a pragmatic solution—one that stirs things up and that, in my view, should now be considered without the demand that the solution be in any sense ideal and with the admission that the current outcomes are unacceptable.

A voucher system need not be an either-or choice. Vouchers could be used in combination with the provision of public schooling. For example, a certain number of vouchers could be given out when school enrollment has temporary spikes. This would reduce the pressures on the existing institutional structures, save the public from building new school facilities, and reduce, rather than increase, the cost pressure on school budgets.

Starting with Policies with Zero Net Cost

A second characteristic of a pragmatic liberal approach to policy would be a more explicit focus on trade-offs. It would focus on policy with zero net cost—a policy or a combination of policies that has no additional costs. To say we should spend more money on a problem is in many ways a cop-out. More money has to come from somewhere, and any policy proposal should include where that money is to come from. The more pragmatic the policy is, the more the money to support the new initiative would come from those groups who are benefited by the proposal—not from currently polit-ically impossible sources, such as increased taxes on the rich or on some other outside group—because the closer that connection, the more likely the policy is to be adopted. Thus, a pragmatic policy includes the politi-cally possible trade-offs that must be made to implement it.

Many modern liberal policy discussions that deal with policy problems start from the position that more money is needed to solve them. One's commitment to solving them is based on whether one is willing to commit more money to solving them. Whether or not more money is needed, that approach is politically divisive. It hides the difficult trade-offs that must be made. It insures that the policies modern liberals advocate are unlikely to get the broad-based support they need if they are to be adopted. In the pragmatic approach I am advocating, more effort would be focused, at least initially, on consideration of policy or a combination of policies that has zero net cost in resources.[6]

Taking this position leads one to look at combining policies to help blacks with innovative reform policies for existing institutions. For exam-ple, vouchers go much further toward government involvement in educa-tion than a cost-benefit approach to economic education would suggest. Voucher plans involve giving government money to individuals to use for their private gain, a policy that, while it also has a public gain, delivers a large private gain for the individual recipient. From a cost-benefit perspec-tive, since much of the benefit of education accrues to the individual, not to the society, part of the payment for that education should come from the student or the family. Some private funding of education—either contribution of time or payment by parents and students through loans that they are to pay back at some point—would create more pressure by parents and students to keep education focused on attaining the goals that the parents and students have.

There are no inherent reasons why students cannot perform many of the functions that make schools operate or why such student provision of services cannot be built into schooling. Older students could provide some of the teaching to younger students. (It is well known that individuals often learn a subject better by teaching it than by studying it—we continually tell that to teaching assistants at our universities.) If one built into our educational system a pyramid of teaching, with older students at each level playing a role in teaching younger students, resources could be saved to use for new initiatives that could benefit blacks. Such an institutional redesign could be part of a larger institutional redesign based on a requirement that some percentage of the costs of education be paid by students in the form of bonds or services, some percent be paid by parents, some percent come from local property taxes, and some percent be contributed by higher levels of government through general taxation. The amounts could vary with the income, wealth, and demographic characteristics of the community. This would be a much better formula for supplying education than we currently have, and it could make it possible to expand what our schools offer. For example, such a change might free up money from the educational budget to allow earlier educational and day-care programs for those who choose them—say from the age of two or three, rather than from the age of five. Such an institutional redesign might do much more for many blacks than slight modifications of our current institutional structure can do.

I am under no illusion that the preceding proposals are likely to get much immediate support. They are not meant to. Instead, they are meant to move the policy discussion toward consideration of more substantial institutional changes than it generally currently includes. One of economists' policy jobs is to stimulate the imagination of the powers who actually decide on policy, and the preceding proposals should be seen in that light.

Indirect Policies

Sometimes the set of policies that are most likely to affect blacks are broader-based policies that only indirectly affect blacks but that are at least partially responsible for imposing the stigma associated with being black. For that reason, consideration of policies toward blacks cannot be judged only, or even primarily, in relation to those policies that directly affect blacks; policies that affect them indirectly are probably more important. For example, the lack of a general incomes policy, such as the market-based incomes policy that I and others have put forward (Lerner and Colander 1980; Colander 1986), keeps the aggregate economy weaker than it otherwise would be and means that blacks cannot move up as fast as they would in a high-pressure economy like that of the late 1990s.[7] Politically, such incomes policies are not currently in the cards, but that should not preclude the realization that such general economic conditions are probably more central to blacks' success than are policies directly aimed at blacks.

Even without an incomes policy, blacks could have been helped by the high-pressure economy of the late 1990s much more than they were. One reason they were not lies in U.S. immigration policy. In fact, when considering blacks' economic status alone, I would argue that the set of policies that play a significant role in preventing blacks in the United States from advancing is the immigration policies that the United States has maintained. The policies have increased competition among workers for entry-level jobs and reduced the incentive that firms have to bring into the workforce U.S. workers currently not in the workforce. High-pressure job markets give incentives to firms to find ways to improve the skills of blacks and to integrate them into the job market. If pressure is taken off because of immigration, the position of blacks will improve less than it otherwise would. I fully recognize that immigration policies raise tragic questions of their own, but I have been amazed by the lack of discussion of those tragic questions in the debate on racial policy.

Another indirect policy that significantly affects blacks involves drugs. As Loury points out, the way recreational drug laws are enforced affects blacks more than whites, and the decision to enforce the laws on sellers rather than buyers is in part responsible for the higher incarceration rates of blacks. Changing that bias in enforcement is highly unlikely, but some type of legalization would reduce the need for any enforcement and should thus be considered. In their chapter in this volume, Gowda and O'Flaherty show the imaginative reasoning that I am advocating. They argue not for simple deregulation, but instead for government's clear specification of goals of drug policy. If the market can meet clear, acceptable drug goals, then allowing the private market to supply recreational drugs makes sense. One then gets the best elements of both regulation and the market.

Conclusion

As I stated at the beginning of this chapter, for me, the importance of the Carlyle-Mill debate is in its implications for modern policy. David Levy and Sandra Peart have played an important role in helping to remove the firewall that has loomed over the discussion of racial policy. Removal of that firewall is necessary because the easy policy task has been accomplished. The legal position of blacks has changed, but the stigma still remains. As long as we distinguish blacks from other groups in a manner different than we distinguish blonds, Germans, or Asians, there is a need for racial policy. Racial policy is too important not to be treated pragmatically, and the best way for that to happen is for the firewall surrounding policy discussions to come down. Discussion of racial policy has to deal with the reality that further advances on racial issues will involve unacceptable, tragic choices.

The pragmatic approach to making policies involves focusing the policy discussion on policies most likely to bring about the results one wants, given the political institutions. To me, one of the interesting aspects of the conference on which this volume is based is how the policy views held by participants often did not fit standard liberal or conservative classifications. The participants had gone beyond those simple confines and had adopted far more sophisticated policy positions. I wrote this chapter in an effort to convey to a broader audience the sense of openness that I felt at the conference and the sense of optimism that it gave me that progress can be made, as long as a pragmatic and imaginative approach to policy is taken.

NOTES

I would like to thank Robert Prasch, Brendan O'Flaherty, and outside reviewers for their suggestions concerning this chapter, many of which I adopted. Responsibility for the ideas in this chapter remains totally with me.

1. A second argument for affirmative action is that it is designed to achieve efficient search mechanisms for bright students who have not been prepped for

being admitted to college and who the normal admissions criteria would miss. This argument, which can lead to a variety of programs of the affirmative action type, is consistent with either approach to liberalism.

2. Clearly, there are disagreements with this assessment; committed modern liberals still object. But the negative effects of the policy that many modern liberals predicted when it was implemented have not materialized, and the number of welfare recipients has fallen significantly.

3. The commitment of modern liberalism to method as opposed to goal has been decreasing in the past decade, but significant vestiges remain. This chapter argues that the process of separation should be encouraged.

4. I am often tempted to believe in a backward induction approach to philosophical foundations of policy, because it seems that bright philosophers can take any policy position and create a set of plausible philosophical arguments to support it.

5. The 70 percent is based on a 1999 survey by a nonpartisan research group, Public Agenda. The 60 percent figure is based on a poll in 1999 by the Joint Center for Political and Economic Studies, which is also a nonpartisan think tank.

6. I am arguing neither that policies that commit new resources are unsupportable nor that pushing for increased funding of programs is wrong; I am only arguing that the problems facing blacks are sufficiently urgent that concentrating on those policies that can draw a broader degree of support because they do not require new resources are more likely to have positive near-term results.

7. We developed market-based incomes policies to demonstrate that incomes policies do not necessarily have to go against the market but can work with the market. In a market-based incomes policy, the aggregate value added of a firm and a measure of inputs are determined, and each firm is allowed to increase its value added per unit input by the average productivity increase in the economy. If the firm increases the value added, it is required to buy additional value-added credits from other firms that have reduced it. Thus, by the structure of the program, inflation is impossible, allowing the central bank to run the economy at a lower unemployment rate than it otherwise could.

Better Recreational Drugs

Unleashing Technology to Win the War on Bad Drugs

Vanita Gowda and Brendan O'Flaherty

The problem with recreational and occupational drugs[1] in the United States today is not the drugs we have but the drugs we do not have. We do not have modern drugs that can satisfy the demand for mood-altering and consciousness-changing experiences in a safe and effective way. Instead, we are saddled with old drugs, both legal and illegal, that generally have rather awful side effects—sometimes for their users, sometimes for others, sometimes for both. The current illicit drug situation is particularly harmful to African-Americans, due to the concentration of negative externalities in minority neighborhoods. Clear government policies would probably give us "better" drugs—better privately and better socially. There is little reason to think that technology is the stumbling block.

Would better recreational and occupational drugs really make the world a better place? We argue that they would, if properly regulated. People have many legitimate nonmedical reasons for using drugs: for instance, to relax, to sleep, to stay awake, to make friends, to forget friends, to concentrate, and just to have fun (an entirely legitimate goal on which Americans spend hundreds of billions of dollars annually). The consumer and producer benefits alone from good new drugs would probably justify investing in the needed research.

Benefits for Everyone

Good recreational drugs are also likely to reduce demand for the lousy drugs we have currently. People drink alcohol to relax and feel inebriated (or because it is expected on the job), not to have hangovers, car crashes, or cirrhosis. They use heroin to get high, not to get AIDS, to suffer overdoses, or to experience withdrawal symptoms. American consumers have generally shown a significant willingness to embrace new products that are better than old ones—as makers of slide rules and buggy whips know—and we expect that users of recreational drugs will be no different.

Reducing demand for alcohol, nicotine, and illicit drugs has numerous advantages. These drugs, especially the licit ones that are used heavily, do great harm to their users and to third parties, and so less use implies less harm. Alcohol contributes to accidents, promotes aggression and violent crime, causes cirrhosis and birth defects, contributes to bad parenting, lowers the probability of high school completion, and, if people become addicted, can severely damage lives and families. Barbiturates probably have similar effects. Marijuana causes clumsiness and promotes personality changes that can lead to paranoia and aggression. Because it is smoked, marijuana contributes to asthma and other respiratory diseases, possibly including cancer. Heroin causes constipation (one of its early uses was as a diarrhea remedy), drowsiness, and, often, severe addiction; overdoses sometimes occur, and unsupervised injection can spread hepatitis and HIV. Cocaine stimulates aggression and possibly crime and can lead to paranoia and other mental illnesses. Perinatal cocaine causes certain developmental problems.

For the illicit drugs, moreover, reducing demand would reduce the harm caused by attempts to suppress them. You would not need a war on illicit drugs if nobody used them, and almost nobody would use them if better alternatives were available. No police force was needed to suppress slide rules.

The Benefits for African-Americans

On average, African-Americans would probably gain more than other Americans from the availability of better recreational drugs. As consumers, African-Americans would probably gain as much on average as other Americans would, and as producers, they might lose some benefits.

The big relative gain comes in the reduction of externalities: current heavy demand for prohibited drugs creates substantial negative externalities disproportionately in neighborhoods inhabited primarily by African-Americans. Moreover, all African-Americans lose from the practice of racial profiling caused in part by the pressure on law enforcement agencies to confiscate drugs and apprehend drug dealers.

There is no evidence that African-Americans' demand for recreational drugs is any different from demand by other Americans. Even for prohibited drugs (for which we would not expect the law of one price to hold), African-American consumption does not differ greatly from general consumption. African-Americans use somewhat more marijuana and cocaine, but other groups use more alcohol, tobacco, hallucinogens, inhalants, and psychotherapeutics (table 1 shows recent comparisons). Thus, better drugs should bring to African-American consumers approximately the same gains that they would bring to other American consumers.

The big racial difference is currently in the anonymous sale of illicit drugs. Booker T. Washington foresaw this phenomenon in 1915 when he argued against residential segregation laws.

A segregated Negro community is a terrible temptation to many white people. Such a community invariably provides certain types of white men with hiding-places—hiding-places from the law, from decent people of their own race, from their churches and their wives and daughters. . . . Now when a Negro seeks to buy a house in a reputable street he does

TABLE I.   Past Month Use of Recreational and Occupational Drugs, 2000 (percentage of population aged 12 and over)

	White (non-Hispanic)	Black (non-Hispanic)	Hispanic
Alcohol	50.7	33.7	39.8
Heavy alcohol use	6.2	4.0	4.4
Cigarettes	25.9	23.3	20.7
Any illicit drug	6.4	6.4	5.3
Marijuana	4.9	5.2	3.6
Cocaine	0.5	0.7	0.8
Hallucinogens	0.5	0.2	0.3
Inhalants	0.3	0.2	0.3
Psychotherapeutics*	1.8	1.2	1.7

Source: U.S. Substance Abuse and Mental Health Services Administration 2002, chaps 2–4, tables 1.1B, 1.31B, 1.36B, 1.41B, 1.46B, F.43
*Nonmedical use of prescription psychotherapeutics

it not only to get police protection, lights and accommodation, but to remove his children to a locality in which vice is not paraded. (Washington 1915)

This "parading of vice" in African-American neighborhoods can be seen in the data on arrests, convictions, and incarcerations. Even though racial disparities in the consumption of prohibited recreational drugs are negligible, disparities in punishment—primarily punishment for distribution—are huge. In 1998, 53 percent of the individuals convicted in state courts of all drug felonies and 57 percent of those convicted for drug-trafficking felonies were African-American (U.S. Bureau of Justice Statistics 2002, table 2.1). Similarly, in 1997, 53 percent of those incarcerated in state and federal prisons due to drug offenses were African-American (U.S. Bureau of Justice Statistics 2000, tables 4.3, 4.4).

By contrast, for crimes involving licit recreational drugs, African-Americans are represented in numbers slightly below their share in the general population. In 2000, 9.6 percent of the people arrested for driving under the influence were African-American, as were 10.6 percent of those arrested for violating liquor laws and 13.7 percent of those arrested for public drunkenness (State University of New York at Albany 2002, table 4.10).

One might be tempted to argue that reducing demand for a service (anonymous sale of prohibited drugs) in which African-Americans appear to enjoy comparative advantage would harm them as producers. This argument would be correct in a neoclassical market, but illicit drugs are not sold in a neoclassical market. Two deviations from neoclassical conditions are important.

First, many of the participants in this market are children. Whether adults can make sufficiently good decisions about actions with uncertain long-term consequences is a matter of some dispute; children almost certainly cannot. To the extent that children systematically underestimate the long-term deleterious consequences of drug dealing—death, disability, incarceration, lack of subsequent employment opportunities—their employment in this market brings them more harm than good, at least on the margin. Reducing demand for illicit drugs might plausibly help, rather than hurt, many of the children who now work in this market.

Second, anonymous sale of prohibited drugs creates huge negative externalities, most of which are borne by African-American and other minority communities. Violence spills over to bystanders, decent people lose the use of their stoops and sidewalks, parents are forced to take extra measures to protect their children's safety and morality, and guns proliferate. Some spillovers are statistical: robbery, for instance, is a more appealing occupation if victims are likely to be reluctant to report the loss of an abundance of cash to the police (within every income class, African-Americans are more than twice as likely as European-Americans to be robbery victims [U.S. Department of Justice 2002a table 15]). Racial profiling is also a statistical spillover: the more that some African-Americans deal drugs, the greater are the indignities that all African-Americans are forced to suffer, rightly or wrongly, because of stereotypes. Thus, on average, African-Americans have more to gain than do other Americans from policies that encourage better drugs.

Policies to Produce Better Drugs

The advantages of reducing demand for the dangerous old recreational and occupational drugs Americans now use are so great that a strong case can be made for subsidizing chemical substitutes.[2] Analogous here is free garbage collection, an activity many cities undertake because midnight dumping produces great negative externalities and is almost impossible to police. But we will not press the case for subsidies. Instead, we will argue only that the government should be neutral—that it should allow reasonably safe, reasonably effective recreational drugs to be sold through normal channels, sales taxes and all.

This argument presumes that in a neutral regulatory environment, pharmaceutical companies would develop these drugs. The evidence in favor of this proposition is strong but not overwhelming. The tremendous technological progress these companies have made with psychotherapeutic drugs during the past half century indicates to us that they have the capacity to develop recreational drugs far superior to any that Americans use today. The size of the market for current recreational and occupational drugs, on the order of magnitude of $200 billion a year in the United States alone, tells us that the companies are likely to find investing in research an attractive option. In more cynical moments, we think that the aggressive marketing of such drugs as Prozac, Oxycontin, and Ritalin shows that companies are not unaware of the profits to be made in this market. But in the worst case, if our presumption is wrong and a neutral regulatory environment fails to spur the development of safe new drugs, nothing will be lost; the status quo will just continue.

The Current Regulatory Regime

Probably the most serious objection to our proposal is that the current regulatory system already permits safe recreational drugs and that any tampering with that system would serve only to introduce unsafe ones. We disagree. While current drug laws do not prohibit recreational drugs, the environment is not impartial; instead, both the convoluted, subjective nature of drug policies and the rhetoric surrounding them discourage the development of more safe recreational drugs. To make our disagreement clear, however, we need first to explain how the United States regulates drugs. Most people do not know how this is done, aside from the names of a few substances that are illegal. In the long run, knowing the names of these illegal drugs is probably the least important aspect of the system.

Suppose you were working to create a new recreational or occupational drug. What would you need to know about federal regulation? First, you might want to consider the Bureau of Alcohol, Tobacco, and Firearms (ATF), which regulates the recreational drugs most commonly used in the market today. The ATF, however, will not be able to oversee the marketing of your drug, because the only drugs it deals with are those containing ethanol (the psychoactive substance in alcoholic drinks) and nicotine. (Even if you found a way of making these drugs healthier, the ATF bars you from advertising health claims.)

Thus, your new drug would come under the purview of the Food and Drug Administration (FDA), the agency that ensures that all drugs sold in the United States are safe and effective for human use, and possibly the Drug Enforcement Agency (DEA), whose mission it is to enforce the country's controlled substances laws. Controlled substances are those drugs that the DEA, FDA, and other related agencies determine to have a "potential for abuse" by the general public. *Potential* is an important word here, because the standards that determine which drugs the DEA regulates and why are sometimes inconsistent and subjective.

Many prescription and over-the-counter drugs—Prozac and caffeine, Tylenol, and most sleeping pills, for instance—are not regulated by the DEA at all. Other prescription drugs—Ritalin and Oxycontin, for instance—are regulated by the DEA because their use for occupational and recreational purposes is prohibited.

Guidelines set by the Controlled Substances Act of 1970 (CSA) determine which drugs are regulated by the DEA and are thus prohibited from being used recreationally or occupationally. The CSA created five "schedules" that classify illicit drugs according to a number of criteria, including a drug's pharmacological effects and its "potential for abuse." Strictly prohibited drugs, such as marijuana, cocaine, and heroin, are listed in Schedule I. Schedule I drugs are considered to have no medical purpose and the highest potential for abuse by users. Schedules II–V list drugs that have medical purposes, with a diminishing "potential for abuse." The schedules serve to group together drugs believed to pose comparable threats to public health. Accordingly, criminal penalties are linked to the schedule system, with the strongest sentences assigned to the possession or sale of Schedule I drugs.

It is important to note that while a drug must have a "potential for abuse" to be controlled by the DEA, the criteria for "potential for abuse" are not defined in law. A drug's addictiveness level is a significant component of the determination, but several other factors also contribute. These include evidence that people use the drug in amounts sufficient to possibly cause a danger to their health or create a public health risk, evidence that significant quantities are diverted from legitimate channels, or proof that individuals take the drug on their own initiative rather than with a doctor's supervision.

These criteria show that the DEA has a good deal of discretion when deciding how various drugs are regulated and, thus, how users and sellers are penalized. While the DEA takes the FDA's medical findings into consideration, there are no clear, specific medical or chemical attributes assigned to each of the schedules; drugs with wildly different effects and pharmacological properties can be in the same schedule. For instance, marijuana and heroin are both Schedule I drugs, despite their vastly different chemical characteristics. Presumably, there are other significant similarities between the two drugs with regard to other factors examined by the DEA. But how the different criteria are considered and applied by the DEA is uncertain.

Currently, many prescription "lifestyle drugs," such as Prozac and Viagra, are not controlled by the DEA, despite reports of their recreational use. It appears that these drugs are not controlled by the DEA primarily because they are not considered addictive enough or physically harmful enough to warrant additional regulation currently; however, if these drugs were marketed as recreational drugs, it is unclear whether they would then satisfy some of the criteria for "potential for abuse." This uncertainty is a large part of the current regulatory environment; unclear rules discourage the development of safe recreational and occupational drugs.

It is, after all, very hard to think of any substances that have literally no "potential for abuse." Knives and tire irons are implicated in many murders and assaults, and people committing suicide use bridges. People fall off stepladders and ingest all sorts of cleaning fluids. Everyone in New York is painfully aware of what can be done with box cutters. Tennis injuries, some of them chronic and severe, afflict millions of Americans. Music, stamp collecting, hang gliding, and Internet-surfing have on occasions obsessed individuals to the point where their careers and family lives suffered.

Thus, you cannot count on marketing a really good occupational or recreational drug unless you can prove it is perfect, and nobody can ever prove anything is perfect. Somebody somewhere would take your drug and do something bad. That is why we have such unsafe recreational drugs now, and that is why we will continue to be stuck with them unless government policies change to create a reasonable standard of safety.

Conclusion

In some ways, cars are like recreational drugs: they kill, maim, injure, pollute, threaten traditional values, and destabilize families. But when we realized this, we did not say that 1937 Model T Fords and ambulances were the only kinds of cars that people could have. If we had done so, we would now be faced every year with alarming newspaper stories about new teenage trends in ambulance abuse and with a coterie of libertarian advocates of legalizing 1923 Packards. Instead, consumer demand, government pressure, and autonomous technological progress have combined to make cars a lot safer and less polluting than they were in 1937—and a lot more fun. Nobody abuses ambulances or 1923 Packards. We should learn from ourselves.

NOTES

1. While alcohol and the illicit drugs are usually referred to as "recreational," they are extensively used as inputs to production as well. About 20 percent of alcohol is purchased by firms (Cook and Moore 2000, 1634), and the fact that light

drinkers earn more than abstainers (ibid., 1654–55) is not inconsistent with the idea that alcohol is a social lubricant that promotes business. Caffeine and amphetamines are used in many industries to fight fatigue and promote alertness, and cocaine, too, once served this purpose (German doctors invented it in the nineteenth century to keep troops from getting tired).

2. Nonchemical substitutes are also imaginable. Roller coasters, for instance, are popular because of the consciousness-altering experiences they produce. Perhaps subsidizing them also has merit. But chemicals are more likely to be substitutes for other chemicals.

Bibliography

Ackerman, Bruce, and Anne Alstott. 1999. *The Stakeholder Society*. New Haven, CT: Yale University Press.

Ackroyd, Peter. *Dickens*. 1990. New York: Harper Collins.

Agassiz, E. C. 1886. *Louis Agassiz, His Life and Correspondence*. 5th ed. Boston: Houghton Mifflin.

Agassiz, L. 1850. The Diversity of Origin of the Human Races. *Christian Examiner* 49:110–45.

Anderson, Elijah. 1990. *Streetwise: Race, Class, and Change in an Urban Community*. Chicago: University of Chicago Press.

Andrews, Marcellus. 1999. *The Political Economy of Hope and Fear: Capitalism and the Black Condition in America*. New York: New York University Press.

Anti-Slavery Reporter. 1850. London.

Arce, Carlos H., Eduard Murguia, and W. Parker Frisbie. 1987. Phenotype and Life Chances among Chicanos. *Hispanic Journal of Behavioral Studies* 9, no. 1:19–33.

Arrow, Kenneth J. 1973. The Theory of Discrimination. In *Discrimination in Labor Markets*, ed. Orley Ashenfelter and Albert Rees, 3–33. Princeton: Princeton University Press.

Atkinson, Anthony. 1995. *Public Economics in Action: The Basic Income/Flat Tax Proposal*. New York: Oxford University Press.

Augustine. 1952. *The City of God*. Trans. G. G. Walsh and G. Monahan. New York: Fathers of the Church.

Aytoun, W. E. 1850. Alton Locke, Tailor and Poet: An Autobiography. *Blackwood's Edinburgh Magazine* 68 (November): 592–610.

Bachman, J. 1850. An Investigation of the Cases of Hybridity in Animals on Record, Considered in Reference to the Unity of the Human Species. *Charleston Medical Journal* 5:168–97.

———. 1855a. *An Examination of Professor Agassiz's Sketch of the Natural Provinces of the Animal World and Their Relation to the Different Types of Man, with a Tableau Accompanying the Sketch*. Charleston, SC: James Williams and Gitsinger.

———. 1855b. *An Examination of the Characteristics of Genera and Species, as Applicable to the Doctrine of the Unity of the Human Race*. Charleston, SC: James Williams and Gitsinger.

Baker, L. D. 1998. *From Savage to Negro: Anthropology and the Construction of Race*. Berkeley: University of California Press.

Bass, W. M. 1987. *Human Osteology*. 3d ed. Columbia, MO: Missouri Archaeology Society.

Battel, A. [1625] 1905–7. In Samuel Purchas, *Hakluytus posthumus, or Purchas his Pilgrimes: Contayning a History of the World in Sea Voyages and Lande Travells by Englishmen and Others*. Glasgow: J. MacLehose and Sons.

Bean, R. B. 1906. Some Racial Peculiarities of the Negro Brain. *American Journal of Anatomy* 5:353–432.

Becker, Gary S. 1971. *The Economics of Discrimination*. 2d ed. Chicago: University of Chicago Press. 1st ed., 1957.

————. 1968. Discrimination, Economic. In *International Encyclopedia of the Social Sciences*, ed. David Sills, 4:208–10. New York: Macmillan.

Beddoe, John. 1870. Anthropology and Politics: Kelts and Saxons. *Anthropological Review* 8:215–16.

Bergmann, Barbara R. 1971. The Effect on White Incomes of Discrimination in Employment. *Journal of Political Economy* 79, no. 2:294–313.

————. 1974. Occupational Segregation, Wages and Profits When Employers Discriminate by Race or Sex. *Eastern Economic Journal* 1:103–10.

Berlin, Isaiah. 1969. Two Concepts of Liberty. In *Four Essays on Liberty*. London: Oxford University Press.

Bernier, F. [1684, trans. 1863–64] 2000. A New Division of the Earth. Trans. Thomas Bendyshe. Reprinted in *The Idea of Race*, ed. R. Bernasconi and T. L. Lott, 1–4. Indianapolis: Hackett.

Bernstein, Michael. 2001. *A Perilous Progress: Economists and the Public Purpose in Twentieth-Century America*. Princeton: Princeton University Press.

Bertrand, Marianne, and Sundhil Mullainathan. 2002. Are Emily and Brendan More Employable Than Lakisha and Jamal? Unpublished manuscript, Graduate School of Business, University of Chicago.

Blackmon, Douglas A. 2001. Hard Time: From Alabama's Past, Capitalism and Racism in a Cruel Partnership. *Wall Street Journal*, July 10, A1, A10.

Blinder, Alan S. 1974. *Toward an Economic Theory of Income Distribution*. Cambridge: MIT Press.

Blumenbach, J. F. [1775] 1865. *De generis humani varietate nativa* (On the natural variety of mankind). In *The Anthropological Treatises of Johann Friedrich Blumenbach*, trans. and ed. T. Bendyshe, 65–144. London: Longman, Green, Longman, Roberts and Green.

————. [1795] 1865. *De generis humani varietate nativa* (On the natural variety of mankind). 3d ed. In *The Anthropological Treatises of Johann Friedrich Blumenbach*, trans. and ed. T. Bendyshe, 145–276. London: Longman, Green, Longman, Roberts and Green.

Borjas, George J. 1994. Long-Run Convergence of Ethnic Skill Differentials: The Children and Grandchildren of the Great Migration. *Industrial and Labor Relations Review* 47:553–73.

Botwinick, Howard. 1993. *Persistent Inequalities: Wage Disparity under Capitalist Competition*. Princeton, NJ: Princeton University Press.

Bound, J., and R. Freeman. 1989. Black Economic Progress: Erosion of Post–1965 Gains in the 1980s. In *The Question of Discrimination: Racial Inequality in the U.S. Labor Market*, ed. S. Shulman and W. Darity Jr., 32–49. Middletown: Wesleyan University Press.

Boyer, George. 1990. *An Economic History of the English Poor Laws, 1750–1850*. Cambridge: Cambridge University Press.

Brighouse, Harry. 2000. *School Choice and Social Justice*. London: Oxford University Press.

Broca, P. 1888. *Memoires sur le cerveau de l'homme et des primates*. Paris: C. Reinwald.

Browne, P. A. 1850. *The Classification of Mankind, by the Hair and Wool of their Heads, with an Answer to Dr. Prichard's Assertion, that The Covering of the Head of the Negro is Hair, Properly so Termed, and Not Wool*. Philadelphia: A. Hart.

Bruno, Giordano. [1591] 1950. On the Infinite Universe and Worlds. Trans. D. W. Singer. In *Giordano Bruno, His Life and Thought*, by D. W. Singer, 225–378. New York: Schuman.

Bryce, J. 1903. *The Relations of the Advanced and Backward Races of Mankind*. 2d ed. Oxford: Clarendon.

Buffon, G. L. L., Comte de. [1749, trans. 1812] 1950. Varieties of the Human Species. In *A Natural History, General and Particular*, trans. W. Smellie, 1:276–86. Reprinted in *This Is Race*, ed. E. W. Count, 3–15. New York: Schuman.

———. 1749–1804. *Histoire naturelle, generelle et particuliere*. Paris: Imprimerie Royal; Plassan.

Burke, Edmund. [1792] 2001. *Reflections on the Revolution in France*. Ed. J. C. D. Clark. Stanford, CA: Stanford University Press.

Burtless, Gary. 1995. International Trade and the Rise in Earnings Inequality. *Journal of Economic Literature* 33:800–816.

Cairnes, J. E. 1865. The Negro Suffrage. *Macmillan's Magazine* 12:334–43.

Campbell, Jay R., Kristin E. Voelkl, and Patricia L. Donahue. 1997. *Report in Brief: NAEP 1996 Trends in Educational Progress*. National Center for Education Statistics, U.S. Department of Education, Office of Educational Research and Improvement, NCES 97–986, August.

Cannadine, David. 1984. The Present and Past in the English Industrial Revolution, 1880–1980. *Past and Present* 103:131–72.

Card, D., and A. Krueger. 1992. School Quality and Black-White Relative Earnings: A Direct Assessment. *Quarterly Journal of Economics* 107:151–200.

Carlyle, Thomas. 1849. Occasional Discourse on the Negro Question. *Fraser's Magazine for Town and Country* 40:670–79.

———. 1850. *Latter-Day Pamphlets*. London: Chapman and Hall.

———. 1867. *Shooting Niagara: And After?* London: Chapman and Hall

———. 1904. *Edinburgh Edition: The Works of Thomas Carlyle in Thirty Volumes*. New York.

———. [1843] 1927. *Past and Present*. New York: Oxford University Press.

———. [1844] 1965. *Past and Present*. Ed. Richard D. Altick. Boston: Houghton Mifflin.

Cartwright, S. A. 1860. Slavery in the Light of Ethnology and the Education, Labor, and Wealth of the South. In *Cotton Is King and Pro-Slavery Arguments: Comprising the Writings of Hammond, Harper, Christy, Stringfellow, Hodge, Bledsoe, and Cartwright on This Important Subject*, ed. E. N. Elliott, 691–728, 879–96. Augusta, GA: Pritchard, Abbott, and Loomis.

Chandler, Alice. 1970. *A Dream of Order: The Medieval Ideal in Nineteenth-Century Literature*. Lincoln: University of Nebraska Press.

Cherry, Robert. 1976. Racial Thought and the Early Economics Profession. *Review of Social Economy* 34, no. 2:147–62. Reprinted in *Economics and Discrimination*, ed. William Darity Jr. (Brookfield, VT: Edward Elgar, 1995), 17–32.

Clark, John Bates. 1899. *The Distribution of Wealth: A Theory of Wages, Interest, and Profit*. New York: Macmillan.

———. 1891. The Industrial Future of the Negro. In *First Mohonk Conference on the Negro Question*, ed. Isabel C. Barrows, 93–96. Boston: George H. Ellis.

———. [1910] 2002. Anarchism, Socialism, and Social Reform. Edited and transcribed by Robert E. Prasch. *Journal of the History of Economic Thought*.

Clark, John Bates, and Franklin H. Giddings. 1888. *The Modern Distributive Process*. Boston: Ginn.

Clark, John Maurice. [1926] 1939. *Social Control of Business*. 2d ed. New York: McGraw-Hill.

Clark, John Maurice. 1960. *Alternative to Serfdom*. 2d ed. New York: Vintage.

Coate, Stephen, and Glenn C. Loury. 1993. Will Affirmative-Action Policies Eliminate Negative Stereotypes? *American Economic Review* 83:1220–40.

Cohen, Gerald A. 1995. Incentives, Inequality, and Community. In *Equal Freedom: Selected Tanner Lectures on Human Values*, ed. Stephen Darwall, 331–98. Ann Arbor: University of Michigan Press.

———. 2000. *If You're an Egalitarian, How Come You're So Rich?* Cambridge: Harvard University Press.

Colander, David, ed. 1986. *Incentive Anti Inflation Plans*. Boston: Ballinger Publishers.

Combe, G., and B. H. Coates. 1840. Review of the *Crania Americana*. *American Journal of Science* 38:341–75.

Commons, John R. 1904. Labor Conditions in Meat Packing and the Recent Strike. *Quarterly Journal of Economics* 19:1–32.

———. 1908. *Races and Immigrants in America*. New York: Macmillan.

———. 1916. *Races and Immigrants in America*. New York: Macmillan.

Commons, John R., and John B. Andrews. 1916. *Principles of Labor Legislation*. New York: Harper and Brothers.

Cook, Philip J., and Michael J. Moore. 2000. Alcohol. In *Handbook of Health Economics*, ed. Anthony J. Culyer and Joseph P. Newhouse, 1B:1629–73. Amsterdam: Elsevier.

Cope's Tobacco Plant. 1878. Liverpool: J. Fraser.

Cordero-Guzman, Hector. 1990. Sociological Approaches to Employment Discrimination. Unpublished manuscript. University of Chicago.

Cotton, Jeremiah. 1993. Color or Culture? Wage Differences among Non-Hispanic Black Males, Hispanic Black Males, and Hispanic White Males. *Review of Black Political Economy* 21, no. 4:53–68.

Cowherd, Raymond. 1977. *Political Economists and the English Poor Laws: A Historical Study of the Influence of Classical Economics on the Formation of Social Welfare Policy.* Athens, OH: Ohio University Press.

Crow, James F. 2002. Unequal by Nature: A Geneticist's Perspective. *Daedalus* 131:81–88.

Culler, A. Dwight. 1985. *The Victorian Mirror of History.* New Haven, CT: Yale University Press.

Currie, Janet, and Duncan Thomas. 1995. Race, Children's Cognitive Achievement, and *The Bell Curve.* Working Paper, no. 5240, National Bureau of Economic Research, Cambridge, MA.

Curtis, L. P., Jr. 1968. *Anglo-Saxons and Celts.* Bridgeport, CT: Conference on British Studies at the University of Bridgeport.

Cutler, David, and Edward Glaeser 1997. Are Ghettos Good or Bad? *Quarterly Journal of Economics* 112 (3):827–72.

Cuvier, G. [1817, trans. 1831] 1950. *The Animal Kingdom Arranged in Conformity with Its Organization.* Trans. H. McMurtie. In *This Is Race,* ed. E. W. Count, 44–47. New York: Schuman.

Dangerfield, George. 1935. *The Strange Death of Liberal England.* New York: H. Smith and Haas.

Darity, William, Jr. 1989a. Introduction to *Race, Radicalism, and Reform: Selected Papers of Abram L. Harris,* ed. William Darity Jr. New Brunswick, NJ: Transactions.

———. 1989b. What's Left of the Economic Theory of Discrimination? In *The Question of Discrimination,* ed. Steven Shulman and William Darity Jr., 335–74. Middletown, CT: Wesleyan University Press.

———. 1994. Many Roads to Extinction: Early AEA economists and the Black Disappearance Hypothesis. *History of Economics Review* 21 (winter): 47–64.

———. 1995. Introduction. *Economics and Discrimination.* Ed. William Darity Jr. Brookfield, VT: Edward Elgar.

Darity, William, Jr., and Patrick L. Mason. 1998. Evidence on Discrimination in Employment: Codes of Color, Codes of Gender. *Journal of Economic Perspectives* 12:63–90.

Darity, William, Jr., and Rhonda Williams. 1985. Peddlers Forever? Culture, Competition, and Discrimination. *American Economic Review* 75:256–61.

Darity, William, Jr., Jason Dietrich, and David Guilkey. 1997. Racial and Ethnic Inequality in the United States: A Secular Perspective. *American Economic Review* 87:301–5.

Darity, William, Jr., David Guilkey, and William Winfrey. 1996. Explaining Differences in Economic Performance among Racial and Ethnic Groups in the USA: The Data Examined. *American Journal of Economics and Sociology* 55, no. 4:411–26.

Darwall, Stephen, ed. 1995. *Equal Freedom: Selected Tanner Lectures on Human Values.* Ann Arbor: University of Michigan Press.

Darwin, C. 1859. *On the Origin of Species by Means of Natural Selection, or the*

Preservation of Favoured Races in the Struggle for Existence. London: John Murray.

———. 1871. *The Descent of Man, and Selection in Relation to Sex*. London: John Murray.

———. 1989. *The Descent of Man, and Selection in Relation to Sex*. Vol. 21 of *The Works of Charles Darwin*, ed. Paul H. Barrett and R. B. Freeman. New York: New York University Press.

Darwin, Leonard. 1916. Quality Not Quantity. *Eugenics Review* 8:297–321.

———. 1919. Eugenics in Relation to Economics and Statistics. *Journal of the Royal Statistical Society of London* 82, no. 1:1–33.

Dealey, James Q., and Lester F. Ward. 1905. *A Text-Book of Sociology*. New York: Macmillan.

Death of the Best Man in England. 1870. *Anthropological Review* 8:97.

Degler, Carl N. 1991. *In Search of Human Nature: The Decline and Revival of Darwinism in American Social Thought*. New York: Oxford University Press.

Deniker, J. 1900. *The Races of Man*. London: Walter Scott.

Denman, Lord. 1853. *Uncle Tom's Cabin, Bleak House, Slavery, and Slave Trade*. 2d ed. London: Longman, Brown, Green, and Longman.

Dhesi, A. Singh, and Harbhajan Singh. 1989. Education, Labour Market Distortions, and Relative Earnings of Different Religion-Caste Categories in India (a case study of Delhi). *Canadian Journal of Development Studies* 9:75–89.

Dickens, William T., and Kevin Lang. 1993. Labor Market Segmentation Theory: Reconsidering the Evidence. In *Labor Economics: Problems in Analyzing Labor Markets*, ed. William Darity Jr., chap. 5. Boston: Kluwer Academic.

Dictionary of National Biography. 1997. CD-rom version 1.1. Oxford: Oxford University Press.

Donner, Wendy. 1991. *The Liberal Self: John Stuart Mill's Moral and Political Philosophy*. Ithaca: Cornell University Press.

Donohue, John J., and James Heckman. 1991. Continuous versus Episodic Change: The Impact of Civil Rights Policy on the Economic Status of Blacks. *Journal of Economic Literature* 29:1603–43.

Douglass, F. [1854] 1979. *The Claims of the Negro, Ethnologically Considered*. In *The Frederick Douglass Papers*, ed. J. W. Blassingame, 2:497–525. New Haven: Yale University Press.

DuBois, W. E. B. [1897] 2000. The Conservation of Races. In *The Idea of Race*, ed. R. Bernasconi and T. L. Lott, 108–17. Indianapolis: Hackett.

———. 1898a. *The Negroes of Farmville, Virginia: A Social Study*. Bulletin, no. 14. Washington, DC: United States Department of Labor.

———. 1898b. The Study of the Negro Problems. *Annals of the American Academy of Political and Social Science* 11:1–23.

———. 1899a. *The Negroes in the Black Belt: Some Social Sketches*. Bulletin, no. 22. Washington, DC: United States Department of Labor.

———. [1899b] 1973. *The Philadelphia Negro: A Social Study*. Millwood, NY: Kraus-Thomson.

———. 1901. *The Negro Landholder of Georgia*. Bulletin, no. 35. Washington, DC: United States Department of Labor.

———. 1906a. The Economic Future of the Negro. *Publications of the American Economic Association*, 3d ser., 7, no. 1:219–42.

———. 1906b. *The Negro Farmer*. In *Supplementary Analysis and Derivative Tables, Twelfth Census of the United States, 1900*, by Department of Commerce and Labor, Bureau of the Census. Washington, DC: U.S. Government Printing Office.

———. 1908. Is Race Separation Practicable? *American Journal of Sociology* 13:834–38.

———. [1911] 1995. The First Universal Races Congress, 1911. In *W. E. B. DuBois: A Reader*, ed. David L. Lewis, 44–47. New York: Henry Holt. Originally published in *The Independent* 70 (August 24, 1911).

———. [1939] 1975. *Black Folk, Then and Now*. Millwood, NY: Kraus-Thomson.

Dworkin, Ronald. 2000. *Sovereign Virtue: The Theory and Practice of Equality*. Cambridge: Harvard University Press.

Dyer, T. G. 1980. *Theodore Roosevelt and the Idea of Race*. Baton Rouge: Louisiana State University Press.

Earle, Jonathan. 2000. *The Routledge Atlas of African-American History*. New York: Routledge.

Early, Gerald. 2002. The Way Out of Here. *New York Times Book Review*, March 3, 12.

Economic Report of the President. 2002. Washington, DC: Government Printing Office.

Economic Science and the British Association. 1877. *Journal of the Statistical Society of London* 40:468–76.

Edgeworth, Francis Y. 1922. Equal Pay to Men and Women for Equal Work. *Economic Journal* 32, no. 128:431–57.

Ehrenreich, John H. 1985. *The Altruistic Imagination: A History of Social Work and Social Policy in the United States*. Ithaca: Cornell University Press.

Elmslie, Bruce, and Stanley Sedo. 1996. Discrimination, Social Psychology, and Hysteresis in Labor Markets. *Journal of Economic Psychology* 17:465–78.

Ely, Richard T. 1903. *Studies in the Evolution in Industrial Society*. New York: Macmillan.

Ennius, Q. 1903. *Ennianae poesis reliquiae*, ed. Johannes Vahlen. Lipsiae: B. G. Teubneri.

Epstein, Richard. 1992. *Forbidden Grounds: The Case against Employment Discrimination Laws*. Cambridge: Harvard University Press.

Ferguson, Ronald. 1995. Shifting Challenges: Fifty Years of Economic Change toward Black-White Earnings Equality. *Daedalus* 124 (winter): 37–76.

Fetter, Frank A. 1916. *Modern Economic Problems*. New York: Century.

Figlio, K. M. 1976. The Metaphor of Organization: An Historiographical Perspective on the Biomedical Sciences of the Early Nineteenth Century. *History of Science* 14:17–53.

Fine, Sidney. 1964. *Laissez-Faire and the General Welfare State: A Study in Conflict in American Thought, 1865–1901*. Ann Arbor: University of Michigan Press.

Fisher, Irving. [1909] 1976. *National Vitality, Its Wastes and Conservation*. New York: Arno.

————. [1930] 1986. *The Theory of Interest*. Fairfield, NJ: Augustus M. Kelly.

Fiske, J. 1884. *The Destiny of Man Viewed in the Lights of His Origins*. Boston and New York: Houghton Mifflin.

Fitzhugh, G. [1854] 1965. *Sociology for the South, or the Failure of Free Society*. Richmond, VA. Reprint, Burt Franklin Research and Source Work Series, no. 102, New York: B. Franklin.

————. [1856] 1960. *Cannibals All! or Slaves without Masters*. Port Royal, Caroline, VA. Ed. C. Vann Woodward. Cambridge: Belknap Press of Harvard University.

Fix, Michael, George C. Galster, and Raymond J. Struyk. 1993. An Overview of Auditing for Discrimination. In *Clear and Convincing Evidence: Measurement of Discrimination in America*, ed. Michael Fix and Raymond Struyk, 1–68. Washington, DC: Urban Institute Press.

Flourens, M. [1847] 1865. Memoir of Blumenbach. In *The Anthropological Treatises of Johann Friedrich Blumenbach*, trans. and ed. T. Bendyshe. London: Green, Longman, Roberts, and Green.

Fogel, R., R. A. Gallantine, R. L. Manning, and N. S. Cardell. 1992. *Without Consent or Contact: The Rise and Fall of American Slavery, Evidence and Methods*. New York: Norton.

Fortin, Nicole M., and Thomas Lemieux. 1997. Institutional Change and Rising Wage Inequality: Is There a Linkage? *Journal of Economic Perspectives* 11:75–96.

Freeman, R. 1973. Changes in the Labor Market for Black Americans, 1948–72. *Brookings Papers on Economic Activity* 1:67–120.

Friedman, Milton. 1962. *Capitalism and Freedom*. Chicago: University of Chicago Press.

Froude, James Anthony. 1885. *Thomas Carlyle: A History of His Life in London, 1834–1881*. New York.

Gallagher, Catherine. 1985. *The Industrial Reformation of English Fiction: Social Discourse and Narrative Form, 1832–67*. Chicago: University of Chicago Press.

Galton, Francis. 1863. Anthropology at the British Association. *Anthropological Review* 1:379–89.

————. 1865. Hereditary Talent and Character. *Macmillan's Magazine* 12:157–66, 318–27.

————. 1908. *Memories of My Life*. London: Methuen.

————. [1892] 1978. *Hereditary Genius: An Inquiry into Its Laws and Consequences*. London: Julian Friedmann.

Garcia, J. L. A. 2002. Race and Inequality: An Exchange. *First Things* 123 (May): 22–26.

Gaskell, Elizabeth. [1848] 1987. *Mary Barton*. Ed. Edgar Wright. New York: Oxford University Press.

Geoffroy St. Hilaire, E., and G. Cuvier. 1795. Histoire naturelle des Orangs-Outans. *Magazin encyclopèdique, ou Journal des sciences, des lettres et des arts* (Paris) 3:451–63.

Gerber, David A. 1976. *Black Ohio and the Color Line, 1860–1915*. Urbana: University of Illinois Press.

Gilman, Charlotte Perkins. [1898] 1966. *Women and Economics: A Study of the Economic Relation between Men and Women as a Factor in Social Evolution*. New York: Harper and Row.

———. 1908. A Suggestion on the Negro Problem. *American Journal of Sociology* 14:78–85.

Girouard, Mark. 1981. *The Return to Camelot: Chivalry and the English Gentleman*. New Haven, CT: Yale University Press.

Glenn, Norval D. 1963. Occupational Benefits to Whites from the Subordination of Negroes. *American Sociological Review* 28, no. 3:443–48.

Gobineau, Arthur. 1963. *Introduction à l'essai sur L'inéqualité des Races Humaines*. Paris: Nouvel Office d'Edition.

Goldberg, David Theo. 2000. Liberalism's Limits: Carlyle and Mill on the Negro Question. *Nineteenth-Century Contexts* 22:203–16.

Goldsmith, Arthur H., Jonathan Veum, and William Darity Jr. 1997. The Impact of Psychological and Human Capital on Wages. *Economic Inquiry* 35:815–29.

———. 2000. Motivation and Labor Market Outcomes. *Research in Labor Economics* 19:109–46.

Gossett, T. F. 1997. *Race: The History of an American Idea*. New ed. New York: Oxford University Press.

Gould, S. J. 1994. The Geometer of Race. *Discover* 15 (11):65–69.

———. 1996. *The Mismeasure of Man*. Rev. ed. New York: Norton.

Gratiolet, P. 1839. *Anatomie comparee du systeme nerveux, considere dans ses rapports avec l'intelligence*. Paris: J. B. Bailliere and Sons; New York: H. Bailliere.

———. 1854. *Memoire sur les plis cerebraux de l'homme et des primates*. Paris: A. Bertrand.

Gray, John A. 1995a. *Enlightenment's Wake: Politics and Culture and the Close of the Modern Age*. New York: Routledge.

———. 1995b. *Liberalism*. 2d ed. Minneapolis: University of Minnesota Press.

Green, Thomas Hill. 1917. *Lectures on the Principles of Political Obligation*. Reprint, London: Longman's Green.

Greg, W. R. 1868. On the Failure of "Natural Selection" in the Case of Man. *Fraser's Magazine for Town and Country* 78:353–62.

———. 1869. The Realities of Irish Life. *Quarterly Review* 126:61–80.

———. 1875. *Enigmas of Life*. Boston.

———. 1876. *Mistaken Aims and Attainable Ideals of the Artizan Class*. London.

Groat, George Gorham. 1924. Economic Wage and Legal Wage. *Yale Law Journal* 33, no. 5:489–500.

Halberstam, David. 1994. *October 1964*. New York: Villard.

Haller, J. S. 1970a. Civil War Anthropometry: The Making of a Racial Ideology. *Civil War History* 16, no. 4:309–24.

———. 1970b. The Physician versus the Negro: Medical and Anthropological Concepts of Race in the Late Nineteenth Century. *Bulletin of the History of Medicine* 40 (March–April): 154–67.

———. 1971. *Outcasts from Evolution: Scientific Attitudes of Racial Inferiority, 1859–1900*. Carbondale: Southern Illinois University Press.

Hamilton, Walton. 1919. The Institutionalist Approach to Economic Theory. *American Economic Review* 9:309–18.

Hannaford, I. 1996. *Race: The History of an Idea in the West*. Baltimore: Johns Hopkins University Press.

Harris, Abram L. 1989. *Race, Radicalism, and Reform: Selected Papers of Abram L. Harris*, ed. William Darity Jr. New Brunswick, NJ: Transactions.

Harris, Abram L., and Sterling D. Spero. 1933. Negro Problem. In *The Encyclopaedia of the Social Sciences*, ed. Edwin R. A. Seligman and Alvin Johnson, 11:335–56. New York: Macmillan.

Harrison, Bennett. 1972. Education and Underemployment in the Urban Ghetto. *American Economic Review* 62:796–812.

Harvie, Christopher. 1988. Revolution and the Rule of Law. In *The Oxford History of Britain*, ed. Kenneth Morgan, 470–517. New York: Oxford University Press.

Hayek, Friedrich v. [1944] 1972. *The Road to Serfdom*. Chicago: University of Chicago Press.

———. 1973. *Law, Legislation, and Liberty*. Vol. 1, *Rules and Order*. Chicago: University of Chicago Press.

———. 1976. *The Mirage of Social Justice*. Chicago: University of Chicago Press.

Heckman, James J. 1997. The Value of Quantitative Evidence on the Effect of the Past on the Present. *American Economic Review* 87:404–8.

Heckman, James J., and Peter Siegelman. 1993. The Urban Institute Audit Studies: Their Methods. In *Clear and Convincing Evidence: Measurement of Discrimination in America*, ed. M. Fix and R. Struyk, 187–258. Washington, DC: Urban Institute Press.

Hepler, Allison L. 2000. *Women in Labor: Mothers, Medicine, and Occupational Health in the United States, 1890–1980*. Columbus: Ohio State University Press.

Herrnstein, Richard, and Charles Murray. 1994. *The Bell Curve: Intelligence and Class Structure in American Life*. New York: Basic.

Hobhouse, Leonard T. [1911] 1994. *Liberalism and Other Writings*. Reprint, ed. James Meadowcroft. New York: Cambridge University Press.

Hobson, John A. 1974. *The Crisis of Liberalism: New Issues of Democracy*. Ed. P. F. Clarke. New York: Barnes and Noble.

Hofstadter, Richard. 1955. *Social Darwinism in American Thought*. Boston: Beacon.

Holt, Thomas C. 1992. *The Problem of Freedom: Race, Labor, and Politics in Jamaica and Britain, 1832–1932*. Baltimore: Johns Hopkins University Press.

Holzer, Harry. 1997. *What Employers Want: Job Prospects for Less-Educated Workers*. New York: Russell Sage Foundation.

Hunt, James. 1863–64. On the Negro's Place in Nature. *Anthropological Society of London: Memoirs* 1:51–52.

———. 1864. *The Negro's Place in Nature: A Paper Read before the London Anthropological Society*. New York: Van Evrie, Horton.

———. 1866a. On the Negro Revolt in Jamaica. *Popular Magazine of Anthropology* 1:14–20.

———. 1866b. Race Antagonism. *Popular Magazine of Anthropology* 1:24–26.

———. 1866c. Race in Legislation and Political Economy. *Anthropological Review* 4:113–35.

Hutchison, Emilie J. 1919. Women's Wages. *Studies in History, Economics, and Public Law* 89, no. 1:1–179.

Huxley, T. H. 1870. *Evidence as to Man's Place in Nature*. New York: D. Appleton.

Irons, Peter. 1999. *A People's History of the Supreme Court*. New York: Penguin.

James, F., and S. W. DelCastillo. 1991. Measuring Job Discrimination by Private Employers against Young Black and Hispanic Males Seeking Entry Level Work in the Denver Metropolitan Area. Unpublished manuscript. Department of Economics, University of Colorado at Denver.

Jenks, Jeremiah W., W. Jett Lauck, and Rufus D. Smith. [1911] 1922. *The Immigration Problem: A Study of American Conditions and Needs*. 5th ed. New York: Funk and Wagnalls.

Jevons, William Stanley. 1869. A Deduction for Darwin's Theory. *Nature*, 2, December 30, 231–32.

———. 1870. Opening Address of the President of Section F Economic Science and Statistics, of the British Association for the Advancement of Science. *Journal of the Royal Statistical Society of London* 33, no. 3:309–26.

———. [1871] 1911. *Theory of Political Economy*. 4th ed. London: Macmillan.

Johnson, Edgar. 1977. *Charles Dickens: His Triumph and His Tragedy*. Rev. ed. New York: Penguin.

Johnson, H. 1891. *The Question of Race: A Reply to W. Cabell Bruce, Esq*. Baltimore: J. F. Weishampel.

Johnson, James H., Jr., and Walter C. Farrell Jr. 1995. Race Still Matters. *Chronicle of Higher Education*, July 7, A48.

Johnson, James H., Jr., Elisa Jayne Bienenstock, and Jennifer A. Stoloff. 1995. An Empirical Test of the Cultural Capital Hypothesis. *Review of Black Political Economy* 23, no. 4:7–27.

Juhn, C., Kevin Murphy, and B. Pierce. 1991. Accounting for the Slowdown in Black-White Wage Convergence. In *Workers and Their Wages: Changing Patterns in the United States*, ed. M. Kosters. Washington, DC: AEI Press.

Kanigel, Robert. 1997. *The One Best Way: Frederick Winslow Taylor and the Enigma of Efficiency*. New York: Penguin.

Kant, I. [1775] 1997. On the Different Races of Man. In *Race and the Enlightenment: A Reader*, ed. E. C. Eze, 38–64. Cambridge, MA: Blackwell.

Kaufman, Bruce E. 1994. *The Economics of Labor Markets and Labor Relations*. 3d ed. Chicago: Dryden.

Keane, A. H. 1896. *Ethnology*. 2d ed. Cambridge: Cambridge University Press.

———. 1908. *The World's People: A Popular Account of Their Bodily Form and Mental Character, Beliefs, Traditions, Political and Social Institutions*. New York: G. P. Putnam's Sons; London: Hutchinson.

Keith, Verna M., and Cedric Herring. 1991. Skin Tone and Stratification in the Black Community. *American Journal of Sociology* 97:760–78.

Kelsey, Carl. 1903. The Evolution of Negro Labor. *Annals of the American Academy of Political and Social Sciences*. 21 (1):55–76.

Kennedy, Randall. 2002. *Nigger: The Strange Career of a Troublesome Word*. New York: Pantheon Books.

Keynes, John Maynard. [1936] 1964. *The General Theory of Employment, Interest, and Money*. New York: Harcourt Brace Jovanovich.

Kingsley, Charles. 1850. *Alton Locke, Tailor and Poet: An Autobiography*. New York: Harper and Brothers.

———. 1863. *The Water-Babies: A Fairy-Tale for a Land-Baby*. Abridged. London and Cambridge: Macmillan.

Kirschenman, Joleen, and Kathryn M. Neckerman. 1991. "We'd Love to Hire Them, But . . .": The Meaning of Race for Employers. In *The Urban Underclass*, ed. Christopher Jencks and Paul E. Peterson, 203–32. Washington, DC: Brookings Institution.

Klinkner, Philip A., and Rogers M. Smith. 1999. *The Unsteady March: The Rise and Decline of Racial Equality in America*. Chicago: University of Chicago Press.

Knight, Frank H. 1931. Professor Fisher's Interest Theory: A Case in Point. *Journal of Political Economy* 39, no. 2:176–212.

Knox, R. 1850. *The Races of Men: A Fragment*. London: Henry Renshaw.

Kolchin, Peter. 1993. *American Slavery, 1619–1877*. New York: Hill and Wang.

Kosters, Marvin, and Finis Welch. 1972. The Effects of Minimum Wages on the Distribution of Changes in Aggregate Employment. *American Economic Review* 62:323–32.

Krueger, Anne O. 1963. The Economics of Discrimination. *Journal of Political Economy* 71, no. 5:481–86.

Lawrence, W. 1822. *Lectures on Physiology, Zoology, and the Natural History of Man*. London: J. Smith.

Leavis, F. R. 1948. *The Great Tradition: George Eliot, Henry James, Joseph Conrad*. London: Chatto and Windus.

Lees, Lynn Hollen. 1998. *The Solidarities of Strangers: The English Poor Laws and the People, 1700–1948*. Cambridge: Cambridge University Press.

Leibnitz, G. W. von. 1718. *Otium Hanoveranum sive Miscellanes ex ore*. Leipzig: Johann Christiani Martini.

Lerner, Abba, and David Colander. 1980. *MAP: A Market Anti-inflation Plan*. New York: Harcourt Brace Jovanovich.

Levine, David P. 1980. Aspects of the Classical Theory of Markets. *Economic Development and Cultural Change* 28 (4): 1–15.

Levy, David M. 1992. *Economic Ideas of Ordinary People: From Preferences to Trade*. London: Routledge.

———. 2001. *How the Dismal Science Got Its Name: Classical Economics and the Ur-Text of Racial Politics*. Ann Arbor: University of Michigan Press.

———. N.d. Metatheoretical Introduction. Center for the Study of Public Choice, George Mason University. Photocopy.

———. N.d. Poets Come Bringing Death to Friends of the Dismal Science. Center for the Study of Public Choice, George Mason University. Photocopy.

Levy, David M., and Sandra J. Peart. 2000. Modeling Non-Abstract Economic Man: Victorian Anthropology, *Punch*, and Piltdown. Paper presented at the University of Toronto History of Economics Workshop, Toronto, Ontario.

———. 2001–2. The Secret History of the Dismal Science: Economics, Religion,

and Race in the Nineteenth Century. Accessed Aug. 4, 2003, at
<http://www.econlib.org/library/columns/LevyPeartdismal.html>.

———. 2002. Galton's Two Papers on Voting as Robust Estimation. *Public Choice* 113:357–65.

———. 2003. Who Are the Canters. Paper presented at the Conference on Visualization and Economics, Montreal.

Lewis, D. L. 1993. *W. E. B. DuBois: Biography of a Race, 1868–1919*. New York: Henry Holt.

———. 2000. *W. E. B. DuBois: The Fight for Equality and the American Century, 1919–1963*. New York: Henry Holt.

Lewis, W. Arthur. 1979. The Dual Economy Revisited. *Manchester School* 47, no. 3:211–29.

Lieberson, Stanley. 1980. *A Piece of the Pie: Black and White Immigrants since 1880*. Berkeley: University of California Press.

Link, William A. 1992. *The Paradox of Southern Progressivism, 1880–1930*. Chapel Hill: University of North Carolina Press.

Linnaeus, C. 1740. *Systema Naturae*. 2d ed. Stockholm: G. Kiesewetter.

———. 1758. *Systema Naturae*. 10th ed. Stockholm: L. Salvii.

———. [1735] 1964. *Systema Naturae*. Nieuwkoop: B. de Graaf.

Litwack, Leon F. 1998. *Trouble in Mind: Black Southerners in the Age of Jim Crow*. New York: Alfred A. Knopf.

Locke, John. [1690] 1952. *The Second Treatise of Government*. New York: Bobbs-Merrill.

Lorimer, D. A. 1997. Race, Science, and Culture: Historical Continuities and Discontinuities, 1850–1914. In *The Victorians and Race*, ed. S. West, 12–33. Brookfield, VT: Scholar.

Loury, Glenn C. 1992. Two Paths to Black Power. *First Things* 26 (October): 18–24.

———. 1994. Self-Censorship and Public Discourse: A Theory of "Political Correctness" and Related Phenomena. *Rationality and Society* 6 (4):428–61. Reprinted in *One by One from the Inside Out* (New York: Free Press, 1995), 145–82.

———. 1998. Discrimination in the Post–Civil Rights Era: Beyond Market Interactions. *Journal of Economic Perspectives* 12:117–26.

———. 2002. *The Anatomy of Racial Inequality*. Cambridge: Harvard University Press.

Lovell, Peggy. 1993. Development and Discrimination in Brazil. *Development and Change* 24:83–101.

Macaulay, Thomas Babington. 1961. *Critical and Historical Essays*. Arranged by A. J. Grieve. London: J. M. Dent and Sons.

———. 1972. Minute on Indian Education. In *Selected Writings*, ed. John Clive and Thomas Pinney, 235–51. Chicago: University of Chicago Press.

Madden, Janice F. 1975. Discrimination—a Manifestation of Male Market Power? In *Sex, Discrimination, and the Division of Labor*, ed. Cynthia Lloyd, 146–74. New York: Columbia University Press.

Maddison, Angus. 1995. *Monitoring the World Economy*. Washington: Organization for Economic Cooperation and Development.

Majeed, Javed. 1992. *Ungoverned Imaginings: James Mill's "The History of British India" and Orientalism*. New York: Oxford University Press.

Mall, F. P. 1909. On Several Anatomical Characters of the Human Brain. *American Journal of Anatomy* 9:1–32.

Margalit, Avishai. 1996. *The Decent Society*. Cambridge: Harvard University Press.

Marks, J. 1995. *Human Biodiversity. Genes, Race, and History*. New York: Aldine de Gruyter.

Marshall, Alfred. 1884. The Housing of the London Poor. *Contemporary Review* 45 (February): 224–31.

———. [1890] 1930. *Principles of Economics*. 8th ed. London: Macmillan.

Marshall, Ray. 1974. The Economics of Racial Discrimination: A Survey. *Journal of Economic Literature* 12:849–71.

Martineau, Harriet. 1837. *Society in America*. London.

Mason, Patrick. 1995. Race, Competition, and Differential Wages. *Cambridge Journal of Economics* 19, no. 4:545–68.

———. 1996. Race, Culture, and the Market. *Journal of Black Studies* 26, no. 6:782–808.

———. 1997a. Race, Culture, and Skill: Interracial Wage Differences among African Americans, Latinos, and Whites. *Review of Black Political Economy* 25, no. 3:5–40.

———. 1997b. Racial Discrimination and the Rate of Return to Cognitive Ability, 1968–1991. Unpublished manuscript, Department of Economics, University of Notre Dame.

———. 1999a. Competing Explanations of Male Interracial Wage Differentials: Missing Variables Models versus Job Competition. *Cambridge Journal of Economics* 23, no. 2: 1–39.

———. 1999b. Male Interracial Wage Differentials: Competing Explanations. *Cambridge Journal of Economics* 23, no. 3:261–99.

———. 2000. Understanding Recent Empirical Evidence on Race and Labor Market Outcomes in the USA. *Review of Social Economy* 58, no. 3:319–38.

Maxwell, Nan. 1994. The Effect on Black-White Wage Differences of Differences in the Quantity and Quality of Education. *Industrial and Labor Relations Review* 47:249–64.

Mayo-Smith, Richmond. 1890. *Emigration and Immigration: A Study in Social Science*. New York: Charles Scribner's Sons.

Mayr, Ernst. 2002. The Biology of Race. *Daedalus* 131:89–106.

McWhorter, John. 2000. *Losing the Race: Self-Sabotage in Black America*. New York: Free Press.

———. 2002. Race and Inequality: An Exchange. *First Things* 123 (May): 26–32.

Meade, James. 1993. *Liberty, Equality, and Efficiency: Apologia pro Agathotopia Mea*. New York: New York University Press.

Merquior, J. G. 1991. *Liberalism: Old and New*. Boston: Twayne.

Michael, J. S. 1988. A New Look at Morton's Craniological Research. *Current Anthropology* 29, 2:349–54.

Mill, John Stuart. 1850. The Negro Question. *Fraser's Magazine for Town and Country* 41:25–31. Reprinted in *Collected Works of John Stuart Mill*, ed. J. M. Robson (Toronto: University of Toronto Press; London: Routledge and Kegan Paul, 1969), 10:87–95.

———. 1862. *Considerations on Representative Government*. New York: Harper and Brothers.

———. [1848] 1965. *The Principles of Political Economy*. Vol. 2 of *Collected Works of John Stuart Mill*, ed. J. M. Robson. Toronto: University of Toronto Press.

———. [1874] 1969. Nature. In *Collected Works of John Stuart Mill*, ed. J. M. Robson, 10:373–402. Toronto: University of Toronto Press; London: Routledge and Kegan Paul.

———. [1859] 1978. *On Liberty*. Ed. Elizabeth Rapaport. Indianapolis: Hackett.

———. [1861] 1979. *Utilitarianism*. Ed. George Sher. Indianapolis: Hackett.

———. [1873] 1989. *Autobiography*. Ed. John Robson. New York: Penguin.

Mill, John Stuart, and Harriet Taylor Mill. 1970. *Essays on Sex Equality*. Ed. Alice Rossi. Chicago: University of Chicago Press.

Miller, Kelly. 1906. The Economic Handicap of the Negro in the North. *Annals of the American Academy of Political and Social Science* 27:81–88.

Mills, Edwin S., and Luan Sendé Lubuele. 1997. Inner Cities. *Journal of Economic Literature* 35:727–56.

Mincy, Ronald B. 1993. The Urban Institute Audit Studies: Their Research and Policy Context. In *Clear and Convincing Evidence: Measurement of Discrimination in America*, ed. Michael Fix and Raymond J. Struyk, 165–86. Washington, DC: Urban Institute Press.

Mirowski, Phillip. 1989. *More Heat than Light*. Cambridge: Cambridge University Press.

———. 1994. *Natural Images in Economic Thought: Markets Read in Tooth and Claw*. Cambridge: Cambridge University Press.

Mitchell, Wesley C. 1919. Statistics and Government. *Journal of the American Statistical Association*, n.s., 125 (March): 223–35.

Moir, Martin, Douglas Mark Peers, and Lynn Zastoupil, eds. 1999. *J. S. Mill's Encounter with India*. Toronto: University of Toronto Press.

Moore, Thomas G. 1971. The Effect of Minimum Wages on Teenage Unemployment. *Journal of Political Economy* 79, no. 4:897–902.

Morley, Henry, and Charles Dickens. 1852. North American Slavery. *Household Words: A Weekly Journal Conducted by Charles Dickens*, September 18:1–6.

Morton, S. 1839. *Crania Americana; or, A Comparative View of the Skulls of Various Aboriginal Nations of North and South America, to Which is Prefixed an Essay on the Varieties of the Human Species*. Philadelphia: J. Penington; London: J. Madden.

Murnane, Richard J., John B. Willett, and Frank Levy. 1995. The Growing Importance of Cognitive Skills in Wage Determination. *Review of Economics and Statistics* 77, no. 2:251–66.

Murray, Charles, and Herrnstein, Richard. 1994. *The Bell Curve: Intelligence and Class Structure in American Life*. New York: Free Press.

Myers, Samuel, Jr., and William E. Spriggs. 1997. Black Employment, Criminal Activity, and Entrepreneurship: A Case Study of New Jersey. In *Race, Markets, and Social Outcomes*, ed. Patrick L. Mason and Rhonda M. Williams, 31–64. Boston: Kluwer Academic.

Myrdal, Gunnar. [1944] 1962. *An American Dilemma: The Negro Problem and Modern Democracy*. Vols. 1–2. New York: Pantheon.

———. [1939] 1962. *Monetary Equilibrium*. New York: Kelley Reprints.

National Center for Education Statistics. 1996. *NAEP 1994 Trends in Academic Progress: Report in Brief*. Washington, DC: Government Printing Office.

Neal, Derek A., and William R. Johnson. 1996. The Role of Pre-market Factors in Black-White Wage Differences. *Journal of Political Economy* 104, no. 5:869–95.

Nearing, Scott. 1929. *Black America*. New York: Vanguard.

Norwood, Stephen H. 2002. *Strikebreaking and Intimidation*. Chapel Hill: University of North Carolina Press.

Nott, J. C., and G. R. Gliddon. 1854. *Types of Mankind: or, Ethnological Researches, Based upon the Ancient Monuments, Paintings, Sculptures, and Crania of Races, and upon Their Natural, Geographical, Philological and Biblical History, Illustrated by Selections from the Inedited Papers of Samuel George Morton and by Additional Contributions from L. Agassiz; W. Usher; and H. S. Patterson*. Philadelphia: J. B. Lippincott Grambo and Company.

Nussbaum, Martha. 2000a. The Costs of Tragedy: Some Moral Limits of Cost-Benefit Analysis. In *Cost Benefit Analysis: Legal, Economic, and Philosophical Perspectives*, ed. Matthew D. Adler and Eric Posner, 169–200. Chicago: University of Chicago Press.

———. 2000b. *Women and Human Development: The Capabilities Approach*. New York: Cambridge University Press.

Oakes, James. 1998. *The Ruling Race: A History of American Slaveholders*. New York: Norton.

O'Neill, June. 1990. The Role of Human Capital in Earnings Differences between Black and White Men. *Journal of Economic Perspectives* 4:25–45.

Owen, R. 1852. Osteological Contributions to the Natural History of the Chimpanzees (*Troglodytes*) and Orangs (*Pithecus*). No. V, Comparison of the Lower Jaw and Vertebrate Column of the *Troglodytes Gorilla, Troglodytes niger, Pithecus Satyrus*, and Different Varieties of the Human Race. *Transactions of the Zoological Society of London* 4, part 4:89–115.

Parrington, Vernon Louis. [1930] 1958. *The Beginnings of Critical Realism in America: 1860–1920*. New York: Harcourt Brace.

Pearson, Karl. 1924. *The Life, Labours, and Letters of Francis Galton*. Cambridge: Cambridge University Press.

Pearson, Karl, and Margaret Moul. 1925. The Problem of Alien Immigration into Great Britain Illustrated by an Examination of Russian and Polish Jewish Children. *Annals of Eugenics* 1:5–127.

Peart, Sandra J. 2000. Irrationality and Intertemporal Choice in Early Neoclassical Thought. *Canadian Journal of Economics* 33:175–88.

———. 2001a. Theory, Application, and the Canon. In *Reflections on the Classical Canon in Economics*, ed. Evelyn L. Forget and Sandra J. Peart, 356–77. London: Routledge.

———. 2001b. "Facts Carefully Marshalled" in the Empirical Studies of William Stanley Jevons. In *The Age of Economic Measurement*, ed. Judy L. Klein and Mary S. Morgan, 252–76. History of Political Economy, annual supplement. Durham: Duke University Press.

Peart, Sandra J., and David M. Levy. 2001. Godwin, Mill, and Ruskin on Human Development. Presented at the History of Economics Society, Winston-Salem, NC.

———. 2003a. Denying Human Homogeneity: Eugenics and the Making of Post-Classical Economics. *Journal of the History of Economic Thought* 25(3):261–88.

———. 2003b. Post-Ricardian British Economics, 1830–1870. In *Blackwell's Companion to the History of Economics*, ed. Jeff Biddle, John Davis, and Warren Samuels, 130–45. Malden, MA: Blackwell.

Persky, Joseph. 1990. Retrospectives: A Dismal Romantic. *Journal of Economic Perspectives* 4:165–72.

Phelps, Edmund. 1972. The Statistical Theory of Racism and Sexism. *American Economic Review* 62:659–61.

Pigou, A. C. 1907. Social Improvement and Modern Biology. *Economic Journal* 17, no. 3:358–69.

———. 1920. *The Economics of Welfare*. 3d ed. London: Macmillan.

Pinker, Steven. 2002. *The Blank Slate: The Modern Denial of Human Nature*. New York: Viking.

The Plenipotent Key to Cope's Correct Card of the Peerless Pilgrimage to Saint Nicotine of the Holy Herb: &c. 1878. Liverpool: J. Fraser.

Porter, Theodore M. 1986. *The Rise of Statistical Thinking*. Princeton: Princeton University Press.

Prasch, Robert E. 1998. American Economists and Minimum Wage Legislation during the Progressive Era, 1912–1923. *Journal of the History of Economic Thought* 20:161–75.

———. 2000. John Bates Clark's Defense of Mandatory Arbitration and Minimum Wage Legislation. *Journal of the History of Economic Thought* 22:251–63.

Prichard, J. C. 1826. *Researches into the Physical History of Mankind*. 2d ed. London: John and Arthur Arch.

Rainger, Ronald. 1978. Race, Politics, and Science: The Anthropological Society of London in the 1860s. *Victorian Studies* 22 (autumn): 51–70.

Ranke, J. [1894] 1938. Der Mensch. In Magnus Hirschfeld, *Racism*, trans. and ed. Eden and Cedar Paul. London: V. Gollancz.

Ransford, H. E. 1970. Skin Color, Life Chances, and Anti-White Attitude. *Social Problems* 18:164–78.

Ransom, Roger L., and Richard Sutch. 1977. *One Kind of Freedom: The Economic Consequences of Emancipation*. New York: Cambridge University Press.

Raphael, Steven. 2002. Anatomy of *The Anatomy of Racial Inequality*. *Journal of Economic Literature* 40:1202–14.

Rawls, John. 1971. *A Theory of Justice*. Cambridge: Harvard University Press.

Ray, J. 1691. *The Wisdom of God Manifested in the Works of Creation.* London.

Reade, W. Winwood. 1864. *Savage Africa: Being the Narrative of a Tour in Equatorial, Southwestern, and Northwestern Africa; with Notes on the Habits of the Gorilla; on the Existence of Unicorns and Tailed Men; on the Slave-Trade; on the Origin, Character, and Capabilities of the Negro, and on the Future Civilization of Western Africa.* New York: Harper and Brothers.

Reich, Michael. 1981. *Racial Inequality: A Political-Economic Analysis.* Princeton: Princeton University Press.

Reid, B. Archdall. 1906. The Biological Foundations of Sociology. With comments by C. W. Saleeby, H. Ashby, and H. Bernard. *Sociological Papers* 3:3–51.

Reuters. 2002. Rights Groups Cites U.S. for Minorities in Prison. Accessed August 19, 2002, at <wysiwyg://81/http://story.news.yah…/20020227/ts_nm /rights_prison_dc_2)>

Riach, Peter B., and Judith Rich. 1991–92. Measuring Discrimination by Direct Experimental Methods: Seeking Gunsmoke. *Journal of Post Keynesian Economics* 14, no. 2:143–50.

Ripley, W. Z. 1899. *The Races of Europe: A Sociological Study.* New York: D. Appleton.

Roberts, David. 1979. *Paternalism in Early Victorian England.* London: Croom Helm.

Robson, J. M., ed. 1969. *Collected Works of John Stuart Mill.* Toronto: University of Toronto Press; London: Routledge and Kegan Paul.

Rodgers, William, III, and William E. Spriggs. 1996. What Does AFQT Really Measure: Race, Wages, Schooling, and the AFQT Score. *Review of Black Political Economy* 24, no. 4:13–46.

Rodgers, William, III, William E. Spriggs, and Elizabeth Waaler. 1997. The Role of Premarket Factors in Black-White Wage Differences: Comment. Unpublished manuscript, Department of Economics, College of William and Mary.

Rossi, Alice. 1970. Sentiment and Intellect. In *Essays on Sex Equality,* by John Stuart Mill and Harriet Taylor Mill, ed. Alice Rossi, 3–63. Chicago: University of Chicago Press.

Rubinstein, Ariel. 2000. *Economics and Language.* Cambridge: Cambridge University Press.

Ruhm, Christopher J. 1989. Labor Market Discrimination in the United States. In *Affirmative Action in Perspective,* ed. F. A. Blanchard and F. J. Crosby, 149–58. New York: Springer-Verlag.

Ruskin, John. [1853] 1985. The Nature of Gothic. In *"Unto This Last" and Other Writings,* ed. Clive Wilmer, 77–109. New York: Penguin.

———. 1893. *Ruskin on Himself and Things in General.* Ed. William Lewin. Illustration by John Wallace. Cope's Smoking-Room Booklets, no. 13. Liverpool: Cope's.

———. 1862. *"Unto This Last": Four Essays on the First Principles of Political Economy.* London: Smith, Elder, and Company.

———. 1893. *Ruskin on Himself and Things in General.* Ed. William Lewin. Illustration by John Wallace. Cope's Smoking-Room Booklets, no. 13. Liverpool: Cope's.

Rutherford, Malcolm. 2000. Understanding Institutional Economics, 1918–1929. *Journal of the History of Economic Thought* 22:277–308.

Said, Edward. 1978. *Orientalism*. New York: Pantheon.

———. 1994. *Culture and Imperialism*. New York: Vintage.

Sanders, Elizabeth. 1999. *Roots of Reform: Farmers, Workers, and the American State, 1877–1917*. Chicago: University of Chicago Press.

Schultz, Harold J., ed. 1972. *English Liberalism and the State: Individualism or Collectivism?* Lexington, MA: D. C. Heath.

Schumpeter, Joseph A. [1942] 1975. *Capitalism, Socialism, and Democracy*. New York: Harper and Row.

Schwab, Stewart. 1986. Is Statistical Discrimination Efficient? *American Economic Review* 76:228–34.

Schweninger, Loren. 1990. *Black Property Owners in the South, 1790–1915*. Urbana: University of Illinois Press.

Seager, Henry Rogers. 1913a. The Minimum Wage as Part of a Program for Social Reform. *Annals of the American Academy of Political and Social Science* 48:3–12.

———. 1913b. The Theory of the Minimum Wage. *American Labor Legislation Review* 3:81–91.

Semmel, Bernard. 1962. *The Governor Eyre Controversy*. London: Macgibbon and Kee.

Sen, Amartya. 1997. From Income Inequality to Economic Inequality. *Southern Economic Journal* 64 (October): 384–403.

———. 1999. *Development as Freedom*. New York: Alfred A. Knopf.

———. 2000. Merit and Justice. In *Meritocracy and Economic Inequality*. ed. Kenneth Arrow, Samuel Bowles, and Steven Durlauf, 5–16. Princeton: Princeton University Press.

Sheth, Falguni A., and Robert E. Prasch. 1996. Charlotte Perkins Gilman: Her Significance for Feminism and Social Economics. *Review of Social Economy* 54, no. 3:323–35.

Sibicky, Mark, and John Dividio. 1986. Stigma of Psychological Therapy: Stereotypes, Interpersonal Relations, and the Self-Fulfilling Prophecy. *Journal of Counseling Psychology* 33, no. 2:148–54.

Silva, Nelson do Valle. 1985. Updating the Cost of Not Being White in Brazil. In *Race, Class, and Power in Brazil*, ed. Pierre-Michel Fontaine, 42–55. Los Angeles: UCLA Center for African American Studies.

Simons, Henry. 1948. *Economic Policy for a Free Society*. Chicago: University of Chicago Press.

Skocpol, Theda. 1992. *Protecting Soldiers and Mothers: The Political Origins of Social Policy in the United States*. Cambridge: Harvard University Press.

Slotkin, J. S. 1944. Racial Classifications of the Seventeenth and Eighteenth Centuries. *Transactions of the Wisconsin Academy of Sciences* 36:459–67.

———. 1965. *Readings in Early Anthropology*. London: Methuen.

Smith, Adam. 1759. *The Theory of Moral Sentiments*. Accessed Aug. 1, 2003, at <http://www.econlib.org>

———. [1776] 1937. *An Inquiry into the Nature and Causes of the Wealth of Nations*. New York: Modern Library.

———. [1776] 1976. *An Inquiry into the Nature and Causes of the Wealth of Nations*. Ed. R. H. Campbell and A. S. Skinner, 2 vols. Oxford: Clarendon.

Smith, Stanhope. 1810. *An Essay on the Causes of the Variety of Complexion and Figure in the Human Species*. 2d ed. New Brunswick: J. Simpson and Company; New York: Williams and Whiting.

Soloway, Richard A. 1995. *Demography and Degeneration: Eugenics and the Declining Birthrate in Twentieth-Century Britain*. Chapel Hill: University of North Carolina Press.

Sowell, Thomas. 1977. *Minimum Wage Escalation*. Stanford: Hoover Institution Press.

———. 1980. *Knowledge and Decisions*. New York: Basic.

———. 1981a. *Ethnic America: A History*. New York: Basic.

———. 1981b. *Markets and Minorities*. New York: Basic.

Spear, Jeffrey. 1984. *Dreams of an English Eden: Ruskin and His Tradition in Social Criticism*. New York: Columbia University Press.

Spencer, Herbert. [1874] 1961. *The Study of Sociology*. Ann Arbor: University of Michigan Press.

Spero, Sterling D., and Abram L. Harris. [1931] 1972. *The Black Worker: The Negro and the Labor Movement*. New York: Atheneum.

Stanton, W. 1960. *The Leopard's Spots: Scientific Attitudes toward Race in America, 1815–1859*. Chicago: University of Chicago Press.

State University of New York at Albany. 2002. Sourcebook of Criminal Justice Statistics. Accessed April 27, 2002, at <http://www.albany.edu /sourcebook/1995/tost_4.html>

Stepan, N. 1982. *The Idea of Race in Science: Great Britain, 1800–1960*. London: Macmillan.

Stigler, George J. 1941. *Production and Distribution Theories*. New York: Macmillan.

———. 1975. *The Citizen and the State*. Chicago: University of Chicago Press.

Stigler, George J., and Gary S. Becker. 1977. De Gustibus Non Est Disputandum. *American Economic Review* 67:76–90.

Stiglitz, Joseph. 1973. Approaches to the Economics of Discrimination. *American Economic Review* 63:287–95.

———. 1994. *Whither Socialism?* Cambridge: MIT Press.

Stokes, Eric. 1959. *The English Utilitarians and India*. London: Oxford University Press.

Stone, Alfred Holt. 1902. The Negro in the Yazoo-Mississippi Delta. *Publications of the American Economic Association*, 3d ser., 3, no. 1:235–72.

———. 1905. A Plantation Experiment. *Quarterly Journal of Economics* 19:270–87.

———. 1906. The Economic Future of the Negro: The Factor of White Competition. *Publications of the American Economic Association*, 3d ser., 7, no. 1:243–94.

———. 1908. Is Race Friction between Blacks and Whites in the United States Growing and Inevitable? *American Journal of Sociology* 13:676–97.

Storing, Herbert. 1964. The School of Slavery. In *100 Years After Emancipation*, ed. Robert Goldwin. Chicago: Rand McNally.

Sugrue, Thomas J. 1996. *The Origins of the Urban Crisis: Race and Inequality in Postwar Detroit*. Princeton: Princeton University Press.

Swinton, David. 1978. A Labor Force Competition Model of Racial Discrimination in the Labor Market. *Review of Black Political Economy* 9, no. 1:5–42.

Telles, Edward, and Nelson Lim. 1998. Does It Matter Who Answers the Race Question? Racial Classification and Income Inequality in Brazil. *Demography* 35, no. 4:465–74.

Telles, Edward, and Edward Murguia. 1990. Phenotypic Discrimination and Income Differences among Mexican Americans. *Social Science Quarterly* 71, no. 4:682–94.

Thomas, K. 1983. *Man and the Natural World*. New York: Pantheon.

Thomson, James. 1879. *Pursuit of Diva Nicotina*. Poem. Fraser Collection, University of Liverpool Library, 1516 (1–2). Accompanies Cope's Key for "Modern Pilgrims." Cope's Card. 1878. Poem accompanies J. Wallace 1878a.

Tiedemann, F. 1816. *Anatomie und Bildungsgeschichte de Gehrins im Foetus des Menschen*. Nuremberg: Steinischen.

———. 1836. On the Brain of the Negro, Compared with That of the European and the Orang-outang. *Philosophical Transactions of the Royal Society of London* 126:497–527.

Tillinghast, Joseph A. 1902. The Negro in Africa and America. *Publications of the American Economic Association*, 3d ser., 3, no. 2:1–231.

Topinard. [1892] 1950. On "Race" in Anthropology. In *This Is Race*, ed. and trans. E. W. Count, 171–77. New York: Schuman.

Tuttle, William M., Jr. 1969. Labor Conflict and Racial Violence: The Black Worker in Chicago, 1894–1919. *Labor History* 10, no. 3:408–32.

Tyree, Andrea. 1991. Reshuffling the Social Deck: From Mass Migration to the Transformation of the American Ethnic Hierarchy. In *Social Roles and Social Institutions: Essays in Honor of Rose Laub Coser*, ed. Judith Blau and Norman Goodman, 195–215. Boulder: Westview.

Unger, Roberto. 1998. *Democracy Realized: The Progressive Alternative*. New York: Verso.

U.S. Bureau of Justice Statistics. 2000. Correctional Populations in the United States, 1997. Accessed April 27, 2002, at <www.ojp.usdoj.gov/bjs/pub/pdf/cpus9704.pdf>

———. 2002. State Court Sentencing of Convicted Felons, 1998. Accessed April 27, 2002, at <www.ojp.usdoj.gov/bjs/pub/pdf/scscf98.pdf>

U.S. Department of Justice. 2002a. Criminal Victimization in the United States, 1999: Statistical Tables: National Criminal Victimization Survey. Accessed June 9, 2002 at <www.ojp.usdoj.gov/bjs/pub/pdf/cvus9902.pdf>.

———. 2002b. Homicide Trends in the U.S. Bureau of Justice Statistics. Accessed August 19, 2002, at <www.ojp.usdoj.gov/bjs/homicide/tables/vracetab.htm>

U.S. Substance Abuse and Mental Health Services Administration. 2002.

National Household Survey of Drug Abuse. Accessed April 26, 2002, at <www.samhsa.gov>.

Vanini, G. C. [1619] 1842. *Oeuvres philosophiques de Vanini*, trans. M. X. Rousselet. Paris: C. Gosselin.

Van Parijs, Philippe. 1995. *Real Freedom for All: What (if anything) Can Justify Capitalism?* New York: Cambridge University Press.

Virchow, R. [1896] 1950. Race Formation and Heredity. In *This Is Race*, ed. and trans. E. W. Count, 178–94. New York: Schuman.

Voegelin, E. [1933] 1998. Species and Race in the Eighteenth Century. In *The History of the Race Idea: From Ray to Carus*, vol. 3 of *The Collected Works of Eric Voegelin*, trans. Ruth Hein, ed. Klaus Vondung, 29–79. Baton Rouge: Louisiana State University Press.

Wakefield, E. G. 1835. Notes to *An Inquiry into the Nature and Cause of the Wealth of Nations*, by Adam Smith, ed. E. G. Wakefield. London: Charles Knight and Company.

Waldinger, Roger. 1996. *Still the Promised City: African-Americans and New Immigrants in Postindustrial New York*. Cambridge: Harvard University Press.

Walker, Francis A. 1881. The Colored Race in the United States. *Forum* 2:501–9. Reprinted in *Economics and Discrimination*, ed. William Darity Jr. (Brookfield, VT: Edward Elgar, 1995), 33–41.

Wallace, A. R. 1864. The Origin of Human Races and the Antiquity of Man Deduced from the Theory of "Natural Selection." *Journal of the Anthropological Society of London* 2:clviii–cixx.

———. 1871. *The Action of Natural Selection on Man*. New Haven, CT: C. C. Chatfield and Company.

Wallace, John. 1878a. *Peerless Pilgrimage to Saint Nicotine of the Holy Herb*. Painting. Owned by David M. Levy, Fairfax, and reproduced in the Fraser Collection, University of Liverpool Library, 1105.

———. 1878b. *In Pursuit of Diva Nicotina*. Poster. On exhibition in the Fraser Collection, University of Liverpool Library, 1105.

Walvin, James. 1973. *Black and White: The Negro and English Society, 1555–1945*. London: Allen Lane the Penguin Press.

Washington, Booker T. 1915. My View of Segregation Laws. *New Republic* 5 (December 4): 113–14.

———. [1895] 1965. The Atlanta Exposition Address, 1895. Reprinted in *Up from Slavery*, 147–57. New York: Avon.

Webb, Sydney. 1910. Eugenics and the Poor Law: The Minority Report. *Eugenics Review* 2, no. 3:233–41.

Weintraub, E. Roy. 2002. *How Economics Became a Mathematical Science*. Durham, NC: Duke University Press.

Wells-Barnett, Ida. [1893] 1991. *Selected Works of Ida B. Wells-Barnett*. Ed. Trudier Harris. New York: Oxford University Press.

Whately, Richard. 1831. *Introductory Lectures on Political Economy*. London.

———. 1832. *Introductory Lectures on Political Economy*. 2d ed. London.

———. 1833. *Easy Lessons on Money Matters; For the Use of Young People*. London.

White, C. 1799. *An Account of the Regular Gradation in Man, and in Different Animals and Vegetables*. London: C. Dilly.

White, Katherine. 1997. Simultaneity Issues in the Relationship of Income and Intelligence. Undergraduate Senior Honors Thesis, Department of Economics, University of North Carolina at Chapel Hill.

Wiebe, Robert H. 1967. *The Search for Order, 1877–1920*. New York: Hill and Wang.

Wiener, Martin J. 1985. *English Culture and the Decline of the Industrial Spirit, 1850–1980*. New York: Penguin.

Willcox, W. F. 1910–11. The Negro. *Encyclopaedia Britannica*. 11th ed. New York: Encyclopaedia Britannica.

Williams, John A. [1960] 1996. *The Angry Ones*. New York: Norton.

Williams, Raymond. 1958. *Culture and Society, 1780–1950*. New York: Columbia University Press.

Wilson, Joseph T. 1888. *The Black Phalanx: A History of Negro Soldiers of the United States in the Wars of 1775–1812, 1861–1865*. Hartford, CT: American Publishing Company.

Wilson, William Julius. 1980. *The Declining Significance of Race*. Chicago: University of Chicago Press.

Wolff, Edward Nathan. 1997. *Economics of Poverty, Inequality, and Discrimination*. Cincinnati, OH: Southwestern Publishing.

Wolpoff, M. H., and R. Caspari. 1997. *Race and Human Evolution*. New York: Simon and Schuster.

Woodbury, Stephen. 1993. Culture and Human Capital: Theory and Evidence or Theory versus Evidence? In *Labor Economics: Problems in Analyzing Labor Markets*, ed. William Darity Jr., 239–68. Norwell: Kluwer Academic.

Word, Carl O., Mark P. Zanna, and Joel Cooper. 1974. The Nonverbal Mediation of Self-Fulfilling Prophecies in Interracial Interaction. *Journal of Experimental Social Psychology* 10:109–20.

Young, Robert J. C. 1995. *Colonial Desire: Hybridity in Theory, Culture, and Race*. London: Routledge.

About the Authors

MARCELLUS ANDREWS is a professor of economics in the School of Public Affairs of Baruch College at the City University of New York. His research interests include macroeconomics, dynamics, crime and punishment, and analytical approaches to economic and social justice. He is the author of *The Political Economy of Hope and Fear: Capitalism and the Black Condition in America* (1999). He was a fellow at the Institute on Race and Social Division at Boston University during the 1997–98 academic year. Professor Andrews has also taught at the University of Denver and at Wellesley College. He received his Ph.D. from Yale University.

DAVID COLANDER has been the Christian A. Johnson Distinguished Professor of Economics at Middlebury College in Vermont since 1982. In 2001–2 he visited Princeton as the Kelley Professor for Distinguished Teaching. He has authored, coauthored, or edited over thirty-five books and over one hundred articles on a wide range of topics. These include *Principles of Economics* (5th ed. 2004); *History of Economic Thought*, with Harry Landreth, (4th ed. 2002); *Why Aren't Economists as Important as Garbagemen?* (1991); *MAP: A Market Anti-inflation Plan*, with Abba Lerner (1980); and his edited volume *The Complexity Vision and the Teaching of Economics* (2000).

He received his Ph.D. from Columbia University in 1976 and has served as a Brookings Policy Fellow and a Visiting Scholar at Nuffield College, Oxford. He is listed in *Who's Who, Who's Who in Education*, and others. He has been on the board of numerous economic societies and has been president of the Eastern Economic Association and History of Economic Thought Society. He is or has been on the editorial boards of the *Journal of the History of Economic Thought*, the *Journal of Economic Methodology*, the *Eastern Economic Journal*, the *Journal of Economic Education*, and the *Journal of Economic Perspectives*. He is also series editor, with Mark Blaug, of the Twentieth-Century Economists series of Edward Elgar Publishers.

WILLIAM A. (SANDY) DARITY JR. is the Cary C. Boshamer Professor of Economics at the University of North Carolina at Chapel Hill and a half-time research professor of public policy studies at Duke University. He has published numerous articles on inequality by race, class, and ethnicity. His research interests also include North-South theories of development and trade and the history of economic thought and political economy. His most recent book, edited with Ashwini Deshpande, is entitled *Boundaries of Class and Color* (2003). Professor Darity received his Ph.D. in economics from the Massachusetts Institute of Technology.

VANITA GOWDA received an M.A. in public administration, with a focus on urban policy, from Columbia University in 2002. For several years, she worked as a journalist in Washington, D.C., where she wrote about federal and local policy issues for publications including *Congressional Quarterly* and *Governing* magazine. She currently works in health communications.

DAVID M. LEVY is a professor of economics at George Mason University. He earned his Ph.D. from the University of Chicago with a dissertation entitled "The Content of Classical Economics." His first publications in the history of economics were on misrepresentations of classical economics: "Ricardo and the Iron Law" (1976) and "Some Normative Aspects of the Malthusian Controversy" (1978) in *History of Political Economy*. His first study of the Romantic critics of classical economics is "S. T. Coleridge Responds to Adam Smith's Pernicious Opinion: A Study In Hermetic Social Engineering" in *Interpretation* (1986). The 2001 article "How the Dismal Science Got Its Name" in the *Journal of the History of Economic Thought* was awarded the prize of Best Article of the Year by the History of Economics Society. As an econometrician, Levy specializes in estimation in nonideal conditions, especially when the researcher has preferences over estimates. He serves on the American Statistical Association's Committee on Professional Ethics and wonders why there is no code of ethics in econometrics. His joint work with Sandra Peart on "Galton's papers on Voting as Robust Estimators" appeared in *Public Choice* (2002). Their essay "Statistical Prejudice: From Eugenics to Immigrants" appeared in the *European Journal of Political Economy* (2003). Their essay

"Denying Homogeneity" appeared in the *Journal of the History of Economic Thought* (2003). Their book *Classical Economics and the Cattle Herders: From the "Vanity of the Philosopher" to Eugenic Central Planning* is forthcoming from the University of Michigan Press.

GLENN C. LOURY is the founder and director of the Institute of Race and Social Division at Boston University, where he has been a professor of economics since 1991. He has published numerous articles on race, discrimination, inequality, and economic policy. His articles have appeared in journals as diverse as the *Journal of Economic Perspectives*, the *American Economic Review*, the *Quarterly Journal of Economics*, the *Journal of Political Economy*, the *Journal of Sociology and Social Work*, *Social Philosophy and Policy*, the *Review of Black Political Economy*, the *Journal of Urban Economics*, *The New Republic*, *The American Prospect*, and the *Georgetown Law Journal*. He is also the author of numerous books, most recently, *The Anatomy of Racial Inequality* (2002). Professor Loury received his Ph.D. from the Massachusetts Institute of Technology.

PATRICK L. MASON is an associate professor of economics at Florida State University. His research interests include racial discrimination in employment, wage differentials among various racial and ethnic groups, and theories of racial identity. His articles have appeared in the *Journal of Post-Keynesian Economics*, the *Review of Black Political Economy*, the *Cambridge Journal of Economics*, and the *Review of Radical Political Economics*, as well as in several books. He is the editor of *African Americans, Labor, and Society: Organizing for a New Agenda* (2001). Professor Mason received his Ph.D. in economics from the New School for Social Research.

BRENDAN O'FLAHERTY is an associate professor of economics at Columbia University. He received his B.A., M.A., and Ph.D. from Harvard and then moved into politics, serving as an aide to the mayor of Newark, New Jersey, as well as in a number of other positions. He returned to academia in the 1980s, and published *Rational Commitment: A Foundation for Macroeconomics* (1985) and *Making Room: The Economics of Homelessness* (1998). His current research is in urban economics, especially homelessness and housing, the economics of race, and in other related areas, including world and national records in track and field.

SANDRA J. PEART is a professor of economics at Baldwin-Wallace College. She received her B.A. and Ph.D. in economics from the University of Toronto in 1982 and 1989. Her dissertation on the economics of W. S.

Jevons was awarded the prize of Best Dissertation by the History of Economics Society. She taught at the University of Toronto and the College of William and Mary before coming to Baldwin-Wallace in 1991. She has published articles on utilitarianism, the methodology of J. S. Mill, rationality and intertemporal choice, economics and eugenics, and the transition to neoclassicism, in such journals as *Manchester School*, the *Canadian Journal of Economics*, the *American Journal of Economics and Sociology*, *History of Political Economy*, the *Journal of Economic Education*, and the *Journal of the History of Economic Thought*. She has also published a four-volume collection entitled *W. S. Jevons: Critical Responses* (2003). In 1998, with Evelyn L. Forget, she organized a conference supported by the Social Sciences and Humanities Research Council of Canada celebrating the work of Samuel Hollander. With Forget, she edited the conference volume, *Reflections on the Classical Canon in Economics* (2001). She currently serves as vice president of the History of Economics Society and on the editorial board of the *Journal of the History of Economic Thought*. With David Levy, she is the senior author of the forthcoming *Classical Economics and the Cattle Herders: From the "Vanity of the Philosopher" to Eugenic Central Planning*.

ROBERT E. PRASCH is an associate professor of economics at Middlebury College. He received a Ph.D. in economics from the University of California, Berkeley, in 1992. He has also taught at Vassar College, the University of Maine, and San Francisco State University. His areas of research and teaching include the history of economic thought, macroeconomics, monetary economics, and American economic history. Some of his more recent articles have appeared in the *Journal of the History of Economic Thought*, the *Review of Social Economy*, the *Journal of Economic Issues*, the *Journal of Economic Perspectives*, and the *Review of Political Economy*. He also serves on the editorial board of the *Review of Political Economy*.

JILL S. SHAPIRO is an assistant professor of anthropology at Columbia University. She is also an adjunct associate professor at New York University's School of Continuing and Professional Education. Her research interests include hominoid systematics and evolution, paleoanthropology, morphometrics, and cultural and biological conceptions of race and human variation. Her publications to date have primarily been in the sphere of biological anthropology, in journals such as the *American Journal of Physical Anthropology*. She received her Ph.D. from Columbia University.

FALGUNI A. SHETH is a visiting assistant professor of philosophy and political theory at Hampshire College. She received a B.A. in rhetoric from the University of California, Berkeley, and an M.A. in philosophy from the New School for Social Research, where she also received her Ph.D. Her dissertation explored several philosophical understandings of work in relation to the public and private spheres in modern society. Her teaching and research interests include various topics in feminist, political, and legal philosophies. She has taught political, moral, and feminist philosophy at Middlebury and Vassar Colleges, at the New School for Social Research, and at several public universities. She has published several articles on topics of public policy, such as the ethics of the minimum wage and educational vouchers, and on the feminism and social economics of Charlotte Perkins Gilman. Her publications have appeared in the *Journal of Economic Issues*, the *Review of Social Economy*, and *Ethics*.

SUSAN ZLOTNICK is an associate professor of English at Vassar College. She received a Ph.D. in English from the University of Pennsylvania. Her areas of research include Victorian studies, gender studies, the novel, and working-class literature. She is the author of several articles that explore the intersections of Victorian literature and culture, as well as of the book *Women, Writing, and the Industrial Revolution* (1998).

Index

abolitionism, in nineteenth-century
Britain, 88
Ackerman, B., and stakeholder
scheme, 234
Adams, C. F., and slow change, 160
adverse selection, and racial bias,
239–42
affirmative action: and merit-based
policies, 221; and racial inequality,
231, 232
African-Americans (*see also* blacks):
and assimilation compared to
Afro-Caribbeans, 81, 172, 181n. 16;
and the Enlightenment, 34; and
equal opportunity, 182; excluded
from social reform, 149; facial characteristics, 48; and fair opportunity,
253; and illicit recreational drugs,
275; implications of their posture,
48–49; improvement of their fate,
50; and incarceration for recreational drugs, 278; and increase in
academic employment, 178; and job
discrimination, 185; and obstacles
to economic success, 171–72; and
productivity, 187, 191; and social
justice, 253; and the vicious circle,
163–64, 246
Africans: and apes, 36, 44; superiority
of, 51; viewed as inferior, 32–34
Afro-Caribbeans: and assimilation
compared to African-Americans,
172, 181n. 16; and job discrimination, 193–94
Agassiz, L.: and "centers of creation,"

3; and monogeny, 37; and polygeny,
38, 41; and rigidity of classification,
36
age discrimination, 183
Alcott, A., and stakeholder scheme,
234
Alexander, G. W., and Anti-Slavery
Society, 65
Alton Locke (Kingsley), 67
American blacks, and ability to affect
market, 15
American slavery, 146
Anatomy of Racial Inequality (Loury),
17–18, 238–55
"ancient candelabra," view of race,
29–30
Anderson, E., and constraint of skill
acquisition, 248
Anglo-Saxons: and job discrimination,
193–94; and superiority, 124, 129
Anthropological Institute, 47
Anthropological Review, and James
Hunt, 124
anthropologists, and evolutionary economics, 152
anthropology: development as a social
science, 21; and evolution, 47–48;
foundation of institutions, 47;
racial, 65; and ranking of races,
47–48
anticapitalism, links to proslavery, 86
antislavery: Carlyle's opposition to,
58–59; and industrial society, 90;
proponents of, 59; and racial theorizing, 123